ABORTION AND THE CONSTITUTION

ABORTION
AND THE
CONSTITUTION
Reversing *Roe v. Wade*
Through the Courts

■

Dennis J. Horan
Edward R. Grant
Paige C. Cunningham
EDITORS

Foreword by
the Honorable Rex E. Lee

GEORGETOWN UNIVERSITY PRESS
Washington, D.C.

Abortion and the Constitution: Reversing Roe v. Wade through the Courts
Copyright © 1987
Americans United for Life Legal Defense Fund

Library of Congress Cataloging-in-Publication Data

Abortion and the Constitution.

  Includes index.
  1. Abortion—Law and legislation—United States.
2. United States—Constitutional law.   I. Horan,
Dennis J.   II. Grant, Edward R.   III. Cunningham,
Paige C. (Paige Comstock)
KF3771.A93   1987   344.73′0419   87-287
ISBN 0-87840-446-5   347.304419
ISBN 0-87840-447-3 (pbk.)

Contents

PART III: STRATEGIES FOR REVERSAL OF *ROE v. WADE*

PART IV: CONCLUSION

PART V: APPENDICES

Contributors

MARTIN ARBAGI, A.B., Georgetown University, M.A., Ph.D., Rutgers University; Associate Professor of History, Wright State University.

THOMAS J. BALCH, B.A., Williams College, J.D., New York University School of Law; Staff Counsel, National Center for the Medically Dependent and Disabled, former Staff Counsel, Americans United for Life Legal Defense Fund.

WILLIAM BENTLEY BALL, A.B., Western Reserve University, J.D. College of Law, University of Notre Dame; Partner, Ball & Skelly, Harrisburg, Penna., constitutional lawyer; lead counsel in litigations in twenty states and in nineteen U.S. Supreme Court cases, including *Wisconsin v. Yoder*.

JOHN R. CONNERY, S.J., B.A., M.A., Loyola University Chicago, Litt. B., Xavier University, S.T.D., Pontifical Gregorian University; Professor Emeritus, Loyola University, Chicago.

PAIGE COMSTOCK CUNNINGHAM, B.A., Taylor University, J.D., Northwestern University School of Law; former Executive Director of Americans United for Life Legal Defense Fund.

JOSEPH DELLAPENNA, B.B.A., University of Michigan, J.D., Detroit College of Law, LL.M., George Washington University, LL.M., Columbia University School of Law; Professor of Law, Villanova University.

JOHN P. EAST, B.A., Earlham College, LL.B., University of Illinois, M.A., Ph.D., University of Florida; United States Senator from North Carolina 1981–1986; Professor of Political Science, East Carolina University, 1964–1980. (Editors' note: Senator East, who, as Chairman of the U.S. Senate Subcommittee on Separation of Powers, conducted the landmark 1981 hearings on the "Human Life Bill," died in 1986.)

JOHN M. FINNIS, LL.B., University of Adelaide, D. Phil. (Oxon.), Rhodes Scholar for South Australia, University College, Oxford; Rhodes Reader in the Laws of the British Commonwealth and the United States; Member, the Catholic Bishops' (of Great Britain and Ireland) Joint Committee on Bio-Ethical Issues.

EDWARD R. GRANT, A.B., Georgetown University, J.D., Northwestern University School of Law; Executive Director/General Counsel, Americans United for Life Legal Defense Fund.

DENNIS J. HORAN, B.S., J.D., Loyola University, Chicago; Partner, Hinshaw, Culbertson, Moelmann, Hoban and Fuller; former Lecturer in Law and Medical Law, University of Chicago Graduate School of Business and the University of Chicago Law School; Chairman, Americans United for Life Legal Defense Fund.

THOMAS J. MARZEN, B.A., University of Illinois, J.D., Illinois Institute of Technology; General Counsel, the National Legal Center for the Medically Dependent and Disabled; former Chief Staff Counsel, Americans United for Life Legal Defense Fund.

RICHARD S. MYERS, B.A., Kenyon College, J.D., University of Notre Dame Law School; Professor of Constitutional Law, Case Western Reserve University; formerly Associate, Jones, Day, Reavis and Pogue, Washington, D.C.

MICHAEL PEARCE PFEIFER, President, Pfeifer Communications, Inc. is an editor and publishing consultant. He first researched abortion and the impact of the Supreme Court decision on congressional elections with Maris Vinovskis at The University of Michigan, Institute for Social Research.

VICTOR G. ROSENBLUM, A.B., LL.B., Columbia University, Ph.D., University of California, Berkeley; Professor of Law and Political Science, Northwestern University; Counsel for intervening defendants in Supreme Court abortion funding cases, *Harris v. McRae* and *Williams v. Zbaraz*. Vice-chairman, Americans United for Life Legal Defense Fund.

STEVEN R. VALENTINE, B.G.S., J.D., Indiana University; Attorney, Washington, D.C.; chief of staff to Senator East, 1985–1986.

LYNN D. WARDLE, B.A., Brigham Young University, J.D., Duke University; Professor of Law, J. Reuben Clark Law School, Brigham Young University.

Editors' Introduction

Compiling the principal criticisms of *Roe v. Wade* and formulating a coherent strategy for bringing about its reversal has challenged our thinking on the status of abortion in American law, and rewarded us with fresh insights into the problem. Many individuals have invested knowledge, wisdom, and energy to bring *Abortion and the Constitution* into fruition.

We are indebted to the contributing authors. On March 31, 1984 most of them presented earlier versions of their chapters at an Americans United for Life sponsored conference, "Reversing *Roe v. Wade* Through the Courts." They have been uniformly patient, generous, and cooperative in revising their works. Steven Baer, former AUL staff member, was primarily responsible for bringing the authors together, for the success of the 1984 conference, and assisted in the original compilation of manuscripts. Laurie Anne Ramsey, AUL Director of Education, has coordinated the final stages of editing and publication. AUL staff members meticulously did proofreading, cite-checking and indexing: Maura Quinlan, Guy Condon, Suzanne Diddams, Clarke Forsythe, Ann-Louise Lohr, Christine Caprio, Thomas Jipping, Kevin Liss, and Richard Bargetto.

John Breslin, S.J., Director, Georgetown University Press, provided essential encouragement and support. Eleanor Waters, Senior Editor at Georgetown University Press, ably performed the final editorial responsibilities on the manuscript and galleys.

Abortion and the Constitution could not have been completed without the thorough editing and wise counsel of Michael Pearce Pfeifer; and the patient manuscript preparation and frequent revision by Jean A. Pfeifer.

The love and support of our spouses and families, especially Dolores Horan, Penny Grant, and Jay Cunningham, have eased and sustained our work. To them go our love and enduring gratitude.

The editors dedicate this work to the memory of Senator John East, and of Dr. Jasper F. Williams, both courageous champions of human life.

Dennis J. Horan
Edward R. Grant
Paige C. Cunningham
Chicago
June 11, 1987

Foreword

This nation is blessed with the world's oldest and most successful written constitution. One of the lessons we have learned from 200 years of experience under that Constitution is that while the Supreme Court from time to time will err in its interpretation, most of the really serious errors will eventually be corrected.

I believe that one such error occurred on January 22, 1973, when the United States Supreme Court decided *Roe v. Wade*. Both in theory and also in application, its deficiencies reach far beyond questions of abortion, and even beyond the existence or nonexistence of a constitutionally based privacy right which entitles a person to control his or her body. The most serious consequence of *Roe v. Wade*, in my view, is its effect on the structure of the Constitution, and therefore on individual rights.

One of the core concepts of our Constitution is that the residual lawmaking authority belongs to the political branches. That is, the power to make policy choices where there is no existing law is vested in Congress and the president (as long as they act within the scope of their delegated powers) and in state legislators and governors in the exercise of their police powers. Courts, by contrast, exercise their powers to decide cases and controversies. And while the ultimate power to say what the Constitution means must rest with the courts, the courts must not use that power as a convenient vehicle for implementing their own policy choices. This means, I believe, that courts, in making constitutional decisions, are limited to interpretation and application of those principles that can fairly be derived either from language used by the constitution-makers or from what the history of their efforts clearly indicates that they intended.

Large numbers of Americans regard the abortion issue as very important. On both sides, participants in the abortion debate base their arguments on moral as well as policy grounds. For some, the issue is whether government is to interfere with the most intimate of personal matters: the control of one's body, and the right to control personal autonomy. For others, life itself is at stake.

The issue is important. But the debate itself is equally important. At stake is a legitimate policy and moral issue; it should be left to the processes by which policy and moral issues are resolved. *Roe v. Wade's* most serious error is that it constitutionalized the issue, thereby removing at least the core from the public debate. This is wrong for at least two reasons. First, the abortion question is complex and multifaceted; its resolution would benefit from the free play of public debate. Second, under our republican form of government, issues of public policy were intended to be, and should be, resolved by the people's elected representatives; they should be removed from that process only where it is clear that the extraordinary requirements of lawmaking by constitutional amendment have been satisfied. It will not do simply to assert that constitutionally guaranteed rights are outside the reach of statutory lawmaking. Of course they are. But this counsels that issues of public importance should be removed from the usual democratic processes only where it is quite clear that the constitution-makers have intended so to remove them.

The abortion question fails this test. There is nothing in the constitutional text that even alludes to abortion, and nothing in the history of First, Ninth, Fourteenth or any other amendment indicating that the constitution-makers had the slightest intent to remove it from the legitimate realm of representative lawmaking.

The years since *Roe v. Wade* have witnessed the development of an accompanying problem, which was quite predictable the day the case was decided. Because the rule came into being without any real constitutional underpinnings, its further development has followed the same pattern as its birth—one series of policy choices building on another. As the development of this "law" has progressed, the choices and resulting rules of "constitutional law" have become more detailed, so that today the list of rules specifying what our elected representatives may or may not do has come to resemble a rather complex statute or administrative regulation. Each time that a new decision is rendered, the statute becomes longer and more complex, and the judicial work product moves even farther away from the basic judicial function of interpreting what the constitution-makers intended.

Lacking any anchorage in the Constitution for this kind of law-making, the Court has turned to another source, current medical opinion. Because the constitutional rules are keyed in large part to medical knowledge and practice, changes in the medical world have effectively been converted into constitutional doctrine. As a result, the ultimate policy-making authority in this area is not only taken away from elected governmental officials, it is effectively exercised by persons who have no governmental authority or responsibility at all.

These deficiencies are so fundamental and so serious that they cannot withstand the long-range test of time. Though history teaches that the Supreme Court sometimes needs decades to correct its largest errors, that same history also assures that the corrections will eventually be made.

For all of these reasons the publication of *Abortion and the Constitution: Reversing* Roe v. Wade *through the Courts* is a propitious event. The scholars and practitioners whose works appear in this volume have set out not only to criticize the historical and jurisprudential flaws of *Roe*, but to suggest a course of responsible and effective litigation to bring about the reversal of *Roe*. They accomplish their purposes with great scholarly precision, and with utmost respect for the constitutional values that have sustained this nation for over two centuries.

The task of convincing the Supreme Court to abandon a doctrine such as that proclaimed in *Roe v. Wade* is severe indeed. The doctrine of stare decisis stands as an immediate barrier, as does the inertial force of a nationwide public policy built on the premise of abortion as a fundamental constitutional right. Furthermore, the advocates charged with this effort must maintain the highest respect for the Court, even as they criticize part of its handiwork.

However, the recent decisions of the Court in the *Akron* and *Thornburgh* cases demonstrate that the Court itself remains divided on the merits of *Roe*. I believe that such tension over landmark constitutional decisions is a sign of health for our system of government. Moreover, I believe that the effort to keep such issues alive through litigation is a necessary and laudable step to assist the courts in their sworn responsibility to uphold and affirm the Constitution.

This volume will enrich its readers with a scholarly analysis of the *Roe* decision and a unique application of lessons learned from two centuries of constitutional adjudication to the pressing issue of abortion. Among their many contributions to the debate, these authors remove from the work of our courts on abortion a veil of secrecy that has often hindered the quality of public debate on this issue. They analyze the prospects for reversal of *Roe*, and candidly suggest the strategy by which this might be accomplished. Thus, they have not only assembled a brief against adherence to *Roe* by the Court, but have also contributed to public understanding of the processes of constitutional litigation by which our rights, liberties, and responsibilities are forged.

If the proper balance in policy-making between the judicial and elected branches of government is to be restored, greater public understanding of the judicial process is essential. *Abortion and the Constitution* adds to our understanding not only of *Roe v. Wade* and abortion, but also of our constitutional system of government.

Provo, Utah
Rex E. Lee
January 14, 1987
J. Reuben Clark School of Law
Brigham Young University

Part I

Background and Perspectives on Abortion

MICHAEL PEARCE PFEIFER

Abandoning Error: Self-Correction by the Supreme Court

IN 1970, an unmarried pregnant woman filed a class action suit in federal district court in Dallas which sought a declaratory judgment that Texas' criminal abortion laws were unconstitutional and an injunction against their enforcement. The Texas law, first enacted in 1854 and basically unchanged since 1856, prohibited abortion except when "procured or attempted by medical advice for the purpose of saving the life of the mother." The district court held that the Texas laws were unconstitutionally vague and overbroad, and infringed on the "fundamental right of single women and married persons to choose whether to have children." Wade, the defendant and district attorney, and Roe, a pseudonym for the plaintiff filing suit, appealed to the Supreme Court of the United States. The case was argued twice before the Court. On January 22, 1973, the Court announced its decision in *Roe v. Wade*, affirming the district court's judgment on the merits and introducing the broad doctrine of abortion privacy into constitutional law.[1]

Seldom, if ever, has a single Supreme Court decision so decisively transformed American constitutional history or so altered the relationship between law and morals—both public and private.[2] *Roe v. Wade* established within the Constitution a doctrine that has entirely legitimized what had previously been almost universally condemned: the practice of abortion on demand throughout the nine months of pregnancy.[3]

Such precedent setting decisions are usually derived from the social, economic, political, and legal philosophy of the majority of the Justices who make up the Court, and also represent a segment of the American population at a given time in history.[4] Seldom has a Supreme Court decision sliced so deeply into the basic fabric that composes the tapestry and direction of American law or instigated such profound changes in cherished rights, values, and personal prerogatives of individuals: the right to privacy, the structure of the family, the status of medical technology and its impact upon law and life, and the authority of state governments to protect the lives of their citizens.[5]

Many legal scholars, on both sides of the *Roe* debate, maintain that the effects of the decision are revolutionary; and, perhaps, the most tantalizing constitutional issue is the privacy right argument. Although a supporter of *Roe*, Laurence H. Tribe has admonished the legal community that *Roe* poses a conflict between important constitutional values and liberties so basic to our everyday lives.[6] John T. Noonan, Jr., a critic of *Roe*, sustained both points and argued that the Supreme Court, on behalf of liberty and of private choice, has revolutionized the legal structure of the family.[7] Tribe asserted that our history has clearly shown that, where controversy is greatest, so also are the dangers of majoritarian excess and the need for protection of privacy rights under the Constitution by an independent and principled judiciary.[8] Noonan claimed that these attributes were not evident in *Roe*; furthermore, he declared that the privacy right liberty established by *Roe* and other abortion cases has no foundation in the Constitution. Its establishment was illegitimate, unprincipled, and reflects the imposition of the personal beliefs of seven justices on the women and men of fifty states and rested on serious errors.[9] Professor Lynn Wardle concurred that incorporating the doctrine of abortion privacy as part of the supreme law of the land resulted from an accident of history, and argued that the Supreme Court should either overhaul the *Roe* doctrine or abandon it as a "derelict in the stream of the law."[10] But the law of the land, the meaning of the Constitution as a legal document, will be what the Court says that meaning is, until it admits its error or is corrected by a constitutional amendment.[11]

In *Thornburgh v. American College of Obstetricians and Gynecologists*, former Chief Justice Burger abandoned his tacit support of *Roe*, writing that his colleagues had gone too far in establishing an absolute right to abortion on demand, and therefore, *Roe* must be reexamined.[12] However, any effort to reexamine and reverse a landmark decision such as *Roe* must be solidly grounded. To determine the legitimacy of such an endeavor several questions must be examined and answered.

First, how often and under what circumstances have reversals of Supreme Court decisions taken place? Second, is there a coherent theory of self-correction by which the Court can admit error and reverse itself on *Roe* and other crucial decisions? Third, are there precedents for reversal sufficiently analogous in historical scope and constitutional importance to justify the expectations voiced by Burger?

A fortiori, admission of mistake goes against both the human grain and the corporate sense of self. For the Supreme Court, a constitutionally established branch of the federal government, to admit mistakes requires a partial repudiation of its historical past which has made the institution what it is; and it involves actively attacking the pose of wise self-sufficiency which the institution regularly assumes as it asserts its special claims to recognition as a corporate entity.

Why, theoretically and practically, should the Court be self-correcting? In the past the Court has erred with tragic consequences for individuals and disastrous results for the nation. *Lochner v. New York* and *Plessy v. Ferguson* were overturned only after great damage to individual citizens and the Republic that an admission of error could never rectify. *Roe v. Wade* has yet to be overturned and its constitutional misinterpretation has not been acknowledged by a majority of the Court. If *Roe* is to become a legitimate part of the constitutional tradition the Court must fashion a more workable doctrine and provide a more convincing justification.

I. A Brief Review of Supreme Court Reversals

WRITING IN 1932, Justice Brandeis used the word "often" to describe the frequency with which the Court had overruled its own constitutional decisions.[13] Brandeis was an experienced, perceptive, circumspect member of the Court whose cogent observation points out that on matters central to the American system of government, in terms of the Court's understanding of itself, its powers and its duties, a fallible Court has experienced failures and made constitutional mistakes. The Court has openly acknowledged error in interpreting the Constitution and admitted judicial error in fundamental areas such as human rights, federalism, and the duties of the various branches of government. It has corrected flawed interpretations and overruled its past constitutional decisions. The Court has explicitly rejected its own earlier reading of the Constitution over one hundred times. This number excludes the silent abandonment of a constitutional reading; cases which have distinguished or qualified or confined past precedents so that they are no longer viable and, although formally unrepudiated, are nonetheless discredited. Also, it does not include cases where the Court has changed the procedural rules in order to produce results which run counter to prior holdings—an efficacious technique as substantive as any pronouncement which abandons a past position.[14]

As the Court's confessions of error demonstrate, interpreting the Constitution can be fraught with risks and difficulties. Justices of intelligence, good will, and professional training have authoritatively misread the Constitution twice as frequently as voters elect presidents. This amounts to one admitted mistake every other year; but it should be noted that the figure is well under one percent of the overall percentage of decisions. However, considering the magnitude of subjects on which the Court has erred, along with the deliberateness with which the error has been proclaimed and the vigor with which it has been enforced, it becomes evident that any constitutional mistake by the Supreme Court has serious consequences for the country.

One argument asserts that when the Court overrules itself, it does not admit error, but brings itself up to date; and is adjusting its interpretation of the Constitution to a changed society. Such a contention supposes that the Constitution lacks specificity on many subjects and thus permits inconsistent interpretations and changes with the changing times; or that the Supreme Court is a constitutional convention permanently in session and free to give the Constitution contextually appropriate meaning. Both suppositions are spurious. Even with this devised interpretation, the Court cannot be acquitted of error when it changes its mind and gives a new interpretation of a prior decision. One prefers John Marshall's view that the Constitution must not be kept in tune with the times; on the contrary, he understood that the times, to the extent possible, must be kept in tune with the Constitution.[15]

One does not always know whether error is being corrected or being committed by the later ruling. What is clear is that, at one time or another, the Court must have been mistaken. In some instances, like *Lochner v. New York* and *Plessy v. Ferguson*, reasonable people agree that the original decisions were erroneous. Eminent Justices, like Marshall, Holmes, Brandeis, Cardozo, Taft, Taney, Stone, and Frankfurter, have given, or joined in, fallacious opinions. Their sole protection against repeating an error was a readiness to reconsider and follow experience and reason. The Court's willingness to revise former doctrines in light of the "lessons of experience and the force of better reasoning" is the best evidence of and best justification for continued confidence in the profound role of the Supreme Court in American government.[16]

Hudson and Smith v. Guestier in 1810, the first case in which the Supreme Court overruled itself, was remarkable, not because of a constitutional issue, but because the Court, supposedly dominated by John Marshall, repudiated an opinion announced as law by the Chief Justice only two years earlier. Marshall, in his stunned dissent to *Guestier*, appears to admit that he had incorrectly counted the votes when he first gave the decision now overruled—an admission of another kind of human fallacy. [17]

The practice of overruling error has been defended by the conservative nineteenth century Chief Justice Roger Brooke Taney and championed by the liberal twentieth century Justice William O. Douglas. The necessity of jettisoning past mistakes is a belief that belongs to the ideology of no party and no faction and is as much an institution accepted by the whole Court as judicial review itself.

In 1959 Albert P.Blaustein and Andrew H. Field calculated that the average life of a constitutional mistake was twenty-four years. [18] Under the Warren Court, which increased the number of reversals to almost two per term, the average life of a mistake declined. [19] The rate of overturning has fluctuated from time to time and reached its high point in the New Deal Court under Chief Justice Harlan Fiske Stone, when President Franklin D. Roosevelt had had a chance to replace most of the Justices who consistently found his legislative measures unconstitutional. [20]

Some cases have had a lengthy history before being repudiated; in fact, *New York v. Miln* was 104 years old when overruled by *Edwards v. California* in 1941. [21] At the other extreme is *Jones v. Opelika*, where a rehearing granted the same parties resulted in an announced opinion being overruled for the same litigants. [22] At least eight decisions have overruled earlier decisions within a year of their publication. [23] The most famous "quick" overruling was *The Legal Tender Cases*, which decided that it is constitutional for the federal government to make paper dollars lawful currency to pay debts. The opposite result, reached on constitutional grounds, had threatened the solvency of thousands of businesses and individuals after the Civil War. Bankruptcy and ruin across the nation were averted when President Ulysses S. Grant appointed two new Justices to the Court on the day on which the decision holding the greenbacks unconstitutional was announced. The new Justices, with the dissenters in the first case, turned the reading of the Constitution around and spared the finances of the nation. [24]

Other, less dramatic, reversals by the Court have nonetheless had far-reaching consequences. In 1842 Justice Joseph Story held, in *Swift v.*

Tyson, that there existed a "federal" common law which federal judges must apply in suits between citizens of different states.[25] Many jurists and lawyers thought *Swift* to be an offensive intrusion upon state sovereignty and principles of federalism. In 1938 in *Erie R.R. v. Tompkins*, one jurist, Louis Brandeis, forged a 5 to 4 majority and the Supreme Court held that the Constitution did not authorize a federal common law, and that federal judges must therefore be bound by the common law of the states. As a result, federal suits among citizens of different states were to be decided according to principles of state common law. Through the viewpoint of the new majority, what had been regularly invoked and applied for almost a century became an unconstitutional ghost whose erroneous existence was now ended. What had become reality by legal fiat in *Swift v. Tyson* ceased to be reality by legal fiat in *Erie*.[26] Moreover, *Erie* has survived in an era marked by the aggrandizement of federal power—often at the expense of the states. Thus, the Court is capable of running counter to prevailing trends in law and society when it recognizes a constitutional error in need of correction. Had Brandeis been unable to convince his brethren to overturn *Swift*, the activist judiciary of the 1960s and 1970s may have been able to accomplish the "federalization" of enormous portions of the common law heretofore entrusted to the states.

Another example of reversal on a matter of technical jurisdiction, but having immense practical effect, was the question of interstate jurisdiction over marriage and divorce. In 1904, the Court held by a 5 to 4 vote in *Haddock v. Haddock* that, absent personal jurisdiction over the parties, a state in which a couple was domiciled did not have power to grant a divorce which would be constitutionally valid in other states of the Union. In *Williams v. North Carolina* in 1942, *Haddock* was formally overruled and Nevada was empowered to give visitors from North Carolina divorces which, as a matter of constitutional doctrine, would be valid elsewhere.[27] However, three years later in *Williams II*, the Court held as a matter of constitutional law that North Carolina could still prosecute for bigamy the remarried spouse who had been lawfully divorced in Nevada.[28] It is unnecessary to trace the Court's subsequent permutations and gyrations as to divorce law except to quote Justice Frankfurter's 1957 statement that the Court had turned "the constitutional law of marital relations topsy-turvy." Justice Jackson turned to Shakespeare and quoted: "Confusion has made his masterpiece." In this area, the willingness to admit error and to start afresh was carried to perhaps an extreme degree.[29]

Of course, reversals were not limited to questions of jurisdiction. Three areas of mistake and correction illustrate instances of error in matters of popular concern where the Court has had to make sensitive appraisals of American values and, by its own later admission, failed. Often, the Court has reversed a decision bearing upon the fundamental rights of citizens vis-à-vis their government. Four prominent examples from the twentieth century illustrate this history.

In 1937, writing for an 8 to 1 majority, Benjamin Cardozo, a brilliant Court jurist with lengthy experience as a state judge in criminal appeals, held in *Palko v. Connecticut* that the Constitution did not forbid retrial of a defendant when a state showed on appeal that the trial court had erred in the defendant's favor. To permit a second trial did not violate fundamental principles of liberty and justice. "The edifice of justice stands," Cardozo wrote, "its symmetry, to many, greater than before."[30] Only Pierce Butler dissented, and did so without opinion. Thirty years later, *Palko* was overruled and Cardozo's approach scorned as "a watered down subjective version of the individual guarantees of the Bill of Rights," which were now read to erect an absolute barrier to retrying a defendant a second time at the state's request.[31]

In 1942, the Court held in *Betts v. Brady* that an indigent defendant on state felony charges was not entitled, as a matter of constitutional right, to a court-appointed lawyer.[32] In a decision ten years earlier, the Court had granted a right to counsel in *capital* cases, but the *Betts* court by a 6 to 3 vote distinguished this precedent. In the words of Justice Owen Roberts, "we are unable to say that the concept of due process incorporated in the Fourteenth Amendment obligates the states, whatever may be their own views, to furnish counsel in every such case."[33] Twenty-one years later, Justice Hugo Black, who dissented in *Betts v. Brady*, wrote for a unanimous Court in *Gideon v. Wainwright* that the Court had strayed in *Betts* from "its own well-considered precedents." He added:

[T]hat government hires lawyers to prosecute and defendants who have the money hire lawyers to defend are the strongest indicators of the widespread belief that lawyers in criminal courts are necessities, not luxuries. The right of one charged with crime to counsel may not be deemed fundamental and essential to fair trials in some countries, but it is in ours.[34]

In 1935 the Court, in *Grovey v. Townsend*, unanimously concluded, in another opinion written by Justice Roberts, that the Texas Democratic Party could exclude blacks from its state primary. It was admitted that, in Texas, Democratic nomination was equivalent to election. However, the Court refused to find that the party's exclusion of blacks was a state action discriminating on the basis of race and in violation of the Fourteenth and Fifteenth Amendments. Even more remarkable, the Texas Democrats had not even bothered to argue *Grovey*.[35] Nine years later, Justice Roberts, the earlier opinion writer now alone in dissent, was outraged when the Court found that the Democratic party conducted its primary under state statutory authority and that its acts were therefore state action violating the Fifteenth Amendment.[36] A greater degree of realism, an enhanced sensitivity to racial injustice, and the replacement of seven Justices since 1935 had led the Court to see the error of its first ruling.

The sanctity of religious belief was addressed in 1940 in *Gobitis v. Minersville School District*. The Court held that Pennsylvania could require a school child to salute the American flag, even though the requirement violated the child's belief as a Jehovah's Witness that the salute was a form of irreligious idolatry condemned by the Bible. Eight members of the Court believed there was no unconstitutional abridgement of the child's freedom of religion. Writing for the Court, Justice Frankfurter said that it would involve the Court "in the pronouncement of pedagogical and psychological dogma" to hold that the salute requirement was "a lawless inroad on that freedom of conscience which the Constitution protects." He treated the issue as one of educational policy and concluded that the Court had no authority to be "the school board for the country."[37] Just three years later, remarkably in the midst of war, *Gobitis* was formally repudiated by a majority of 6 to 3 in *West Virginia v. Barnette*. In the often quoted words of Justice Jackson, the Court declared, "If there is any fixed star in our constitutional constellation, it is that no official, high or petty, can prescribe what shall be orthodox in politics, nationalism, religion, or other matters of opinion or force citizens to confess by words or act their faith therein." The matter was now seen not as one of legislative policy in education but as one withdrawn by the First Amendment from legislative discretion. The conclusive reasoning of 1940 was decisively rejected as erroneous in 1943.[38]

II. Stare Decisis and Theories of Reversal

THUS, ERROR IS committed, and often abandoned, by the Court. Theory is needed to justify this self-corrective process because of the existence of a doctrine in all Anglo-American courts which favors reliance on precedents and accordingly creates a presumption in their favor. Shorthand for this doctrine, stare decisis, is a truncation of a longer Latin phrase, *stare decisis et quieta non movere*—"to stand by what has been decided and not disturb what is at rest."[39]

Some consider the issue of stare decisis as a particularly compelling reason why the Supreme Court should reconsider *Roe v. Wade*. First, as Justice Powell reminded the Court in 1974, it is not only the Court's prerogative but also its duty to reexamine a precedent where its reasoning or understanding of the Constitution is fairly called into question. And if the precedent or its rationale is of doubtful validity, then it should not stand. Second, the fundamental principle of consistency that underlies the doctrine of stare decisis should impel the Court to review its abortion privacy doctrine in order to achieve harmony in the law regarding the status of prenatal human life. [40]

Yet, even where the case for reversal is compelling, it is still a departure from this maxim of judicial behavior and, often enough, the dissenter who is objecting to the overruling will be found evoking stare decisis as a principle which the Court should be following. [41] It has been shrewdly observed that few instances can be found of a justice "embracing a constitutional principle he seriously disagrees with because of the compulsion of stare decisis." [42] In other words, most constitutional decisions remain good law because the justices still agree with them, not because of any independent force in the doctrine of stare decisis. But the maxim, useful in other branches of law, may work to keep the Justices from re-examining too many consititutional issues with a fresh mind. Agreeing with this view, Professor Tribe considers Justices who look upon precedents as divine edicts inscribed on stone tablets as lacking in a "sufficient appreciation of the evolutionary nature of constitutional law. It is sometimes more important that the court be right than that it be consistent." [43] Given these attributes of stare decisis, why has the Court, in Stone's words, "consistently maintained that the doctrine of precedent has less force in the realm of constitutional interpretation than in other areas of the law?" [44]

Stanley Reed, when Solicitor General under Roosevelt, tersely gave four reasons: "because the court must test its conclusions by the organic document, rather than precedent; because constitutional doubt must be personal . . . ; because legislation is often powerless to overcome questionable constitutional decisions; and finally because of the extreme difficulty in rectifying judicial error by amendment." [45] The first two reasons may be collapsed into one. Justices take an oath to uphold the Constitution—not the glosses of their predecessors. They have a sworn obligation to be personally faithful to the original document. They cannot shirk this duty by pointing to someone else's mistaken interpretation. [46] Indeed, Justices of the Supreme Court always have a right and duty of recourse to the Constitution to correct any later gloss upon it; and are called to control the text of "the organic document."

Reed's other two reasons may also be collapsed into a single point: for anyone except the Court, constitutional mistakes are difficult to correct. Since the Court is not insensible to congressional action, Congress may assist the process. However, after Congress has acted, the Court has the last word. It has to admit that Congress was right, and it was wrong. The Court occasionally must overrule its earlier cases because legislative correction of a constitutional decision is all but impossible. Some opponents of *Roe* learned this lesson through bitter experience when they attempted to attack *Roe* through congressional statute in 1981 and constitutional amendment in 1982 and 1983. Only four decisions have been reversed and corrected by constitutional amendment: *Chisholm v. Georgia* (1793) was reversed by the Eleventh Amendment; *Dred Scott v. Sanford* (1857) was overturned by the Thirteenth Amendment in 1865 and the Fourteenth Amendment in 1868; *Pollack v. Farmers Loan and Trust* (1865) was nullified by the Sixteenth Amendment in 1913; and the Twenty-sixth Amendment voided the Court's holding in *Oregon v. Mitchell* (1970).[47]

Compared with correction by the Court itself, amendment is a time-consuming, cumbersome business. "It is not the constitution-amending power that plays the major role in the American system in resolving the dilemma of stability and change in constitutional law," writes a professor of constitutional law. "It is the Supreme Court. And this is not an innovation. It has been the guiding principle since the establishment of the doctrine of judicial review."[48] If the Supreme Court has displaced the amending process in amending the Constitution, the Court also has the obligation to amend its constitutional errors. If, as Justice Brandeis pointed out, "correction through legislative action is practically impossible," the Court has the duty to correct itself.[49] Since the Constitution is so difficult to amend, the Court has a special duty to correct itself when it has misread the document.

There is a final reason, not stated by Reed, which could apply to the correction of any error; and which has peculiar force when the meaning of our basic governmental document is in question. It is wrong to go on being wrong. As Justice Black put it in a particularly bold challenge to precedent (the issue was whether a corporation was a person under the Fourteenth Amendment): "A constitutional interpretation that is wrong should not stand."[50] The Court cannot command respect by invoking precedent to maintain a position that is seen by informed observers as contrary to experience and reason. As Justice Brandeis expressed it, when arguing for overruling a line of bad precedents, the Court should bring itself "into agreement with experience and with facts newly ascertained," so that its judicial authority may, as Chief Justice Taney said, "depend altogether on the force of the reasoning by which it is supported."[51]

Reed outlined his theory of stare decisis and the Constitution during a pivotal era in the Court's interplay with American political life. Since then, matters, such as the process of screening candidates for the judiciary, the role of the Senate in the judicial appointment procedure, and the appropriateness of the executive branch seeking reversal of landmark precedents, have become a battleground between the White House and Congress. While *Roe* is not the sole precipitant of the debate, it seems the most vulnerable of the landmarks under attack. Not surprisingly, the status of *Roe* has keenly influenced the theories of constitutional interpretation during the current decade. These theories, unfortunately, have often blurred the reality that the Court is capable of—and in fact, has often committed objectively determined—identifiable error. Thus, the Court's record of reversal has been rationalized not as admission of error, but as an alteration of constitutional interpretation which coincides with the views of contemporary American society. In Dean Stone's words, "[e]xcept in the most extraordinary of circumstances, a prior interpretation can be said to be 'wrong' not in any definitive sense, but only in the sense that the process of constitutional interpretation is a process of evolution. It is a dynamic process through which constitutional law comes . . . to express the ideas of the community."[52]

This view has several prominent adherents who cite *Roe* as the archetype of a decision where the Court exercised a prophetic function by simultaneously discerning and shaping the values of the community. They argue that a reversal of *Roe* would be expedited through "raw judicial power." Ironically, the other side of the legal community in this debate, discussed in this volume by Horan and Balch, argue that *Roe* itself was the exercise of raw judicial power.

This essentially relativist view of constitutional interpretation does not adequately explain the Court's historical record of reversing its interpretation. First, the view supposes that the Constitution lacks specificity on important topics and the Court must sit as a permanent constitutional convention empowered to amend the Constitution by interpretation of inherently vague terms. Professor Raoul Berger's trenchant analysis of the Fourteenth Amendment, *Government By Judiciary*, demonstrated that this viewpoint has encouraged Supreme Court decisions which may be contrary to the plain meaning and history of the Constitution's text and not merely a questionable reading of that text.[53] Second, even under this view of the Court's role, the Court cannot be acquitted of error every time it reverses a prior decision; for that prior decision may have itself created or exaggerated the unjust institutions or practices which impelled the Court later to reconsider its error. Can these modern theoreticians sincerely believe that there ought to be no sense of "rightness" or "wrongness" inherent in the terms of the Constitution to guide the judges in its interpretation? John Marshall's view, that the times must be kept in tune with the Constitution, is preferred.[54] Thus, neither the traditional common law understanding of stare decisis, nor the relativist view of constitutional values shields the Court from the obligation to identify and to correct error in constitutional interpretation.

III. *Lochner, Plessy,* and *Roe:* Three Egregious Errors

REASON, SWORN DUTY, and the lack of other convenient ways to redress an error converge in justification of the Court's pattern of self-correction in constitutional cases. Six instances have been examined. Two were in the domain of judicial expertise; and four in the sphere of political values and human rights where self-correction was needed and was achieved. Another three examples where the error was deepest and most pernicious in its consequences will conclude the analysis. Rectification of error in two of these cases affords reason for hope that the third mistake will also be abandoned.

First, the Court made a fallacious judgment that "the liberty" conferred by the Fourteenth Amendment had been violated by the states' regulation of working conditions, hours, and wages. This error was initiated in the 1905 *Lochner v. New York* ruling by a divided Court.[55] Justice Holmes denounced the ruling in a classic dissent, which is as pertinent now as when written: "I think that the word liberty in the Fourteenth Amendment is perverted when it is held to prevent the natural outcome of a dominant opinion, unless it can be said that a rational and fair man necessarily would admit that the statute proposed would infringe fundamental principles as they have been understood by the traditions of our people and our law."[56] Holmes' criticisms were echoed by law professors and in law reviews.[57] Nonetheless, in 1922, *Lochner* was still considered good precedent. It was confidently invoked by a 5 to 3 split Court holding unconstitutional the action of Congress in setting a minimum wage for the District of Columbia.[58] Liberty of contract was still a sacred shibboleth. Not until 1937 was it decisively put to rest.[59] For about thirty years, *Lochner* had been a block to the regulation of wages and hours and to the protection of the health and working conditions of the ordinary worker.

Later opinions of the Court have ritualistically acknowledged the error of *Lochner*.[60] The mistake arose from lack of judicial restraint, from reading personal opinions into the Constitution, from supposing that the majority Justices were wiser and more virtuous than their dissenting brethren or any legislators, and from a perverse expansion of the term "liberty" in the Fourteenth Amendment. Between the 1937 expulsion of *Lochner* and *Roe v. Wade* in 1973, the notion of substantive due process—the notion that the Court could give a substantive social meaning to liberty in the Fourteenth Amendment— had few defenders off the Court or on. It was in the light of *Lochner* that Justice Douglas could conclude, "From age to age the problem of constitutional adjudication is the same. It is to keep the power of government unrestrained by the social or economic theories that one set of judges may entertain.... It is when a judiciary with life tenure seeks to write its social and economic creed into the Constitution that instability is created."[61]

Notice that those who reflected critically on *Lochner* did not speak simply of economic theories, but of social theories read into the Constitution. The lesson of *Lochner* is a powerful one; in *Roe v. Wade* we see a parallel decision using the rubric of liberty to deny the power of a state to protect its inhabitants. Professor Archibald Cox criticized *Roe v. Wade* because the Court failed to establish the legitimacy of the decison by not articulating a precept of sufficient abstractness to lift the ruling above the level of a political judgment. "Constitutional rights ought not to be created under the Due Process Clause unless they can be stated in principles sufficiently absolute to give them roots throughout the community and continuity over significant periods of time, and to lift them above the level of the pragmatic political judgments of a particular time and place."[62]

It is sometimes believed that the Court has never corrected itself in order to diminish or impair a constitutional liberty. The repudiation of *Lochner* is evidence to the contrary. Liberty of contract, a liberty as dear to employers and to academic defenders of laissez-faire as the liberty of abortion is dear to abortionists and their media supporters, was sharply curtailed. Liberty was limited in order to protect more basic human rights.

Plessy v. Ferguson was the second consequential and socially extensive mistake that, though ultimately corrected by the Court, denied blacks full participation in American life. *Dred Scott*, and its monstrous holding that a descendant of black slaves could never be a citizen of the United States, was undone within a decade by the Civil War and the amendments that the war made possible.[63] In 1896 the Court held, in *Plessy v. Ferguson*, that the Fourteenth Amendment was not violated when the state segregated its facilities by race. The case involved a man "of one-eighth African blood" criminally prosecuted for travelling in a railroad coach reserved for whites. The Court invoked for justification a pre-Civil War decision in Massachusetts upholding segregated schools in Boston. A majority of 7 to 1 found nothing wrong in "the enforced separation of the two races." "Absolute equality before the law" was compatible with segregation.[64]

The academic community acquiesced in the error. The most relevant *Harvard Law Review* article on the subject prior to 1912 seriously contended that the Fifteenth Amendment giving blacks the vote was actually void as an infringement of sovereignty irrevocably possessed by the states.[65]

As late as 1927, *Plessy v. Ferguson* was formally applied to schools and upheld by the Court. In the 1927 case, Martha Lum, a nine-year-old girl of Chinese descent, was denied admission to the "white" school in her Mississippi neighborhood and allowed only to enter the "colored" school. The Court found nothing unconstitutional in the action of the school board and even added that segregation on railroads was "a more difficult question" than in schools. The unanimous opinion was written by Chief Justice, and former President, William Howard Taft for a Court which included Holmes and Brandeis—men not afraid of dissenting. Their joining in the opinion and judgment must be taken to reflect their reading of the Constitution.[66]

More than forty years after its adoption, *Plessy v. Ferguson* was alive and well. Using its formal criteria of equal though separate facilities, the white majority was able with equanimity to disregard reality and see segregated churches, restrooms, eating facilities, streetcar seats, schools, and colleges as though black persons in America were treated equally with white. Reality was seen through the blinders the Court had provided.

In 1954, *Brown v. Board of Education* ended the farce of formal equality and actual discrimination. Again, the Court was unanimous. What Taft and Holmes and Brandeis could not see in 1927, everyone on the Court saw in 1954: that segregation of children in the public schools deprived the minority children of "equal educational opportunities" in violation of the equal protection clause of the Fourteenth Amendment. It had been more than 100 years since a famous state judge, Lemuel Shaw, had given the Boston school segregation decision.[67]

Whether the time is measured from that early date or from the beginning of the twentieth century when other eminent judges could see nothing discriminatory in segregation, certain lessons can be drawn. The law can be used as a powerful screen keeping out reality. The law proclaimed by the Supreme Court can blind the nation and the Justices themselves for long stretches of time. Yet, hope should never die. The foundational work of lawyers, law professors, teachers, and the interested public was instrumental in changing the firmly established error. A powerful single-issue group, the National Association for the Advancement of Colored People (NAACP), which had been in existence for almost fifty years, played a critical part in the agitation and litigation that removed the Court's blinders on race. Such organizations played a significant role in helping the Court to recognize error.[68] In the end, the Court put itself in accord with "newly-ascertained facts" and made its authority depend not on raw judicial power but on reason. Indeed, the Court's strength in repudiating its half-century-old reading of the Constitution, and the vigor with which desegregation has become an agenda for our society, are happy auguries of what can happen if *Roe v. Wade* is corrected.[69]

As in *Lochner*, the dissent in *Roe* was at pains to tell the majority how it was not only wrong but had exceeded the judicial mandate. Also, academic criticism has regarded *Roe* as being as wrong as *Lochner*.[70] Like *Lochner*, in the name of some secret superior wisdom of the majority Justices, the case profoundly inhibits the states in their lawful exercise of their power to protect their inhabitants. No rule would be violated, no constitutional authority would be subverted, and no revolutionary precedent would be created, if the Court allows the states to protect the unborn.[71]

Worse than *Lochner*, *Roe* inhibits this power at the fundamental level of life itself. In its devastating consequences for individuals it can be compared to *Plessy v. Ferguson*. Like *Plessy*, *Roe* is profoundly disrespectful of the minority it subjects to discriminatory treatment. Noonan's emotion and intellect compelled him to say:

> *Roe* strains reality through formal legal blinders preventing the relevant reality from being seen. The moving, growing, pain-conscious child in the womb becomes a "theory of life," an abstraction, a zero in the constitutional weighing. And that blindered perception has been forced upon every federal judge, and shields the Court itself, as well as large numbers of our fellow citizens, from facing the real fact that abortion is the taking of the life of a human child.[72]

Stare decisis et quieta non movere—in the last analysis, wrongly decided constitutional questions are never quiet, but are always open to discussion. The major cases which have been overturned were opinions whose grounds were tenuous, which were against the most profound values in American history, and which were already crumbling because they were seen as wrongly reasoned and blind to reality. As Justice Jackson memorably noted, "Power should answer to reason none the less because its fiat is beyond appeal." [73] In fact, the fiat of the Court is not beyond appeal. Appeal from Supreme Court error always lies, not in the wrongly decided case, but in the wrongly decided issue heard by a subsequent Court possessed of the truth. Lessons of experience and the force of better reasoning lead one to conclude that what was done by raw judicial power in *Roe* must answer to reason—and it will ultimately do so.[74]

Notes

1. Roe v. Wade, 410 U.S. 113 (1973). The concept for this chapter was taken from an address delivered by John T. Noonan, Jr., then Professor of Law at The University of California, Berkeley, at an AUL Conference on March 31, 1984. Professor Noonan was later appointed to the United States Court of Appeals for the Ninth Circuit and began service as a court of appeals judge in 1986. Professor Noonan had no responsibility subsequent to 1984 in the conceptualization or final version of this paper. For an excellent, critical overview of the *Roe* decision see Lynn D. Wardle, *Rethinking Roe v. Wade*, 1985 B.Y.U.L. Rev., at 231. Discussion and criticism of *Roe* is standard in constitutional law texts and treatises as well as many other monographs. *See, e.g.,* A. Bickel, The Morality of Consent 27–29 (1975); A. Cox, The Role of the Supreme Court in American Government 113 (1976); G. Gunther, Constitutional Law 517–47 (11th ed. 1985); H. Krause, Family Law: Cases, Comments, and Questions 327–30 (2d ed. 1983); J. Nowak, R. Rotunda & J. Young, Constitutional Law 630–35 (1978); L. Tribe, American Constitutional Law 886–990 (1978). For comprehensive and reliable information on abortion cases and the law in America, contact The AUL Legal Defense Fund, 343 South Dearborn, Suite 1804, Chicago, IL 60604.

2. In his seminal treatment of religion and politics in the United States, Richard John Neuhaus remarked about the dispute spawned by *Roe v. Wade* that "no other dispute so clearly and painfully illustrates the problematic of the naked public square." R.J. Neuhaus, The Naked Public Square, 28 (1984).

3. For a discussion of the precise holdings in *Roe v. Wade, see* Horan and Balch, Roe v. Wade: *No Justification in History, Law or Logic* in this volume.

4. W. Berns, *Judicial Review and the Rights and Laws of Nature,* The Supreme Court Review (1982) at 49, 51.

5. *See* L. Wardle, The Abortion Privacy Doctrine (1981).

6. Laurence H. Tribe, God Save This Honourable Court: How the Choice of Supreme Court Justices Shapes Our History, 17 (1985). He felt that the greatest impact of privacy right ruling in *Griswold* was felt in the *Roe* case.

7. John T. Noonan, Jr., A Private Choice: Abortion in America in the Seventies, 3 (1979).

8. Brief of *Amici Curicae* Sen. Bob Packwood, Rep. Don Edwards, et al., *Thornburgh* v. *American College of Obstetricians and Gynecologists,* 106 S. Ct. 2169 (1986) at 7. *See, e.g., United States* v. *Nixon,* 418 U.S. 683 (1974); *New York Times* v. *United States,* 403 U.S. 713 (1971); *Cooper* v. *Aaron,* 358 U.S. 1 (1958). Tribe goes

on to assert that for the Court to overrule *Roe* v. *Wade* would not only be a significant step backward but a repudiation of the fifty-year path along which the Court located its 1973 abortion ruling. "The central question to be addressed, then, is whether an overruling of *Roe* v. *Wade* would, as the Government asserts, merely turn the clock back to 1973 by erasing what it calls 'an erroneous point of departure,' ... 'from the generally propitious journey,' ... along which constitutional law had traveled up to 1973—or whether *Roe* v. *Wade* was instead a natural step along that journey, so that its overruling would entail a far more substantial retreat, propelling the Court and country onto a legal landscape from which not only *Roe* but many of its important antecedents, and the protections they provide for us all, would tragically be absent." Brief Amici Curiae, *supra* at 10.

9. Noonan, *supra* note 7 at 189. Noonan notes that "Harry Blackmun found in the Ninth Amendment's reservation of power to the People or in the Fourteenth Amendment's reference to liberty—he was not entirely sure in which—a liberty to consent to an abortion. On that date the Constitution came to mean that abortion was an American freedom." *Id.* at 9. The constitutional right to privacy, first announced in *Griswold*, was located, in Justice Douglas's expressive phrase, in the "penumbra" of several Amendments; and was a right to marital privacy. "The right of privacy was an offshoot of the holiness of marriage. . . . How quickly marital privacy became procreative privacy." *The Family and the Supreme Court*, 23 Cath. U. L. Rev. 256, 266 (1973).

10. Wardle, *supra* note 1. In the 1973 *Roe* opinion, written by Justice Blackmun, the Court declared that a woman's right to abortion privacy was a fundamental constitutional right; thus, state regulations "restricting abortion could be sustained only if necessary to effectuate a compelling state interest." 235, 245. North Dakota State Bd. of Pharmacy v. Snyder's Drug Store, Inc., 414 U.S. 156, 167 (1973). Wardle wrote, "It is time for the Supreme Court to reexamine and revise *Roe v. Wade*. The doctrine of abortion privacy should be modified to provide more workable standards and more reasonable analysis." The Supreme Court now has an excellent opportunity to correct the excesses without rejecting the positive principle of *Roe*, at 263.

11. Noonan, *supra* note 7, at 8. He also strongly feels that the abortion cases subverted the Ninth and Fourteenth Amendments and violated the organic distribution of powers made by Article I.

12. 106 S. Ct. 2169, 2190–2192 (1986) (Burger, C.J. disssenting).

13. Burnet v. Coronado Oil and Gas Co., 285 U.S. 393, 407 (Brandeis, J., dissenting).

14. *See* Blaustein and Field, *'Overruling' Opinions in the Supreme Court*, 57 Mich. L. Rev. 152, 161, 167 (1958) (90 overruling decisions as of 1958, 60 of them on constitutional questions); Noland, *Stare Decisis and the Overruling of Constitutional Decisions in the Warren Years* (30 overruled, 1954–1968). Subtracting 4 decisions counted twice, there were 86 constitutional overrulings as of 1969. For an example of an apparent *sub silentio* overruling, *see* City of Akron v. Akron Center for Reproductive Health, Inc., 462 U.S. 416 (1983), *overruling* Gary-Northwest Indiana Women's Services, Inc. v. Orr, 451 U.S. 134 (1981); the overruling is pointed out by Justice O'Connor in dissent. *Akron*, 462 U.S. at 455

n. 3. For examples of qualifying decisions, *see* Burnet v. Coronado Oil and Gas Co., 285 U.S. 393, 408 (1932) (Brandeis, J., dissenting). For discussion of the effect of procedural changes, see Neuborne, *The Procedural Assault on the Warren Legacy:* A Study in Repeal by Indirection, 5 Hofstra L. Rev. 545 (1977). *See also* Wardle, *supra* note 1, at 234.

15. Berns, *supra* note 4, at 51.

16. Wardle, *supra* note 1, at 257. Burnet v. Coronado Oil & Gas Co., 285 U.S. 393, 407–08 (Brandeis, J., dissenting); *see also* United States v. Scott, 437 U.S. 82, 101 (1978) (Brennan, J., dissenting).

17. Hudson and Smith v. Guestier, 10 U.S. (6 Cranch) 280 (1810), *overruling* Rose v. Himely, 8 U.S. (4 Cranch) 241 (1808). For dissenting opinion of Justice Marshall, see *Hudson*, 6 Cranch at 285.

18. Blaustein and Field, *supra* note 14 at 161.

19. Noland, *supra* note 14 at 119.

20. Douglas, *Stare Decisis*, 49 Col. L. Rev. 735, 743 (1949).

21. Edwards v. California, 314 U.S. 160 (1941), *overruling* City of New York v. Miln, 11 Pet. (36 U.S.) 102 (1837).

22. Jones v. Opelika 319 U.S. 103 (1943), *overruling* Jones v. Opelika 316 U.S. 584 (1942).

23. Blaustein and Field, *supra* note 14 at 160.

24. The Legal Tender Cases, 79 U.S. (12 Wall). 457 (1870) *overruling* Hepburn v. Griswold. 75 U.S. (8 Wall). 604 (1869).

25. Swift v. Tyson, 41 U.S. (16 Pet.) 1 (1842).

26. Erie R.R. Co. v. Tompkins, 304 U.S. 64 (1938).

27. Williams v. North Carolina, 317 U.S. 287 (1942), *overruling* Haddock v. Haddock, 201 U.S. 562 (1906).

28. Williams v. North Carolina, 325 U.S. 226 (1945).

29. Vanderbilt v. Vanderbilt, 354 U.S. 416, 425 (1957) (Frankfurter, J., dissenting); Rice v. Rice, 336 U.S. 674, 680 (1949) (dissenting opinion of Jackson, J., quoting *Macbeth*, Act II, iii, 65. *See generally*, Noonan, *The Family and the Supreme Court*, 23 Cath. U. L. Rev. 256 (1973).

30. Palko v. Connecticut, 308 U.S. 319, 328 (1937).

31. Benton v. Maryland, 395 U.S. 784, 794 (1968), *overruling* Palko v. Connecticut, 308 U.S. 319 (1937).

32. Betts v. Brady, 316 U.S. 455 (1942).

33. Powell v. Alabama, 287 U.S. 45 (1932); Betts v. Brady, 316 U.S. at 455.

34. Gideon v. Wainwright, 372 U.S. 335 (1963).

35. Grovey v. Townsend, 295 U.S. 45, 46 (1935) (no appearance for respondent); *Id.* at 54 (admission that primary win meant election).

36. Smith v. Allwright, 321 U.S. 649 (1944).

37. Minersville School District v. Gobitis, 310 U.S. 586, 597–598 (1940).

38. West Virginia State Board of Education v. Barnette, 319 U.S. 624, 642 (1943), *overruling Minersville*, 310 U.S. 586. Having pointed to the decisive impact of new presidential appointees in the *Legal Tender Cases* and in the New Deal Court's rulings, one should note that in the party primary case Justice Stone changed his mind on the merits between the first and second decision;

and that in the flag salute cases, Justices Black, Douglas, and Murphy shifted their votes and made error what they had embraced as truth only three years earlier.

39. *See* McKay, *Stability and Change in Constitutional Law*, 17 Vand. L. Rev. 203, 213 (1964). McKay renders *"quieta"* as "what is established." "What is at rest" seems more accurate.

40. Wardle, *supra note* 1 at 252. Mitchell v. W.T. Grant Co., 416 U.S. 600, 627–28 (1974) (Powell, J., concurring). Professor Llewellyn noted many years ago that: "no phase of our law is so misunderstood as our system of precedent. The basic false conception is that a precedent or the precedents will in fact (and in a "precedent-system" ought to) simply dictate the decision in the current case.... Now the truth is this: only in times of stagnation or decay does an appellate system even fairly resemble such a picture of detailed dictation by the precedents." Wardle at 256, *citing* K. Llewllyn, The Common Law Tradition 62 (1960).

41. *See, e.g.*, Roberts, J., dissenting in Smith v. Allwright, 321 U.S. at 666.

42. *See* Kadish, *Judicial Review in the United States Supreme Court and the High Court of Australia*, 37 Texas L. Rev. 133, 153 (1958).

43. Tribe, *supra* note 6 at 123.

44. Stone, *Precedent, The Amendment Process, and Evolution in Constitutional Doctrine*, Address to the Federalist Society Convention, Jan. 31, 1987, at 8 (copy on file with the author).

45. Reed, *Stare decisis and Constitutional Law*, Pa. Bar. Assoc. April 1938 at 134, *quoted in* Noland, *supra* n. 13 at 108.

46. *Cf.* Douglas, *supra* n. 20 at 736.

47. Tribe, *supra* note 6 at 123; Stone, *supra* note 44 at 3.

48. Williams, *Stability and Change in Constitutional Law*, 17 Vand. L. Rev. 221, 237 (1964).

49. *Burnet*, 285 U.S. 406–407. (Brandeis, J., dissenting).

50. Connecticut General Co. v. Johnson 303 U.S. 77, 85 (1938) (Black, J., dissenting).

51. *Burnet*, 285 U.S. at 412–413 (Brandeis, J., dissenting).

52. Stone, *supra*, note 44 at 9.

53. R. Berger, *Government By Judiciary* (1976). For discussion of just such an error, and the legal strategy to reverse it, *see* Myers, *Prolife Litigation and the American Civil Liberties Tradition* in this volume. *See also* C. Wolfe, *The Rise of Modern Judicial Review* (1986).

54. Berns, *supra note* 4 at 51.

55. Lochner v. New York, 198 U.S. 45 (1905).

56. *Id.* at 76 (Holmes, J., dissenting).

57. *See, e.g.*, Hand, *Due Process of Law and the Eight-Hour Day*, 21 Harv. L. Rev. 495 (1910).

58. Adkins v. Children's Hospital, 261 U.S. 525, 545 (1923).

59. West Coast Hotel v. Parrish, 300 U.S. 379 (1937) (overruling explicitly only *Adkins, supra* n. 58).

60. *See, e.g.*, Ferguson v. Skrupa, 372 U.S. 726 (1963). *See also* Justice Stewart's remarks in Dandridge v. Williams, 397 U.S. 471, 484 (1970).

61. Douglas, *supra* note 20 at 754.

62. A. Cox, The Role of the Supreme Court in American Government (New York, 1976) at 113,114. Other respected scholars have echoed this criticism. *See, e.g.,* A. Bickel, *supra* note 1, at 27–29; Blasi, *The Rootless Activism of the Burger Court,* in The Burger Court: The Counter-Revolution That Wasn't 198, 212 (v. Blasi ed. 1983); Ely and Epstein are also quoted in Wardle, *supra* note 1. Wardle, *The Gap Between Law and Moral Order: An Examination of the Legitimacy of the Supreme Court Abortion Decisions,* 1980 B.Y.U. L. Rev. 820–27; Noonan, *supra* note 7.

63. Dred Scott v. Sanford, 60 U.S. (19 How.) 393, 403, 427 (1857).

64. Plessy v. Ferguson, 163 U.S. 537, 538 (1896) (description of appellant); *Id.* at 544 ("absolute equality before the law"); *Id.* at 551 ("enforced separation").

65. Machem, *Is the Fifteenth Amendment Void?* 23 Harv. L. Rev. 169 (1912).

66. Gong Lum v. Rice, 275 U.S. 78 (1927).

67. Brown v. Board of Education, 347 U.S. 483, 493 (1954).

68. *See* The Black Revolt, 65 (Geschwender ed. 1971). The NAACP was founded in 1909.

69. Roe v. Wade, 410 U.S. 113 (1973).

70. *Id.* at 222 (White, J., dissenting). *See* Noonan, *supra* note 7 at 29–32.

71. Noonan, *supra* note 7 at 178.

72. J. Noonan, Abandoning Error, Speech delivered to a conference sponsored by Americans United for Life, Chicago, Illinois, March 31, 1984, Unpublished. Speech on file with AUL.

73. Jewell Ridge Coal Corp. v. Local No. 6167, 325 U.S. 161, 196 (1945).

74. Noonan, *supra* note 72.

RICHARD S. MYERS*

Prolife Litigation and the American Civil Liberties Tradition

Introduction

AMERICANS UNITED FOR LIFE LEGAL DEFENSE FUND sponsored a March, 1984 conference on "Reversing *Roe v. Wade* through the Courts"; while a historic moment in the prolife movement, the event was hardly unique in the contemporary history of American constitutional litigation. The conferees, like other Americans attempting to secure protection for individuals and groups who are without a voice in American political society, focused on understanding the dynamics of the process of constitutional litigation. They then explored how they could meaningfully participate in that process.

Indeed, there is a particularly striking parallel between the present effort to secure rights for the unborn and the fight for racial equality, which has occupied our judicial system for most of this century. The parallel can be seen by first describing the now-famous litigation which culminated in the overruling of *Plessy v. Ferguson* in *Brown v. Board of Education*.[1] This chapter isolates and discusses several key lessons flowing from that earlier civil rights experience. Finally, the intention

---

*An earlier draft of this chapter was completed in September, 1984. I coauthored that version with Kenneth F. Ripple, who was then a Professor of Law at the University of Notre Dame. John M. Maciejczyk, Notre Dame Class of 1984, provided helpful research assistance in preparation of the September, 1984 draft. Professor Ripple's participation in the project ended in September, 1984. Professor Ripple was later appointed to the United States Court of Appeals for the Seventh Circuit, and began service as a federal court of appeals judge in June, 1985. In November, 1986, I substantially revised the September, 1984 draft. That revision was undertaken without the participation of Judge Ripple.

is to analyze how these lessons have been applied in the various submissions of the AUL conference.

I. *Brown v. Board of Education* and Its Lessons

WHEN A DEDICATED GROUP of NAACP lawyers set out in earnest to secure the eventual overruling of *Plessy v. Ferguson,* they had before them the now famous Margold Report—a report which in many ways was not all that different from the work product of the AUL conference. The Margold Report attempted to set forth a long-term strategy for the eventual overruling of the separate but equal doctrine.[2] That report was based on a brilliant understanding of the process of constitutional litigation and represented an act of faith in the American judicial system's capacity for self-correction and vindication of human rights.

Why was this group confident that, in the long term, it would achieve justice for its cause within the context of the American judicial system? Earlier decisions of the Court had given them little cause for hope. Indeed, *Plessy v. Ferguson* appeared to be just as insurmountable a barrier then as *Roe v. Wade* appears today.[3] While most Americans remember the decision in *Plessy v. Ferguson,* the absolute sterility of its analysis and the Court's blindness to the decision's impact on the lives of black Americans have been blunted by intervening events. Consider, however, the following passage from *Plessy*:

> We consider the underlying fallacy of the plaintiff's argument to consist in the assumption that the enforced separation of the two races stamps the colored race with a badge of inferiority. If this be so, it is not by reason of anything found in the act, but solely because the colored race chooses to put that construction upon it.[4]

Faced with this judicial work product, the NAACP lawyers still put their faith in the capacity of the American judicial system to self-correct.[5] In using the litigation process to bring about constitutional change, the NAACP lawyers displayed an understanding of two basic principles of the process of constitutional litigation. First, even as it performs the important task of constitutional adjudication, the American judiciary is still a child of the common law. It rarely takes a giant step to establish a new doctrine or definitively reject an old one. On the rare occasions when it radically departs from an established precedent, the system still articulates its new course as an outgrowth of older, deemphasized strains in the case law. Second, advances in constitutional doctrine, even more than changes in other areas of the common law, are based not only on the facts of the case but also on a broader understanding of the issue's significance and impact.

In the series of school desegregation cases between *Plessy* and *Brown*, the NAACP lawyers, led by Thurgood Marshall, observed and adhered to fundamental principles of the American constitutional litigation system. First, they accepted the current state of the law and worked with it. They did not argue immediately for a reversal of *Plessy v. Ferguson*. Rather, they argued that if segregation were to continue, absolute equality between the races was constitutionally mandated. In the words of the Margold Report, "we are in effect choosing only to compel the states which desire segregation to provide for it in a form which will render equality imperative and provide Negro parents with effective, practicable means of forcing derelict educational officers to perform their duties properly."[6] Or, as Marshall asserted, "the best overall strategy seemed to be an attack against the segregation system by lawsuits seeking absolute and complete equalization of curricula, faculty, and physical equipment in white and black schools on the theory that the extreme cost of maintaining two equal school systems would eventually destroy segregation."[7]

In 1936, *Pearson v. Murray*, one of the most prominent early cases, involved the attempt of a young black man to attend the then segregated University of Maryland Law School.[8] The major thrust of the litigation was aimed at this limited goal of obtaining equal educational facilities for black law students. The trial court and, on appeal, the Court of Appeals of Maryland ordered Murray's admission to the University of Maryland. Although *Plessy* permitted separate facilities for each race, the court concluded that Maryland was required under the Fourteenth Amendment to provide *substantially equal* treatment to citizens of different races. The court ruled that the principle of "substantial equality" required that Maryland either provide an equal education within the state of Maryland or admit the student to the University of Maryland.[9] To a casual observer, victory in *Pearson* may have seemed insignificant in terms of the ultimate goal of overruling *Plessy v. Ferguson*. Yet, it accomplished a great deal by assuring black citizens the professional education they sought and needed if they were to obtain leadership positions in the community. Moreover, *Pearson* created a situation that required state authorities and courts to think through whether "separate but equal" had any rational basis. Finally, the decision set the stage for even more significant advances.

The second fundamental principle observed by the NAACP lawyers was that, while accepting and dealing with the reality of current precedent, Marshall and his colleagues suggested the need for reevaluation of the current rule. For instance, while the major thrust of the *Pearson* litigation was toward securing equality of treatment within the rule of *Plessy v. Ferguson*, evidence was also submitted to support the claim that it was not possible for any professional school to be segregated by race and still be considered equal. For example, Roger Howell, Dean of the University of Maryland Law School, testified that, for a student aspiring to a practice in Maryland, attendance at any other law school but the University of Maryland Law School was not an equivalent legal education.[10]

The NAACP's methodology of presenting the court an easy way of deciding the case within the established rule of law and, simultaneously, offering the court an opportunity to reexamine its precedent to forge a more just rule, was particularly prominent in later professional school cases. For instance, in *Sipuel v. Board of Regents*, Marshall argued that the University of Oklahoma had to provide the plaintiff with a separate but qualitatively equivalent education.[11] He also argued, through the testimony of leading professors from Harvard, Chicago, Columbia, and Wisconsin, that an all black law school separated from the dominant white population could never provide an equivalent legal education. Again, in *Sweatt v. Painter*, a great effort was made to demonstrate that, no matter how similar the schools might be from the point of view of physical facilities or faculty, a black law school could not give an inherently equal education.[12] In *McLaurin v. Oklahoma State Regents*, Marshall argued that a segregated environment deprived a graduate student of an integral part of graduate education—the opportunity to interact with other equally qualified students.[13]

This approach bore fruit when both *Sweatt* and *McLaurin* finally came before the Supreme Court of the United States. Writing for the Court, Chief Justice Fred Vinson accepted the argument that, no matter how equal the schools might be in terms of physical facilities, separate professional education was still an unequal education. In the *Sweatt* case, he wrote:

> Moreover, although the law is a highly learned profession, we are well aware that it is an intensely practical one. The law school, the proving ground for legal learning and practice, cannot be effective in isolation from the individuals and institutions with which the law interacts. Few students and no one who has practiced law would choose to study in an academic vacuum removed from the interplay of ideas and the exchange of views with which the law is concerned.[14]

Therefore, by accepting and dealing with the reality of incremental change, Marshall was able to move constitutional doctrine from the insensitivity of *Plessy v. Ferguson* to a realization that "separate but equal" could never be equal. He set the stage for a final assault on racially segregated schools.

A third basic principle was that, in suggesting that the law evolve from the status quo, Thurgood Marshall relied on the maxim *ex facto oritur jus*. In each case, the record was carefully developed to establish the factual predicate for the suggested position. Marshall was attentive both to the "adjudicative facts" and to the "constitutional" or "legislative facts" of the case.[15] For instance, in *Pearson*, Marshall relied on the testimony of the Dean of the University of Maryland Law School with respect to the "prestige factor" of attending a recognized institution. In *Sipuel*, Marshall relied on the testimony of professors from leading law schools with respect to the impossibility of receiving a quality education in a segregated environment. This same strategy was even more evident in *Sweatt* as Marshall described his own approach:

> Experts in anthropology were produced and testified that given a similar learning situation a Negro student tended to react the same way as any other student and that there were no racial characteristics which had any bearing whatsoever to the subject of public education. Experts in the field of legal education testified that it was impossible for a Negro student to get an equal education in a Jim Crow law school because of the lack of the opportunity to meet with and discuss their problems with other students of varying strata of society.[16]

The lessons learned in the earlier litigation were especially valuable in the elementary school desegregation cases. Beginning in *Briggs v. Elliott*, one of the companion cases to *Brown v. Board of Education*, Marshall presented a detailed picture of the school system in question. He also introduced substantial social science information showing that segregated schools contributed to a black person's "feelings of insecurity, self hate, . . . [and] . . . undermine [] his ego, make him feel inferior and warp his outlook on life. . . ."[17]

In presenting this data, Marshall was cognizant of the Court's traditional sensitivity to charges of "judicial legislation." He carefully structured his presentation so that traditional sources of information were offered prior to the unique forms of evidence drawn from the social sciences. Even in his presentation to the Supreme Court of the United States, Marshall was aware of the traditional judicial mistrust of evidence based on the social sciences. Marshall placed the more unique material in an appendix and not in the body of the brief.

A fourth NAACP strategy was careful case selection. Marshall selected situations that easily permitted portrayal of the values at stake. He avoided contexts that might lead the Court to focus on nonessential issues.

In *Pearson*, Marshall chose a plaintiff who clearly had all the necessary qualifications for admission to the University of Maryland Law School. In fact, the choice of law schools as the primary battleground in the early cases was not an accident. A law school admissions case was clearly a favorable environment in which to demonstrate to *judges* the impossibility of receiving an equal legal education in a segregated atmosphere. All judges have attended law school and understand that legal education is received through formal classroom instruction, clinical work, *and* intellectual and social interaction with other aspiring attorneys. Again, in the *McLaurin* case, the plaintiff's age was a significant consideration. At that time, one of the popular objections to school integration was that it would lead to miscegenation. McLaurin was over fifty years old, and, therefore, did not present the image of someone who was about to marry one of his younger, white classmates.[18]

Marshall's adherence to these basic principles of constitutional litigation and their corollaries was not an easy task. He was under constant pressure from his constituency to move faster. Marshall and the other attorneys who had dedicated a good portion of their lives to the careful process of putting these cases together were occasionally tempted to succumb.

Richard Kluger, in his outstanding account of the *Brown* litigation, recounted an incident during the *Sweatt* case in which Marshall, angered over what he believed to be the trial judge's partiality for the opposing side, confided in a colleague that he was going to "tell that judge what I think of him today." The colleague later recalled: "He said nothing in court, but after the case was over and we were heading for the cars, there was Thurgood standing in the corner apparently muttering to himself. When he came back to join us, I asked him what that was all about, and he said, 'I told you I was gonna tell that judge what I thought of him—and I just did.'"[19]

On at least one occasion, Marshall succumbed to the temptation to assert the ultimate goal directly—even when his understanding of the system called for a more cautious approach. Four days after oral argument in *Sipuel v. Board of Regents*, the Supreme Court issued a brief *per curiam* opinion which simply recited the case's procedural history and, on the basis of its earlier holding in the *Gaines* case, required that the state afford the plaintiff an in-state education at either an in-state law school for blacks or the University of Oklahoma "as soon as it does for applicants of any other group."[20] The Oklahoma Board of Regents replied to the holding of the Court by roping off a section of the state capitol and calling it a state law school for blacks.

Predictably, Marshall filed a notice for leave to file a petition for writ of mandamus, claiming that the "law school" set up by the Board of Regents did not comply with the mandate of the Court. An education given in such an arrangement would never be comparable to that given at the University of Oklahoma. He even went further and wrote: "Exclusion of any group on the basis of race automatically imputes a badge of inferiority to the excluded group."[21] The Court denied relief because the case did not raise the question, according to the justices, of whether the equal protection clause could be fulfilled by the maintenance of separate schools for black students.[22] In his anger over the Board of Regents' ultraliteral interpretation of the Court's mandate, Marshall had proceeded too far, too fast, within the judicial system. The Court was not prepared to go any further than its earlier precedent; nor was it willing to confront the argument that "separate but equal" could never really be equal.

Marshall's miscalculations, with respect to what Justice Frankfurter referred to as the "rhythm of constitutional litigation," were few and far between.[23] In building a record, Marshall was constantly aware of the justices' sensitivity to the lessons of history. He exhibited a particularly keen sense of the Court's belief that it forges constitutional doctrine within the context of the overall American historical experience. He understood that the process of building constitutional doctrine takes place within a wider context of a dialogue throughout American society on the values that are to characterize its political and social relationships. He realized that the justices are constantly buffeted by the crosscurrents of American political and intellectual life and that the position taken by the parties in a case before the Court must deal realistically with those crosscurrents.

II. Reversing *Roe v. Wade*: A Parallel Road to *Brown*

THE EXPERIENCE OF the NAACP lawyers in developing a litigation strategy that culminated in *Brown v. Board of Education* provides an important perspective on the nature of the American judicial process as it deals with constitutional issues. The AUL conferees appreciated the lessons of the NAACP's earlier experience, and, consequently, structured and focused their deliberations on the lessons of the NAACP experience.

A. AN ASSESSMENT OF THE CURRENT SITUATION

1. The Current Judicial Perspective.   The first step in applying the lessons of the *Brown* litigation to the abortion issue was a dispassionate assessment of the current situation. In examining *Roe* and the first decade of subsequent case law, the conferees simultaneously proceeded on three different levels.

First, there was a doctrinal assessment. Upon what principles did the Court base its *Roe v. Wade* decision? In the years after *Roe v. Wade*, what principles has the Court repeatedly emphasized? What principles were either rejected or reconsidered?

Second, AUL conferees went beyond doctrinal concerns and dealt with the underlying policy themes that induced the Court to accept or reject a particular doctrinal construct. In short, what values have been most important to the Court in developing its current position with respect to abortion? What values has it constantly rejected? What values has it simply failed to realize, understand, or deal with comprehensively?

Lastly, there was a "linguistic analysis"—a careful evaluation of the decisions of the Court in search of language that might indicate the possibility of a shift in the Court's direction. This latter approach must be regarded as supportive of the first two inquiries rather than having an independent justification. In brief, language is important only insofar as it indicates a shift in philosophical perspective or in a doctrinal exposition of that philosophical perspective.

An assessment of the last ten years centers upon two questions: What is the Court's present view of its holding in *Roe v. Wade* and what themes from the Court's earlier opinions offer the best hope of serving as a vehicle for altering the Court's present view and setting a new direction? In dispassionately assessing current judicial perspective, the AUL inquiry focused on the abortion cases of the Supreme Court's 1982 October Term.[24] These cases appear to be a rather inauspicious basis for further litigation aimed at protecting prolife interests. Regarding the particular state regulations at issue, the cases can hardly be considered a victory for prolife advocates. Indeed, the basic tone of the majority opinion can best be described as demonstrating an impatience with the efforts of prolife citizens and state legislatures to circumscribe the holding of *Roe v. Wade.*

Any dispassionate assessment of the current situation requires that such a reality be accepted and confronted. The Court's decision in *Akron v. Akron Center for Reproductive Health* did, however, contain two more positive elements. First, Justice Sandra Day O'Connor's powerful dissent made a forceful attack on *Roe v. Wade.*[25] Justice O'Connor dealt not only with the correctness of the Court's balancing of the woman's right to an abortion and the state's interest in the preservation of life, but she also questioned the legitimacy of the Court's methodology—most notably, the Court's trimester approach. Pivotal to Justice O'Connor's critique of *Roe v. Wade* was her assertion that the balancing of these constitutional values cannot be based on changing scientific data. She cogently demonstrated that *Roe v. Wade* is on a "collision course with itself."[26] Justice O'Connor emphasized that inevitable changes in medical technology threaten the foundation of the trimester framework established in *Roe*:

> It is apparent from the Court's opinion that neither sound constitutional theory nor our need to decide cases based on the application of neutral principles can accommodate an analytical framework that varies according to the "stages" of pregnancy, where those stages and their concomitant standards of review, differ according to the level of medical technology available when a particular challenge to state regulation occurs.[27]

Both before and after Justice O'Connor's dissent in *Akron*, commentators have noted that the Court's focus on viability, as the point at which the state has a compelling interest in protecting the unborn, threatens to undermine *Roe*.[28] In fact, the language of the Court's abortion decisions appears to leave open the possibility that advances in medical technology, improvements in prenatal care, and new technologies such as artificial wombs and fetal implantation, may entirely eliminate a woman's right to an abortion.[29]

Second, the majority opinion of Justice Lewis Powell in the *Akron* case did not squarely meet Justice O'Connor's dissent and relied on the doctrine of stare decisis to reaffirm the holding of *Roe v. Wade*.[30] This refusal to confront directly Justice O'Connor's criticism and the reliance on stare decisis could be an indication that the current majority is unable to address her arguments. More importantly, the Court's reliance on stare decisis could be construed as an acknowledgment of *Roe*'s weakness. The Court does not resort to stare decisis when it has confidence in its doctrinal approach. The Court's invocation of the doctrine in *Akron*, as well as some of its more recent abortion decisions—particularly the funding cases[31]—may well indicate a growing sense of insecurity in this area.[32]

Since the March, 1984 AUL Conference, the Supreme Court has decided another important case involving state restrictions on abortion. In *Thornburgh v. American College of Obstetricians*,[33] the Court, in a 5-4 decision, struck down most of Pennsylvania's Abortion Control Act. In an opinion by Justice Blackmun, the majority "reaffirm[ed] the general principles laid down in *Roe* and in *Akron.*"[34] In fact, although the Court still emphasized the role of the pregnant woman's physician,[35] the *Thornburgh* case probably represents the Court's strongest statement in support of a woman's right to choose an abortion.[36] In addition, the Court's opinion expresses a growing impatience with efforts to restrict abortions and contains a forceful message that the majority of the Court will simply not tolerate efforts it interprets as designed "to intimidate women into continuing pregnancies."[37]

The *Thornburgh* decision did, however, contain some promising features. The extreme nature of the majority opinion prompted former Chief Justice Warren Burger, who had joined the majority in *Roe*, to suggest that the Court "should reexamine *Roe.*"[38] More importantly, Justice Byron White (who was joined by Justice William Rehnquist) wrote a powerful dissent, which argues that "the time has come to recognize that *Roe v. Wade* . . .'departs from a proper understanding' of the Constitution and to overrule it."[39]

Justice White gave two basic reasons for this position. First, he rejected the Court's conclusion that the abortion liberty should be regarded as "fundamental." Justice White did not reject the entire notion of substantive due process. Rather, because of his concern that this doctrine creates the risk that the Court will engage "in the unrestrained imposition of its own, extraconstitutional value preferences, . . ."[40] Justice White described two approaches the Court has used to limit the scope of the doctrine.[41] According to Justice White, "either of these two basic definitions of fundamental liberties, taken seriously, indicates the illegitimacy of the Court's decision in *Roe v. Wade.*"[42] Justice White's second reason for urging the Court to overrule *Roe v. Wade* was his conviction that the Court had arbitrarily denigrated the state's interest in the fetus. According to Justice White, the state has a compelling interest in preserving the fetus, and this interest exists prior to viability.[43]

Although the abortion decision of the 1982 Term appeared to indicate that the Court was not inclined to return to the issue of abortion, the Court has continued to accept review of cases in the area. Indeed, the Court will decide another abortion case during the 1986 Term.[44] The majority opinion in *Thornburgh* indicates that *Roe v. Wade* will not be reversed by the current Supreme Court. The powerful dissents of Justice O'Connor in *Akron* and Justice White in *Thornburgh* have, however, provided extended analysis of the errors of *Roe v. Wade*, and suggested the most promising avenues for attacking *Roe*.

2. Identifying the Promising Themes. After considering the current judicial perspective, AUL conferees identified those themes offering the best hope of serving as a vehicle for reconsideration of *Roe v. Wade*.

Central to this discussion was Professor Victor G. Rosenblum's excellent essay, which suggests three possible thematic options: the "privacy option," the "personhood option," and the expansion of the state's interest in protecting the unborn through, in part, a critical examination of *Roe*'s reliance on the concept of viability.[45]

AUL conferees generally agreed that the third approach is the most advantageous starting point. Without squarely confronting the holding of *Roe v. Wade*, such an approach permits an initial attack upon what some of the justices apparently perceive to be the most vulnerable aspects of *Roe*. Developing this theme permits counsel to argue that the current state of scientific evidence compels the reconsideration of the trimester framework and a reassessment of the balancing of interests based on the concept of viability. Existing evidence shows that modern scientific advances can save unborn life, prematurely expelled from the uterus, at a much earlier stage of development than was previously possible. Therefore, it can be argued, the state's interest in preserving that life must begin at a much earlier stage of development. This approach also directly attacks the *Akron* majority's reliance on the doctrine of stare decisis. The *Akron* majority acknowledged that stare decisis has never been considered as formidable a barrier to the overruling of constitutional holdings as it has in the area of statutory or common law decisions.[46] Just as important, the Court should be open to the reconsideration of this particular aspect of *Roe*. Justice Brandeis's dissenting opinion in the *Burnet* case noted that the Court should be willing to reexamine its holdings when they are based on factual assumptions that are subject to change.[47] Prolife counsel would not be asking the Court to reevaluate a doctrinal holding in the abstract; rather, the approach would be to urge the Court to reexamine the factual premises for that holding—factual premises that have clearly changed with the advancement of scientific knowledge during the last decade.

This strategy, if adopted, is quite compatible with the central lessons of the school desegregation litigation. Advancing incrementally, it relies on deliberate factual development for its success in altering the Court's doctrinal approach to the issue of abortion. As in *Pearson v. Murray*, this tactic requires that counsel acknowledge, at least for the time being, the continued vitality of the precedent that is the ultimate object of attack. Marshall did not squarely confront *Plessy v. Ferguson* in *Pearson*; rather, he insisted on its full and fair application. Prolife counsel would not, under this approach, directly attack the woman's right to an abortion; instead, counsel would concentrate on enforcing one aspect of *Roe*—the state's interest in life that can be preserved outside the uterus.

This is hardly an "Uncle Tom" position. *Pearson v. Murray* demanded equality in separate education for the races. Thus, it demonstrated the absurdity of the argument that separate education could really ever be equal. Similarly, this strategy, which would acknowledge a woman's right to an abortion but insist on the state's right to preserve life capable of existence outside the womb, would also set the stage for further inquiry into the nature of the fetus, which clearly has, at a very early stage of its development, a distinctly human identity separate from that of the mother.[48] It is also important to note that, just as *Pearson v. Murray* secured the education of many black Americans, expanding the state's interest in protecting the unborn may prevent a significant number of abortions.

The argument that the concept of viability, as understood in the *Roe* decision, is no longer a principled basis for reconciling constitutional interests, is merely a beginning. Candidly, it must be acknowledged that it is a starting point with significant limitations. Substantial success in abolishing the viability criterion will be meaningless unless the Court also reexamines its current view that, at every stage of development, the state's interest in the preservation of unborn life must be subordinate to the woman's interest in life or health, however broadly defined.[49] Here too, the lessons of the school desegregation cases provide a reasonable approach. Rather than dealing in broad strokes with the issue of maternal health or the relative rights of the mother and child with respect to the entire period of pregnancy, the initial cases ought to confront expansive definitions of maternal health. Courts must question whether the woman's health interest can always be considered superior to the state's interest in the life of the unborn, especially when the maternal health claim is based on relatively minor conditions of emotional or psychological discomfort.

The "health claim" based solely on the psychological discomfort or disappointment with respect to the gender of the unborn is markedly vulnerable. With the heightened consciousness of gender-based discrimination,[50] such a claim appears especially weak.[51] A court, faced with new scientific studies showing an unborn child with recognizable human traits and capable of being sustained outside the uterus, ought to be unimpressed with an argument preferring the mother's discomfort about the gender of the fetus to the right of an unborn female to retain her individuality and live to develop her full potential.

In summary, it seems realistic to suggest that the judiciary, as it is confronted with more specific information about the identifiable human characteristics and human destiny of the unborn at an early stage, will become less receptive to the position that the mother's health, broadly defined, is to be given precedence under all circumstances.

The school desegregation cases starkly demonstrated that abstract questions must be supported by a firm factual record before they can provide the appropriate foundation for significant changes in doctrinal perspective. Thurgood Marshall certainly experienced the reality of this point. The Court summarily rejected his petition for mandamus in the *Sipuel* case and declined to rule on the question of whether separateness in education could ever be equal on a record that, in the Court's opinion, did not squarely raise the issue.[52] The question of personhood in abortion litigation is a similarly abstract question. Moreover, as Professor Rosenblum states, it is an abstract question which has, up until this point, elicited a distinctly unfavorable judicial reaction.[53] Emphasis on the state's interest in protecting the unborn will not only achieve a significant amount of success in itself, but will also place the personhood issue in a far more tangible context when the Court ultimately confronts the question again. Biological evidence will demonstrate the separateness and the humanity of the fetus at earlier stages of development and will indirectly bolster the personhood argument.

The importance of exercising a great deal of caution, before confronting the personhood argument, becomes obvious when recalling the importance of the personhood argument to achieving complete success for those who are attempting not only to establish the state's right to protect the unborn, but also to secure affirmative protection for the unborn. Even with the biological foundation established in earlier stages of litigation, counsel should prudently acknowledge the wisdom of the basic maxims learned in the *Brown* litigation—the need to proceed incrementally. Here, John R. Connery suggests an approach compatible with Justice O'Connor's dissent in the *Akron* case. Rather than confront the issue of whether the unborn is a "person" for purposes of the Fourteenth Amendment, he suggests the following approach:

> The basic argument against abortion has always been that the conceptus has a *human destiny* and this is what makes it sacred. It has this destiny right from the beginning, whatever one may consider its early status to be. We know right from the beginning that it is destined to be a human being.[54]

In other words, whether one considers the unborn a person or a "potential person," the state's interest in preserving this future member of society has undeniable significance.[55]

Expanding the state's interest in protecting the unborn and linking it to the personhood argument is compatible with the basic characteristics of constitutional litigation. This strategy permits the Court gradually to adjust its doctrinal position on the basis of factual reassessment and creates, at each step, a significant basis for further protection of the unborn.

The attractiveness of an incremental approach, coupled with the development of a sound factual record, becomes apparent when one turns to the third possible approach—the "privacy approach." If abstract arguments are particularly poor bases for effectuating major doctrinal shifts, abstract arguments aimed at currently favored philosophical positions are especially doomed to failure.

The right of privacy, once restricted to sexual behavior within the bond of marriage, has been, for the past fifteen years, extended to afford substantive protection against a variety of governmental actions.[56] At first glance, the privacy question raised in the abortion cases appears to involve an area near the "core concerns" of the right of privacy—matters of sexuality.[57] These considerations require prolife counsel to adopt an approach that is both specific and narrow, so that the state's interest in protecting the unborn does not run counter to the impenetrable barrier of the mother's "privacy" right to make personal decisions with respect to childbearing.

The Court's conclusion that a right of privacy does exist under the Constitution, and that "this right of privacy ... is broad enough to encompass a woman's decision whether or not to terminate her pregnancy ... " has typically been attacked on two grounds.[58] First, some have explained that the Court's opinion in *Roe* is an essay on substantive due process,[59] and subject to condemnation for that reason alone.[60] According to this critique, it is simply not permissible for the Court to protect "fundamental" values that are not traceable to the Constitution. Second, the Court's discovery of a "right to an abortion" can be attacked in the following manner: even if the Court can legitimately protect certain areas of personal liberty through the doctrine of substantive due process, the "right to an abortion" should not be included on the list of things considered sufficiently "fundamental" to be free from governmental restraint.[61]

Currently, it is unlikely that either approach will be successful. Although the first approach, i.e., attacking the entire notion of substantive due process, has significant appeal, the Court appears unlikely to abandon the doctrine of substantive due process. The Court's views on what aspects of personal liberty are sufficiently fundamental to warrant heightened scrutiny under this theory have changed over the years, but the doctrine has been embraced by conservative and liberal justices for quite some time.[62] Any direct attack on the doctrine will encounter resistance from a Court which believes that protecting "rights" it considers "fundamental" is an important part of its mission.

The second approach, attacking the Court's conclusion that the right of privacy includes the right to an abortion, is also likely to be unsuccessful, at least in the short term. This approach does, however, offer significantly more promise. The Court's view of tradition and history heavily influences its consideration of whether certain aspects of personal liberty are entitled to heightened protection.[63] The Supreme Court's decision upholding the Georgia sodomy statute is perhaps the most prominent recent example.[64] In *Bowers v. Hardwick*, Justice White emphasized the role of tradition and history in the Court's substantive due process cases and stressed that the long history of laws condemning homosexual sodomy counseled against affording special protection to the conduct.[65] Similarly, Chief Justice Burger's concurring opinion emphasized that "the proscriptions against sodomy have very 'ancient roots, . . . ' [and that t]o hold that the act of homosexual sodomy is somehow protected as a fundamental right would be to cast aside millenia of moral teaching."[66] Obviously, the same arguments could be made with respect to abortion, as Justice Rehnquist indicated in his dissent in *Roe*.[67] The historical work presented at the AUL conference would be particularly useful in making the argument that our legal and moral traditions have consistently condemned abortion.

More narrowly, the argument should be made that abortion is not a matter of "privacy." The Court recognizes that the presence of the fetus makes the abortion issue qualitatively different from the issues it faced in earlier "privacy" cases.[68] Abortion does, however, appear to involve a decision near the core concerns of the right to privacy—matters of sexuality—and, therefore, a direct attack on the abortion privacy right is, at least at the present, likely to meet with considerable hostility.

In view of all this, an "indirect" assault on this "right" to an abortion is far more promising. It will be necessary to make a basic distinction between the decision to abort the conceptus, clearly identified as having at least the potential for human existence, and other decisions involving sexual activity currently protected by the constitutional right of privacy. [69] The Court will probably not entertain the distinction unless it is convinced that the countervailing interest of the state in the potential of the unborn is legitimate. The reality of that countervailing concern to the mother's privacy can be demonstrated if appropriate factual foundations have been established.

B. IMPLEMENTING THE APPROACH

THE INITIAL step in formulating a sound litigation strategy to an important public policy issue such as abortion is to establish a theoretical approach that is compatible with the basic characteristics of the process of constitutional litigation and that deals realistically with the current state of the law. Implementing this theoretical approach, however, requires that both client and counsel also address many more pragmatic questions and resolve them in a manner compatible with the foregoing considerations. The task in the present effort will be to identify the most significant issues and suggest how the work of the AUL conferees is compatible with the "rhythm" of constitutional litigation.[70]

1. The Need for Legislation.   First, legislation is needed to serve as a vehicle for further development of the foregoing litigation theory. It seems certain that the most favorable litigation circumstances would occur when a legislature has specifically undertaken to protect the unborn and has bolstered its position by specific legislative findings on the nature of prenatal life. In this context, a reviewing court would be confronted with the explicit legislative finding that life, capable of existence outside the uterus, is present. The court would be forced to confront the findings of that legislature and driven to address the issue of whether it owes deference to the findings of that legislature.[71] Particular attention must be given to the legislative efforts of the last decade and the judicial response to those efforts. Several factors are of key importance.

(a) The Need for Detailed Information and Conclusions.   While courts have long recognized the superior fact-gathering and evaluative ability of the legislative branch, recent constitutional cases do not always support such a conclusion.[72] Sometimes the courts cannot be faulted for declining to show deference because the fact-finding process of the legislature is not always evident in its work product. Care must be taken to ensure that the legislative record is comprehensive, with detailed information on the unborn, the consequences of various situations on maternal health, and the impact of circumstances relating to the decision to have an abortion on the woman's freedom of choice. Additionally, information submitted by opponents to legislation must be carefully scrutinized.

Legislation ought to express, as precisely as possible, the legislature's conclusions regarding the nature of the unborn life at issue. Precise conclusions ought to be expressed with respect to the other issues as well. These precise findings will permit counsel to argue that the legislature did in fact make a conscious choice to protect the life in question.

(b) The Need to Avoid "Legislative Overreaction." In reviewing the state statutes regulating abortion, the Court has repeatedly stressed the need for "certainty" and "carefully drawn regulations," particularly when there is a risk of criminal liability.[73] In addition, the Court has shown a special interest in ensuring that statutes imposing sanctions contain a clear *scienter* requirement so that good faith errors are not penalized.[74]

The design of the legislative package must serve as a vehicle for judicially wrought constitutional change. Therefore, the legislation must reflect the same considerations that dominate the constitutional litigation process. It is imperative that the legislation be based on data which has a scientific consensus and which is relevant to the state interest the statute is attempting to serve. Legislation that rests on a controversial factual basis or that can be viewed as tangential to the legitimate state interest involved will likely encounter significant obstacles. For example, the provision in several test statutes requiring a physician to advise the mother of the possibility of fetal pain during the abortion procedure might be counterproductive.

In fact, the Court has indicated that it looks with disfavor on statutes that are "designed not to inform the woman's consent but rather to persuade her to withhold it altogether."[75] Moreover, requiring that specific information be conveyed is likely to run afoul of the Court's desire to prevent the state from "intru[ding] upon the discretion of the pregnant woman's physician."[76] In *Akron*, the Court repeated its earlier warning "against placing the physician in just such an undesired and uncomfortable straitjacket."[77] The majority opinion in *Thornburgh* indicates even greater hostility to "informed consent" provisions.[78] Thus, a requirement that fetal pain be disclosed will likely be viewed as a direct challenge to the Court's more recent holdings. Although the sentiment behind pressing the fetal pain issue is surely commendable, requiring that this information be conveyed to the pregnant woman is likely to make the *indirect* assault on *Roe* more difficult. Presenting the information on fetal pain in the legislative hearings would be more helpful in supporting the state's interest in protecting the unborn.

2. The Need for Careful Factual Development of the Record. Accurate factual development of the legislative record must be paralleled by prudent development of the litigation record. As Thurgood Marshall understood in the school desegregation litigation, this process involves the attentive compilation of adjudicative facts as well as developing legislative or constitutional facts to supply the court with sufficient information to permit an appreciation of the values at stake and of the impact of the court's holding. Factual material from prolife litigators would be used in the classic Brandeisian sense, i.e., to support the judgment of the legislature.[79] Therefore, there will be a certain parallelism in the fact gathering of the legislative process and the evidence assembled by counsel.

Theoretically, such a factual basis can be developed at trial or on appeal. Because of the great notoriety given the "Brandeis Brief," many often associate this process primarily with the appeal. Indeed, at least at first glance, there seems to be a sound reason for preferring the appeal context to the trial context for the development of constitutional or legislative facts. Material presented at trial is subject to much greater impeachment and to counter submissions. There is, however, a more sophisticated perspective. As Thurgood Marshall demonstrated in the school desegregation litigation, information submitted at trial can take on an added aura of credibility precisely because it has been submitted through the adversary process. On at least one occasion, the Supreme Court has remarked that such material is preferably submitted at the trial level.[80]

Of course, there are other considerations in determining whether to submit such material at trial or on appeal. As Judge Jack Weinstein pointed out in his treatise, judges who favor a narrow view of the judicial role and are therefore more fearful of encroaching on the legislative prerogative, will probably feel more comfortable with a trial submission as opposed to an *ex parte* submission in appellate briefs.[81] Such trial submission of constitutional evidence also permits counsel to take full advantage of closely related adjudicative facts. Often, the best constitutional facts are actually the adjudicative facts of the case which, if they are accepted by the trial court, can rest under the protection of the so-called clearly erroneous standard.[82]

No matter how scrupulously counsel complies with traditional notions of judicial methodology, infusing the trial record with large doses of constitutional or legislative facts introduces elements that are hardly the daily fare of the trial judge. Civil rights cases arising in a federal district court require wide ranging factual inquiry. Encountering judicial reluctance, grounded partially in the case or controversy requirement and partially in the pressures of current judicial work load, is to be expected.[83] Therefore, prolife counsel must carefully establish a firm foundation of adjudicative facts before presenting more extensive, supportive information.

Counsel must also decide what evidence should be initiated by live testimony, and what evidence should be introduced through documentation. In *Legislative Facts in Constitutional Litigation*, Professor Kenneth Karst suggested that the expected value of cross-examination ought to be central to any decision as to whether to proceed with testimony on a particular issue or to rely on documentation.[84] Since testimony followed by cross-examination is not a very effective way of educating the court with respect to general principles, documentary evidence is just as effective for conveying broader social or philosophical processes.

On the other hand, the impact of a particular rule or suggested rule of law in a particular context is probably best demonstrated through the drama of live testimony. Perhaps, in forthcoming abortion litigation, historical information may be best presented through documentary evidence. However, clinical advances in neonatology will probably be more effectively presented by a practicing physician.

Since many constitutional cases involve very little controversy with respect to the actual adjudicative facts, counsel must be prepared to face the possibility that judgment will be entered on the pleadings or on the basis of a motion for summary judgment. There may, therefore, be limited opportunities to develop a full record or present constitutional facts. Counsel must be sure to use the mechanisms of the pretrial stage to develop the best possible factual record. Even with the modern rules of pleading, it is possible to develop pretrial submissions to enable counsel properly to support his legal position.[85]

3. The Need for Careful Attention to History. In highly value-oriented constitutional litigation, such as abortion litigation, one particular form of constitutional fact has a unique value. The Court places particular significance on historical analysis in properly balancing competing constitutional values.[86] The Supreme Court's decision in *Bowers v. Hardwick* is an important recent example.

The importance of history is understandably compatible with the judiciary's basic approach of reconciling competing ideals on the basis of historical experience. Actually, in value-oriented constitutional cases, history is to a great degree a substitute for judicial precedent. Judicial adoption of a particular historical perspective can assume the aura of earlier case law. For this reason, one must be aware of the difficulty in overcoming the Court's earlier historical assessment. History, once reviewed by the Supreme Court and memorialized in its decisions, tends to take on an aura of credibility that is not easily disparaged. This circumstance justifies the significant amount of time spent at the AUL conference evaluating the historical underpinnings of *Roe v. Wade.* If the Court is to reassess this aspect of *Roe v. Wade,* the contrary evidence must be overwhelming.

The strong "precedential" effect of historical analysis in the Court's constitutional opinions makes John Connery's approach especially important. He suggests an approach to the "personhood" argument that renders most of the Court's earlier historical analysis in *Roe v. Wade* irrelevant. He implies that one should not directly confront the question as to whether, historically, the unborn has been considered a "person." Rather, one ought to prove that throughout history the law has continually recognized the unborn as having the confirmed potential to develop into a complete human personality.

4. The Need to Deal Carefully with Stare Decisis.   Admittedly, a proper understanding of constitutional litigation dictates that both client and counsel understand the difficulty of reversing an existing precedent. It is accurate, as Justice Brandeis pointed out in the *Burnet* case, that the Court has announced it will not rigidly apply the doctrine of stare decisis in constitutional cases as it might in statutory and common law cases.[87] However, there remains a tendency to underestimate the importance of the rule. As Justice John Stevens has written, "[t]he decisional process invariably involves a study and analysis of relevant precedents. In conference deliberation precedents regularly provide the basis for analysis and discussion. The framework for most Court opinions is created by previously decided cases." Indeed, he suggested that, while several of the Court's rulings per term are significant, "it must be remembered that the Court disposes of literally thousands of cases every year; repeatedly, the Court's action involves nothing more than the application of old precedent to a new controversy."[88]

More importantly, on the abortion issue in the *Akron* case, the Court justified its reliance on the doctrine of stare decisis by suggesting that *Roe* had in fact been considered "with special care."[89] The Court mentioned that *Roe* had been argued, reargued, and evaluated over the ten-year interval. However, because reargument of a case simply indicates that the issue is difficult and that the Court is sharply divided, prolife counsel must argue that reliance on a "special care" exception to the general constitutional rule for reliance on stare decisis is questionable.

Justice Stevens's discussion of stare decisis in *Thornburgh* also needs to be addressed. There, he stated that "[t]here is a strong public interest in stability, and in the orderly conduct of our affairs, that is served by a consistent course of constitutional adjudication."[90]

Prolife counsel should invoke Justice Brandeis's remark that reliance on stare decisis is especially inappropriate in constitutional cases based on ascertainable but changing data.[91] Additionally, counsel could argue that, when an *asserted* life interest is involved, the Court has a special duty constantly to reevaluate the basis of its holding. The Court had previously admitted that "when a defendant's life is at stake, the Court has been particularly sensitive to ensure that every safeguard is observed."[92] By analogy, even if the life interest asserted has not yet been established, the mere assertion of the life interest requires the Court to make a more searching reexamination of its prior cases than it might undertake if the interest asserted were less significant.[93]

5. *The Need to Appreciate the "Dialogue" Element of American Constitutional Adjudication.* As Justice Marshall appreciated so well throughout the *Brown* litigation, the Supreme Court does not decide constitutional law cases in a vacuum. Doctrinal developments result from the stimuli of the adjudicative and constitutional facts produced by the litigation, coupled with the active forces spawned by other branches of government and by the political process.[94]

For instance, in the *Minersville School District v. Gobitis* case,[95] Justice Felix Frankfurter's realization of President Roosevelt's almost insurmountable responsibility in mobilizing the country for war influenced his decision to uphold the flag salute requirement imposed by a local Pennsylvania school board on its pupils.[96] The Court has often explicitly acknowledged interactive dialogue. In *Frontiero v. Richardson*, Justice Powell candidly noted that the controversy over the proper standard of review of legislative gender-based classifications was debated before the background of the pendency of the Equal Rights Amendment.[97] More recently, in *Committee for Public Education v. Regan*, Justice White, writing of the Court's effort to forge a principled approach to the question of aid to religiously oriented public schools, predicted that a "continuing interaction between the courts and the States—the former charged with interpreting and upholding the Constitution and the latter seeking to provide education for their youth ... [would produce] a single, more encompassing construction of the Establishment Clause."[98]

Lawyers are also well aware of the dialogue that continually takes place between the Supreme Court of the United States and both state and federal lower courts. Broad propositions of constitutional law, established in earlier Supreme Court cases, are critiqued and modified by lower courts as they seek to apply the rulings.[99]

In large-scale, protracted, constitutional litigation, the constant dialogue among these institutions of government cannot be ignored; to the contrary, its reality must be affirmatively addressed. Political and legislative activity, in addition to creating the necessary building blocks of litigation, emits significant tremors which are felt throughout the judicial system and collectively affect the litigation atmosphere and the judicial perspective. The Court's methodology in *Roe* invites this type of interactive dialogue. State legislatures can legitimately spend money on research demonstrating that, at an earlier stage than previously believed, the unborn meets the Court's viability criteria. The state's governing assemblies are also free to explore means of protecting the viable unborn during an abortion.[100]

Consequently, the political activity of prolife organizations is an essential element in educating the judiciary about values in the abortion controversy. Political and legal strategy must be coordinated. Ill-timed or ill-conceived legislative or political efforts can cast a detrimental shadow on litigation efforts. Even isolated instances of "moving too far, too fast" can create significant problems for the sympathetic or uncommitted judge. For example, a broadside legislative attack on the abortion right can impede a litigation effort precisely focused on the state's interest in protecting the viable unborn child. Litigation efforts must be coordinated, because even the most obscure case can have a significant impact on this constant dialogue of values.

6. The Need to Deal Effectively with the Cross-Currents of Constitutional Values. Abortion litigation is part of a wider-ranging controversy within the political community. This understanding ought to concentrate on a further realization that the entire debate is an extensive dialogue on the basic values of our constitutional system. The continuing discourse on values, as it appears in other contexts, will inevitably affect the final resolution of the abortion issue.

For instance, can a society that is tolerating various forms of infanticide value the separate identity and destiny of an unborn child? Would advances in scientific and medical evidence change jurisprudence within such an environment?[101] Will it really make any difference to prove that a conceptus is a human being if society permits the killing of a baby two weeks after birth because the "quality of its life" is deemed to be relatively insignificant?[102] Unless the tide is stemmed with respect to the shifting values of our society toward the value of human life in other contexts—whether in its deformed young or its infirm aged—it will be difficult to arouse much sensitivity for the life of the unborn. The value choice for American society in both the infanticide and euthanasia situations is essentially the same value choice presented in the abortion context. Lost ground in either of these two areas, where the countervailing life interest is so easily identifiable, can easily doom the more difficult task of stopping abortion.[103]

Prolife advocates must also confront the criticism that recognizing the inviolability of unborn human life constitutes the imposition of a particular moral view on a pluralistic society.[104] This appeal to democratic ideals can exercise tremendous influence in the ultimate resolution of the abortion issue. The "pluralism" argument is, however, simply a restatement of the question; the real issue, what are the appropriate social limits on individual choice, "must be decided one way or the other...."[105] Regardless of how the issue is decided, that decision represents the imposition of a particular moral view.

Another aspect of the broader dialogue that needs to be addressed is the role of religiously based values in the legal process.[106] Justice Stevens's opinion in *Thornburgh* expresses a common concern, namely, that a legislative decision to prohibit abortions would necessarily be based on a theological argument.[107] Justice White's dissent in *Thornburgh* contains an effective rebuttal to this argument.[108] The broader point is that prolife advocates need to be careful about the type of dialogue they conduct, both in the legislative and judicial arenas. A recent article by Professor Kent Greenawalt contains some useful advice: religious and moral principles properly play a role in the lawmaking process, but there should be great care about the way in which the dialogue is conducted. As Professor Greenawalt states, "argument in religious terms is often an inapt form of public dialogue."[109]

It can be argued that *Roe's* creation of "a constitutional barrier to state efforts to protect human life" is "an improvident and extravagant exercise of the power of judicial review."[110] Thus, *Roe* represents the real barrier to the resolution of the issues through the democratic process. This approach will have a widespread, initial appeal since many feel the federal judiciary has continually second-guessed the policies and intentions of the state legislatures.[111]

However, definitive reliance on this "states' rights" approach contains significant limitations for the prolife advocate. If the matter is left to the political processes, one cannot be sure that the unborn will be protected. Absolute security for the unborn requires that the Court eventually hold that the Constitution protects the inviolability of all human life. Given the current judicial and social perspectives, accomplishing such a change will be a formidable task.

Prolife advocates must give more thought to the reconciliation of these methodologies and objectives. Perhaps the lessons of the *Brown* litigation can again be helpful. In initial litigation strategies, the focus will be on legislative efforts to protect unborn life. Key issues will be the nature of unborn life and the interest of the state in protecting that life. Here, prolife advocates should recommend that deference be paid to the work of the legislature. Then, one can argue that the prevailing judgments of the legislatures are actually *evidence* that the Constitution affirmatively protects all life interests—including unborn life.[112] If the ultimate objective is to establish the principle that all life is protected by the Constitution, then it cannot be conceded that the legislature has the constitutional authority to "strike a balance" between that life interest and other concerns.[113]

Failure to appreciate fully the dynamics of this "dialogue" element in constitutional adjudication results in the tendency by some prolifers to place the *total* responsibility for *Roe v. Wade* on the justices of the Supreme Court. Unfortunately, that misdirected blame has been expressed in rather harsh ad hominem attacks on particular members of the Court.

Obviously, responsibility for the decision must rest with the justices. Yet, that decision was also the product of many intellectual, cultural and political cross-currents. Prolifers were not exempt from the responsibility of directing the broader dialogue about our society's basic values. *Roe v. Wade* was lost in these forums long before it was lost in the courtroom. Those seeking to reverse *Roe v. Wade* cannot continue to lay total blame for the decision on the judiciary.

While the Court is stimulated from many quarters, the most important dialogue remains the one the Court carries on with the litigants before it. The quality of that dialogue in long-term constitutional litigation depends on the continued relationship between the judiciary and the institutional litigants regularly appearing before it. The channels of communication must remain open. Stridency by the litigants will retard the Court's receptivity to the facts and values it must understand and appreciate if the goal is to be realized. Litigants expect the judiciary to be open to their arguments. Likewise, the judiciary expects litigants to approach the system with an understanding of its ways and an appreciation that the process of judging, especially in the value-oriented area of constitutional law, is a difficult responsibility.

With this clearly in mind, prolife advocates must walk the same road traveled by other civil rights advocates. The path is not without its twists and turns. Fortunately, because of the judicial system's capacity for self-correction, there is hope for change.

Notes

1. Of course, *Brown v. Board of Education*, 347 U.S. 483 (1954) did not expressly overrule *Plessy v. Ferguson*, 163 U.S. 537 (1896). The Court held only "that in the field of public education the doctrine of 'separate but equal' has no place." 347

U.S. at 495. A series of cases following *Brown* made it clear, however, that the separate but equal doctrine no longer retained any vitality. *See* J. Nowak, R. Rotunda & J. Young, *Constitutional Law* 574–76 (3rd ed. 1986). The text, therefore, discusses *Brown* as having overruled *Plessy*, since *Brown* effectively brought the separate but equal doctrine to an end.

2. *See generally* Ripple, *Thurgood Marshall and the Forgotten Legacy of* Brown v. Board of Education, 55 Notre Dame L. Rev. 471 (1980).

The Court established the separate but equal doctrine in *Plessy*. There, the Court held that a Louisiana statute requiring railroad companies to provide separate but equal accommodations for the "white and colored" races, and forbidding passengers to sit in a section other than that to which their race had been assigned, did not violate either the Thirteenth or Fourteenth Amendments.

3. 410 U.S. 113 (1973).

4. 163 U.S. at 551.

5. This faith in the system's ability to self-correct was undoubtedly based on the belief that the courts would be moved by the power of ideas, perhaps sooner than other segments of society. Judge Bork has expressed this belief well: "Absent a constitutional amendment, a general means to ensure that courts stay within the limits the Constitution provides for them can only be intellectual and moral. That may seem a weak control. It does not seem so to me. Intellectual criticism in the short run may be quite ineffective. In the long run, ideas will be decisive. That is particularly true with respect to courts, more so perhaps than with any other branch of government." Bork, *The Struggle Over The Role of The Court*, 34 Nat'l Rev. 1137 (Sept. 17, 1982).

6. J. Greenberg, Judicial Process and Social Change: Constitutional Litigation 57 (1977) (quoting Margold, Preliminary Report to the Joint Committee Supervising the Expenditure of the 1930 Appropriation by the American Fund for Public Services to the NAACP) (unpublished report, copy on file in the New York Public Library).

7. Marshall, *An Evaluation of Recent Efforts to Achieve Racial Integration in Education Through Resort to the Courts*, 21 J. Negro Educ. 316, 318 (1952).

8. 169 Md. 478, 182 A. 590 (1936). Interestingly, it was segregation at this law school that had caused Marshall to commute daily from his home in Baltimore, Maryland to attend Howard University's law school in the District of Columbia.

9. This principle of "substantial equality" reached the Supreme Court of the United States two years later when the Court specifically ratified the Maryland court's holding in *Pearson* and made it clear that the "substantial equality" criterion could not be satisfied by providing scholarships to out-of-state schools. Missouri *ex rel.* Gaines v. Canada, 305 U.S. 337 (1938).

10. R. Kluger, Simple Justice 190 (1975).

11. 199 Okla. 36, 180 P. 2d 135 (1947), *rev'd per curiam*, 332 U.S. 631 (1948).

12. 339 U.S. 629 (1950). For a comprehensive discussion of *Sweatt*, see Entin, Sweatt v. Painter, *The End of Segregation, and the Transformation of Education Law*, 5 Rev. Litigation 3 (1986).

13. 339 U.S. 637 (1950).

14. *Sweatt*, 339 U.S. at 634.

15. *See generally* Karst, *Legislative Facts in Constitutional Litigation*, 1960 Sup. Ct. Rev. 75.

16. Marshall, *supra* note 7, at 319–20.

17. Marshall, *supra* note 7, at 322. For Briggs v. Elliott, *see* 347 U.S. 483 (1954) (decided with *Brown*).

18. *See* Entin, *supra* note 12, at 41 n. 231.

19. R. Kluger, Simple Justice 263 (1975).

20. 332 U.S. 631, 633 (1948), *citing* Missouri *ex rel.* Gaines v. Canada, 305 U.S. 337 (1938).

21. R. Kluger, Simple Justice 260 (1975).

22. Fisher v. Hurst, 333 U.S. 147, 150 (1948).

23. Frankfurter, *The Supreme Court*, reprinted in P. Kurland, Felix Frankfurter On the Supreme Court: Extrajudicial Essay on the Court and the Constitution 448 (1970). The original version of this essay was published in 1939 in the *Encyclopedia of Social Sciences*. The later version was prepared for publication in the Hansard Society's *Aspects of American Government* (1950).

24. Simopoulos v. Virginia, 462 U.S. 506 (1983); Planned Parenthood Ass'n v. Ashcroft, 462 U.S. 476 (1983); Akron v. Akron Center for Reproductive Health, Inc., 462 U.S. 416 (1983).

25. *Akron*, 462 U.S. at 452 (O'Connor, J., dissenting).

26. *Akron*, 462 U.S. at 459 (O'Connor, J., dissenting).

27. *Akron*, 462 U.S. at 453 (O'Connor, J., dissenting).

28. *See, e.g., The Supreme Court, 1982 Term*, 97 Harv. L. Rev. 70, 78 (1983); Note, *Technological Advances and* Roe v. Wade: *The Need to Rethink Abortion Law*, 29 U.C.L.A. L. Rev. 1194 (1982); Comment, *Fetal Viability and Individual Autonomy: Resolving Medical and Legal Standards for Abortion*, 27 U.C.L.A. L. Rev. 1340 (1980). *See generally*, Rhoden, *Trimesters and Technology: Revamping* Roe v. Wade, 95 Yale L. J. 639 (1986).

29. *See, e.g., The Supreme Court, 1982 Term*, 97 Harv. L. Rev. at 85–86. As one commentator has stated: "Conditioning women's abortion rights on the medical technology of the moment threatens to permit those rights to evaporate altogether." *Id.* at 86 (footnote omitted). This argument—that there is an inherent instability in an artificial trimester framework based on rapidly changing medical technology—is further bolstered by the recognition that the Court has often stated its view of a woman's right to an abortion in narrow terms. Many who favor abortion rights have bemoaned the Court's failure to rest its abortion jurisprudence exclusively on a women's rights approach. *Id.* at 84; *see* Law, *Rethinking Sex and the Constitution*, 132 U. Pa. L. Rev. 955, 1020 (1984); Ginsburg, *Some Thoughts on Autonomy and Equality in Relation to* Roe v. Wade, 63 N. Car. L. Rev. 375 (1985). Indeed, on certain occasions the Court has not described a woman's right to an abortion with the same enthusiasm it uses in describing fundamental rights such as free speech or free exercise of religion. *See The Supreme Court, 1982 Term*, 97 Harv. L. Rev. at 83 (footnotes omitted) (The Court's abortion decisions of the 1982 Term "illustrate the essentially limited nature of the right declared fundamental in *Roe*, and continue the erosion of women's abortion rights begun in cases involving public funding and

minors."). The Court often describes a woman's right to an abortion in cautious, somewhat hesitant terms; for example, in certain instances the Court has given at least equal emphasis to the doctor's role in the process, *Akron*, 462 U.S. at 445; Colautti v. Franklin, 439 U.S. 379, 387 (1979), and in other cases the Court has allowed the government to take action intended to encourage alternatives to the exercise of a "fundamental" right, Harris v. McRae, 448 U.S. 297 (1980); Maher v. Roe, 432 U.S. 464 (1977). In fact, the Court's emphasis on the importance of the physician-patient relationship and the Court's support of government action based on the immorality of abortion may ultimately make it easier to attack *Roe* successfully. Indeed, some have suggested that the Court's decisions upholding governmental limits on abortion funding undermine the foundation of the rules announced in *Roe*. As one noted commentator has stated:

> [t]he Connecticut welfare regulation [*Maher*] and the Hyde Amendment [*Harris*] reflect an understanding of the moral ideals of the community different from the understanding that informs *Roe v. Wade*. By sustaining the constitutionality of these two provisions, the Court has undermined the foundation for the rules it announced in *Roe v. Wade*. It has implied that its earlier understanding of the moral ideals of the community was mistaken. *Roe v. Wade*, accordingly, should be seen as a shaky precedent, and the Court should see itself as under an obligation to reexamine the breadth of that 1973 decision.

Wellington, *The Nature of Judicial Review*, 91 Yale L. J. 486, 517–18 (1982) (footnote omitted).

30. *Akron*, 462 U.S. at 420 & n. 1.

31. Harris v. McRae. 448 U.S. 297 (1980); Maher v. Roe, 432 U.S. 464 (1977).

32. The weakness of *Roe* is also suggested by the continuing efforts to "rewrite" the opinion. *See, e.g.*, Rhoden, *supra* note 28; Regan, *Rewriting* Roe v. Wade, 77 Mich. L. Rev. 1569 (1979).

33. 106 S. Ct. 2169 (1986). See Appendix 2, p. 269.

34. 106 S. Ct. at 2178, *infra* at 274.

35. *See id.*

36. *See id.* at 2184–85, *infra* at 282–83.

37. 106 S. Ct. at 2178, *infra* at 274.

38. 106 S. Ct. at 2192 (Burger, C.J., dissenting), *infra* at 298.

39. 106 S. Ct. at 2193 (White, J., dissenting)(quoting *Garcia v. San Antonio Metropolitan Transit Authority*, 105 S. Ct. 1005, 1021 (1985)). *Infra* at 301.

40. 106 S. Ct. at 2196 (White, J., dissenting). *Infra* at 304.

41. *See id.* at 2194–95 (discussing the "implicit in the concept of ordered liberty" approach of *Palko v. Connecticut*, 302 U.S. 319, 325 (1937) and the "history and tradition" approach used in Justice Powell's opinion in *Moore v. City of East Cleveland*, 431 U.S. 494, 503 (1977)). *Infra* at 301-303.

42. 106 S. Ct. at 2195 (White, J., dissenting). *Infra* at 303.

43. 106 S. Ct. at 2197 (White, J., dissenting). *Infra* at 305.

44. *See* Hartigan v. Zbaraz, 763 F. 2d 1532 (7th Cir. 1985), *jurisdiction postponed*, 107 S. Ct. 267 (1986)(No. 85–673).

45. *See* Rosenblum & Marzen chapter in this volume, p. 195.

46. *See Akron,* 462 U.S. at 419–420; *see also Akron,* 462 U.S. at 458-59 (O'Connor, J., dissenting).

47. Burnet v. Coronado Oil & Gas Co., 285 U.S. 393, 412 (1932) (Brandeis, J., dissenting).

48. *See Thornburgh,* 106 S. Ct. at 2195 (White, J., dissenting). *Infra* at 304.

49. *Akron,* 462 U.S. at 428; *Doe v. Bolton,* 410 U.S. at 192, 215-16.

50. *See generally* Mississippi University for Women v. Hogan, 458 U.S. 718 (1982); Craig v. Boren, 429 U.S. 190 (1976).

51. *See* Rhoden, *supra* note 28, at 686.

52. Fisher v. Hurst, 333 U.S. 147, 150 (1948).

53. As Justice Stevens stated in *Thornburgh,* "[n]o member of this Court has ever suggested that a fetus is a 'person' within the meaning of the Fourteenth Amendment." 106 S. Ct. at 2188, n.8 (Stevens, J., concurring). *Infra* at 293. Although it is certainly possible that this position can be changed through the judicial process, a constitutional amendment would be the most straight-forward way of accomplishing complete protection for the unborn. *See* Destro, *Abortion and the Constitution: The Need for a Life-Protective Amendment,* 63 Calif. L. Rev. 1250 (1975).

54. The quote was taken from Connery's original manuscript for this volume. See *infra* at 126-127.

55. *See also* Kommers, *Liberty and Community in Constitutional Law: The Abortion Cases in Comparative Perspective,* 1985 B.Y.U.L. Rev. 371, 408 (discussing the West German Federal Constitutional Court's decision to afford constitutional protection to the fetus without examining the personhood question).

56. *See* Griswold v. Connecticut, 381 U.S. 479 (1965). The Supreme Court and lower courts have expanded the "privacy" doctrine over the years. For example, the "privacy" rationale has been used frequently in the following contexts: (1) the termination or withholding of medical treatment, *see, e.g.,* In re Quinlan, 70 N.J. 10, 355 A.2d 647 (1976); In re Phillip B., 92 Cal. App. 3d 796, 156 Cal. Rptr. 48 (Cal. Ct. App. 1979), *cert. denied sub nom.* Bothman v. Warren B., 445 U.S. 949 (1980); (2) in challenges to laws proscribing homosexual conduct, *see, e.g.,* People v. Onofre, 51 N.Y. 2d 476, 415 N.E. 2d 936, 434 N.Y.S. 2d 947 (1980), *cert. denied,* 451 U.S. 987 (1981); and (3) in defining the limits on the disclosure of confidential records, *see e.g.,* Tarlton v. Saxbe, 507 F.2d 1116 (D.C. Cir. 1974). *See generally,* J. Nowak, R. Rotunda & J. Young, Constitutional Law 711-721 (3d ed. 1986). Indeed, many of these advances have been hailed as having a salutary impact in striking the proper balance between individual liberty and state authority. On occasion, the Supreme Court has set forth the right of privacy in rather sweeping terms. In Whalen v. Roe, 429 U.S. 589 (1977), Justice Stevens placed the Court's prior privacy cases into three categories: (1) freedom from governmental surveillance and intrusion as protected by the Fourth Amendment; (2) the interest in avoiding public disclosure of personal matters; and (3) the interest in making independent personal decisions in matters relating to marriage, procreation, and childrear-ing. 429 U.S. at 599–600. Despite the developments in the lower courts and the

broad language in Justice Stevens's opinion for a unanimous Court in *Whalen*, the Supreme Court has not further expanded the right of privacy, at least not beyond the core concerns of family and sexuality. *See generally*, Bell v. Wolfish, 441 U.S. 520 (1979); Posner, *The Uncertain Protection of Privacy by the Supreme Court*, 1979 Sup.Ct. Rev. 173. In these areas, however, the right of privacy is firmly entrenched.

57. Posner, *The Uncertain Protection of Privacy by the Supreme Court*, 1979 Sup. Ct. Rev. 173, 214.

58. Quote is from *Roe*, 410 U.S. at 153.

59. *See* Posner, *supra* note 57, at 198; Rehnquist, *Is an Expanded Right of Privacy Consistent with Fair and Effective Law Enforcement? Or: Privacy, You've Come a Long Way, Baby*, 23 Kan. L. Rev. 1, 4–6 (1974) (noting similarities between *Lochner* and *Roe*).

60. Ely, *The Wages of Crying Wolf: A Comment on* Roe v. Wade, 82 Yale L. J. 920 (1973); Epstein, *Substantive Due Process By Any Other Name: The Abortion Cases*, 1973 Sup. Ct. Rev. 159; Bork, *supra* note 5, *The Struggle Over the Role of the Court.*

61. *See generally* A. Cox, The Role of the Supreme Court in American Government 114 (1976); A. Bickel, The Morality of Consent 27–28 (1975).

62. *Compare* Lochner v. New York, 198 U.S. 45 (1905) *with* Roe v. Wade, 410 U.S. 113 (1973). As Archibald Cox has stated: "The Court's persistent resort to notions of substantive due process for almost a century attests to the strengths of our natural law inheritance in constitutional adjudication, and I think it unwise as well as hopeless to resist it." A. Cox, The Role of the Supreme Court in American Government 113 (1976).

63. *See generally* Hafen, *The Constitutional Status of Marriage, Kinship, and Sexual Privacy—Balancing the Individual and Social Interests*, 81 Mich. L. Rev. 463 (1983) (discussing the importance of history and tradition in the Court's substantive due process cases). And as Justice Harlan stated in dissent in Poe v. Ullman, 367 U.S. 497, 542 (1961):

> Due process has not been reduced to any formula; its content cannot be determined by reference to any code. The best that can be said is that through the course of this Court's decisions it has represented the balance which our Nation, built upon postulates of respect for the liberty of the individual, has struck between that liberty and the demands of organized society. If the supplying of content to this Constitutional concept has of necessity been a rational process, it certainly has not been one where judges have felt free to roam where unguided speculation might take them. The balance of which I speak is the balance struck by this country, having regard to what history teaches are the traditions from which it developed as well as the traditions from which it broke. That tradition is a living thing. A decision of this Court which radically departs from it could not long survive, while a decision which builds on what has survived is likely to be sound.

64. Bowers v. Hardwick, 106 S. Ct. 2841 (1986).

65. *Bowers*, 106 S. Ct. at 2844–46.

66. *Bowers*, 106 S. Ct. at 2847 (Burger, C.J., concurring).

67. Roe v. Wade, 410 U.S. at 174–77 (Rehnquist, J., dissenting).

68. The pregnant woman cannot be isolated in her privacy. She carries an embryo and, later, a fetus, if one accepts the medical definitions of the developing young in the human uterus.... The situation is inherently different from marital intimacy, or bedroom possession of obscene mater-

ial, or marriage, or procreation, or education, with which *Eisenstadt* and *Griswold, Stanley, Loving, Skinner,* and *Pierce* and *Meyer* were respectively concerned.

Roe v. Wade, 410 U.S. at 159 (citation omitted); *see also Thornburgh*, 106 S. Ct. at 2195, n. 2 (White, J., dissenting). *Infra* at 318.

69. This approach has the considerable merit of not challenging the whole line of the Court's substantive due process cases. As Professor Hafen has explained: "The *Roe* Court could logically have concluded that the state interest in protecting the unborn was strong enough to override a pregnant woman's right of privacy, without seriously challenging the parental and other family rights established in the line of cases stretching from *Meyer v. Nebraska* to *Eisenstadt.*" Hafen, *The Constitutional Status of Marriage, Kinship, and Sexual Privacy—Balancing the Individual and Social Interests,* 81 Mich. L. Rev. 463, 533 n. 341 (1983). This approach also avoids a direct challenge to the interest in personal sovereignty that some have found in the Court's "privacy" cases. "[I]f the fetus is a person with its own right to life, then the decision to terminate pregnancy is *not* a wholly self-regarding one, hence within the zone of the pregnant woman's sovereignty." Feinberg, *Autonomy, Sovereignty, and Privacy: Moral Ideals in the Constitution?*, 58 Notre Dame L. Rev. 445, 487 n. 60 (1983); *see* Epstein, *Substantive Due Process By Any Other Name: The Abortion Cases,* 1973 Sup. Ct. Rev. 159, 171–72.

70. Frankfurter, *supra* note 23.

71. Of course, the Court has stated that "[v]iability is reached when, *in the judgment of the attending physician on the particular facts of the case before him,* there is a reasonable likelihood of the fetus' sustained survival outside the womb, with or without artificial support." Colautti v. Franklin, 439 U.S. 379, 388 (1979) (emphasis added). Thus, the state is not permitted to determine the point at which its interest becomes compelling. *Id.* at 388–89. A narrowly tailored state regulation that preserved some role for the physician in the viability determination is probably as much as the Court would countenance.

72. *See generally* Monaghan, *The Supreme Court, 1974 Term—Foreword: Constitutional Common Law,* 89 Harv. L. Rev. 1, 28 (1975) (footnote omitted) ("Congress has, for example, a special ability to develop and consider the factual basis of a problem.")

73. *Akron,* 462 U.S. at 451, 452 & nn. 44 & 45. In *Akron,* the Court struck down Akron's ordinance requiring physicians performing abortions to "insure that the remains of the unborn child are disposed of in a humane and sanitary manner." 462 U.S. at 451. The Court distinguished a case that had upheld a Pennsylvania statute governing the humane disposal of fetal remains. As the *Akron* Court stated: "That decision [Planned Parenthood Ass'n v. Fitzpatrick, 401 F. Supp. 554 (E.D. Pa. 1975), *aff'd mem. sub nom.* Franklin v. Fitzpatrick, 428 U.S. 901 (1976)] is distinguishable because the statute did not impose criminal liability, but merely provided for the promulgation of regulations to implement the disposal requirement." 462 U.S. at 451 n. 44.

74. *See Harris,* 448 U.S. at 311, n. 17.

75. *Akron,* 462 U.S. at 445.

76. *Id.*

77. *Id.* at 445 (quoting Planned Parenthood v. Danforth, 428 U.S. 52, 67 n. 8 (1976)).

78. See Edward Grant's chapter in this volume, p. 245.

79. *See, e.g.,* Muller v. Oregon, 208 U.S. 412, 419 & n. 1 (1908) (describing brief filed by Louis D. Brandeis in support of an Oregon statute limiting the hours of employment of women).

80. *See* Borden's Farm Products Co. v. Baldwin, 293 U.S. 194, 210 (1934).

81. *See* 1 J. Weinstein & M. Berger, Weinstein's Evidence Para. 200 [01] (1982).

82. *See* Fed. R. Civ. P. 52(a). Even if the constitutional facts submitted by counsel at trial are not accepted by the trial court and incorporated in the court's findings, their presence in the trial record makes it somewhat easier to point out to a reviewing court that an adverse decision was necessarily based on something other than an objective view of the record.

83. *See* K. Ripple, Constitutional Litigation 86 *et seq.* (1984).

84. Karst, *Legislative Facts in Constitutional Litigation,* 1960 Sup. Ct. Rev. 75; *see generally* Shaman, *Constitutional Fact: The Perception of Reality by the Supreme Court,* 35 U. Fla. L. Rev. 236 (1983).

85. *See* Ripple, *supra* note 83, at 236.

86. For example, in *Moore v. City of East Cleveland,* Justice Powell stated: "Appropriate limits on substantive due process come not from drawing arbitrary lines but rather from careful 'respect for the teachings of history [and] solid recognition of the basic values that underlie our society.'" 431 U.S. 494, 503 (1977) (opinion of Powell, J.)(footnotes omitted) (quoting Griswold v. Connecticut, 381 U.S. 479, 501 (1965) (Harlan, J., concurring)). Although it has often been criticized for its reliance on history, *see generally* Gaffney, *Political Divisiveness Along Religious Lines: The Entanglement of the Court in Sloppy History and Bad Public Policy,* 24 St. Louis L. J. 205, 212–224 (1980); Kelly, *Clio and the Court: An Illicit Love Affair,* 1965 Sup. Ct. Rev. 89, 155–58, the Court continually resorts to history in resolving questions of broad public significance. *See, e.g.,* Lynch v. Donnelly, 465 U.S. 668 (1984); Marsh v. Chambers, 463 U.S. 783 (1983). The role of history and tradition has played a significant role in the literature and the cases considering whether homosexual conduct is protected by the right of privacy. *See generally* Hafen, *The Constitutional Status of Marriage, Kinship, and Sexual Privacy—Balancing the Individual and Social Interests,* 81 Mich. L. Rev. 463 (1983). In a decision rejecting the contention that the right of privacy protects private consensual homosexual activity, Judge Bork noted that this form of behavior had "never before [been] protected, and indeed [had been] traditionally condemned...." Dronenburg v. Zech, 741 F. 2d 1388, 1396 (D.C. Cir.), *suggestion for rehearing en banc denied,* 746 F. 2d 1579 (D.C. Cir. 1984).

87. *See* Burnet v. Coronado Oil & Gas Co., 285 U.S. 393, 405–10 (1932) (Brandeis, J., dissenting) (noting that stare decisis is more strictly applied in England).

88. Steven, *The Life Span of a Judge-Made Rule,* 58 N.Y.U. L. Rev. 1, 4 (1983).

89. *Akron,* 462 U.S. at 420 n. 1.

90. *Thornburgh,* 106 S. Ct. at 2189 (Stevens, J., concurring). Dean Bennett has also made this point: "*Roe* has aroused expectations and induced patterns of

behavior, so that, quite apart from one's views of the merits of the abortion controversy, any move to overrule brings social costs that must be taken into account." Bennett, *Judicial Activism and the Concept of Original Intent*, 69 Judicature 219, 223 (1986).

91. Burnet v. Coronado Oil & Gas Co., 285 U.S. 393, 412 (1932) (Brandeis, J., dissenting).

92. Gregg v. Georgia, 428 U.S. 153, 187 (1976) (opinion of Stewart, Powell,and Stevens, JJ.).

93. For a useful discussion of stare decisis and *Roe v. Wade*, see Wardle, *Rethinking* Roe v. Wade, 1985 B.Y.U.L. Rev. 231, 251-57.

94. Dean Wellington has described this aspect of constitutional litigation in this fashion: "Moreover, the process has its own built-in dynamics of evaluation. Of course Justices are fallible. But when they make mistakes, they hear about them: signals are sent, groups are formed, legislation is proposed, and the public forum is heavily used. New cases will afford the Court opportunities for reevaluation. The doctrine of stare decisis is not strong in the constitutional realm." Wellington, Book Review, 97 Harv. L. Rev. 326, 335 (1983).

95. Minersville School District v. Gobitis, 310 U.S. 586 (1940), *overruled,* West Virginia State Board of Education v. Barnette, 319 U.S. 624 (1943).

96. Danzig, *How Questions Begot Answers in Felix Frankfurter's First Flag Salute Opinion*, 1977 Sup. Ct. Rev. 257, 268-269.

97. 411 U.S. 677, 692 (1973) (Powell, J., concurring in the judgment).

98. 444 U.S. 646, 662 (1980).

99. *See generally*, Murphy, *Lower Court Checks on Supreme Court Power*, 53 Amer. Pol. Sci. Rev. 1017 (1959); Wilkes, *New Federalism in Criminal Procedure: State Court Evasion of the Burger Court*, 62 Ky. L. J. 421 (1974). *See Margaret S. v. Edwards*, 794 F. 2d 994, 995-96 (5th Cir. 1986)(acknowledging the criticism of the Supreme Court's abortion jurisprudence). In *Margaret S.*, Judge Higginbotham stated: "Although we have not undertaken to criticize the Supreme Court, we do not believe it would be improper to do so . . . . Indeed, the Supreme Court itself has implicitly encouraged the lower courts to offer it responsible criticisms of its decisions." *Id.* at 996 n. 3(citations omitted).

100. In *Ashcroft*, the Court upheld a Missouri statute requiring the attendance of a second physician at the abortion of a viable fetus. *Ashcroft*, 462 U.S. at 485-486. *See also* Tribe, *The Abortion Funding Conundrum: Inalienable Rights, Affirmative Duties, and the Dilemma of Dependence*, 99 Harv. L. Rev. 330, 341 (1985). The activity of governmental and private groups in providing assistance to poor women may help to alleviate "equal protection" concerns that existed prior to *Roe v. Wade*, i.e., that state prohibitions on abortion had particularly harsh effects on the poor.

101. *See generally* Kuzma, *The Legislative Response to Infant Doe*, 59 Ind. L. J. 377 (1983-84); Infanticide and the Handicapped Newborn (Horan & Delahoyde ed. 1982).

102. In a newspaper article, the chief of neonatology at Johns Hopkins was quoted as saying: " 'If it's ethical to interrupt a pregnancy at 20 weeks because of Down's syndrome, then what is the difference if the same child is allowed to

die at 38 weeks?' he asks. 'It's all a compromise with your conscience.'" *'Baby Doe' is dividing the medical community*, Wash. Times, July 9, 1984, p. 5A, Col. 4. *See* Aloia, *The Treatment of Handicapped Infants*, New Oxford Review 18 (March 1984) (arguing that in the last decade, "[t]here has been a systematic erosion of the traditional belief in the sanctity of each human life, and a gradual transformation to another, relativistic standard"). *See also* Koop and Grant, *The "Small Beginnings" of Euthanasia: The Erosion of Legal Prohibitions Against Mercy-Killing*, 2 Notre Dame J. L. Ethics & Pub. Pol'y 585 (1986); Hentoff, "Barriers Against Killing Are Coming Down," Wash. Post, March 30, 1986 (describing the American Medical Association's adoption of "the euthanasia principle," and quoting a statement by Dr. Alexander (who was with the Office of the Chief Counsel for War Crimes at Nuremberg) in response to the growing acceptance of euthanasia that: "'It is much like Germany in the 20's and 30's, the barriers against killing are coming down.'").

103. For an excellent discussion of these issues, see Destro, *Quality-of-Life Ethics and Constitutional Jurisprudence: The Demise of Natural Rights and Equal Protection for the Disabled and Incompetent*, 2 J. Contemp. Health L. & Pol'y 71 (1986).

104. *See generally* Law, *Rethinking Sex and the Constitution*, 132 U. Pa. L. Rev. 955, 1026 (1984) (arguing that values of our pluralistic society support the result in *Roe*); Chemerinsky, *Rationalizing the Abortion Debate: Legal Rhetoric and the Abortion Controversy*, 31 Buff. L. Rev. 107, 142–45 (1982) (same).

105. Epstein, *Substantive Due Process By Any Other Name: The Abortion Cases*, 1973 Sup. Ct. Rev. 159, 172. *See also Thornburgh*, 106 S. Ct. at 2196 n. 3 (White, J., dissenting). *Infra* at 318.

106. That is, of course, a complex issue. For enlightening discussions, see Greenawalt, *Religious Convictions In Lawmaking*, 84 Mich. L. Rev. 352 (1985); R. Neuhaus, *The Naked Public Square* (1984).

107. *Thornburgh*, 106 S. Ct. at 2188 (Stevens, J., concurring). *See also Bowers v. Hardwick*, 106 S. Ct. at 2854–55 (Blackmun, J., dissenting)(arguing that traditional religious condemnation of sodomy argued against the constitutionality of Georgia's sodomy statute).

108. *Thornburgh*, 106 S. Ct. at 2197 n. 4 (White, J. dissenting); *see* Greenawalt, 84 Mich. L. Rev. at 371–80.

109. Greenawalt, 84 Mich. L. Rev. at 357.

110. *Doe v. Bolton*, 410 U.S. 179, 222 (1973) (White, J., dissenting).

111. In his dissent in *Thornburgh*, Justice White noted these criticisms in stating that the Court's substantive due process decisions risk opening the Court "to the accusation that, in the name of identifying constitutional principles to which the people have consented in framing their Constitution, the Court has done nothing more than impose its own controversial choices of value upon the people." *Thornburgh*, 106 S. Ct. at 2194 (White, J. dissenting). According to Justice White, the abortion issue should be "resolved by the will of the people...." *Id.* at 2197 (White, J., dissenting). *Infra* at 302, 305.

112. *See City of Cleburne v. Cleburne Living Center*, 105 S. Ct. 3249, 3268–69 (1985)(Marshall, J., concurring in the judgment in part and dissenting in part). Justice Marshall noted how "[s]hifting cultural, political, and social patterns" affect the Court's constitutional interpretation. 105 S. Ct. at 3269. Justice

Marshall stated: "It is natural that evolving standards of equality come to be embodied in legislation. When that occurs, courts should look to the fact of such change as a source of guidance on evolving principles of equality." *Id.* at 3269.

113. Justice White's dissent in *Thornburgh* appears to adopt a states' right approach; his opinion simply advocated "return[ing] the issue to the people. . . ." 106 S. Ct. at 2197 (White, J., dissenting).

Dennis J. Horan and
Thomas J. Balch

Roe v. Wade: No Justification in History, Law, or Logic

I. Roe and Its Critics

IN THE HISTORY of American constitutional jurisprudence, few Supreme Court decisions have come to be recognized as so faulty, and with such damaging social consequences that history has branded them not only as controversial or erroneous but also as watersheds of ignominy.

Dred Scott v. Sanford ruled that blacks were not citizens, Plessy v. Ferguson upheld racial segregation, and Lochner v. New York said that legislatures could not enact maximum hour laws to protect workers from the superior bargaining power of employers. Roe v. Wade is in this unenviable tradition.[1] It is difficult to find a contemporary decision whose reasoning is more universally questioned by the community of legal scholars. It is attacked by thinkers who, like John Hart Ely, support legal abortion as a matter of legislative policy, and criticized by those who support its result as a matter of constitutional law.[2]

After surveying the decision, editors of the Michigan Law Review, introducing a Symposium on the Law and Politics of Abortion, wrote that "the consensus among legal academics seems to be that, whatever one thinks of the holding, the opinion is unsatisfying."[3] Richard Morgan notes:

> Rarely does the Supreme Court invite critical outrage as it did in Roe by offering so little explanation for a decision that requires so much. The stark inadequacy of the Court's attempt to justify its conclusions... suggests to some scholars that the Court, finding no justification at all in the Constitution, unabashedly usurped the legislative function.... Even

some who approve of *Roe*'s form of judicial review concede that the opinion itself is inscrutable.[4]

Joseph Dellapenna has asserted that the opinion is so poorly written that even its defenders begin by apologizing for the difficulties in following the reasoning of the Court.[5] Heymann and Barzelay, although they defend *Roe*'s consistency with "principles that are justified in both reason and precedent," regret that "these principles were never adequately articulated by the opinion of the Court.""This failure," they write, "leaves the impression that the abortion decisions rest in part on unexplained precedents, in part on an extremely tenuous relation to provisions of the Bill of Rights, and in part on a raw exercise of judicial fiat."[6]

The Court's articulation of its position is so embarrassing that the invariable approach of legal scholars writing in support of *Roe*'s holdings is to "rewrite" the opinion, suggesting some constitutional rationale not proffered by the Court which attempts to justify its conclusions.[7] Archibald Cox speaks for many: "The failure to confront the issue in principled terms leaves the opinion to read like a set of hospital rules and regulations, whose validity is good enough this week but will be destroyed with new statistics upon the medical risks of child-birth and abortion or new advances in providing for the separate existence of a foetus."[8]

Virtually every aspect of the historical, sociological, medical, and legal arguments Justice Harry Blackmun used to support the *Roe* holdings has been subjected to intense scholarly criticism. The unprecedented extremity of the Court's opinion is well known. After Justice Blackmun announced the Court's opinion on January 22, 1973, not a single abortion statute in any state of the Union still stood. Even the law of New York, the "abortion capital of the country," which allowed abortion on demand through the twenty-fourth week of pregnancy, was too protective of the unborn for the majority of the United States Supreme Court.[9] For under *Roe*, it is constitutionally impossible for any state to prohibit abortions at any time during pregnancy.

The Court held:

(a) For the stage prior to approximately the end of the first trimester, the abortion decision and its effectuation must be left to the medical judgment of the pregnant woman's attending physician.

(b) For the stage subsequent to approximately the end of the first trimester, the State, in promoting its interest in the health of the mother, may, if it chooses, regulate the abortion procedure in ways that are reasonably related to maternal health.

(c) For the stage subsequent to viability, the State in promoting its interest in the potentiality of human life may, if it chooses, regulate, and even proscribe, abortion except where it is necessary, in appropriate medical judgment for the preservation of the life *or health* of the mother.[10]

On the same day that the Court decided *Roe*, it also decided the companion case *Doe v. Bolton*. The Court emphasized, in *Roe*, "That opinion and this one, of course, are to be read together." In *Doe*, the Court, making reference to its earlier decision in *United States v. Vuitch*, construed the meaning of "mother's life or health."

That . . . has been construed to bear upon psychological as well as physical well-being. . . . [T]he medical judgment may be exercised in the light of all factors— physical, emotional, psychological, familial, and the woman's age—relevant to the well-being of the patient. All these factors may relate to health. This allows the attending physician the room he needs to make his best medical judgment. And it is room that operates for the benefit, not the disadvantage, of the pregnant woman.[11]

In *Roe* the Court expanded on the factors the physician might consider.

Maternity, or additional offspring, may force upon the woman a distressful life and future. Psychological harm may be imminent. Mental and physical health may be taxed by child care. There is also the distress, for all concerned, associated with the unwanted child, and there is the problem of bringing a child into a family already unable, psychologically and otherwise, to care for it. In other cases . . . the additional difficulties and continuing stigma of unwed motherhood may be involved. All these are factors the woman and her responsible physician necessarily will consider in consultation.[12]

Thus it is clear that, under the Supreme Court's abortion decisions, no state may constitutionally prohibit abortion at any time during pregnancy. After the end of the first trimester (first three months), it may make some regulations to protect *maternal* health, but not to impede abortion. After viability, the state may "proscribe" abortion only when the woman considering abortion can find no physician willing to say that her mental health would, for example, be "taxed by child care" or suffer "distress . . . associated with the unwanted child."[13] In effect, "[t]he statutes of most states must be unconstitutional *even as applied to the final trimester.* ... [E]ven after viability the mother's life *or health* (which presumably is to be defined very broadly indeed, so as to include what many might regard as the mother's convenience ...) must, as a matter of constitutional law, take precedence over ... the fetus's *life.* ... "[14]

The lower courts have followed this analysis. In *American College of Obstetricians and Gynecologists v. Thornburgh*, a federal court of appeals was quite explicit:

> [A] physician may perform an abortion even after viability when necessary "to preserve maternal life or health." It is clear from the Supreme Court cases that "health" is to be broadly defined. As the Court stated in *Doe v. Bolton*, the factors relating to health include those that are: "physical, emotional, psychological, familial, [as well as] the woman's age." 410 U.S. at 192.

> ... [I]t is apparent that the Pennsylvania legislature was hostile to this definition. Section 3210(b) [of the state's abortion law] contains the statement, "The potential psychological or emotional impact on the mother of the unborn child's survival shall not be deemed a medical risk to the mother." Had the legislature imposed this qualification on the language "maternal ... health." ... we would have no hesitation in declaring that provision unconstitutional.[15]

Similarly, in *Schulte v. Douglas*, a federal district court declared unconstitutional a Nebraska statute that attempted to prohibit abortion after viability unless it was necessary to protect the woman from imminent peril substantially endangering her life or health. This, Judge Warren Urbom held, prevents postviability abortions "even when in the physician's judgment a different course should be undertaken to preserve the mother ... from a *non-imminent* peril that endangers her life or health *less than substantially* ... This the state has no authority to do."[16]

In effect, as long as a woman can find a physician willing to perform the abortion, she has a constitutional right to obtain an abortion at *any* time during pregnancy. When the Court asserts that such an extreme position is required by the Constitution, one expects an especially compelling rationale. Few have found *Roe* convincing.

II. Historical Critiques of *Roe*

AFTER JUSTICE BLACKMUN recited the case history and disposed of the procedural questions of justiciability, standing, and abstention, he did not launch directly into analysis of the substantive issues at stake.

Instead, he began with a lengthy discussion of the history of legal and societal attitudes toward abortion. Why? Justice Blackmun maintained that, until the mid-nineteenth century, abortion was generally and freely available and not forbidden by the law and should be recognized as an aspect of the liberty the framers of the Fourteenth Amendment intended to protect.[17] Thus, a historical discussion must be seen as a predicate for the Court's holding that the right of privacy incorporated by the Fourteenth Amendment into the U.S. Constitution should be deemed to encompass abortion as a time-treasured right.[18]

Before considering Justice Blackmun's version of the history of abortion, it is worth putting that history in perspective. Today, virtually all who oppose abortion do so because abortion kills unborn human life. Therefore, in examining the history of abortion it is natural to focus our understanding on the attitudes of previous historical eras toward the child in the womb. To what extent, and at what point in gestation, did each epoch recognize the child as a human person? Did they, on that ground, condemn abortion as a form of homicide?

Regarding these important questions, scholarly research reveals that recognition of the unborn as "persons in the whole sense" was largely determined by the biological and medical knowledge of each historical era. The ovum and the actual nature of fertilization were discovered in the nineteenth century. Prior to this, scientists and contemporaneous jurists supposed that human life commenced at "formation," "animation," or "quickening." Abortion was seen as unquestionably homicidal only after the gestational point at which, in light of the science of the time, human life was finally understood to be present.

Justice Blackmun's conclusion that in prior eras abortion in early pregnancy was not seen as homicidal is irrelevant. Indeed, an approach coinciding with historical continuity, *pace* Blackmun, would be to protect the unborn from the time of fertilization because that is when modern science teaches us that the life of an individual human organism comes into being.[19]

Another aspect important to an historical analysis of abortion is that there was widespread disapproval and prohibition of abortion during early pregnancy before, in the view of the science of the time, human life had been infused. The motives for this repudiation of early abortion may not be the same as those that would appeal to today's society as justifying legal interdiction.[20]

Our ancestors' biologically incorrect notions of when human life begins led Blackmun to assert that, historically, "abortion was viewed with less disfavor than under most American statutes currently in effect" (in January, 1973) and "[p]hrasing it another way, a woman enjoyed a substantially broader right to terminate a pregnancy than she does . . . today."[21] Examination of the condemnation of abortion, apart from views on the beginning of human life, proves this conclusion incorrect.

A. ANCIENT AND MEDIEVAL ATTITUDES

BLACKMUN'S RECOUNTING of the history of abortion began with ancient attitudes and the Hippocratic oath. Relying exclusively for both areas on the dated work of historian Ludwig Edelstein, he concluded that the ancient Greeks and Romans had resorted to abortion with great frequency and that it had met with widespread approbation.[22] Conversely, Martin Arbagi demonstrates that temple inscriptions and other ancient writings disclose considerable opposition to abortion in the Greco-Roman world. Opposition spread and intensified from earlier to later ancient times—a tendency which manifested itself long before Christianity had any influence.[23]

Apart from remarking that the Persian Empire banned abortion, Justice Blackmun's survey of the ancient world was limited to Greece and Rome. Yet, it is significant that abortion was condemned in the twelfth century B.C. by Assyrians, Hittites, early Hindus, Buddhists of India, and Indian law. There is some evidence that the ancient Egyptians took a similar attitude. Most of this information was available in the epical work of Eugene Quay, which Blackmun cited but failed to incorporate into his opinion.[24]

Justice Blackmun recognized that the oath of Hippocrates, composed in ancient Greece, forbade the practice of abortion. Apparently, in view of the longstanding honor paid to the Hippocratic oath, Blackmun felt the need to diminish its importance. In fact, he brought this question up *sua sponte*, because, "Although the Oath is not mentioned in any of the principal briefs in this case or in [the companion case of] *Doe v. Bolton* . . . , it represents the apex of the development of strict ethical concepts in medicine, and its influence endures to this day."[25] Citing Edelstein, Blackmun argued that the oath, rather than establishing significant pre-Christian opposition to abortion, was merely the manifesto of an idiosyncratic and unrepresentative sect of Pythagoreans. However, as noted in Professor Arbagi's chapter, the oath's condemnation is not out of step with ancient attitudes.[26] Harold Brown makes a further point:

> The unspoken implication of the Court's argument seems to be that the Hippocratic Oath need not be taken seriously as an expression of medical

ethics because, at the outset, it was the view of a minority ... and later, when it came to enjoy majority acceptance, this only took place because the majority by that time had embraced Christianity. Edelstein's conclusion is somewhat different ... In all countries, in all epochs, in which monotheism, in its purely religious or its more secularized form, was the accepted creed, the Hippocratic Oath was applauded as the embodiment of truth. Not only the Jews and the Christians, but the Arabs, the medieval doctors, men of the Renaissance, scholars of the enlightenment and scientists of the nineteenth century embraced the ideals of the oath.[27]

In short, the Court's discussion of the oath amounts to a *non sequitur*: even were its scholarship and conclusions about the oath's origins unassailable, the Court did not diminish the significance of the Hippocratic oath as a longstanding and near universal condemnation of abortion by the organized medical profession.[28]

Despite the fact that studies and commentaries on that period were available to the Court, Justice Blackmun left a historical gap of more than a thousand years when he leaped directly from ancient attitudes and the Hippocratic oath to Anglo-American common law; John Noonan, in 1970, wrote about the rejection of abortion as *An Almost Absolute Value in History*.[29] During that period, the ethics and law of Western civilization were dominated by the Judeo-Christian perspective; in fact, every adequate survey of historical attitudes toward abortion has to come to terms with the longstanding opposition to abortion by Jews and Christians. True, there was both ignorance and debate, appropriate to the science of the time, about "ensoulment" and what was viewed as the coming of full humanity to the fetus. But opposition to abortion, with minor exceptions, was constant.

The Septuagint, the Greek version of the Hebrew Bible used by third century B.C. Jews of the Diaspora, contained a version of Exodus which decreed capital punishment for one who aborted a formed fetus.[30] The Didache (first century A.D.), known as the "Teaching of the Twelve Apostles," proclaimed to the early Christian Church, "You shall not slay the child by abortions. You shall not kill what is generated." Other early Christian writings such as the Epistle of Barnabas and the Apocalypse of Peter contained similiar prohibitions.[31] In the West, the Fathers of the Church, from second century Clement of Alexandria through Tertullian and Jerome to Augustine, condemned abortion. In the East, St. John Chrysostom and St. Basil of Cappadocia preached against all abortion. These early teachings were concretized in the prohibitions of penitentials and of canons enacted by synods and councils which, in turn, found their way into the law of the state, such as the Frankish kingdom of Charlemagne. These were followed by canon law. A decretal of Gregory IX grouped the penalty for abortion with that for means of sterilization. Of both it was said, "[l]et it be held as homicide."[32]

This treatment of abortion and contraception as crimes demanding severe punishment was coupled with a general attitude that abortion was not "true" homicide until the fetus was "ensouled"—something held to occur at formation or quickening.[33] That distinction, taken from Aristotle, was introduced by theologians in the fifth century and was dominant until the seventeenth century.[34] John Connery describes Aristotle's essentially biological theory of "delayed animation":

> To Aristotle...life at conception came from a vegetative soul. After conception, this would eventually be replaced by an animal soul, and the latter finally by a human soul. The difficult question was when this human soul was infused, or as it is sometimes put, when the fetus became a human being. Aristotle held that this occurred when the fetus was formed, 40 days after conception for the male fetus and 90 days for the female. Aristotle also used the criterion of movement. If the aborted fetus showed signs of movement, it was considered human. But since this coincided with the time of formation, the time estimate was the same...It was easy to argue for delayed animation when one thought that semen gradually turned into blood and then into flesh and bone and eventually into a human fetus.[35]

Through the Middle Ages, civil law on the continent of Europe was based on the Roman law. Connery notes that from the end of the second century through the thirteenth century, that law applied the same punishment to abortion throughout pregnancy. In the thirteenth century, the Italian jurist Accursio first interpreted the law to impose a higher punishment for abortion after formation: such abortion was classified as homicide and incurred capital punishment.[36] This late application to the civil law of the Aristotelian view that had long dominated church penitential discipline did not eliminate or lessen the penalty for preformation abortion; it only heightened it for postformation abortion.

B. THE COMMON LAW ON ABORTION

IGNORING THIS CIVIL law background, which was important for its relation to the beginnings of the English common law, the Supreme Court paid considerable attention to the content of English common law. From the thirteenth through the sixteenth centuries, the common law courts coexisted with the ecclesiastical courts in England—much as state courts coexist with federal courts today. Just as state and federal courts have independent jurisdiction over some matters and concurrent jurisdiction over others, so it was with the medieval, royal, and church courts. The ecclesiastical courts dealt with many secular matters such as wills, slander, and informal contracts.[37] As Dellapenna's research discloses, "at least prior to 1600, royal courts did not concern themselves about abortion, but . . . royally-sustained ecclesiastical courts did."[38]

Justice Blackmun's view of the common law focused almost exclusively on the royal courts. He followed the position of Cyril Means, legal counsel to the National Association for the Repeal of Abortion Laws, and concluded that it is "doubtful that abortion was ever firmly established as a common-law crime even with respect to the destruction of a quick fetus."[39] Means's and Blackmun's position has been resoundingly refuted in articles by Dellapenna, Robert Byrn, and Robert Destro.[40] Essentially, Means's position rests on his attribution of deceit and distortion to Chief Justice Sir Edward Coke. He was the great sixteenth and seventeenth century jurist who successfully led the fight to capture, for the common law courts, most of the jurisdiction exercised up to then by the ecclesiastical courts. In the process, Coke was a leader in systematizing, expanding and recording the common law. In his famous *Institutes* he declared that, while not "murder," abortion of a woman "quick with childe" was a "great misprision."[41]

Means, based upon his interpretation of two fourteenth century cases he called *The Twinslayer's Case* and *The Abortionist's Case*, and two sixteenth century commentaries, Sir William Stanford's *Les Plees del Coron* and William Lamborde's *Eirenorcha, or of The Office of the Justice of the Peace*, concluded that Coke was mistaken.[42] He asserted that these sources established that abortion was never a crime at common law. He brushed aside the earlier evidence of the thirteenth century commentators Bracton and Fleta, who described abortion of a formed and animated fetus as homicide.[43] He scornfully accused Coke of distorting the law to fit the view of abortion he had taken as attorney general in a case argued in 1601; and he dismissed Blackstone, whose name was synonymous with "law" for eighteenth and nineteenth century American lawyers, as an uncritical follower of Coke.[44] Blackstone's work, well known by the framers of the Constitution and the architects of the Fourteenth Amendment, called it a "great misprision" "[t]o kill a child in its mother's womb."[45]

The intricacies of legal history and the explication of the scanty texts of these decisions and commentaries are complex. Means's interpretation of *The Twinslayer's Case* and *The Abortionist's Case* rested on the assumption that the dismissals of charges brought against abortionists in those cases were due to the fact that abortion was not a crime at common law. Instead, as Byrn, Dellapenna and Destro have demonstrated, the dismissals were clearly based on problems of proof.[46] Robert Destro argued from the text of the cases, and included a key paragraph in *The Twinslayer's Case* ignored by Means. He concluded, and the documents affirm, that as a matter of substantive law, post-quickening abortion was a common law crime. The same can be said of Stanford's commentary.[47]

The primitive nature of biological knowledge and abortion technology made it next to impossible to prove that the child was alive before the supposed abortion *and* that the abortion was the cause of death. It was compounded by rigidly technical procedural requirements, and led to the conclusion by the sixteenth century commentary that abortion was not punished as a crime.[48]

In the 1601 *Sims Case*, a solution to some of these difficulties in proof was offered: when a child was born alive, but showed the marks of an abortion, and subsequently died, murder could be proved.[49] This position was adopted by Coke and carried through to Blackstone. There is a plethora of cases since Coke holding postquickening abortion a common law crime—cases ignored by Means or dismissed by him as being based on Coke's "distortion."[50] Yet, as Destro asks, "[e]ven assuming that Coke's view was completely at variance with the earliest common law precedents...one question remains to be answered: Why did Coke's view persevere and gain acceptance by virtually every court which considered the matter?"[51] Suppose someone were to contend today that racial segregation was "never" unconstitutional because *Brown v. Board of Education* was inconsistent with *Plessy v. Ferguson* and other precedents, and that the many subsequent desegregation cases in the Supreme Court and other federal courts were based on an uncritical acceptance of *Brown*. Justifiably, the argument would be laughed out of court.[52]

Coke's views became so firmly established from the seventeenth through the nineteenth century that it takes a remarkably selective vision to deny that abortion of a quickened fetus was a common law crime at the time of the adoption of the Constitution or the Fourteenth Amendment. In the words of Robert Byrn, "For the Supreme Court in *Roe v. Wade* to cite the 'lenity' of the common law as a basis for holding that unborn children do not possess a fundamental right to live and to the law's protection at any time up to birth, is a perversion of Bracton, Coke, Hawkins and Blackstone. The whole history of the common law cries out against the jurisprudence of *Wade*."[53]

C. NINETEENTH CENTURY STATUTORY REFORM

AFTER EVALUATION of the common law, Justice Blackmun described the nineteenth century English and American statutory enactments on abortion. Then, after charting the changing positions of the American Medical Association, the American Public Health Association, and the American Bar Association on abortion, he analyzed reasons behind the nineteenth century enactment of statutes against abortion throughout pregnancy.[54]

Following Cyril Means's thesis, Blackmun maintained that the nineteenth century's statutory prohibitions of abortion, even back to the moment of conception, were enacted not to aid prenatal life but to protect maternal health against the danger of unsafe operations.[55] Blackmun made several key factual errors and completely failed to mention the important scientific developments that prompted the statutory changes. As Victor Rosenblum has noted:

> Only in the second quarter of the nineteenth century did biological research advance to the extent of understanding the actual mechanism of development. The nineteenth century saw a gradual but profoundly influential revolution in the scientific understanding of the beginning of individual mammalian life. Although sperm had been discovered in 1677, the mammalian egg was not identified until 1827. The cell was first recognized as the structural unit of organisms in 1839, and the egg and sperm were recognized as cells in the next two decades. These developments were brought to the attention of the American state legislatures and public by those professionals most familiar with their unfolding import—physicians. It was the new research finding which persuaded doctors that the old "quickening" distinction embodied in the common and some statutory law was unscientific and indefensible.[56]

Beginning about 1857, the American Medical Association (AMA) led a "physicians' crusade" to enact laws protecting the unborn from the time of conception.[57] These vigorous physicians rested their argument primarily upon the living nature of the fetus in early pregnancy, and it was their efforts that passed the laws. As Dellapenna noted, twenty-six of thirty-six states had prohibited abortion by the end of the Civil War, and six of the ten territories. "The assertion by Justice Blackmun that such legislation did not become widespread until after the 'War Between the States' is simply wrong."[58] Justice Blackmun ignored this clear history—an extraordinary omission in light of his quotation, in *Roe*, of statements from the principal resolutions of the AMA during "the 'physicians' crusade."[59]

Blackmun gave three reasons for the notion that the laws were enacted to protect maternal health rather than the child. All have been rebutted. First, citing only one New Jersey decision, he said: "The few state courts called upon to interpret their laws in the late nineteenth and early twentieth century did focus on the state's interests in protecting the woman's health rather than in preserving the embryo and fetus."[60] To the contrary, John Gorby has demonstrated that there are eleven state court decisions explicitly affirming that protection of the unborn was a purpose of their nineteenth century abortion statutes, and nine others that imply the same position. Robert Destro and Gorby have both independently demonstrated that the isolated New Jersey citation misstates the purpose even of that jurisdiction's law.[61]

Second, Blackmun argued: "In many States . . . by statute or judicial interpretation, the pregnant woman herself could not be prosecuted for self-abortion or for cooperating in an abortion performed upon her by another."[62] John Gorby replies:

> The explanation for this legal phenomenon is that there are special circumstances surrounding the commitment of an act, circumstances which the lawmaker may properly and reasonably consider in formulating means to protect state interests and values . . . in the abortion situation, the assumed stresses on the woman burdened by an unwanted pregnancy. These factors may justify and explain different treatment of the woman or even the physician in the abortion context, just as they justify or explain different treatment of the child of tender years or even of one who kills another under severe provocation.[63]

Finally, Blackmun contended: "Adoption of the 'quickening' distinction through received common law and state statutes tacitly recognizes the greater health hazard inherent in late abortion and impliedly repudiates the theory that life begins at conception."[64] Robert Sauer demolishes this notion:

> Although a number of the initial state laws contained a distinction based on quickening which gave lower value to early foetal life, the large majority of state laws never made this distinction, and most of these laws referred to a woman as "being with child" or some similar phrase which attributed a human status to the foetus. Furthermore, many of the states which initially had this distinction written into their law later dropped it and also referred to a woman at any period of her pregnancy as "being with child."[65]

Common law was not the only means available or used to prevent abortion. In the ecclesiastical courts and in church law, the notion, based on the inaccurate biology of the time, that the fetus became a human being only at formation or quickening did not prevent the authorities from condemning abortion during all stages of gestation. Although problems of proof prevented the common law from punishing abortion of an unquickened fetus, they allowed society to use other endeavors to prevent abortion throughout pregnancy.

Professor Dellapenna has made a valuable contribution to accurately understanding the history of abortion by pointing out the varying technical methods used to attempt abortion at different periods in history. Historically, these methods involved the use of drugs, potions (often either ineffectual or fatally poisonous), beatings, or other risky efforts to induce trauma that would trigger abortion. After 1750, methods involving the insertion of objects into the uterus were introduced; and surgery, initially highly dangerous, was used sometime later.[66]

Today, we naturally think of abortive surgical procedures being performed by physicians. Yet into the nineteenth century, midwives attended women during childbirth and pregnancy and performed most abortions.[67] Following the institution of similar systems in continental Europe in the fifteenth century, England developed a system of regulating and licensing midwives in the early sixteenth century. These regulations required midwives' oaths swearing that they would not give advice or medicines to women enabling them to abort. No distinction was made on the basis of the stage of pregnancy. A similar practice was instituted in colonial America: records exist of a New York City ordinance requiring midwives to take such an oath as early as 1716.[68] Possibly the nineteenth century "physicians' crusade" extended the protection of statutory law back to conception because midwives had lost their prominence as abortion providers.

Evidence is overwhelming that the Court's abortion history is fatally flawed. Contrary to Justice Blackmun's assertion that "restrictive criminal abortion laws . . . are of relatively recent vintage . . . not of ancient or even of common-law origin," abortion was condemned even in ancient times and the consensus of Western civilization was opposed to abortion throughout the duration of pregnancy.[69] True, the precise penalties varied, depending on what science held to be the point at which human life began. As the result of nineteenth century biological discoveries the existence of human life from the time of conception became clear. Members of the American medical community were aware of new evidence and the increasing frequency of abortion resulting from technological developments in abortion methodology. They successfully led a reform movement which extended the full protection of the criminal law to the time of fertilization. These statutory amendments were neither anomalous nor explained by motivations other than fetal protection; they were the logical outgrowth of the interaction of "an almost absolute value in history" and the teachings of evolving science.[70]

History provides no excuse for Justice Blackmun's conclusion that "at common law, at the time of the adoption of our Constitution, and throughout the major portion of the 19th century...a woman enjoyed a substantially broader right to terminate a pregnancy" than in most states immediately before *Roe v. Wade*.[71] That "right" was *never* present in America until 1973. That erroneous conclusion is of paramount importance, since it is from its misguided version of abortion history that the Court implicitly draws what meager support it can for the notion that abortion is time-treasured and incorporated into the Fourteenth Amendment.

III. Abortion as a Constitutional Right

IMMEDIATELY AFTER HIS historical survey, Justice Blackmun turned to the essence of what he found to be the abortion right. "The Fourteenth Amendment's concept of personal liberty," the Court ruled, "is broad enough to encompass a woman's decision whether or not to terminate her pregnancy."[72] This textually unsupported assertion has been subjected to an avalanche of criticism—some of it from the most respected legal minds in the country. Indeed, this portion of the opinion has stimulated more negative jurisprudential evaluation than any other section and the critique comes from various parts of the ideological spectrum.

Listing cases recognizing some form of a "right of privacy," Justice Blackmun acknowledged that "[t]hese decisions make it clear that only personal rights that can be deemed 'fundamental' or 'implicit in the concept of ordered liberty'...are included in this guarantee of personal privacy." What makes abortion "implicit" in the very nature of "ordered liberty"? Justice Blackmun wrote that the right of privacy has been deemed to encompass marriage, procreation, contraception, family relationships, and child rearing and education. Without abortion a woman may suffer direct harm, distressful life and/or psychological harm. Mental and physical health may be taxed by child care, also the distress associated with the unwanted child and the additional difficulties and continuing stigma of unwed mothers.[73]

This is the entirety of Blackmun's argument. Norman Vieira, one of many critics, said in response:

> No elaborate discussion is required to expose the glaring non sequitur in the Court's argument. Plainly the fact that *some* family matters are constitutionally protected does not demonstrate that abortion is constitutionally

protected. Nor does the added fact that abortion laws disadvantage pregnant women establish their invalidity. Legal restrictions are placed on family autonomy in fields ranging from divorce to euthanasia despite the heavy costs thereby exacted from the individuals concerned.[74]

In 1973 John Ely made an early and telling attack on *Roe*'s postulation of this right. Referring to the Court's delineation of the difficulties of undesired pregnancy, he wrote:

> All of this is true and ought to be taken very seriously. But it has nothing to do with privacy in the Bill of Rights sense or any other the Constitution suggests...What is unusual about *Roe* is that the liberty involved is accorded...a protection more stringent, I think it is fair to say, than that the present Court accords the freedom of the press explicitly guaranteed by the First Amendment. What is frightening about *Roe* is that this super-protected right is not inferrable from the language of the Constitution, the framers' thinking respecting the specific problem in issue, any general value derivable from the provisions they included, or the nation's governmental structure. Nor is it explainable in terms of the unusual political impotence of the group judicially protected vis a vis the interest that legislatively prevailed over it. And that, I believe...is a charge that can responsibly be leveled at no other decision of the past twenty years.[75]

Remember that Ely has written that, were he a legislator, he would vote for a bill legalizing abortion nearly to the the extent allowed by the Supreme Court.

Vieira and Ely are not alone. Archibald Cox wrote, "The Court failed to establish the legitimacy of the decision by not articulating a principle of sufficient abstractness to lift the ruling above the level of a political judgment."[76] Judge Richard Posner warns that "*Wade* raise[s] ...the question whether we have a written Constitution, with the limitations thereby implied on the creation of new constitutional rights, or whether the Constitution is no more than a grant of discretion to the Supreme Court to mold public policy in accordance with the Justices' own personal and shifting preferences."[77]

At least two commentators have noted the incoherence of the striking contrast between the Court's treatment of privacy with regard to abortion, which the justices clearly like, and with regard to sexually explicit material, which they just as clearly do not.[78] Indeed, the very notion that abortion should be subsumed under a right of "privacy" is strange. As Joseph O'Meara objects, "[T]here is nothing private about an abortion." It occurs not at home, like sex or the reading of obscenity, but in a public clinic.[79]

IV. Abortion and Human Personhood

HAVING READ INTO the Constitution a right that was not in the text, Justice Blackmun then proceeded to read out of the Constitution the application of a right basic to that text. Recognizing that if the Fourteenth Amendment's protection of the right to life is extended to the unborn the case for abortion collapses, he developed the argument for his conclusion that "the word 'person'...does not include the unborn."[80] As John Hart Ely has noted, after employing the most imaginative possible construction of the Fourteenth Amendment to find a right of abortion, the Court resorted to the most literalistic possible form of strict construction to avoid finding the unborn to be persons.[81]

Professors Byrn, Destro, and Gorby have independently provided comprehensive, point-by-point rebuttals of the Court's objections to unborn personhood.[82] The opinion argued that the word "person," as used in clauses elsewhere in the Constitution, has application only postnatally.[83] Ely wrote that the Court "might have added that most of them were plainly drafted with *adults* in mind, but I suppose that wouldn't have helped."[84] As John Gorby has pointed out:

> [T]hese other clauses...do not provide an answer to the question of the scope of constitutional personhood. In the clauses mentioned by the Court, the concept of "person" was broad and undefined and the function of the specific constitutional clause was to limit the broader class of persons for a particular purpose. For example, for a person to be...a representative, a senator or the President, he must be twenty-five, thirty and thirty-five years of age respectively...The fact that a 24-year-old is not qualified for these offices suggests only that there are "persons" who are not qualified for the House, Senate or the Presidency...; it does not suggest when the 24-year-old became a "person," or that he became a person at birth.[85]

For example, the Court says, "[w]e are not aware that in the taking of any census a fetus has ever been counted."[86] As one commentator put it:

> The Court seems to be saying that, because a word is narrowly defined in the context of a practical application (census taking) due to the impracticability or susceptibility to large error of including fetuses within the meaning of the term, that it should also be narrowly defined, to the exclusion of an entire class of potential "persons," when determining what persons are deserving of constitutional protection of the right to life.[87]

The Court fails to recognize that the Apportionment Clause merely provides for a decennial census "in such manner as [Congress] shall by law direct."[88] "Although Congress has never done so, it would be neither irrational nor unconstitutional for it to direct that account also be taken of the unborn whenever the census-taker is made aware of their existence," writes Destro. "The fact that Congress has never done so is irrelevant." He and Byrn observe that corporations are not counted in the census, yet they are Fourteenth Amendment persons.[89]

Blackmun objects that, under the challenged Texas law, the existence of an exception to save the life of the mother is inconsistent with regard to the unborn as persons entitled to equal protection with their mothers.[90] But the doctrines of self-defense and legal necessity allow persons acting out of self-protection to kill another human being, releasing themselves from the liability for killing a born person. "'Balance of interest' tests are commonplace," Epstein points out. "That process of balancing can take place even if the unborn child is treated as a person under the Due Process Clause. . . . We might as well conclude that self-defense should never be treated as a justification for the deliberate killing of another person under the law of either crime or tort. No one could believe that the constitutional right to life extends that far."[91]

Blackmun raises what the Court regards as "two other inconsistencies between Fourteenth Amendment status [of the unborn as a person] and the typical abortion statute."[92] The first is that the woman who submits to an abortion is not liable for punishment for the abortion. But this says nothing about the personhood of the unborn child; it represents a societal judgment about the degree of culpability of the mother. The law provides very different penalties for the secretive, hardened assassin who kills for cash, the angered spouse who kills during a family quarrel, the driver who causes the death of another by accident, or the individual whom duress or disturbance has made incapable either of avoiding the killing or of appreciating the significance of the act. The punishment ranges from death to probation to nothing at all; but this represents no judgment by the legislature or the judiciary that any of the victims were other than persons equal before the law.

In the context of abortion, society may reasonably conclude that most women who seek it are in a situation of immense stress and pressure, and that few of them are aware of the full humanity of the child within the womb.[93] It may reasonably choose to regard the woman as a second victim rather than a perpetrator and instead punish the professional who performs abortions for money. Since anyone who performs an abortion is culpable, this does not diminish protection for the unborn child. Indeed, as a practical matter it may increase that protection for it allows a prosecutor to employ the woman's testimony against the abortionist.[94]

The second "inconsistency" is explained by the response to the first. Justice Blackmun objected that the penalty for abortion is less than that for murder. "If the fetus is a person, may the penalties be different?"[95] As Byrn responds:

> The law recognizes "degrees of evil" and states may treat offenders accordingly. Killing an unborn child may, in legislative judgment, involve less personal malice than killing a child after birth even though the result is the same—just as, for instance, a legislature may choose to categorize, as something less than murder, intentional killing under the influence of extreme emotional disturbance or intentionally aiding and abetting a suicide. Such legislative recognitions of degrees of malice in killing have nothing to do with the fourteenth amendment personhood of the victims.[96]

The Court opined that together with its observation that "throughout the major portion of the nineteenth century prevailing legal practices were far freer than they are today," these four arguments led to the conclusion that the unborn are not Fourteenth Amendment persons.[97] The Court's historical flaws have been amply documented and, as shown, the four arguments that comprise its "strict constructionist" approach to the Fourteenth Amendment's use of "person" fail on their own grounds.

How *should* the Court have construed the term "person" in the Fourteenth Amendment? It could have referred to the test for personhood it had previously enunciated in *Levy v. Louisiana*: persons are those who "are humans, live, and have their being."[98] It could have looked at the legislative history of the Fourteenth Amendment and to the words of its sponsor, John Bingham. Under the Amendment, he said during the congressional debates, "[a] State has not the right to deny equal protection to every human being."[99] In reaction to the exclusion of blacks from constitutional protection, the post-Civil War Congress sought to establish once and for all that every biological human being within the national jurisdiction could be entitled to the equal protection of the laws, without allowing any other discriminating criteria. A number of law review articles have carefully argued this point.[100] Unfortunately, all of this argument and evidence was totally ignored by the Supreme Court.

V. The Beginning of Human Life

JUSTICE BLACKMUN ACKNOWLEDGED that even if the unborn lack Fourteenth Amendment protection, a legislature might still assert a compelling interest in prenatal life. In response he argued that no consensus exists on the temporal origin of human life. His effort "to note...the wide divergence of thinking" on "when life begins" is sprinkled with factual errors: incorrect citation of a medical textbook concerning the range of gestational ages associated with viability,[101] a mistaken statement of "Roman Catholic dogma,"[102] a rendering of the decision of certain influential medical advocates of abortifacients who wanted to redefine "conception" to mean "implantation" as "new embryological data that purport to indicate that conception is a 'process' over time," and thus posing "substantial problems" for the view that life begins at conception.[103]

Its larger failure lies in a basic misunderstanding of the nature of the debate. Two pages purporting to summarize the views of the Stoics, various religions, and physicians, together with a cursory summary of the treatment of the unborn in various areas of the law, constitute the evidence mustered in support of what are probably the two best known sentences in *Roe*:

> We need not resolve the difficult question of when life begins. When those trained in the respective disciplines of medicine, philosophy, and theology are unable to arrive at any consensus, the judiciary, at this point in the development of man's knowledge, is not in a position to speculate as to the answer.[104]

The Court's conclusion, together with the jumbled "divergence of thinking" it cites on the matter, confuse two distinct questions.[105] One is the strictly scientific question of when a human being comes into existence. The other is the ethical, sociological, and legal question of what value to place on that existence: whether all human beings ought to be regarded as equal in their entitlement to rights or whether those rights should be accorded only to human beings who possess certain qualities such as certain levels of self-consciousness, societal inter-action, or the like. The first question was a subject of legitimate dispute before the scientific discoveries of the nineteenth century— which explains some of the "diversity" Justice Blackmun recounts. The second question is admittedly being disputed today, and that accounts for the bulk of the "diversity."

The first question is now settled, however. There is an unequivocal consensus among informed scientists that fertilization constitutes the coming into existence of an individual human organism.[106] And the second question, although far from settled in contemporary America, ought as a legal matter to be regarded as settled by the value judgment incorporated in the Fourteenth Amendment that all biological human beings are to be accorded equal protection of law. As Dr. Harrison has warned, "[t]o substitute consensus for soundness as the criterion by which to decide the worth of an argument is to admit a principle of irrationality into the decision-making process. That the issue being decided is as farreaching in its consequences as is the abortion problem only compounds the damage."[107]

Even taking the Court at its word about the unsettled and unsettlable nature of the controversy, a number of commentators have found the implications of its reasoning extraordinary and its derived holdings inconsistent. One commentator writes:

> What the Court does seem to have said is that the question of when life begins is an extremely unsettled and controversial issue, and for that reason alone, any legislative purpose that is based on a purported resolution of the issue is irrational. . . . This is an extremely strict requirement that affords the judiciary a powerful weapon to use against legislation that it finds offensive in some manner, for few issues that reach the Supreme Court are demonstrably non-controversial.[108]

Taking note of Blackmun's ultimate conclusion, that no legislature may "by adopting one theory of life . . . override the rights of the pregnant woman that are at stake," Richard Epstein protests "this formulation of the issue begged the important question; because it assumes that we know that the woman's rights must prevail even before the required balance takes place. We could as well claim that the Court, by adopting another theory of life, has decided to override the rights of the unborn child which the law of Texas tries to protect. . . . [I]t is simple fiat and power that gives his position its legal effect."[109]

Indeed, Blackmun's laconic assumption that the lack of consensus means not that the matter must be left to the legislatures, but that abortion must be permitted has been subject to as much criticism as the initial holding that the right of privacy includes abortion. Commentator after commentator has noted that his balancing as presented by the Court is quite arbitrary, and has no warrant in the Constitution.[110] "[T]he Court's decision lacks legitimacy," writes Erwin Chemerinsky, who is sympathetic to its result, "because it seems to be an arbitrary, unjustified set of choices."[111] "The quintessence of a balancing test," Elliott Silverstein points out, "is the formulation of the rights and interests on both sides. If one side is ignored or slighted, the judicial process becomes a mere exercise in sophistry....If the Court really means, when it says it need not decide when life begins, that it need not recognize the State's valid interest in instilling respect for life, then *Roe* is, indeed, a dangerous precedent."[112]

VI. The Trimester Approach: Judicial Legislation

THE FINAL PORTION of the decision, with its line drawing by convenient trimesters, and its weighting of state interests by medical statistics, has been almost universally recognized as legislation pure and simple. "Neither historian, layman, nor lawyer," says Archibald Cox, "will be persuaded that all the details prescribed in *Roe v. Wade* are part of either natural law or the Constitution."[113]

The decision is an excellent example of the problems with the judiciary as legislature. As Ely says, the opinion draws "lines with an apparent precision one generally associates with a commission's regulations. A commissioner can readily redraw regulations on the basis of a better understanding of the facts or purely for administrative convenience. However, what the Court writes is graven in constitutional stone and can only be altered by constitutional amendment or Court reversal. The Court's lines in *Roe*, where they are not arbitrary, are grounded in questionable or changeable data."[114]

Why did the Court conclude that the state could regulate on behalf of maternal health only after the second trimester? Apparently because it was persuaded that abortion is safer than childbirth during the first trimester.[115] Yet, Hilgers and O'Hare have shown that the mortality statistics relied upon by the Court give an inaccurate measure of the comparative safety of abortion and childbirth.[116] The Court's exclusive reliance on mortality figures quite ignored the question of morbidity and there is abundant evidence of physical and psychological problems short of death associated with abortion.[117] Even were they correct, the assumptions provide no basis for concluding that there is no state interest in health regulations during the first trimester. "The Court gave no reason why it should make a difference whether it is safer to undergo an abortion or carry the pregnancy to full term," writes one commentator. "[T]hough it may be safer for a particular patient to undergo open heart surgery than to forego the operation and do nothing, the state still has an interest in ensuring that if the patient chooses to have the operation, it is performed as safely as possible."[118] Thus, as Arnold Loewy says, "[t]he fact that abortion [during the first trimester] is safer than childbirth is irrelevant unless the Court is also holding that such regulation in regard to childbirth would be unconstitutional."[119] John Hart Ely's comment is written in tones of astonishment: "[e]ven a sure sense that abortion during the first trimester is safer than childbirth would serve only to blunt a state's claim that it is, for reasons relating to maternal health, entitled to *proscribe* abortion; it would not support the inference the Court draws, that *regulations designed to make the abortion procedure safer during the first trimester are impermissible.*"[120]

The only plausible basis for the Court's ruling that the first trimester remain free of health regulation is what Robert Destro calls, "the Court's concern that state health regulations might turn into 'roadblocks' barring access to legalized abortion."[121] Because medical practices and skills change over time, a practical effect of the Court's analysis is to render this aspect of the constitutional test of abortion statutes subject to a variable technological standard. An abortion statute that is constitutional today may be unconstitutional tomorrow as a result of changes in medical techniques.[122]

The Court went on to choose viability as the point in pregnancy after which states could actually prohibit abortion, unless a physician then judged it necessary for the life or health of the mother.[123] As we have seen, this distinction is illusory; with "health" as broadly defined as the Court requires, there is no practical difference between it and abortion on demand. However, the Court clearly sought to give the impression that viability does make a difference, and commentators have persistently observed that Justice Blackmun did not, or could not, say *why*.[124] The opinion says that "the fetus then presumably has the capability of meaningful life outside the mother's womb" and therefore drawing a line at viability "thus has both logical and biological justifications."[125] The ruling made no attempt to detail what "meaningful life" is, why the capability for it is significant, or what the "logical and biological justifications" might be. If the capacity for independent life was to be the criterion, that capacity certainly does not occur at viability. Any newborn infant is totally dependent on others for food, shelter and care. Certainly, when the Court recognized that "artificial means" might be used to make a newborn "viable," it contemplated incubators and other extraordinary medical support systems on which the child would be utterly dependent.[126]

The changeability of the capacity of medical science is even more pronounced in the case of viability than in that of abortion and childbirth safety. Remarkable progress has been made in recent decades in pushing back the time of viability.[127] This means that a child of the same intrinsic development is subject to disposal or protection depending solely upon when he or she is conceived.[128] Such an arbitrary dependency on things wholly extrinsic to the individual in determining whether the individual has value and is worthy of protection is wholly indefensible.

VII. Conclusion

THE COURT'S MAJORITY opinion in *Roe v. Wade* is riddled with factual errors and logical incongruities. Its analysis is as poor as its results are tragic. The thoroughness and breadth of the criticisms directed at *Roe* fully justify the conclusion of Justice Sandra Day O'Connor that "*Roe*...is clearly on a collision course with itself...[It has] no justification in law or logic."[129]

Notes

1. Dred Scott v. Sandford, 60 U.S. (19 How.) 393 (1857); Plessy v. Ferguson, 163 U.S. 537 (1896); Lochner v. New York, 198 U.S. 45 (1905); Roe v. Wade, 410 U.S. 113 (1973).

2. *Compare* Ely, *The Wages of Crying Wolf:A Comment on* Roe v. Wade, 82 Yale L.J. 920, 926 (1973), *with* Heymann & Barzelay, *The Forest and the Trees*: Roe v. Wade *and Its Critics*, 53 B.U.L. Rev. 765 (1973), *see also* Perry, *Abortion, the Public Morals, and the Police Power: The Ethical Function of Substantive Due Process*, 23 U.C.L.A. L. Rev. 689 (1976); Regan, *Rewriting* Roe v. Wade, 77 Mich. L. Rev. 1569 (1979); Tribe, *Toward a Model of Roles in the Due Process of Life and Law*, 87 Harv. L. Rev. 1 (1973). The volume of legal commentary on *Roe* is massive. The Index to Legal Periodicals through May 1984 lists 107 law review articles largely devoted to substantive criticism of *Roe v. Wade*. This does not encompass commentary in books or in articles which cover *Roe* along with other topics. There are also a number of articles and notes which merely report on the decision and its implications, without engaging in meaningful analysis of its reasoning. These include: Uda, *Abortion:* Roe v. Wade *and the Montana Dilemma*, 35 Montana L. Rev. 103 (1974); Swan, *Compulsory Abortion: Next Challenge to Liberated Women?*, 3 Ohio N.U.L. Rev. 152 (1975); Young, *Supreme Court Report*, 59 A.B.A.J. 407 (1973); Note, *Abortion* Cases: A Return to Lochner, *or a New Substantive Due Process?*, 37 Alb. L. Rev. 776 (1973); Note, *Criminal Law—Texas Abortion Statute—Criminality Exceptions Limited to Life-Saving Procedures on Mother's Behalf Without Regard to Stage of Pregnancy Violates Due Process Clause of Fourteenth Amendment Protecting Right to Privacy*, 2 Am. J. Crim. L. 231 (1973); Note, *Implications of the Abortion Decisions: Post* Roe *and* Doe *Litigation and Legislation*, 74 Colum. L. Rev. 237 (1974); Comment, *Abortion: The Five Year Revolution and Its Impact*, 3 Ecology L.Q. 311 (1973); Note, *Abortion Decisions:* Roe v. Wade, Doe v. Bolton, 12 J. Family L. 459 (1972–1973); Notes and Comments, *Perspectives on the Abortion Decision*, 9 N.M.L. Rev. 175 (1978–1979); Comment, *Landmark Abortion Decisions: Justifiable Termination or Miscarriage of Justice? Proposals for Legislative Response*, 4 Pac. L.J. 821 (1973); *The Supreme Court, 1972 Term*, 87 Harv. L. Rev. 1, 75 (1973); and Comment,

Constitutional Law—Abortion—Right of Privacy—State Statutes Permitting Abortion Only for Life Saving Procedure on Behalf of Mother Without Regard for Other Interests Violate Due Process Clause of the Fourteenth Amendment, 3 Memphis State U.L. Rev. 359 (Spring 1973).

3. *Editors Preface, Symposium on the Law and Politics of Abortion,* 77 Mich. L. Rev. unpaginated preceding 1569 (1979).

4. Morgan, Roe v. Wade *and the Lesson of the Pre-*Roe *Case Law,* 77 Mich. L. Rev. 1724, 1724 (1979) (footnotes omitted).

5. Dellapenna, *The History of Abortion: Technology, Morality, and Law,* 40 U. Pitt. L. Rev. 359, 361 n. 11 (1979).

6. Heyman and Barzelay, *supra* note 2, at 784. *See also* Perry, *supra* note 2, at 690 ("[I]t is difficult to find a case that raises methodological problems as severe as those left in the wake of *Roe*"); Regan, *supra* note 2, at 1569; Silverstein, *From Comstockery Through Population Control: The Inevitability of Balancing,* 6 N.C. Cent. L.J. 8, 36 (1974); Tribe, *supra* note 2, at 7 ("One of the most curious things about *Roe* is that behind its own verbal smokescreen, the substantive judgment on which it rests is nowhere to be found."); and Wheeler & Kovar, Roe v. Wade: *The Right of Privacy Revisited,* 21 U. Kan. L. Rev. 527, 527 (1973) ("Unfortunately, the decisions themselves fail to yield a reasonable justification of the constitutional basis for protection of the woman's interest in terminating her pregnancy.").

7. *See* Chemerinsky, *Rationalizing the Abortion Debate: Legal Rhetoric and the Abortion Controversy,* 31 Buffalo L. Rev. 107 (1982); Heymann & Barzelay, *supra* note 2; Perry, *supra* note 2; Regan, *supra* note 2; Tribe, *supra* note 2; Wheeler and Kovar, *supra* note 6. Analysis and criticism of these "rewritings" of *Roe* is beyond the scope of this article. For brief critical analyses of Heymann & Barzelay, Tribe, and Perry, see J. Noonan, A Private Choice 20–32 (1979).

8. Cox, The Role of the Supreme Court in American Government 113-114 (1976); *see also* Epstein, *Substantive Due Process by Any Other Name,* 1973 Sup. Ct. Rev. 159, 184; Ely, *supra* note 2, at 947.

9. N.Y. Penal Law §125.05 (3) (1977). Commentators emphasizing how extreme the Court was, include Chering, *Abortion Decision—A Qualified Constitutional Right in the United States—Whither Canada,* 51 Can. B. Rev. 643, 646 (1973); Moore, *Moral Sentiments in Judicial Opinions on Abortion,* 15 Santa Clara L. Rev. 591, 627, 633 (1975); Note, *Haunting Shadows From the Rubble of* Roe's Right to Privacy, 9 Suffolk U.L. Rev. 145, 152–53 (1974); Comment, Roe v. Wade *and the Traditional Legal Standards Concerning Pregnancy,* 47 Temple L.Q. 715, 726 (1974).

10. *Roe,* 410 U.S. at 164–65 (emphasis added).

11. Doe v. Bolton, 410 U.S. 179, 191–192 (1973), *citing,* United States v. Vuitch, 402 U.S. 62, 71–72 (1971).

12. *Roe,* 410 U.S. at 153.

13. *Doe,* 410 U.S. at 191–92; In *Colautti v. Franklin,* 439 U.S. 379, 388 (1979), the Court held, "Viability is reached when, in the judgment of the attending physician on the particular facts of the case before him, there is a reasonable likelihood of the fetus' sustained survival outside the womb, with or without artificial support."

14. Ely, *supra* note 2, at 921 n. 19 (emphasis in original).

15. American College of Obstetricians and Gynecologists v. Thornburgh, 737 F.2d 283, 299 (3rd Cir. 1984), aff'd, 106 S. Ct. 2169 (1986).

16. 567 F. Supp. 522, 526 (D. Neb. 1981) (emphasis in original). See also Margaret S. v. Edwards, 488 F. Supp. 181, 196 (E.D. La. 1980) (holding unconstitutional a Louisiana statute permitting postviability abortions only if necessary to prevent "permanent impairment" of maternal health).

17. Tribe offers this interpretation of the Court's intent. Tribe, supra, note 2, at 3 n. 13. Some scholars have deemed the historical excursus quite irrelevant. "The Court does not seem entirely clear," writes Ely, "as to what this discussion has to do with the legal argument . . . and the reader is left in much the same quandary. It surely does not seem to support the Court's position. . . . " Ely, supra note 6, at 925 n. 42. According to Professor Epstein, "It is difficult to see what comfort [Justice Blackmun] could draw from his researches, for at no point do they lend support for the ultimate decision to divide pregnancy into three parts, each subject to its own constitutional rules. All that the study accomplished was to prove what we already knew, that legal rules and social attitudes on the question of abortion vary much by place and time." Epstein, Substantive Due Process by Any Other Name: The Abortion Cases, 1973 Sup. Ct. Rev. 159, 167. Accord, Riga, Bryn and Roe: The Threshhold Question and Juridical Review, 23 Cath. Law 309, 311 (1978). See also Dellapenna, supra note 11, at 424 ("The Court's discussion of history is . . . unrelated to its later conclusions."); Note, Roe and Paris: Does Privacy Have a Principle, 26 Stan. L. Rev. 1161, 1181 & n.110 (1974) ("[T]he Court's labored historical sketch . . . is most remarkable for its failure to relate the discussion to the Court's analysis.").

Elizabeth Moore goes so far as to suggest that the Court's "gratuitous historical references" were primarily a "public relations technique" to "calm the predictable excited reaction to the result [Roe] reached" by demonstrating "that abortion was not the universally condemned act which many opponents had believed"—that "certain Christians seem to be the only deviates in the whole history of abortion." Moore, supra note 9, at 626–27.

18. Some have found even the Court's version of abortion history to point in the opposite direction from that holding. "The Court . . . seemed to ignore 'the "traditions and [collective] conscience of our people,"'" wrote one commentator. "[T]he Court's holding was decidedly more lenient than the American attitudes indicated by the legislative trends and professional opinions discussed in the course of its opinion." Comment, Roe v. Wade and In Re Quinlan: Individual Decision and the Scope of Privacy's Constitutional Guarantee, 12 U.S.F.L. Rev. 111, 142 (1977) (quoting Griswold v. Connecticut, 381 U.S. 479, 493 [1965], quoting Powell v. Alabama, 287 U.S. 45, 67 [1932]. See also Regan, supra note 2, at 1621 ("[T]he Court has rarely oveturned as much history all at once as it did in Roe v. Wade. That surely ought to give us pause.").

19. See Lewis, Homo Sapienism: Critique of Roe v. Wade and Abortion, 39 Alb. L. Rev. 856, 865 n. 5 (1975). For the discovery of the ovum see, L. Arey, Developmental Anatomy 3–6 (Rev. 7th ed. 1974); Sauer, Attitudes to Abortion in America, 1800–1973, 28 Population Stud. 53, 58–59 (1974).

20. Soranos, Gynecology, in 4 Corpus Medicorum Graecorum 1.19.60 (J. Ilberg ed. 1927), cited in Noonan, An Almost Absolute Value in History, in The Morality of Abortion 5 n.5 (J. Noonan ed. 1970).

21. 410 U.S. at 140.

22. 410 U.S. at 130–132.

23. *See* Arbagi's chapter; and also consult S. Krason & W. Hollberg, The Law and History of Abortion: The Supreme Court Refuted (1984); and Special Project, *Survey of Abortion Law*, 1980 Ariz. St. L. J. 67, 77.

24. Quay, *Justifiable Abortion—Medical and Legal Foundations* (Pt. 2), 49 Geo. L. J. 395 (1961), *cited in Roe*, 410 U.S. 130 n.9. For accounts of ancient attitudes largely compatible with that expressed by Justice Blackmun, see Joling, *Abortion—The Breath of Life*, 22 Med. Tr. T.Q. 199, 199–201, 202–206 (1975), and Littlewood, *Abortion in Perspective* (Pt. 1), N.Z.L.J. 488, 488–89 (1974). *See generally* de Agullo, *Abortion Polemic: A Restatement of Pros and Cons*, 42 Rev. Jur. U.P.R. 247, 249–51 (1973).

25. 410 U.S. at 131.

26. *See also* Brown, *What the Supreme Court Didn't Know: Ancient and Early Christian Views on Abortion*, 1 Human Life Rev. 5, 11 (1975).

27. Brown, *supra* note 26, at 13, *quoting* L. Edelstein, The Hippocratic Oath, in *Supplements to the Bulletin of the History of Medicine*, No.1, 10, 64 (1943).

28. *Cf.* Ely, *supra* note 2, at 925 n. 42.

29. Noonan, *supra* note 20.

30. *See* Arbagi's discussion on pp. 167-168 of this volume.

31. Noonan, *supra* note 20, at 9,10.

32. *Id.* at 11–21.

33. For a careful and comprehensive history of the attitude of medieval Christendom toward abortion, *see* J. Connery, Abortion: The Development of the Roman Catholic Perspective (1977).

34. *See* Special Project, *Survey of Abortion Law*, 1980 Ariz. St. L. J. 67, 84.

35. *See* Connery, *The Ancients and the Medievals on Abortion*, *infra* at 124. Quotation is from text delivered at Americans United For Life conference in Chicago, March 31, 1984.

36. *Id.*

37. Dellapenna, *supra* note 5, at 367 & n. 46 (1974).

38. *Id.* at 368.

39. 410 U.S. at 136; Means, *The Phoenix of Abortional Freedom: Is a Penumbral or Ninth Amendment Right About to Arise from the Nineteenth Century Legislative Ashes of a Fourteenth Century Common-Law Liberty?*, 17 N.Y.L.F. 335 (1971). *See also* Dellapenna, *supra* note 5, at 366 n. 37.

40. Dellapenna, *supra* note 5, at 366–89; Byrn, *An American Tragedy: The Supreme Court on Abortion*, 41 Ford L. Rev. 807, 815–27 (1973); Destro, *Abortion and the Constitution: The Need for a Life-Protective Amendment*, 63 Calif. L. Rev. 1250, 1267–73 (1975). *See also* article cited at p. 261, n.54, at 105-109.

41. E. Coke, Third Institute *50; Dellapenna, *supra* note 5, at 381–82, 384–86.

42. Cited in Means, *supra* note 39, at 337–341.

43. 2 H. Bracton, The Laws and Customs of England 279 (Twiss ed. 1879); Fleta, Book I, c. 23 (Selden Soc. ed. 1955).

44. Means, *supra* note 39, at 345–48.

45. 4 W. Blackstone, Commentaries *198.

46. Byrn, *supra* note 40, at 817–19; Dellapenna, *supra* note 5, at 366–67, 369–71, 387–89; Destro, *supra* note 40, at 1268–71.

47. Destro, *supra* note 40, at 1269–70.

48. Byrn, *supra* note 40, at 819 & n. 88.

49. R. v. Sims, 75 Eng. Rep. 1075 (K. B. 1601).

50. Means, *supra* note 39, at 348–49.

51. Destro, *supra* note 40, at 1273.

52. Plessy v. Ferguson, 163 U.S. 537 (1896); Brown v. Bd. of Education, 347 U.S. 483 (1954).

53. Byrn, *supra* note 40, at 827.

54. As Morgan, *supra* note 4, at 1726, notes, the Court's own discussion demonstrated that the AMA and ABA had only recently changed from a policy of opposition to abortion, and those changes were controversial within their memberships.

55. 410 U.S. at 151–52, *citing* Means, *supra* note 39, and Means, *The Law of New York Concerning Abortion and the Status of the Foetus, 1664–1968: A Case of Cessation of Constitutionality,* 14 N.Y.L.F. 411 (1968).

56. *The Human Life Bill: Hearings on S. 158 Before the Subcomm. on Separation of Powers of the Senate Comm. on the Judiciary,* 97th Cong., 1st Sess. 474 (statement of Victor Rosenblum, Professor of Law, Northwestern Univ.); *see also* Dellapenna, *supra* note 5, at 402–404.

57. J. Mohr, Abortion in America, The Origins and Evolution of National Policy 200 (1978).

58. Dellapenna, *supra* note 5, at 389.

59. 410 U.S. at 141–42.

60. *Id.* at 151 n. 48, *citing* State v. Murphy, 27 N.J.L. 112, 114 (1858).

61. Gorby, *The "Right" to an Abortion, the Scope of Fourteenth Amendment "Personhood" and the Supreme Court's Birth Requirement,* 1979 So. Ill. L. Rev. 1, 16–17 n. 84; Destro, *supra* note 40, at 1273–75.

62. 410 U.S. at 151.

63. Gorby, *supra* note 61, at 20.

64. 410 U.S. at 151–52.

65. Sauer, *supra* note 19, at 58.

66. Dellapenna, *supra* note 5, at 371–76, 394–95.

67. Horan & Marzen, *Abortion and Midwifery: A Footnote in Legal History,* in New Perspectives on Human Abortion 199, 200 (Horan & Mall, ed. 1981).

68. "Minutes of the Common Council of the City of New York" 3 (1712–1729) *reprinted in* Horan & Marzen, *supra* note 67, at 199.

69. Blackmun's quote is found at 410 U.S. at 129.

70. Noonan, *supra* note 20.

71. 410 U.S. at 140.

72. *Id.* at 153.

73. *Id.* at 152–53.

74. Vieira, Roe *and* Doe: *Substantive Due Process and the Right of Abortion,* 25 Hastings L. J. 867, 873 (1974).

75. Ely, *supra* note 2, at 932, 935–36 (footnotes omitted).

76. Cox, *supra* note 8, at 113.

77. Posner, *The Uncertain Protection of Privacy by the Supreme Court*, 1979 Sup. Ct. Rev. 173, 199 (footnotes omitted).

78. Loewy, *Abortive Reasons and Obscene Standards: A Comment on the Abortion and Obscenity Cases*, 52 N.C.L. Rev. 223 (1973); Note, Roe *and* Paris: *Does Privacy Have a Principle*, 26 Stan. L. Rev. 1161 (1974).

79. O'Meara, *Abortion: The Court Decides a Non-Case*, 1974 Sup. Ct. Rev. 337, 340.

80. 410 U.S. at 156, 158. Blackmun began by stating that the attorney for Texas was unable to cite any case holding the unborn to be persons under the Fourteenth Amendment. In fact, Steinberg v. Brown, 321 F. Supp. 741, 746–47 (N.D. Ohio, 1970), stated, "Once human life has commenced, the constitutional protection found in the Fifth and Fourteenth Amendments impose upon the state the duty of safeguarding it." The court cited medical authority that this occurs "at the moment of conception." *Id.* at 747.

81. Ely, *supra* note 2, at 926. *Accord*, Chemerinsky, *Rationalizing the Abortion Debate: Legal Rhetoric and the Abortion Controversy*, 31 Buffalo L. Rev. 107, 124 (1982) ("Why should the intent of the Constitution be controlling in deciding whether 'persons' includes fetuses, if intent is not controlling in deciding whether the Constitution intended to protect a right to abortions?"); Destro, *supra* note 40, at 1338; Morgan, *supra* note 4, at 1737 ("irony of the Court's sudden allegiance to the letter of the Constitution"); Notes and Comments, Roe v. Wade *and* Doe v. Bolton: *Compelling State Interest Test in Substantive Due Process*, 30 Wash. & Lee. L. Rev. 628, 637 (1973).

82. Byrn, *supra* note 40, at 852–57; Destro, *supra* note 40, at 1283–86; Gorby, *supra* note 61, at 11–13.

83. 410 U.S. at 157.

84. Ely, *supra* note 2, at 925–26.

85. Gorby, *supra* note 61, at 11–12.

86. 410 U.S. at 157 n. 53.

87. Comment, Roe v. Wade—*The Abortion Decision—An Analysis and Its Implications*, 10 San Diego L. Rev. 844, 855 (1973).

88. U.S. Const. art. I, Sec. 2, cl. 3, 4.

89. *See* Santa Clara County v. Southern Pacific Railroad Co., 118 U.S. 394, 396 (1886); Destro, *supra* note 40, at 1284; Byrn, *supra* note 40, at 852–53.

90. 410 U.S. at 157–58 n. 54.

91. Epstein, *Substantive Due Process by Any Other Name*, 1973 Sup. Ct. Rev. 159, 180. *See also* Byrn, *supra* note 40, at 853–54; Destro, *supra* note 40, at 1256 n. 30. Charles Rice argues that the defense of necessity does not justify killing another who is innocent to save one's own life, but that the right of self-defense does, as when the attacker is insane. Rice, *The Dred Scott Case of the Twentieth Century*, 10 Hous. L. Rev. 1059, 1081–82 (1976). But see the more nuanced discussion in his earlier article, making clear his individual view that the unborn should not "be considered an aggressor so as to justify the use of such principles of defense against him" but noting that "where the abortion is allegedly performed to save the life of the mother, there is a parity of values: one life for another." Rice, *Overruling* Roe v. Wade: *An Analysis of the Proposed Constitutional Amendments*, 15 B.C. Ind. & Com. L. Rev. 307, 326–327 (1973). *See generally*, Conley & McKenna, *Supreme Court on Abortion—A Dissenting Opinion*, 19 Cath. Law. 19, 26 (1973).

92. 410 U.S. at 158 n. 54.

93. *See* Gorby, *supra* note 61, at 20.

94. *See* Byrn, *supra* note 40, at 854–55; Destro, *supra* note 40, at 1256 n. 30; Moore, *Moral Sentiments in Judicial Opinions on Abortion*, 15 Santa Clara L. Rev. 591, 598–599 (1975).

95. 410 U.S. at 158 n. 54. *See also* Chemerinsky, *supra* note 7, at 113.

96. Byrn, *supra* note 40, at 855. *See also* Destro, *supra* note 40, at 1256 n. 30; and Gorby, *supra* note 61, at 20.

97. 410 U.S. at 158.

98. Levy v. Louisiana, 391 U.S. 68, 70 (1968).

99. Cong. Globe, 39th Cong., 1st Sess. 1089 (1866) (statement of Rep. Bingham).

100. Boyle, *That the Fetus Should Be Considered a Legal Person*, 24 Am. J. Juris, 59 (1979); Destro, *supra* note 40, at 1332 n. 399, 1334 & n. 406; Gorby, *supra* note 61, at 22–24; Rice, *The Dred Scott Case of the Twentieth Century, supra* note 91, at 1063–72, 1074–76; Rice, *Overruling* Roe v. Wade: *An Analysis of the Proposed Constitutional Amendments, supra* note 91, at 313–19; Riga, *supra* note 17, at 315–16, 319–20, 330; Note, *Haunting Shadows From the Rubble of* Roe's *Right of Privacy, supra* note 9, at 148–49.

101. 410 U.S. at 160–161. Blackmun wrote, "Viability is usually placed at about seven months (28 weeks) but may occur earlier, even at 24 weeks," *Roe*, 410 U.S. at 160 n. 59, citing L. Hellman & J. Pritchard, *Williams Obstetrics* 493 n. 59 (14th ed. 1971). In fact, the text describes viability as varying from *20*, not 24, to 28 weeks. This error has been remarked by Note, *Haunting Shadows from the Rubble of* Roe's *Right of Privacy, supra* note 9, at 151–52 n.39 and Note, Roe v. Wade *and the Traditional Legal Standards Concerning Pregnancy*, 47 Temple L.Q. 715, 736 (1974).

102. Blackmun describes the Roman Catholic Church as holding "until the 19th century" the "Aristotelian theory of 'mediate animation'" as "dogma." 410 U.S. at 160. In fact, according to Connery, the Church has never taken a position as a matter of dogma on either "mediate animation" or "immediate animation"; it has, however, always condemned abortion for all stages of pregnancy throughout its history. *Infra* at 126.

The Court is misleadingly partial concerning the "attitude of the Jewish faith," in which it describes the "view that life does not begin until live birth" as being "predominant." *Roe*, 410 U.S. at 160. While Jewish law (Halakah) does make a sharp distinction between the status of the fetus and the newborn infant, in the predominant view of the rabbis it condemns abortion except when the mother's life or perhaps her health is threatened. There is disagreement concerning the abortion of a handicapped fetus. Bleich, *Abortion and Jewish Law*, in New Perspectives on Human Abortion (Hilgers, Horan & Mall, eds. 1981) 405–419. Rabbi Bleich writes, "It should be clearly understood that the question of whether or not a fetus is a 'person' or a 'full human being' is largely irrelevant in a halakhic context. Judaism regards all forms of human life as sacred. . . . It is the nature of the prohibition and the specific regulations which are significant, not matters of nomenclature which have no halakhic significance." *Id.* at 418.

For a more detailed account of the Protestant perspective than that given by the cursory sentence in *Roe*, 410 U.S. at 160, see B. Nathanson, Aborting

America, 294 (1979); Nelson, *The Divided Mind of Protestant Christians*, in New Perspectives on Human Abortion *supra* at 387–404 (1981).

103. 410 U.S. at 161. Littlewood, *supra* note 24, at 104, echoes Blackmun's argument. Joseph Lewis observes:

> It is perfectly legitimate and, in fact, logically necessary to define the first meeting of the egg and sperm as the point of both legal as well as biological conception.... The Court's contention that conception is a process over time...cannot be confirmed by embryologic observation. The Court is not observing but defining....Development, not conception, occurs over time. Conception occurs when the sperm first penetrates the egg. When penetration of the egg by the sperm is accomplished, conception has ended and development has begun.

Lewis, *supra* note 19, at 870. The Court was entirely unclear about why "new medical techniques such as menstrual extraction, the 'morning after' pill, implantation of embryos, artificial insemination, and even artificial wombs" were held to be "[s]ubstantial problems for precise definition" of the view that individual human life begins at conception. *Roe*, 410 U.S. at 161. *See* Harrison, *The Supreme Court and Abortion Reform: Means to an End*, 19 N.Y.L.F. 685, 687–688 (1974). Did the Court perhaps really mean it the other way around: that acceptance of such a view would pose "substantial problems" for societal acceptance of the new techniques, and hence would be expedient?

104. 410 U.S. at 159.

105. *Id.* at 160.

106. The evidence for the existence of individual human life from the time of fertilization has been set forth in cogent detail in the 1981 report of the Senate Judiciary Committee's Subcommittee on Separation of Powers on the Human Life Bill. Subcomm. on Separation of Powers, Senate Comm. on the Judiciary, The Human Life Bill—S. 158, 97th Cong., 1st Sess. 7–13 (1981).

107. Harrison, *supra* note 103, at 691 n. 32.

108. Comment, Roe v. Wade—*The Abortion Decision—An Analysis and Its Implications*, *supra* note 87, at 850–51.

109. Epstein, *supra* note 91, at 182.

110. In addition to the authors quoted below, critical commentary on the Court's striking of the balance and its justification (or lack thereof), much of which is from scholars who support *Roe*'s results, includes: Boyle, *supra* note 100, at 61; Cincotta, *The Quality of Life: From Roe to Quinlan and Beyond*, 25 Cath. Law. 13, 20, 24–25, 27 (1979); Destro, *supra* note 40, at 1251, 1261 n. 45. Ely, *supra* note 2, at 21, 946–47; Loewy, *supra* note 78, at 229, 232, 233–34, 241–43; Moore, *supra* note 94, at 609–12, 629; Morgan, *supra* note 4, at 1740, 1742–48; Regan, *supra* note 2, at 1141–42; Rice, *The Dred Scott Case of the Twentieth Century*, *supra* note 91, at 1076–77; Rubin, *The Abortion Cases: A Study in Law and Social Change*, 5 N.C. Central L. J. 215, 218–19, 245–47; Tribe, *supra* note 2, at 5; Note, *Current Technology Affecting Supreme Court Abortion Jurisprudence*, 27 N.Y.L. Sch. L. Rev. 1221, 1260 (1982); Comment, Roe v. Wade—*The Abortion Decision—An Analysis and Its Implications*, *supra* note 87, at 856; Note, Roe and Paris: *Does Privacy Have a Principle*, *supra* note 17, at 1183–84; Note, *Haunting Shadows From the Rubble of Roe's Right of Privacy*, *supra* note 9, at 151; Note, *Abortion Decision: Right of Privacy Extended*, 27 U. Miami L. Rev. 481, 486 (1973).

111. Chemerinsky, *supra* note 7, at 142.

112. Silverstein, *supra* note 6, at 39–40.

113. Cox, *supra* note 8, at 114.

114. Ely, *supra* note 2, at 921 n. 19 (emphasis in original).

115. 410 U.S. at 163.

116. Hilgers & O'Hare, *Abortion Related Maternal Mortality: An In-Depth Analysis*, in New Perspectives on Human Abortion *supra* note 102 at 69–91. *See also* Destro, *supra* note 40, at 1296–98 n. 245, 1301–1303; Hellegers, Wade *and* Bolton: *Medical Critique*, 19 Cath. Law. 251, 253–54 (1973). *Cf.* Ely, *supra* note 2, at 942 n. 117 (pointing out Court's assumptions about relative safety not shared by all physicians).

117. *See* Destro, *supra* note 40, at 1298–1301.

118. Comment, *Technological Advances and Roe v. Wade: The Need to Rethink Abortion Law*, 29 U.C.L.A. L. Rev. 1194, 1199 n. 41 (1982). *See also* Tribe, *supra* note 2, at 4.

119. Loewy, *supra* note 78, at 233 n. 58.

120. Ely, *supra* note 2, at 942 n. 117 (emphasis in original). *But see* Jones, *Abortion and the Consideration of Fundamental, Irreconcilable Interests*, 33 Syracuse L. Rev. 565, 578 (1982) (attacking as paternalistic Supreme Court's willingness to allow state regulation of abortion for maternal health at *any* stage of pregnancy).

121. Destro, *supra* note 40, at 1294.

122. Comment, Roe v. Wade—*The Abortion Decision—An Analysis and Its Implications*, *supra* note 87, at 848. *See also* Moore, *supra* note 94, at 621; Notes and Comments, Roe v. Wade and Doe v. Bolton: *Compelling State Interest Test in Substantive Due Process*, *supra* note 81, at 643–44. Indeed, this is exactly what happened in City of Akron v. Akron Center for Reproductive Health, 462 U.S. 416 (1983), where the Court struck down a second trimester hospitalization requirement on the basis of developments in the safety of clinic abortions since *Roe*, in which the Court had expressly indicated that states might require hospitalization for second trimester abortions. *Roe*, 410 U.S. at 163.

123. 410 U.S. at 163–64.

124. *See* Chemerinsky, *supra* note 7, at 125; Ely, *supra* note 2, at 924 (The Court "seems to mistake a definition for a syllogism"); Erickson, *Women and the Supreme Court: Anatomy is Destiny*, 41 Brooklyn L. Rev. 209, 250 (1974); Gorby, *supra* note 61, at 32; King, *The Juridical Status of the Fetus: A Proposal for Legal Protection of the Unborn*, 77 Mich. L. Rev. 1647, 1656 (1979) ("The Court offered no justification for this position, perhaps because any justification would have exposed the thinness of its claim that it was taking no position on when life begins."); Tribe, *supra* note 2, at 4 ("One reads the Court's explanation several times before becoming convinced that nothing has inadvertently been omitted.... [I]t offers no reason at all for what the Court held."); Special Project, *Survey of Abortion Law*, *supra* note 34, at 128; Comment, *Fetal Viability and Individual Autonomy: Resolving Medical and Legal Standards for Abortion*, 27 U.C.L.A.L. Rev. 1340, 1341 (1980). *But see* Perry, *supra* note 2, at 734 ("The fact that this distinction does not proceed inexorably from textually demonstrable first principles is beside the point; the distinction is drawn by the existing moral

culture [at least arguably] and the Court, in assaying conventional moral culture, should be sensitive to such distinctions.").

125. 410 U.S. at 163.

126. *Id.* at 160.

127. "A review of outcome studies on infants born over the past 20 years indicates a significant decline in the mortality of very low birthweight infants. In the 1960s and early 1970s, the survival rate of infants with birthweights between 1000 g and 1500 g increased greatly. Since 1975, there has been an important rise in the percentage of survivors who are less than 1000 g (extremely low birthweight)." Ross, *Mortality and Morbidity in Very Low Birthweight Infants,* 12 Pediatric Annals 32, 32 (1983). *See, e.g.,* Saigal, Rosenbaum, Stoskopf, and Milner, *Follow-up of infants 501 to 1,500 gm birth weight delivered to residents of a geographically defined region with perinatal intensive care facilities,* 100 J. Ped. 606, 608 at Table II (1982) (survival rate of approximately 38% for infants weighing 501–750 grams); Kopelman, *The Smallest Preterm Infants: Reasons for Optimism and New Dilemmas,* 132 Am. J. Diseases Children 461 (1978) (survival rate of 42% for infants with weight of 1000 g or less).

128. Law review articles taking note of the dependency of the viability criterion on changing medical technology include: Byrn, *supra* note 40, at 807 n. 5; Chemerinsky, *supra* note 7, at 125; Cincotta, *supra* note 110, at 30 n. 109; Dellapenna, *supra* note 5, at 360 n. 10; Destro, *supra* note 40, at 1311–13; Ely, *supra* note 2, at 924 n. 34; Erickson, *supra* note 124, at 254–55; Gorby, *supra* note 61, at 32 n. 151; Hughes, *Who is a Victim?,* 1 Dalhousie L. J. 425, 433; King, *supra* note 124, at 1684–86; Note, *Genetic Screening, Eugenic Abortion, and* Roe v. Wade: *How Viable is Roe's Viability Standard?,* 50 Brooklyn L. Rev. 113, 128 (1983); Comment, *Towards a Practical Implementation of the Abortion Decision: The Interests of the Physician, the Woman and the Fetus,* 25 De Paul L. Rev. 676, 678, 692–95 (1976); Comment, *Viability and Abortion,* 64 Ky. L. J. 146, 146, 160–63 (1975–76); Note, *Current Technology Affecting Supreme Court Abortion Jurisprudence, supra* note 110, at 1258; Comment, *Fetal Viability and Individual Autonomy: Resolving Medical and Legal Standards for Abortion, supra* note 124, at 1359–61; Comment, *Technological Advances and* Roe v. Wade: *The Need to Rethink Abortion Law, supra* note 118, at 1202; Notes and Comments, Roe v. Wade *and* Doe v. Bolton: *Compelling State Interest Test in Substantive Due Process, supra* note 81, at 643–45.

129. *City of Akron,* 462 U.S. at 458 (O'Connor, J., dissenting).

John P. East and
Steven R. Valentine

Reconciling *Santa Clara* and *Roe v. Wade*: A Route to Supreme Court Recognition of Unborn Children as Constitutional Persons

In *Roe v. Wade*, the United States Supreme Court decided two principal constitutional issues. First, the Court held that the constitutional right to privacy is broad enough to encompass a woman's decision about whether to undergo an abortion. Second, the Court determined that the word "person," as used in the Fourteenth Amendment, does not include the unborn child. Although it has been argued that the personhood holding really is only a dictum, Justice Harry A. Blackmun, the author of the majority opinion in *Roe*, regarded it as a condition precedent to the Court's determination on the right to privacy issue. Justice Blackmun wrote that a contrary holding on the question of whether the unborn child is a person would have caused the conclusion that the abortion decision is constitutionally protected to collapse, because then his or her life would be specifically protected by the Fourteenth Amendment.[1]

Assuming that Justice Blackmun's observation is correct, the reversal of the Court's second holding would be tantamount to the overruling of the entire case.[2] The current Supreme Court justices who oppose *Roe v. Wade* do so because they disagree with the first holding, but not necessarily with the second one. Therefore, it seems likely that Court recognition of a right to have an abortion will fall before a reversal of the Fourteenth Amendment personhood holding is achieved.[3] Nonetheless, as the opponents of *Roe v. Wade* map a reversal strategy, it is important to evaluate possible routes toward the eventual recognition of constitutional personhood for the unborn by the Supreme Court.[4]

The Supreme Court has decided the meaning of the word "person," as used in the Fourteenth Amendment, only twice. In 1886, the *Santa Clara County v. Southern Pacific Railroad Company* decision held that the corporation is a person.[5] And in *Roe*, the Court ruled that the unborn child is not a person.[6] A comparison of the two decisions can produce a rhetorical formulation that is useful to *Roe's* political opponents because it makes the Court appear to be hauntingly Orwellian—something can be a person without being human, and can be human without being a person.[7]

Does the Court's corporate constitutional personhood doctrine have serious legal implications for efforts to overturn *Roe's* denial of the same status to the unborn? We will argue that it does. Further we will demonstrate that reconciling the *Santa Clara* and *Roe* decisions may be one means by which Supreme Court recognition of unborn children as constitutional persons can be achieved.

Examining each case individually provides a useful foundation for considering how to reconcile *Santa Clara* and *Roe*. The intention of the framers of the Fourteenth Amendment with regard to the status of corporations and of unborn children will be analyzed. Next, an overview of the circumstances under which the decisions were made will be provided. Then a critique of each ruling will be offered, in the context of recent challenges to their validity.[8]

Having laid this foundation, we will discuss possible means by which the two cases could be reconciled. Finally, a legal argument will be distilled for reconciling *Santa Clara* and *Roe* in a manner that would favor recognition of unborn children as Fourteenth Amendment constitutional persons.

I. The Personhood of Corporations: Origins and Case Law

AS NOTED, the corporation became a Fourteenth Amendment person in 1886. But, it had become a "citizen" of the state in which it was incorporated several decades earlier. In *Louisville, Cincinnati and Charleston Railroad v. Letson*, the Court said, "A corporation created by a state to perform its function under the authority of that state and only suable there, though it may have members out of the state, seems to us to be a person, though an artificial one, inhabiting and belonging to that state." Such a "person," observed the Court, "is therefore entitled, for the purpose of suing and being sued, to be deemed a citizen of that state."[9]

Commenting on this Court-created legal citizenship for corporations, Justice Peter Daniel later declared that corporations became citizens by unwarranted and unconstitutional judicial baptism.[10] But, the *Charleston Railroad* case was not to be read too broadly. "Although a corporation, being an artificial body created by legislative power is not a citizen within several provisions of the Constitution," said Justice Stephen Field, "yet it has been held . . . that, where rights of action are to be enforced, it will be considered as a citizen of the State where it was created, within the clause extending the judicial power of the United States to controversies between citizens of different States."[11]

Recognition of corporations as citizens, no matter in what limited sense, however, was not beyond judicial controversy. In 1854, for instance, Justice John Campbell argued that a "corporation is not a citizen."

> It may be an artificial person, a moral person, a juridical person, a legal entity, a faculty, an intangible, invisible being; but Chief Justice Marshall employed no metaphysical refinement, nor subtlety, nor sophism, but spoke the common sense, "the universal understanding," as he calls it, of the people, when he declared the unanimous judgment of this court, "that it certainly is not a citizen."[12]

Laconically, Professor Dudley McGovney observed, that "A deemster may adjudge a mouse to be a cat and in a story for children that make-believe would be amusing." On a more serious note, McGovney noted that the absence of an explicit recognition of corporate citizenry for diversity and jurisdictional purposes in the Constitution does not justify "filling the gap by judicial fiat."[13]

Thus, the Supreme Court had recognized limited citizenship status for the corporation by the time, immediately following the Civil War, at which Congress considered the Fourteenth Amendment. In drafting the Amendment, the framers differentiated between a "citizen" and a "person." Defining "citizens" as all "persons born or naturalized in the United States," the Amendment protected citizens under the Privileges and Immunities Clause, while protecting persons under the Equal Protection and Due Process Clauses.[14] Thus, it can be logically said that the framers understood that, although corporations cannot be "born or naturalized in the United States," their use of the term "citizens," which already included corporations under Court precedent, would incorporate protection of corporations into the Privileges and Immunities Clause.

But, since the Court had not, at that point, recognized corporations as "persons" in a constitutional sense, the same cannot be said for the Equal Protection and Due Process Clauses. Considered in light of the fact that aliens in the United States would be "persons" but not "citizens," it is obvious that the framers intended for the former to be a larger class than the latter within the context of the Fourteenth Amendment. But, as we will see, there is no evidence in any accepted legislative history of the Fourteenth Amendment to suggest that the framers intended for corporations to fall within that larger class.[15]

1886, the Supreme Court decided *Santa Clara*. Chief Justice Morrison Waite acted as if corporate personhood under the Fourteenth Amendment were beyond all dispute. Before the majority opinion in the case even began, Waite announced: "The Court does not wish to hear argument on the question of whether the provision in the Fourteenth Amendment to the Constitution, which forbids a State to deny any person within its jurisdiction the equal protection of the laws, applies to these corporations." Without any further comment, the Chief Justice declared: "We are all of opinion that it does."[16]

As Justice Douglas was to observe sixty-three years later, "The Court was cryptic in its decision, . . . so sure of its ground that it wrote no opinion on the point." "There was," wrote Douglas, "no history, logic, or reason given to support that view. Nor was the result so obvious that exposition was unnecessary."[17] It may be true, as Justice Douglas suggests, that history, logic, and reason are the parents of holdings. If it is, then the *Santa Clara* corporate personhood doctrine may be illegitimate.[18]

Professor John D. Gorby has stated a succinct formulation of the canons of constitutional construction as applied to the interpretation of an operative term such as "person." "The commonly accepted approaches to the construction of legal documents very generally include interpreting the term at issue in good faith according to (1) the natural and ordinary meaning of the term; (2) the context of the whole legal document in which the term is found; (3) the historical background, including preparatory work; and (4) the function to be attributed to the term."[19]

There can be no doubt that the "natural and ordinary use" of the term "person" would be to consider it to include all human beings. It had never been held otherwise by the Supreme Court. The Court did not even do so in the infamous 1857 *Dred Scott v. Sandford* case. *Dred Scott*, decided ten years before the adoption of the Fourteenth Amendment, involved construction of the term "citizen," not "person," as used in the Constitution.[20] While the Court's opinion in the case had the effect of excluding a human group from the enjoyment of certain constitutional privileges and immunities that are due United States citizens, it did not concern the scope of the term "person" as used in the Fifth Amendment. Despite the Court's holding in *Dred Scott*, slaves, as well as being entitled to its protection, were considered to be persons under the criminal law and were held to be responsible for their acts under the criminal law.[21]

The "context" of the Fourteenth Amendment is clear. Congressman John Bingham, who was the Amendment's chief sponsor in the House of Representatives, said that his measure was intended to be "universal" in its application, extending its scope to include "any human being."[22] Senator Jacob Howard, the main Senate sponsor of the Amendment, emphasized that the constitutional language would be applied to even the "humblest, the poorest, the most despised of the human race."[23]

The Supreme Court subscribed to this general view of the Fourteenth Amendment in the 1873 *Slaughter House Cases*. Writing for the majority, Justice Samuel Miller made references to "events 'almost too recent to be called history' to show that the purpose of the Amendment was to protect human rights."[24] Professor Arthur T. Hadley agreed. He wrote: "The Fourteenth Amendment was framed to protect the negroes from oppression by the whites, not to protect corporations from oppression by the legislature." "It is doubtful," Hadley wrote, that "a single one of the members of Congress who voted for it had any idea that it would touch the question of corporate regulation at all."[25]

Justice Black followed the Hadley line of thinking in his 1938 dissent to the majority holding in *Connecticut General Life Insurance Company v. Johnson*. "Neither the history nor the language of the Fourteenth Amendment justifies the belief that corporations are included within its protection.... The records of the time can be searched in vain for evidence that this Amendment was adopted for the benefit of corporations."[26]

Justice Douglas was even more emphatic in his dissent to the majority holding in the 1949 case, *Wheeling Steel Corporation v. Glander*. "Persons in the first sentence of the Fourteenth Amendment, includes only human beings, for corporations are not 'born or naturalized.'" Citing Supreme Court decisions in *Western Turf Associaton v. Greenberg* (1908) and *Selover, Bates and Company v. Walsh* (1919), Douglas added that "corporations are not 'citizens' within the meaning of the first clause of the second sentence" either.[27]

Continuing his analysis of the proper construction of the term "person" in the context of the Fourteenth Amendment, Douglas pointed out that "it never has been held that they [corporations] are persons whom a state may not deprive of 'life' within the meaning of the second clause of the second sentence." " 'Liberty' in that clause," he continued, is the "liberty of natural, not artificial, persons." The term "property," however, noted Douglas, "as used in that clause has been held to include that of a corporation since 1889 when *Minneapolis and St. Louis Railroad Company v. Beckwith* . . . was decided."[28] Concluding his line of attack on the legitimacy of the *Santa Clara* doctrine, Douglas observed, "It requires distortion to read 'person' as meaning one thing then another within the same clause and from clause to clause."[29] Quoting Justice William Woods in *Insurance Company v. North Dakota*, he argued that "the plain and evident meaning of the section is, that the persons to whom the equal protection of the law is secured are persons born or naturalized or endowed with life and liberty, and consequently natural and not artificial persons."[30]

The weight of the argument against the idea that the accepted canons of constitutional construction could produce a conclusion that corporations fit within the meaning of the term "persons" in the Fourteenth Amendment makes one wonder why the Supreme Court reached such a conclusion in the *Santa Clara* case. Suspicions are heightened when one considers that Chief Justice Waite issued the ruling without benefit of even a minimal attempt at such an analysis. What, then, lay behind the Court's decision? Perhaps the most interesting and detailed analysis is Professor Howard J. Graham's *Yale Law Journal* article "The 'Conspiracy Theory' of the Fourteenth Amendment."[31]

Roscoe Conkling appeared before the Supreme Court in 1882 to argue the case of *San Mateo County v. Southern Pacific Railroad Company*.[32] As a former member of the joint congressional committee that drafted the Fourteenth Amendment, he introduced a manuscript journal of the deliberations.[33] During his oral arguments, Conkling utilized extensive references to, and quotations from, these previously unknown documents to convey the unmistakable impression that, in drafting the Amendment, he and his colleagues deliberately had used the word "person" in a manner so as to encompass corporations. "At the time the Fourteenth Amendment was ratified," he argued, "individuals and joint stock companies were appealing for congressional and administrative protection against invidious and discriminating State and local taxes." "One instance," said Conkling, "was that of an express company, whose stock was owned largely by citizens of the State of New York. . . . "[34] Conkling's unspoken inference was that the Joint Committee had "taken cognizance of these appeals and had drafted its text with particular regard for corporations."[35]

Graham argues that Conkling's comments greatly impressed the Court: "Coming from a man who had twice declined a seat on the Supreme Bench, who spoke with first hand knowledge, and who submitted a manuscript record in support of his stand, so dramatic an argument could not fail to make a profound impression." Within the next several years, notes Graham, the Supreme Court became increasingly liberal in its interpretation of the Fourteenth Amendment.[36]

Professor Graham notes that the joint committee on which Conkling served had consistently employed the term "person" in Fourteenth Amendment clauses that applied to property rights while it used the term "citizen" in clauses that applied to specifically political rights. By 1886, "the force of this distinction seemed plain: corporations as artificial persons had indeed been among the intended beneficiaries of the Fourteenth Amendment." Historians developed the "conspiracy theory" because they were convinced of this hidden intention by the framers.[37]

The "conspiracy theory" of the Fourteenth Amendment holds that the drafting committee had assumed the characteristics of a conspiracy, which resulted in the Due Process and Equal Protection Clauses being written as double entendres. Ostensibly working in the interests of the recently freed blacks, cunning lawyers who comprised the committee had intentionally used language that gave greatly enhanced judicial protection to corporations, as against state legislatures.[38]

Graham identifies Charles and Mary Beard's *Rise of American Civilization* (1927) as the foremost scholarly proponent of the conspiracy theory. The lawyers on the committee, argued the Beards, had restored protection for property to the Constitution which Jacksonian judges had been eroding for decades. They made it more sweeping by forbidding states to deprive any "person" of life, liberty, or property without due process of law. With those words, say the Beards, every act of each state and local government that adversely touched the rights of persons and property was made subject to revision or outright annullment by the United States Supreme Court. This theory, reports Graham, has been supported by other eminent scholars.[39]

Graham asserts that the Beards, other historians, scholars, and the Supreme Court were taken in by the deceptive Conkling. Nowhere in his argument in the *San Mateo* case "does Conkling explicitly say that the Committee regarded corporations as persons; nowhere does he say that the members framed the due process and equal protection clauses with corporations in mind." "These are," he says, "simply the casual yet unmistakable impressions gained from dozens of hints, intimations, and distinctions made throughout his argument." Conkling was simply trying to win a case for his client without committing the impropriety of lying to the Supreme Court.[40]

Justice Black's dissent in the *Connecticut General Life Insurance* case supports Graham's view of the "conspiracy theory." "A secret purpose on the part of the [drafting] Committee," wrote Black, "even if such be the fact . . . would not be sufficient to justify any such construction [that corporations are 'persons']. The history of the Amendment proves that the people were told that its [the Fourteenth Amendment's] purpose was to protect weak and helpless human beings and were not told that it was intended to remove corporations in any fashion from the control of state governments."[41]

In his *Glander* dissent, Justice Douglas wrote, "the *Santa Clara* case was wrong and should be overruled. . . . It may be most desirable to give corporations this protection from the operation of the legislative process. But that question is not for us. It is for the people. If they want corporations to be treated as humans are treated, if they want to grant corporations this large degree of emancipation from state regulation, they should say so. The Constitution provides a method by which they may do so."[42]

The idea that the *Santa Clara* doctrine of corporate constitutional personhood is illegitimate is sustained by the fact that it has had no intellectual defenders on the Court. As Chief Justice Waite did when he created it, successor justices have followed it blindly in accordance with the doctrine of *stare decisis*. Justices Black and Douglas have been the lone dissenters. Critical studies accept *Santa Clara* as a fact of life, and then argue that its enormous economic importance must not be endangered by questioning its legitimacy.[43]

The doctrine of corporate personhood is a manifestly simple one, says Graham, which "involves construction of only a single word, and then nothing more than a minor interpolation or transfer of meaning." Corporations for centuries have been regarded effectively as "artificial legal 'persons.'" Countless statutes, decisions, and treatises refer to them in this manner. Thus, "the constitutional term ought to be—and is—given its inclusive, generic construction."[44] Abolitionists, he observed, attempted to have slaves regarded as persons, which they were. Likewise, corporation lawyers in the pre-Civil War era unsuccessfully utilized the "fiction" of the citizenship of corporations under the Diversity Clause to attain corporate citizenship under the Comity Clause.

Graham recognized the significance of the victory that corporations won in the *Santa Clara* case. Holding corporations to be Fourteenth Amendment persons, which are entitled to the equal protection and due process of the laws, was tantamount to winning approval of two constitutional amendments. First, corporations became empowered to challenge any governmental action that opposed their interests as violative of some protected legal right of persons. Second, the Supreme Court attained the power to review all governmental actions, on the local, state, and federal levels, that pertain to corporations; and to veto any such actions that it would deem to be arbitrary or unreasonable.[45]

Professor Graham underscores the great importance of *Santa Clara*. Since 1886, corporate personality has enhanced enormously the power and economic authority of the Supreme Court by expanding its jurisdiction and discretion. In producing these important results, the doctrine of corporate personality reversed the position of the corporation vis-à-vis the government. This is because once corporations were declared to be Fourteenth Amendment persons, they were able to challenge the constitutionality of any government action that affected their interests in a negative manner. Before *Santa Clara*, corporations were agencies of the state and were subject to tight legislative supervision. After *Santa Clara*, they were immediately transformed into legal entities capable of compelling government to justify its regulations over them. "Where beforehand corporate business could challenge only such action as conflicted with the more specifically-worded Commerce or Contracts Clauses," Graham reports, "after 1886 it was possible for almost any law to be attacked, and of course a great many more laws were judicially overthrown."[46]

Graham does posit a *caveat*. Possibly, he says, corporate citizenship under the Privileges and Immunities Clauses of Section One of the Fourteenth Amendment may have served corporate interests almost as effectively as corporate personhood has under the Due Process and Equal Protection Clauses. Moreover, the same results might have been attained by filing lawsuits in the names of individual natural persons who were stockholders of the corporation affected by the governmental action at issue.[47]

Graham places the *Santa Clara* ruling in perspective. The nation "already had committed its destinies to limited, representative, federal government; to judicial review; and finally and increasingly of late, to corporate enterprises...." "Courts and judges were torn between traditional solicitude for corporate and property rights on the one hand," he argues, "and deference to the police power on the other." If not explicitly, "at least implicitly, the Constitutional and public law status of the corporation became ever more insistent and central."[48]

Whatever the true nature of its origins, it is clear that the *Santa Clara* doctrine is of great importance and has been remarkably durable. It has been reaffirmed by the Supreme Court as a threshold issue in at least thirteen cases that have treated state actions affecting the interests of corporations.[49] Most recently, in the 1978 case of *First National Bank of Boston v. Bellotti*, the Court, without comment, cited *Santa Clara* doctrine as binding precedent.[50]

The challenges to the *Santa Clara* doctrine by Justices Black and Douglas were cogent, well argued, and intellectually convincing. Nonetheless, the Supreme Court has witnessed no further challenge in the intervening thirty-eight years. Graham acknowledges that "Corporate personality today is much more than an established or an accepted fact. It also is a doctrine—perhaps more accurately, a part of a doctrinal complex—the collective potentialities and misuse of which, in the hands of judges who pushed its elements 'to dryly logical extremes' have proved to a large degree judicially self-correcting."[51]

The importance of the corporation to the economic nature and vitality of the United States is obvious. As of 1973, when *Roe v. Wade* was decided, there were almost two million active corporations. Over three hundred thousand new ones were being formed each year. Corporations made about 98 percent of all manufacturing sales, comprised 57 percent of all service-oriented business operations, and 22 percent of all agricultural and forestry enterprises. Measured by their assets, there were three hundred "billionaire" corporations. One hundred thousand were "millionaires," and one million corporations owned at least $1,000 in assets.[52]

It would be difficult to imagine how this nation's legal system could cope with disputes involving large, multi-investor enterprises if corporations did not exist. As Professor Detlev Vagts has observed, "... try to think of a grade crossing accident involving a Penn Central train and a General Motors delivery truck." "Treated as partnerships," he continued, "... these two firms would implicate some 2,000,000 'partners' with at least some hundreds changing every day and having to be dropped out or substituted as parties to the resulting litigation."[53] This example teaches the importance of the legal entity known as the corporation.

The Supreme Court, in the 1819 case of *Dartmouth College v. Woodward*, stated:

> A corporation is an artificial being, invisible, intangible and existing only in contemplation of law. Being the mere creature of law, it possesses only those properties which the charter of its creation confers upon it, either

expressly, or as incidental to its very existence. These are such as are supposed best calculated to effect the object for which it was created. Among the most important are immortality, and, if the expression may be allowed, individuality; properties, by which a perpetual succession of many persons are considered as the same, and may act as a single individual. They enable a corporation to manage its own affairs, and to hold property, without the perplexing intricacies, the hazardous and endless necessity, of perpetual conveyances for the purpose of transmitting it from hand to hand. It is chiefly for the purpose of clothing bodies of men, in succession, with these qualities and capacities, that corporations were invented, and are in use. By these means, a perpetual succession of individuals are capable of acting for the promotion of the particular object, like one immortal being.[54]

Thus, it is nearly out of the realm of possibility that the Court ever would reverse *Santa Clara.* "Surely for a nation so thoroughly committed to judicial review, it would be a strange self-doubt or mistrust that would call at this date for *judicial* renunciation of the corporate person as needed security against future *judicial misuse.*" "The corporate person," Graham concludes, "has come of age."[55] The corporation's status as a constitutional "person," then, seems as secure as it approaches its one hundredth anniversary as if it really were written into the text of the Fourteenth Amendment to the Constitution.

II. The Personhood of the Unborn: *Roe* and the Forgotten Lessons of *Santa Clara*

ALTHOUGH CONGRESS DID not debate the abortion issue during its consideration of the Fourteenth Amendment,[56] it did discuss the scope of the word "person" under the provisions of the amendment in a manner that has serious implications for the question of whether the unborn are encompassed by that term. Contemporaneously, the states that ratified the Fourteenth Amendment were changing their abortion laws in a way that also suggests implications for the unborn personhood question as well.

Representative Bingham, author and primary sponsor of Section 1 of the amendment in the House, spoke of the rights guaranteed by the amendment as applying to "every human being."[57] Senator Howard of Michigan, the amendment's Senate sponsor, said that its provisions would protect the rights of "common humanity."[58] Thus it can be said that these leading framers of the Fourteenth Amendment intended for the word "person" to mean "human being."

While Congress debated the Fourteenth Amendment, and the states were deciding on ratification, nearly all of the states were changing their abortion laws to conform to a new view of the issue by the medical profession.[59] Previously, the common law protected only unborn children who had "quickened," which is the point in gestation at which the mother first perceives the movement of her unborn child.[60]

Reacting to advances in the knowledge of embryology, the medical profession rejected the quickening doctrine and adopted the view that the life of a new human being begins at conception. Acting on this belief, the American Medical Association undertook a campaign for more strict antiabortion laws that would protect the unborn through pregnancy. The AMA sought to persuade the states to protect every unborn child because abortion was the "unwarrantable destruction of unborn life."[61]

From 1848 to 1876, nearly all of the states enacted statutes that embodied the AMA view. These new state abortion laws explicitly accepted the assertions of leaders of the AMA that interruption of gestation at any point in a pregnancy should be a crime.[62]

Professor Rosenblum best states one conclusion to which the available evidence on the intention of the framers points:

> Since the 14th Amendment with its broad protection of the lives of all persons was ratified by State legislatures, while these very same legislatures, persuaded by newly discovered scientific and medical evidence, were extending the protection of the criminal law to encompass *all* the unborn from the time of conception or fertilization, it is a fair assumption that the unborn were not excluded from those "persons" covered by the Amendment.[63]

But, even if it can be said that the framers of the Fourteenth Amendment did not intend to exclude the unborn child from the scope of the legal protection that they accorded to a "person," neither can it be convincingly argued that they intended to *include* the unborn. As noted, the Supreme Court recognized the paramount importance of the personhood issue to the disposition of the *Roe* case. "If this suggestion of personhood is established," noted the Court, "the case for a right to abortion . . . collapses, for the fetus' right to life is then guaranteed specifically by the Amendment."[64]

After observing that the "Constitution does not define 'person' in so many words," the Court proceeded to note the points in the Fourteenth Amendment, as well as the other constitutional contexts, in which the word "person" was used.[65] It cited the listing of qualifications for representatives and senators, the Apportionment Clause, the migration and importation provision, the Emolument Clause, the electors provisions, the listing of qualifications for the presidency, the extradition provisions, and the Fifth, Twelfth, and Twenty-second Amendments.[66] The Court concluded that none of these uses of the word person "indicates, with any assurance, that it has any possible pre-natal application."[67]

Having thus analyzed the use of the word "person" in the Constitution, the Court noted that it had decided elsewhere in its opinion that "throughout the major portion of the 19th century prevailing legal abortion practices were far freer than they are today."[68] In that part of the Court's opinion, it noted that "...in the middle and late 19th century, the quickening distinction disappeared from the statutory law of most states and the degree of the offense and the penalties were increased." The Court also observed that "throughout the major portion of the 19th century,...a woman enjoyed a substantially broader right to terminate a pregnancy than in most states today."[69]

On this basis, primarily from its analysis of the use of the word "person" elsewhere in the Constitution and secondarily from its findings on state abortion laws in the nineteenth century, the Court concluded that "the word 'person,' as used in the Fourteenth Amendment, does not include the unborn."[70] Thus, no unborn child, at any point from conception until birth, can be considered a constitutional person.

In making its observations about the state of the law toward abortion "throughout the major portion of the nineteenth century," the Court gave no indication that it even considered the reasons why antiabortion laws were growing stricter contemporaneously with the period in which the Fourteenth Amendment was being drafted, passed, and ratified. Nowhere in its analysis of the word "person" as used in the Fourteenth Amendment did the Court explicitly consider the intention of the framers. Perhaps most important, it never considered whether the framers intended the word "person" to have the same meaning as the words "human being," and, if so, how that might influence its conclusion.

In general, the Supreme Court offered very little analysis of any kind in support of its holding that the unborn child is not a "person" under the Fourteenth Amendment. What it did say, as we have seen, was that the holding rested on two conclusions. First, said the Court, of the other uses of the word "person" in the Constitution, "nearly all" seem to apply only postnatally, and "[n]one indicates, with any assurance, that it has any possible pre-natal application."[71] The second conclusion, said Justice Blackmun, was that "throughout the major portion of the nineteenth century prevailing legal abortion practices were far freer than they are today...."[72] Both conclusions, and hence the holding that they support, have come under sharp criticism.

Professor Basile Uddo argues that there is "probably no more weakly reasoned part of *Roe*" than its approach to defining the term "person" in the context of the Fourteenth Amendment. "Rather than look to commonsense, common law, medical data, or tradition," Justice Blackmun "chose to see how else the word 'person' was used in the Constitution. He found that it was always used postnatally...." Observing that "virtually the entire Constitution was written about adult activities," Uddo contends that if carried to its logical conclusion, "Justice Blackmun's technique for defining 'person' would include only adult white males, since that is what was contemplated by most of the other references to 'person' in the body of the Constitution."[73]

But Professor Robert Destro's criticism cuts even deeper. He argues that a thorough examination of the uses of the word "person" in the Constitution reveals that the meaning of the term is generally derived from the context in which it is used.[74] But, he notes, there is an exception. The only clauses of the Constitution in which context does not supply the meaning of the word "person" are the Due Process Clause of the Fifth Amendment and the Due Process and Equal Protection Clauses of the Fourteenth Amendment.[75] Thus, even if it is assumed that the use of the word "person" in other sections of the Constitution does not include the unborn, it does not follow that the same then is true for these three clauses as well. Furthermore, if the Court was trying to establish that the use of the word "person" in the other sections *precludes* any possible prenatal application, then it failed to support that proposition by merely offering citations to the other passages.[76]

Professor Destro offered an example to illustrate the weakness of the Court's analysis. By its terms, the Twenty-second Amendment prohibits the election of any "person" to the office of president more than twice. It is apparent, observes Destro, that the use of the word "person," in this case, derives its meaning from the context. But, under the Court's analytical scheme, in a future case involving the meaning of the word, a "person" might be deemed to mean only one who has attained the age of 35 and is a natural born citizen.[77]

Professor John T. Noonan agrees with this analysis. "The entire burden of the Court's reasoning is that an unborn child cannot be an elector; and yet 'person' is used as to elector in the Constitution." "[A]n unborn child cannot be a Senator or a Representative,... and yet person is used in that clause; nor can an unborn child be a fugitive slave, yet persons are talked about in that clause." What the Court effectively said in *Roe* is that "it is ridiculous to take unborn children as persons because they cannot be persons in these contexts."[78]

By far the most effective way in which constitutional scholars have attacked the first part of the Court's rationale for its unborn personhood holding in *Roe* is through use of *Santa Clara*. Because, as we have seen, *Santa Clara* represents the Court's only other construction of the word "person," as used in the Fourteenth Amendment, its importance as an analytical tool vis-à-vis *Roe* naturally rises above that of the employment of ordinary logic and reasoning. Professors Noonan and Destro make particularly effective use of *Santa Clara* in their critique of *Roe*. Professor Destro does so in conjunction with another example of the Court's faulty analytical method of looking to the use of the word "person" elsewhere in the Constitution. The Apportionment Clause directs that both congressional representation and taxes must be allocated by "adding to the whole number of free Persons, and excluding Indians not taxed, three-fifths of all other Persons," such enumeration to be made every ten years "in such Manner as [Congress] shall by Law direct."[79] The Court, notes Destro, observed that it was "not aware that in the taking of any census under this clause, a fetus has ever been counted."[80]

If being counted during the census is a primary prerequisite for personhood, Destro argues, then it is difficult to comprehend how a corporation can be a "person" within the meaning of the Fourteenth Amendment. "This writer," notes Destro in a sardonic mimic of Justice Blackmun, "is not aware that in any census a corporation has ever been counted."[81] Professor Noonan agrees. Having argued that an unborn child cannot be a "person" as that term is used in constitutional clauses other than the Fourteenth Amendment, "what the Court did not advert to was that each one of these clauses would be equally effective for showing that a corporation is not a person within the ... Amendment."[82] For example, notes Noonan, a corporation cannot be a fugitive slave, and cannot be a representative, or a senator, or a presidential elector.[83]

Noonan draws an impassioned conclusion. Alluding to the *Santa Clara* decision, he asserts that "here we deal not with a hypothesis requiring the artificial extension of the meaning of 'person' but with real creatures of flesh and blood, whose brains are working, whose hearts are pumping, whose legs are kicking, but which the Court has found not to be persons because they could not vote, be a Senator or Congressman, or become a runaway slave."[84] We can see that *Santa Clara* demolishes the first half of the Court's justification for the personhood holding of *Roe*. For what the Court found that the unborn cannot be in other constitutional contexts where the term "person" is used applies with equal force to the corporation. Thus, *Roe* and *Santa Clara* are inconsistent on this major point.

We turn now to the second half of the Court's justification for its *Roe v. Wade* holding that unborn children are not constitutional persons. Justice Blackmun's statement that "throughout the major portion of the nineteenth century prevailing legal abortion practices were far freer than they are today..."[85] does not reflect an awareness of the true nature of the historical evolution of nineteenth century abortion law. As a report of the U.S. Senate Separation of Powers Subcommittee has noted, "the relatively permissive attitude toward abortion prior to quickening that prevailed in the early nineteenth century was overwhelmingly rejected by the very legislatures which adopted strict antiabortion laws."[86] These laws, as we have seen, resulted from a consensus in the medical profession, arising from new scientific discoveries, that the unborn child is a human being from the time of conception. As the subcommittee observed, although the Court mentioned these scientific and political developments in another part of its opinion, "it did not discuss their relevance to an understanding of the consensus at the time of the adoption of the fourteenth amendment on whether the word 'person' includes the unborn."[87]

Professor Destro draws a sharp conclusion. Since the second part of the Court's justification for its personhood holding "is based upon an alleged lack of statutory and common law concern with prenatal life in the period prior to the ratification of the Constitution and the addition of the fourteenth amendment, a demonstration that nineteenth century common and statutory law were committed to the preservation of unborn life casts substantial doubt on the validity of the Court's view." Simultaneously, "such a showing lends credence to the proposition that neither the words of the fourteenth amendment itself, nor the provisions of any other section of the Constitution, require that the unborn be excluded from the protection of the due process clause and thereby denied the right to life."[88]

Beyond the criticisms of the Court's own rationale for its personhood holding, legal scholars have discovered additional fundamental flaws with that aspect of the *Roe* decision. Professor Byrn cites the Court's 1968 *Levy v. Louisiana* ruling, in which the constitutional rights of illegitimate children were upheld.[89] In the course of its analysis of these children's status under the Constitution in *Levy*, the Court declared that "[W]e start from the premise that illegitimate children are not 'nonpersons.' They are human, live, and have their being." "They are," said the Court, "clearly within the meaning of the Equal Protection Clause of the Fourteenth Amendment."[90]

It can be argued that the Court's definition of personhood in the context of the *Levy* case was only a *dictum*, and that therefore the Court was under no obligation to employ, or to distinguish it, in *Roe*. But, considered in light of the fact that the Court made no effort to define the word "person" in *Roe*, or to explain why it decided not to employ the *Levy* criteria, Professor Robert Byrn believes that it nonetheless is a significant weakness in the Court's analysis. "Had the *Levy* standard been applied in *Wade*," argued Byrn, "the Court could not have avoided passing on the factual, 'biological' question of whether unborn children are live human beings."[91] Asserting that "unborn children in fact are human beings," Byrn says that recognition of that status on the part of the Court would have required it "to take the next step and find all unborn children to be human persons within section one of the fourteenth amendment." Concludes Bryn: "Instead, the Court omitted *Levy* completely. Indeed, having decided not to pass on the crucial question of fact, it has no choice but to ignore *Levy*."[92]

In a 1973 New York Appeals Court case, Judge Charles Breitel applied the *Levy* criteria in the abortion context. Writing for the majority, Judge Breitel granted that unborn children were "human" and unquestionably "alive." But, Breitel continued, "[i]t is not true that the legal order corresponds to the natural order." Who is legally a person is "for the law, including of course, the Constitution, to say."[93] Professor Destro believes that what the Constitution says is clear. "[T]hose most familiar with the purpose of the fourteenth amendment, its authors, rejected any but a biological standard by which to judge the existence of personal rights." An appraisal of "who is or is not a person," Destro concludes, "...is foreign to the essentially egalitarian philosophy upon which its provisions concerning individual rights are based."[94] And Professor Uddo agrees. The concern of the framers of the Fourteenth Amendment "for common humanity, for the sanctity, not the quality of life—for the inalienable right to life," argues Uddo, "would certainly have caused them to resoundingly reject any notion that only certain lives are protected in the Constitution."[95]

Despite the strong logic of Professors Rosenblum's and Destro's argument, that the framers of the Fourteenth Amendment did not intend to exclude the unborn child from the constitutional protection that they provided to a "person," the fact remains that the legislative history does not reflect a positive, explicit intention to include the unborn. However, as the U.S. Senate Separation of Powers Subcommittee has noted, it is no less true that the framers did not address themselves to a constitutional "right of privacy," or to "whether the due process clause prohibited the states from outlawing abortion, pornography, prayer in the public schools, searches and seizures of illicit drugs in the glove compartments of automobiles, and countless

other activities that the courts have held to be under the aegis of the
Fourteenth Amendment."[96] The subcommittee quoted Chief Justice
Marshall:

> A constitution, to contain an accurate detail of all the subdivisions of
> which its great powers will admit, and of all the means by which they may
> be carried into execution, would partake of the prolixity of a legal code,
> and could scarcely be embraced by the human mind. It would probably
> never be understood by the public. Its nature, therefore, requires, that
> only its great outlines should be marked, its important objects desig-
> nated, and the minor ingredients which compose those objects be
> deduced from the nature of the objects themselves. That this idea was
> entertained by the framers of the American Constitution, is not only to
> be inferred from the nature of the instrument but from the language . . .
> we must never forget, that it is a constitution we are expounding.[97]

Applying Marshall's lesson to the Supreme Court's *Roe* personhood
holding, the Senate subcommittee drew a compelling conclusion. To
interpret the term "person" in the strictest manner, while insisting
that it does not include the unborn because the framers neglected to
debate the abortion issue, "makes no more sense than to argue that
infants or senior citizens are not 'persons' within the meaning of the
amendment because the framers never discussed infanticide or
euthanasia."[98]

If we ignore *Santa Clara*, and apply a strict construction to the use of
the word "person" in the Fourteenth Amendment, then a strong case
can be made that the term does not include unborn children. This case
rests on the simple fact that the framers, in the legislative history,
never explicitly said that they intended to include them. Such a narrow
and strict interpretation would reject the inference suggested by
Rosenblum and Destro that, by not excluding unborn children from
the scope of Fourteenth Amendment personhood, the framers implicitly intended to include them. As long as *Santa Clara* stands,
however, it cannot be ignored. And *Santa Clara* stands for nothing if it
does not stand for the principle that the word "person" in the
Fourteenth Amendment is *not* to be construed in the strictest or
narrowest sense.

III. Toward A Unified Theory of Personhood

THE FIRST AND primary basis on which the Supreme Court determined
the issue of whether the unborn child is a "person," for purposes of the
Fourteenth Amendment, was its analysis of the usage of the term
elsewhere in the Constitution. But, as we have concluded, the

strongest and most compelling refutation of Justice Blackmun's rationale was provided by the *Santa Clara* case. For as Professor Joseph O'Meara notes, all of the "provisions enumerated by the learned Justice, containing the word 'person,' which he declared 'do not include the unborn,' are equally and obviously inapplicable to corporations." Professor O'Meara pleads for consistency. "The Court," he said, "cannot have its cake and eat it." "It can," he concludes, "make no pretense at consistency unless and until it holds that a corporation is *not* a person or that a fetus *is*."[99]

Thus, when taken in combination with the fact that the Court erred in its conclusions about the nature of the legal regulation of abortion in the nineteenth century, *Santa Clara* provides the means by which the Supreme Court's personhood holding in *Roe v. Wade* is stripped of the rationale that the Court offered to justify it. If the Supreme Court is to perform its assumed role as the ultimate arbiter of what the Constitution means in an honest and responsible manner, then it must reconcile *Santa Clara* and *Roe*. Professor O'Meara's suggestions for how such a reconciliation can be accomplished do not exhaust the possibilities for using *Santa Clara* to reverse the unborn personhood determination in *Roe*. Principally, there are two. The Supreme Court could reverse the Fourteenth Amendment personhood holdings of both its *Santa Clara* and *Roe v. Wade* decisions. Or, it could preserve *Santa Clara* while reversing *Roe*.

As we have demonstrated, the available evidence points irrefutably towards the conclusion that the framers of the Fourteenth Amendment intended that the term "person" means the same as "human being." This is the conclusion reached by Justice Douglas's critique of *Santa Clara*, and, certainly more important, it is how the Court defined the term in its relatively recent *Levy* decision. *Santa Clara* and *Roe* can be reconciled, if the Court were to hold, in effect, that the term "human being" is constitutionally synonymous with the term "person," and that the former term provides the latter with its exclusive meaning.

Such a holding by the Court would necessitate the reversal of the *Santa Clara* case, which is the course of action urged by Justice Douglas in his *Glander* dissent. Corporations are not, as the Court said in *Levy*, "humans, [who are] live, and [who] have their being."[100] And it would set the stage for the reversal of the personhood holding of *Roe*, and hence the recognition of unborn children as constitutional persons as well. In light of its own professed inability to determine whether the unborn child is a human being, the Court could defer to a legislative determination of fact that the unborn are human beings. Or, the Court could take judicial notice of the scientific fact that unborn children are biologically human at all points in their gestation.[101]

But this scenario is, perhaps, fatally flawed. As we have noted, it is extremely unlikely, from a practical standpoint, that the Court ever would reverse the *Santa Clara* case; and it certainly would not be disposed to do so only as a means of reversing the personhood holding of *Roe v. Wade*. After all, the circumstance in which the Court could consider overruling the personhood aspect of its *Roe* decision would be its review of a lower court ruling on the constitutionality of a legislative act regulating abortion. *Santa Clara*, quite simply, would not be at issue.

Given the fact that it is not realistic to suppose that the Court would reverse *Santa Clara* as a means of reversing *Roe*, how might the Court overrule *Roe*'s personhood holding while preserving *Santa Clara*? Professor Destro suggests the answer. He criticized the Court for interpreting the word "person," as used in the Fourteenth Amendment, so loosely in the *Santa Clara* case, while rigidly doing so in *Roe*. "If the constitutional usage of 'person' is too inflexible to include the unborn, it cannot reasonably be thought flexible enough to include a corporation."[102] But Destro's formulation can be turned around. If the constitutional usage of "person" is flexible enough to include a corporation, then it cannot reasonably be thought too inflexible to include the unborn.

In *Roe v. Wade*, the Court implicitly found that the "viable" unborn child, at least, is a human being. Certainly, then, if the term "person" in the Fourteenth Amendment can be construed broadly enough to admit a nonhuman fictional entity such as a corporation into its protection, it also can be read to include viable, unborn children whom the Court concedes are human beings. Likewise, even if the Court were to determine that the humanity of previable unborn children is subject to dispute, the term "person" must also be read broadly enough to encompass those whom legislatures rationally regard as human beings or that science at least admits might be human beings.[103]

The Supreme Court's doctrine that corporations are constitutional persons, as first established by its 1886 decision in the *Santa Clara* case, has serious implications for the effort to reverse the denial of the same legal status to unborn children by its 1973 ruling in *Roe v. Wade*. Reconciling *Santa Clara* and *Roe*, by the only practically feasible of the two alternative means, is one important route by which the goal of the Supreme Court recognition of unborn children as constitutional persons can be reached.

Notes

1. Roe v. Wade, 410 U.S. 113, 156–157 (1973). The term "the unborn child," rather than "fetus," will be used throughout this paper. According to the Concise Oxford Dictionary (Fifth Edition), the word "fetus" (or "foetus") means a "(f)ully developed embryo in (the) womb." Thus it refers only to a particular stage of human gestation in the womb. Moreover, in *Roe v. Wade*, the Court itself made frequent use of the term "unborn" to describe the nascent human being at all points of gestation. For instance, the personhood holding itself reads: "All this . . . persuades us that the word 'person,' as used in the Fourteenth Amendment, does not include *the unborn*." *Id.* (emphasis added). Later in its opinion, the Court asserts that "*the unborn* have never been recognized in the law as persons in the whole sense." *Id.* at 162 (emphasis added).

2. Professor Ely does not believe that Justice Blackmun is correct. According to Ely, " . . . the argument that fetuses lack constitutional rights is simply irrelevant. For it has never been held or even asserted that the state interest needed to justify forcing a person to refrain from activity whether or not that activity is constitutionally protected, must implicate either the life or the constitutional rights of another person. Dogs are not 'persons in the whole sense' nor have they constitutional rights, but that does not mean the state cannot prohibit killing them. It does not even mean the state cannot prohibit killing them in the exercise of the First Amendment right of political protest. Come to think of it, draft cards aren't persons either." Ely, *The Wages of Crying Wolf: A Comment on Roe v. Wade*, 82 Yale L.J. 920, 926 (1973). Other legal scholars strongly disagree. For example, Professor Destro notes: "That the unborn were found to be excluded from the protection of the Constitution was the keystone of the Court's argument that the state has no interest in protecting them through the use of criminal or civil sanction." Destro, *Abortion and the Constitution: The Need for a Life-Protective Amendment*, 63 Calif. L. Rev. 1250, 1258 (1975).

3. Roe v. Wade, 410 U.S. 113, 221 (1973) (White, J., dissenting); *Id.* at 171 (Rehnquist, J., dissenting); Thornburgh v. American College of Obstetricians and Gynecologists, 106 S.Ct. 2169, 2192 (White, J., dissenting); *Id.* at 2206 (O'Connor, J., dissenting). The arguments against the Court's majority opinion in *Roe* by Justices White, Rehnquist, and O'Connor are directed at the right to privacy holding of the Supreme Court. At no point do these justices challenge the Court's *Roe* holding with respect to the personhood of the unborn. However, in *Thornburgh*, Justice White admonishes the majority to recognize "that the fetus is an entity that bears in its cells all the genetic information that characterizes a member of the species *homo sapiens* and distinguishes an individual member of that species from all others," and "that there is no nonarbitrary line separating a fetus from a child or, indeed, an adult human being." 106 S.Ct. at 2195 (White dissenting). White adds that the state

interest at issue in abortion regulation "is in protecting those who will be citizens if their lives are not ended in the womb." *Id.* at 2196. This line of argument may, or may not, suggest an openness to arguments for the personhood of the unborn.

4. *See, e.g.,* "Foes of Abortion Study Strategies Used by N.A.A.C.P. in Integration," N.Y.Times, Apr. 2, 1984, at A9, col. 1.

5. The Court held that the corporation is a "person" for the purposes of the Equal Protection Clause ("No state shall . . . deny to any person within its jurisdiction the equal protection of the laws." U.S. Const. amend. XIV, Sec. 1). Santa Clara County v. Southern Pacific Railroad Company, 118 U.S. 394, (1886). Three years later, the Court applied the Due Process Clause ("No state shall . . . deprive any person of life, liberty, or property, without due process of law." U.S. Const. amend. XIV, Sec. 1) to corporate persons as well. Minneapolis and St. Louis Railway Co. v. Beckwith, 129 U.S. 26 (1889). The Court has held that aliens are protected by the Fourteenth Amendment, but that decision did not concern the scope of personhood *per se.* Home Ins. Co. v. Dick, 281 U.S. 397, 411 (1929). In the course of a 1968 opinion on the legal rights of illegitimate children, the Supreme Court offered the following dictum: "We start from the premise that illegitimate children are not 'non-persons.' They are humans, live and have their being." Levy v. Louisiana, 391 U.S. 68, 70 (1968). This apparent definition of personhood by the Court was not, however, a holding on which the resolution of the case turned. Recently, two circuits of the United States Court of Appeals have decided issues relating to whether constitutional personhood may continue after death. After death, one is no longer a person within our constitutional framework and has no rights of which he may be deprived or which may form the basis of a lawsuit complaining of the deprivation of such rights. Whitehurst v. Wright, 592 F. 2d 834 (5th Cir. 1979). A "deceased" person is no longer a "person" for purposes of constitutional rights protected by the Fourteenth Amendment. Guyton v. Phillips, 606 F. 2d 248 (9th Cir. 1979).

6. Roe v. Wade, 410 U.S. 113, 158 (1973).

7. It is, of course, beyond dispute that corporations are not human beings. But in *Roe v. Wade,* the Supreme Court seems to concede that, at least by the time in pregnancy at which the unborn child becomes "viable" outside his or her mother's womb, the unborn are human beings. "We need not resolve the difficult question of when life begins," says the Court. "When those trained in the respective disciplines of medicine, philosophy, and theology are unable to arrive at any consensus, the judiciary, at this point in the development of man's knowledge, is not in a position to speculate as to the answer." *Id.* at 159. The Court, however, also determined that "(w)ith respect to the State's important and legitimate interest in potential life, the 'compelling' point is viability. This is so because the fetus then presumably has the capacity of meaningful life outside the mother's womb." *Id.* at 163. By definition, a human being who would be "viable" outside the womb is no less a human being only because he or she remains inside the womb. This, in the view of at least one critic of the *Roe* decision, the Court seems prepared to grant. Ely, *The Wages of*

Crying Wolf: A Comment on Roe v. Wade, 82 Yale L.J. 920, 924 (1973). Thus, when taken in conjunction with the Court's holding that even viable unborn children are not "persons," it is fair to say that *Roe v. Wade* stands for the proposition that one may be a human being, but not a "person," under the Fourteenth Amendment.

8. Connecticut General Life Insurance Company v. Johnson, 303 U.S. 77, 87 (1938) (Black, J., dissenting) (hereinafter *Johnson*); Wheeling Steel Corporation v. Glander, 337 U.S. 562, 576-577 (1949) (Douglas, J., dissenting) (hereinafter *Glander*).

9. 43 U.S. (2 How.) 497, 555 (1844).

10. Rundle v. Delaware & Raritan Canal Co., 55 U.S. (14 How.) 80, 96-103 (1852) (Daniel, J., dissenting). *See also*, Marshall v. Baltimore & Ohio R. Co., 57 U.S. 53) (1853) (16 How.) 314, 338 (Daniel, J., dissenting).

11. Railway Co. v. Whitton's Adm'r., 80 U.S. (13 Wall) 270, 283 (1872).

12. Marshall v. Baltimore & Ohio R.R., 57 U.S. (16 How.) 314, 351 (1854) (Campbell, J., dissenting).

13. McGovney, *A Supreme Court Fiction*, 56 Harv. L. Rev. 853, 873, 898 (1943).

14. "No State shall make or enforce any law which shall abridge the privileges or immunities of citizens of the United States." U.S. Const. amend. XIV, sec. 1.

15. *See, generally, Johnson*, 303 U.S. at 87 and *Glander*, 337 U.S. at 577. *See* the discussion of the "conspiracy theory of the Fourteenth Amendment," pp. *infra*, for some unaccepted "legislative history" on this point. See also Home Ins. Co. v. Dick, 281 U.S. 397, 411 (1930) for the proposition that aliens are persons.

16. 118 U.S. at 396.

17. *Glander*, 337 U.S. at 576-577.

18. In reaching its decision, the Court implicitly overruled a contrary precedent of an inferior federal court. In this 1871 case, a corporation claimed that the State of Louisiana had imposed on it a tax that violated the Equal Protection Clause of the four-year-old Fourteenth Amendment. Writing for the court, Justice Woods, then a circuit court judge of the United States, held that "person," as used in the amendment, did not include a corporation. "This construction of the section," Woods argued, "is strengthened by the history of the submission by Congress, and the adoption by the States of the Fourteenth Amendment, so fresh in all minds as to need no rehearsal." 1 Woods 85, 88 (1871).

19. Gorby, *The "Right" to an Abortion, the Scope of Fourteenth Amendment "Personhood," and the Supreme Court's Birth Requirement*, 1979 So. Ill. U. L.J. 1, 11, n. 62 (1979).

20. 60 U.S. (19 How.) 393 (1857).

21. *See* Kent, Commentaries on American Law, at 253-255 (12th ed. 1973).

22. Remarks of Rep. Bingham, Cong. Globe, 39th Cong., 1st Sess. 2766 (1866).

23. Remarks of Sen. Howard, Cong. Globe, 39th Cong., 1st Sess. 2766 (1866).

24. 83 U.S. (16 Wall.) 36, 71 (1873).

25. A. Hadley, *The Constitutional Position of Property in America*, 64 Independent 834, 836 (1908), *cited in* Wheeling Steel Corp. v. Glander, 337 U.S. 562 (1949).

26. 303 U.S. 77, 85-86 (1938) (Black, J., dissenting).

27. 337 U.S. 562, 579 (1949) (Douglas, J., dissenting) [citing Greenberg, 204 U.S. 359, 369 (1907), and *Walsh*, 226 U.S. 112, 126 (1912)].

28. *Glander*, 337 U.S. at 579.

29. *Id.*

30. *Id.*

31. 47 Yale L.J. 371 (1938).

32. 116 U.S. 138 (1885).

33. "A printed copy of the *Oral Argument of Roscoe Conkling* is preserved·in a volume entitled *San Mateo Case: Arguments, and Decisions*, in the Hopkins Railroad Collection of the Library of Stanford University." Graham, *The 'Conspiracy Theory' of the Fourteenth Amendment*, 47 Yale L.J. 371 (1938) (hereinafter Graham).

34. *Id.* at 371.

35. *Id.*

36. *Id.*

37. *Id.* at 372.

38. *Id.*

39. *Id.* at 373.

40. *Id.* at 378.

41. 303 U.S. at 87.

42. *Glander*, 337 U.S. at 580-581.

43. *See*, Graham, "An Innocent Abroad: The Constitutional Corporate Person," 2 U.C.L.A. L. Rev. 155 (1954).

44. *Id.* at 160-161.

45. *Id.* at 163.

46. *Id.*

47. *Id.* at 165.

48. *Id.* at 178-179.

49. Missouri Pacific Railway Company v. Mackey, 127 U.S. 205, 209 (1888); Minneapolis and St. Louis Railway Company v. Beckwith, 129 U.S. 26 (1889); Charlotte, Columbia, and Augusta Railroad Company v. Gibbes, 142 U.S. 386, 391 (1892); Covington and Lexington Turnpike Road Company v. Sandford, 164 U.S. 578, 592 (1896); Gulf, Colorado and Santa Fe Railway Company v. Ellis, 165 U.S. 150, 154 (1897); Smyth v. Ames, 169 U.S. 466, 522 (1898), Blake v. McClung, 172 U.S. 239, 259 (1898); Southern Pacific Railroad Company v. United States, 183 U.S. 527 (1902); Kentucky Finance Corporation v. Paramount Auto Exchange Corporation, 262 U.S. 544, 550 (1923); Power Manufacturing Company v. Saunders, 274 U.S. 490, 493 (1927); Wheeling Steel Corporation v. Glanders, 337 U.S. 562 (1949); Bell v. Maryland, 378 U.S. 226 (1964); and First National Bank of Boston v. Bellotti, 435 U.S. 765, 780 (1978).

50. 435 U.S. 765, 780, n. 15 (1978).

51. Graham, *supra* note 43, at 210.

52. Vagts, Basic Corporation Law 5 (1973); Conard, Corporations in Perspective 152-159 (1976).

53. Vagts, *supra* note 52, at 34.

54. Dartmouth College v. Woodward, 17 U.S. (4 Wheat.) 518, 637 (1819).

55. Graham, *supra* note 43, at 211.

56. *The Human Life Bill—S. 158: Report ... by ... (the) Subcomm. on Separation of Powers, Senate Comm. on the Judiciary,* 97th Cong. 1st Sess. 24 (1981) (hereinafter HLB Report).

57. *Cong. Globe,* 39th Cong., 1st Sess. 1089 (1866).

58. *Id.* at 2766.

59. States acted to restrict abortion throughout the Civil War and postbellum period: 1860—Connecticut, Pennsylvania; 1861—Colorado, Nevada; 1864—Arizona, Idaho, Montana, Oregon; 1866-67—Alabama; 1867—Illinois, Ohio, Vermont; 1868—Florida, Maryland; 1869—Massachusetts, Wyoming; 1870—Louisiana; 1872—California, New Jersey; 1873—Virginia, Michigan, Minnesota, Nebraska; 1875—Arkansas; 1876—Georgia. Mohr, Abortion in America(:) The Origins and Evolution of National Policy 200–225 (1978), as cited in *The Human Life Bill: Hearings on S. 158 Before the Subcommittee on Separation of Powers, Senate Comm. on the Judiciary,* 97th Cong., 1st Sess. 475 (1981) (prepared statement of Victor G. Rosenblum) (hereinafter HLB Hearings).

60. HLB Report, *supra* note 56, at 24.

61. 12 American Medical Association, *The Transactions of the American Medical Association* 75, 78 (1859), as cited in HLB Report, *supra* note 56, at 25.

62. HLB Report, *supra* note 56, at 24; *see also* note 58, *supra*; Mohr, *supra* note 59, at 200, as cited in HLB Report *supra* note 56, at 25.

63. HLB Hearings, *supra* note 59, at 480.

64. Roe v. Wade, 410 U.S. 113, 156–157 (1973).

65. Section 1 of the Fourteenth Amendment, noted the Court, contains three references to "person." The first, in defining "citizens," speaks of "persons born or naturalized in the United States." The word "person" also is included in both the Due Process and Equal Protection Clauses of Section 1, as well as in Sections 2 and 3 of the Amendment. *Id.* at 157.

66. U.S. Const. Art. 1, sec. 2, cl. 2, and sec. 3, cl. 3 (qualifications for representatives and senators).; *Id.* at sec. 2, cl. 3 (Apportionment Clause); *Id.* at sec. 9, cl. 1 (migration and improvision); *Id.* at sec. 9, cl. 8 (emolument clause); U.S. Const. Art. II, sec. 1, cl. 2 (electors); *Id.* at sec. 1, cl. 5 (qualifications for presidency); U.S. Const. Art. IV. sec. 2, cl. 2 (extradition).

67. Roe v. Wade, 410 U.S. 113, 157 (1973).

68. *Id.* at 158.

69. *Id.* at 139–140.

70. *Id.* at 158.

71. *Id.* at 157.

72. *Id.* at 158.

73. HLB Hearings, *supra* note 59, at 353 (statement of Basile Uddo).

74. Destro, *Abortion and the Constitution: The Need for a Life-Protective Amendment,* 63 Calif. L. Rev. 1250, 1283 (1975) (hereinafter Destro).

75. U.S. Const. amend. V. The operative wording of the Due Process Clause of the Fifth Amendment is identical to that of the Fourteenth

Amendment. *See* note 14, *supra*. The Fifth Amendment, though, applies to the federal government, while the Fourteenth applies to the states.

76. Destro, *supra* note 74, at 1283.

77. *Id.* at 1284.

78. HLB Hearings, *supra* note 59, at 259 (statement of John T. Noonan, Jr.) (hereinafter Noonan).

79. U.S. Const. art. I, sec. 2, cl. 3, 4 *quoted in* Destro, *supra*, note 73, at 1284.

80. *Roe* 410 U.S. at 157 n. 53, *quoted in* Destro, *supra* note 73, at 1284.

81. Destro, *supra* note 74, at 1284.

82. Noonan, *supra* note 78, at 259.

83. *Id.*

84. *Id.* at 274.

85. *Roe*, 410 U.S. at 158.

86. HLB Report, *supra* note 56, at 5, n. 5.

87. *Id.*

88. Destro, *supra* note 74, at 1278.

89. 391 U.S. 68 (1968), *cited in* Byrn, *An American Tragedy: The Supreme Court on Abortion*, 41 Fordham L. Rev. 807 (1973) (hereinafter Byrn).

90. 391 U.S. at 70.

91. Byrn, *supra* note 89, at 842–843.

92. *Id.* at 843.

93. Byrn v. New York City Health and Hospitals Corporation, 286 N.E. 2d 887 (1972); *appeal dismissed*, 410 U.S. 949 (1973), *quoted in* Noonan, A Private Choice: Abortion in America in the Seventies 16 (1979).

94. Destro, *supra* note 74, at 1334–1335.

95. HLB Hearings, *supra* note 59, at 353 (statement of Basile Uddo).

96. HLB Report, *supra* note 56, at 24.

97. McCulloch v. Maryland, 17 U.S. (4 Wheat.) 316, 407 (1819), *quoted in* HLB Report, at 24.

98. HLB Report, *supra* note 56, at 24.

99. O'Meara, "Abortion: The Supreme Court Decides A Non-Case," 1974 Sup. Ct. Rev. 355.

100. *Levy*, 391 U.S. at 70.

101. *See generally*, HLB Report, *supra* note 56.

102. Destro, *supra* note 74, at 1284.

103. *See generally*, HLB Hearings, *supra* note 59, and HLB Report, *supra* note 56.

John M. Finnis

Natural Law and the Rights of the Unborn

A VOCATION TO the philosophy of law involves one in the philosophy of morality and politics. In this province, deep and far-reaching questions concerning life in the human community are investigated, meditated, and debated. During Oxford's academic year, I participate in a weekly meeting of professional philosophers and philosophers of law to discuss ethics and political theory. In this forum, ancient and contemporary philosophical ideas and arguments are discussed and evaluated by senior and junior philosophers drawn from every intellectual persuasion.

Recently, a young philosopher read a paper which he had successfully presented to medical groups, adult education classes, and friends. Exhibiting great confidence in his conclusions, he authoritatively asserted: human life, or the human person, does not begin at conception—human life does not begin until the brain is sufficiently developed to support consciousness. His "reasoned" idea was that everyone admits that a person is dead when he is "brain dead." Therefore, everyone should admit that a being is not yet a human being as long as its brain will not yet support consciousness. Such was the supposed completeness of the argument.[1]

I sat back and gleefully watched the demolition of that argument by two of the best-known philosophers of our time. They contended his argument was both out of line with reality and logically inconsistent. It was unrealistic because the reality of brain death is *not* loss of neocortical functions and consciousness. Rather, it is the loss of integrated organic functioning which occurs with the irreversible collapse of all brain stem functions, and the complete and irreversible collapse of the entire brain. As a result, the entire human organism is unable to function, even though individual organs or portions of its physical mass can be kept functioning by mechanical or quasi-mechanical means.[2]

Today, biologists and philosophers acknowledge as did Aristotle that one of the principal signs of organic integration is that the organism can take in nutriment and, by digestion or other metabolic processes, convert it into the material and the energy constituting the entire organism.[3] But when does a human organism begin to be able to take in nutrients and convert them into material and energy constituting the organism? When does its metabolism *begin* functioning? On the day of its conception? The day its mother's ovum was fertilized?

Obviously, his argument was false because it violated the common understanding of human physiological reality and failed the test of logical consistency. If food and warmth were made available to the dead for six weeks, there would be neither the slightest restoration of function, nor the arrest of decay and disintegration. On the other hand, when food and warmth are made available to the human conceptus for six weeks, a visible brain develops with detectable brain waves; a few more weeks of feeding permits consciousness; after a few more months smiles and protests are noticed; and so on, until there is viable human life—perhaps even a future philosopher.

When we discuss the physiological facts which govern human life, we are talking about natural law. When philosophers discuss natural law, they are talking about the fact that there is a reality which *is* what it *is* whether one personally likes it or not. Also, they mean that individuals can more or less understand that reality; that understanding involves questions, hypotheses and arguments or reasoning toward answers; that reasoning requires consistency whether we like it or not, that answers can be right or wrong whether we like it or not.

The phrase "natural law" may not convey what philosophers want to communicate. Moreover, much of what they wish to convey may seem to be incongruous or removed from what is taken for sophistication, learning, smart philosophy, and the advance of science. For example, the sort of philosophy or world view undergirding abortion and other antilife ethics is in serious intellectual trouble. Their ethics seem dominant in universities, journals, and the media; but thinkers who really understand its foundations know, even if they do not want to abandon its convenient conclusions, that from top to bottom their ideas are in jeopardy. Their ideational foundations have deteriorated.

Proabortionists know and accept Jeremy Bentham's guiding principle: "pursue the greatest good for the greatest number."[4] For philosophers, that idea is a nonsensical proposal. Attention to logic shows that one cannot conjoin superlatives in that manner. One cannot, for example, sensibly offer a prize for the person who says the *most* words in the *shortest* time.[5] One could be concerned with increasing well-being *or* with distributing well-being more extensively, but telling someone to pursue them *both* is incoherent advice.[6]

Supporters of abortion know that, even by itself, the idea of maximizing good is incoherent. It is absurd to say that pleasure, or any other single good, is the only good. There are essential human goods which cannot be reduced one to another, and which cannot be added up on some simple, measurable scale: human life itself, truth, knowledge, wisdom, skill in work and play for its own sake, friendship and community with others, or reasonableness, consistency and authenticity in practice.[7] Someone possessing these "goods" flourishes.

People prosper in different ways. Some people's talent is contemplation or scholarship; for others it is friendship and collaboration, or arts and skills, or devotion to sustaining human life and alleviating disease and suffering. No person can be everything. The "goods" cannot simplistically be totaled as if they were entries in an accountant's ledger. When we look at these different ways or aspects of human thriving, we are looking at one common human nature capable of integrating these forms.

Those supporting abortion accept the premise that differing human customs, as revealed by history and anthropology, show there is no single, unified human nature. However, they seem to ignore the observation that people from varying cultures recognize and acknowledge basic forms of human good. Individual free choice and social action, acting under the guidance of perceived practical reasoning, have generated differing customs, mores, and values.[8]

Intelligent supporters of abortion know there are rational standards of practical reasonableness. Philosophers often have myopic perceptions. One might build philosophy or ethics around fairness, another around contemplation, another around authenticity, another around constancy or fidelity, another around respect-in-every-act for the basic aspects of humanness. If one conscientiously takes all these ethical constructs, and gives each its due place, then there may be a valid and comprehensive picture of the foundational principles of practical reason (i.e. of the *natural law*).[9] Since societies are biased, one can trace reasons why contradictory customs and mores, even unreasonable or wrongful ones, have come into being in different times and places, or indeed in the same period and locality.[10]

Philosophers recognize that it is an elementary error of logic and of scientific method to say that because people and societies disagree on their practices there is no truth therefore about human action, no right and no wrong.[11] Also, they understand that each person has a vocational responsibility to do right in theory and in life. They also know that one can deliberately do wrong by choice.

It is precisely at this point that another shattering incoherence in the dominant utilitarianism or consequentialism of our age is revealed. If it were possible to add up human behavior in morally significant situations and to identify one of the alternatives as simply promising "greater good" or "lesser evil," then *morally* wrong choice would be *impossible*. For no one can morally and sanely choose what he can see to be simply the lesser good.[12] In fact, human behaviors are not commensurable. Utilitarians and other consequentialists are incorrect in their thinking that human behaviors can be added into tidy summations. Personal choices have to be guided by principles other than the principle of maximization. These other principles, as mentioned above, are: do not be arbitrary; do not be inattentive to any basic human behaviors; do not arbitrarily prefer good-for-oneself to the same human good in other people; do not abdicate your commitments; and, finally, do not unfairly or directly attack any basic good in any human being.[13]

Philosophers know that utilitarianism systematically loses sight of individual people; regrettably, aggregates, not individuals, matter.[14] They also realize that utilitarianism is not merely sinister, but actually unreasonable, devoid of real justification, and arbitrary. They know that when utilitarianism (under whatever guise or name) denies the rights of the unborn, it is really denying the rights of everyone. Consistency will win out. One can expel the order of nature, but it will eventually return to settle the score. Principles may be hidden under public relations or subsumed under language, but they will emerge.

Originally, prolifers predicted with confidence that in a few years what was being said about the unborn would be said about the newly born and the elderly. The operators, public relations men, their philosophers, and decent, complacent people laughed and denied it. But, as predicted, they are recognizing the original prolife assertion. When one sees the courts' reasoning, "right of privacy," which has, on the part of the fetus, a liability to be killed and, on the part of doctors and parents, a duty to kill, we know that consistency is making its demands.[15] Each of us knows that we have to trace the reasoning back to its defective source, change that basis, and expunge that originating error—which was hidden under the erroneous guise that one could decide a question of human rights without deciding who is human.

Philosophers who understand the situation know that it is not just some abstract species-nature which is jeopardized. Quite the contrary, the identity and vocation or destiny of every human being is at stake.

The dead have no humanly discernible vocation to which to respond. Animals, however lovable, have no vocation, and no moral or philosophical responsibilities. Humane quality, on the basis of which we reject racism, is an equality of having-a-vocation, of existing as a being who can be responsible. Natural law is ultimately talk about vocation and responsibility.

The animal rights publicists, who are generally the same people who defend abortion and infanticide, are denying humane quality when they accuse "prolifers" of "speciesism." They are laying foundations of a new range of discrimination and denial of rights more devastating than racism. Also, they are denying the identifying core of each and every person. Our identity is not as a mere temporal locus of sensations and consciousness. Human integrity and identity is to exist as a unique being with a unique personal history.

Everyone knows that history and identity began, for each and every one of us, on the day we were conceived. We inherited a vocation that could be frustrated only from external sources and by some denial of right, which is also a denial of the basic arguments of human reason. For this reason, abortion is one of the most destructive philosophical and practical errors perpetuated by modern culture.

Notes

1. For an earlier working out of this notion, see, e.g., Baruch Brody, *Abortion and the Sanctity of Human Life: A Philosophical View* (Cambridge, Mass.: MIT Press, 1975), 100–115.

2. For the concept of death as the irreversible loss of integrated organic functioning, see Germain Grisez and Joseph M. Boyle Jr., *Life and Death with Liberty and Justice* (Notre Dame: University of Notre Dame Press, 1979), 77. For the thesis that it is organic integration, not *merely* genetic singularity, that is the basis of the human and personal identity of the human being from conception, see *In Vitro Fertilisation: Morality and Public Policy, Evidence Submitted to the Government Committee of Inquiry into Human Fertilisation and Embryology by the Catholic Bishops' Joint Committee on Bio-Ethical Issues on behalf of the Catholic Bishops of Great Britain* (Catholic Information Services, Abbots Langley, England: 1983), para. 9.

3. Aristotle, *De Anima* II, 4:41523–24, 4169.

4. Jeremy Bentham, *An Introduction to the Principles of Morals and Legislation* (1789; ed. J.H. Burns and H.L.A. Hart, New York and London: Methuen, 1982), para. 13, note d (added by Bentham in 1822).

5. G.E.M. Anscombe, "On the Frustration of the Majority by Fulfilment of the Majority's Will," *Analysis* 36 (1976), reprinted in *The Collected Philosophical*

Papers of G.E.M. Anscombe, vol. III, *Ethics, Religion and Politics* (Oxford: Basil Blackwell, 1981), 129; P.T. Geach, *The Virtues* (Cambridge: Cambridge University Press, 1977), 91–94; John Finnis, *Natural Law and Natural Rights* (Oxford and New York: Oxford University Press, 1980), 116.

6. Germain Grisez, "Against Consequentialism," *American Journal of Jurisprudence* 23 (1973): 21; Finnis, *Natural Law and Natural Rights*, 112–15; Finnis, *Fundamentals of Ethics* (Washington, D.C.: Georgetown University Press, 1983), 87–94.

7. Finnis, *Natural Law and Natural Rights*, 85–97, 113–14, 60–90; Finnis, *Fundamentals of Ethics*, 88–89.

8. Finnis, *Natural Law and Natural Rights*, 127; Finnis, *Fundamentals of Ethics*, 76–77.

9. Finnis, *Natural Law and Natural Rights*, chap. V.

10. Ibid., 81–85, 97, 127.

11. Ibid., 79 and sources cited therein.

12. Finnis, *Fundamentals of Ethics*, 89–90.

13. Ibid., 74–75.

14. This critique of utilitarianism is advanced in, e.g., John Rawls, *A Theory of Justice* (Cambridge: Harvard University Press, 1971), 22–24, 27, 181, 183, 187; Robert Nozick, *Anarchy, State and Utopia* (Oxford: Blackwell, 1974), 32–33; H.L.A. Hart, "Between Utility and Rights," 79 *Columbia Law Review*, 828, 829–31 (1979), reprinted in Hart, *Essays in Jurisprudence and Philosophy* (Oxford: Oxford University Press, 1983), 199–202.

15. *See, e.g.*, Turpin v. Sortini 182 Cal. Reptr. 337, 345 (19). *See also* Park v. Chessin, 88 Misc. 2d 222, 387 N.Y.S. 2d 204 (Sup. Ct. 1976), *modified and aff'd*, 60 App. Div. 2d 80, 400 N.Y.S. 2d 110 (1977), *modified subnom.* Becker v. Schwartz, 46 N.Y. 2d 401, 386 N.E. 2d 807, 413 N.Y.S. 2d 895 (1978). As to the genesis of identical twins, see, e.g., William E. May, *Human Existence, Medicine and Ethics* (Chicago: Franciscan Herald, 1977), 100–102; Finnis, "IVF and the Catholic Tradition," *The Month* (February 1984), 55 (commenting on Finnis, *In Vitro Fertilisation*, Evidence submitted on behalf of Catholic Bishops of Great Britain).

PART II

Historical Evaluations of Roe v. Wade and Abortion

JOHN R. CONNERY, S.J.

The Ancients and the Medievals on Abortion: The Consensus the Court Ignored

ONE OF THE most garbled and error-laden parts of *Roe v. Wade* is that section dealing with the history surrounding the morality and legality of the practice of abortion in the Western world. It must not go unchallenged, because it was one of the supportive positions the Supreme Court used regarding the constitutionality of abortion laws in the United States. The Court's version of history is so defective that it serves no useful purpose and the accurate account, far from validating the position of the Court, offers a very convincing argument against it.

The Court's first error was in attempting to take refuge behind what has never been a decisive issue regarding the morality of abortion—the question concerning the beginning of human life. The Court assumed that it would have to establish prenatal beginnings to human life before it could justify legal protection for the fetus.[1] Since philosophers and theologians in the past were unable to agree as to when human life begins, the Court concluded that there was no legal duty to protect the fetus. In fact, it declared that giving such protection would be contrary to the Constitution. Practically speaking, although pretending to distance itself from the controversy, the Court operated on the presumption that the fetus did not become a human being until birth. So it opted for the negative side of what it considered an unresolved debate. We expect to show that there is no historical precedent for making abortion legislation hinge either on the presence of the human soul or on the beginning of human life.

Even in attempting to establish such a connection, the Court failed to ask the proper question.[2] It spoke of "the difficult question of when life begins." Historically, this was never a difficult question. Even Aristotle admitted that life began at conception and said that life existed in the semen antecedent to conception. To Aristotle, however, life at conception came from a vegetative soul.[3] After conception this would eventually be replaced by an animal soul and the latter finally by a human soul. The difficult question became: when was this human soul infused, or when does the fetus become a human being? Aristotle thought this occurred when the fetus was formed—forty days after conception for the male fetus and ninety days for the female fetus. Aristotle also used the criterion of movement; that is, if the aborted fetus showed signs of movement it was considered human. But since this coincided with the time of formation, the time estimate was the same. At any rate, the difficult question was not when life began, but when human life begins.

Historically, the earliest thinking associated the beginnings of human life with breathing; thus, human life did not begin until birth— when the child first began to breathe.[4] Prior to birth the fetus was not an independent human being but part of the mother. Its life was similiar to that of other organs in the woman's body. From the Hebrew version of Exodus 21:22 it would seem that the early Jews adopted this more primitive view. To them the fetus became a fully human being only when it was born. Before that it was part of the mother. Later Jews seemed to adopt the Aristotelian viewpoint (Exodus 21:22, LXX version) associating the beginnings of human life with formation. Human life began when the fetus was formed and could be recognized as a human being. Although many Jews still maintained the earlier view, it was this concept which continued into the Christian era.

Whatever differences of opinion there may have been about the beginnings of human life in the pre-Christian Jewish tradition, they had nothing to do with basic judgments on the morality of abortion. One can argue indirectly that the early Jews considered abortion wrong because of the value they put on fertility and child-bearing and the horror with which they viewed barrenness. It can be argued more directly that abortion was considered wrong from the law itself. In the Book of the Covenant, causing an abortion (even accidentally) was penalized. What is clear in the legislation is that the question regarding the beginning of human life was not a relevant consideration. Even though the Jews held that human life did not begin until birth, they condemned abortion and penalized it. When later Jews accepted the Aristotelian view of the beginning of human life, they still condemned abortion.

With the acceptance of the Aristotelian opinion, time became a factor in grading the crime of abortion. If the abortion took place after formation, it was considered homicide and the penalty was a capital sentence—"a life for a life." If the abortion took place before formation, it was still penalized, although the penalty was not as severe. Whatever the Jews thought about the beginning of human life, whenever abortion was induced they continued to condemn it as immoral. Nor did they hesitate to penalize abortion because it occurred prior to the beginning of human life. Clearly, we can find no justification in Jewish history to warrant the scruples of the Supreme Court when it says that legislation arose from doubt that the fetus is a human being.

There is no historical evidence that associating the beginning of human life with birth ever influenced early Christian thinking. Actually, a number of the early Fathers believed in immediate infusion of the human soul.[5] But the Aristotelian opinion, linking infusion of the human soul to formation, prevailed and continued to be generally accepted until the seventeenth century. However, the existing agreement on delayed animation did not affect the basic judgment about the morality of abortion prior to that time and it continued to be condemned—just as it was by Old Testament Jews.

Because it is no longer possible to speak of law in the same sense as used in antiquity, we must take note of one development that occurred in the Christian era. In the Book of the Covenant there are no neat distinctions between religion, morality, and law. Civil penalties were attached to violations of the Covenant and were looked upon as God's law. Jews, like their neighbors in the Mideast, used the *lex talionis* (the law of retaliation) as their norm for punishing crime. However, the early church, unlike its Jewish forerunners, never functioned as a theocracy and, consequently, never resorted to the kind of penalty civil society uses against wrongdoing.

On the moral level, it is quite clear that the church considered all abortion wrong. In the Didache, a late first century or early second century catechism, there is an explicit condemnation of abortion and infanticide: "Thou shalt not kill the child before birth by abortion or after birth by infanticide."[6] This quote is from a section which was taken from a catechism used by the Jews in proselytizing. It is quite evident that the Jewish condemnation of abortion continued into the Christian era, becoming part of the Christian tradition.[7] So, in this regard, there is an obvious continuity between the Jewish and Christian traditions.

Although the church seldom had recourse to civil penalties, it did impose spiritual penances for wrongdoing or sin; consequently, the mind of the church is better expressed in her penitential legislation. Legislative history is long and involved; but the church constantly condemned abortion as a serious sin. The penances attached to it were initially quite severe and involved exclusion from the church for as long as ten years.[8] Sometimes these penances were imposed for abortion without qualification. Increasingly, lesser penances, although still quite severe, were imposed for abortion before formation. More severe penances were imposed for abortion after formation because it was considered homicide.[9]

Initially, reconciliation was granted only after penances were completed. But as penitential discipline developed in the church, although penances were still attached to sins, absolution or reconciliation was given immediately.[10] The faithful were no longer excluded from communion with the church until their penance was completed. At this time the practice of attaching an "excommunication" to certain serious transgressions began.[11] This special penance was usually attached only to abortion of the formed fetus because this was considered homicide. But abortion at any time was still judged to be a serious sin and was subject to ordinary penitential discipline. Thus, in the Christian era, abortion has always been considered a serious sin even though it may have been induced prior to formation, that is, prior to the time when it was generally thought the human soul was infused. The basic judgment of the morality of abortion never hinged on the presence or absence of the human soul. There is not a single precedent in the entire Christian era for the kind of paralysis regarding protection of the fetus that the Supreme Court judged to be inherent in the inability to establish the beginning of human life.

That the time question was never really relevant to the basic morality of abortion is quite clear from the fact that the Roman Catholic Church, and probably other Christian churches, has never defined the beginning of human life. There is no truth in the Court's statement that the Aristotelian theory of mediate animation continued to be "official Roman Catholic dogma" until the middle of the nineteenth century and that immediate animation is now the "official belief of the Catholic Church."[12] The church has never declared such a dogma or belief. Her consistent condemnation of abortion has always been independent of the question of the beginning of human life. The only conclusion one can come to on the level of church teaching is that the human soul is infused sometime prior to birth. Such teaching would not be sufficiently precise for legal purposes.[13] Although the church did not teach the Aristotelian opinion as doctrine, her penal legislation simply followed the accepted thinking of the time.

The basic argument against abortion has always been that the conceptus has a human destiny and this is what makes it sacred. Whatever one may consider its early status to be, it has this destiny, right from the beginning, to be a human being. As Tertullian said: "He is a man who will be a man."[14] Without hesitation, based on this kind of argument, the church condemned abortion. Over the centuries, the argument against abortion has never been based on an assumption of immediate infusion of the human soul.

The Court claims that a large segment of the Protestant community held that life did not begin before birth.[15] I know of no evidence to support this claim. I can understand how the Jews might consider it part of their tradition, but the Protestants have no such tradition. They come out of a tradition which for centuries followed the Aristotelian opinion. Moreover, the more primitive view was based largely on the supposition that the fetus was part of the mother until birth. With our current knowledge of fetology, there is absolutely no basis for holding such a position. And the recent achievement of *in vitro* fertilization makes it an obvious anachronism. As an authority on genetics recently testified, the fetus is no more part of the mother than an astronaut is part of the space machine in which he is carried.[16]

For some curious reason the Court never explicitly asks the basic question about the morality of abortion in the Judeo-Christian tradition. Yet, the answer to this question is the key to the whole legal tradition in the Western world. The answer is that in the Judeo-Christian tradition abortion has been consistently condemned as immoral.

Without in any way confusing morality with law, it can be said that this is the fundamental reason behind the laws enacted against it. This does not imply that everything that is immoral should be a matter for penal legislation. But what is immoral may also be against the welfare of the community. Thus, homicide has always been penalized and abortion, even when not classified as homicide, has always been considered analogous to it in the sense that it is harmful to the community as well as the fetus. This is precisely why abortion legislation has been common in the Western world.

Roe v. Wade considers it apparent that prior to the mid-nineteenth century abortion was viewed with less disfavor than afterward. It interprets this to mean that, at that time, a woman enjoyed "a substantially broader right to terminate a pregnancy." Becoming more specific, it says that "with respect to the early stage of pregnancy, and very possibly without such limitation, the opportunity (to choose abortion) was present in this country well into the nineteenth century."[17]

It is not easy to handle this kind of scatter-shot claim but this much can be said. In the whole Judeo-Christian tradition abortion was considered immoral and looked upon with disfavor. Far from being a substantial right in the eighteenth century, there is no evidence that any such right to abortion existed. The fact that abortion was considered immoral would preclude any such right. Even if the Court were speaking of some kind of "civil right," it is doubtful that any jurist would allow one to conclude its existence automatically from the absence of penal legislation. Certainly, there is no explicit mention of any such right.

Implications, well into the nineteenth century, from the absence of legislation against early abortion can be grossly misleading. The Court actually makes the claim that abortion laws "are not of ancient or even of common law origin."[18] The truth is that there has been abortion legislation in the Western world since the end of the second century. It goes back to an early third century application of the Cornelian law (de sicariis) to abortion by the Roman jurist, Julius Paulus.[19] According to Paulus, if anyone gave to another an abortifacient (poculum abortionis), he would be sentenced to work in the mines or be exiled and lose part of his property. If the victim died, a capital sentence would be imposed. A decree by Severus and Antoninus also attached a penalty for a self-induced abortion; any woman inducing an abortion upon herself would be exiled.[20]

There is nothing in these laws about early or late abortion. Thus, one must conclude that the penalty was incurred whenever the abortion took place. It must be admitted that until recent times there was no certain way of detecting early pregnancies. There were indeed "signs" that people have always used, but none of them were unambiguous.[21] One must also acknowledge that it was difficult to detect and, therefore to prove, early abortion. But inability to prosecute early abortions because of evidentiary problems should not be confused with toleration or acceptance.

One may want to argue that the concern of the Cornelian law when applied to abortion was for the mother and that the concern about an abortion caused by the woman herself was for the rights of the husband.[22] Certainly, there was concern about the mother in a case where she was deceived by another. But the law clearly applied as well to a case in which the mother knowingly took the drug. But even if the concern in this legislation was primarily for the mother, and not the father, it must have arisen because the fetus was considered something of value and its loss a tragedy in their lives. In reality, the concern for the fetus became more explicit when later abortions began to be classified as homicide. Even though early abortions may not have been classified as homicide, there is reason to believe that the concern for the fetus in these instances was serious.

What is important from our viewpoint is that these laws came into existence at a time when Roman law still associated human life with birth and when the fetus was considered part of the mother before birth.[23] The basis for such legislation may have been a well-known legal axiom: *conceptus pro iam nato habetur*.[24] According to this axiom, whenever some benefit to the fetus was at stake it was to be treated like a person already born. Whatever the reason may have been, the Romans were in no way inhibited in legislating against abortion by the fact that the fetus was not considered a human being until birth. Again, the reluctance of the Supreme Court to acknowledge abortion legislation is historically unwarranted.

We are uncertain when the Aristotelian opinion, which associated the beginning of human life with formation, was introduced into Roman law. Accursio, a thirteenth century Italian jurist, in his gloss on Paulus seems to have been the first claiming that the distinction between the formed and unformed fetus applied to the law.[25] As noted above, the distinction appeared much earlier in the penitential discipline of the church. The practical consequence of applying the distinction to the law was that capital punishment was imposed for abortion of the formed fetus. Since then, the distinction became part of Roman law and was the basis for imposing capital punishment for abortion performed after formation. Accursio made no comment about abortion before formation, so it was presumed that the traditional punishment of forced labor, fine, or exile was imposed for such abortions. Also, we are quite certain that the forty/ninety-day estimate was used for the time of formation and, therefore, of animation with a human soul.

This distinction was continually applied into the seventeenth century and capital punishment remained the punishment for abortion of a formed fetus. An exception to the law did develop where abortion was permissible to save the life of the mother; however, for other abortions of a formed fetus, capital punishment was imposed.

Our own law is based on English common law and not Roman law. So the status of abortion in English common law may be more pertinent to our tradition. If we look at English common law, we find a close tie to the general Western tradition, which is undoubtedly due to the fact that both stem from the Judeo-Christian culture: More specifically, the bond is between Sir Henry Bracton and the Spanish jurist, Raymond of Penaforte.[26] Bracton's suggested penalties for abortion parallel quite closely Raymond's response in his *De Penitentia*.[27] Actually, the English would find nothing new in Bracton's assimilation of Penaforte's distinction between the formed and unformed fetus because this distinction was already seen as early as the seventh century English penitentials found in Canon law.[28] What may have been new was the application of the distinction to civil law. As we have already seen, it was at about this time that Accursio first applied it to Roman law. From the end of the second century the punishment in the Roman law was the same for all abortion. While severe, it did not go as far as capital punishment. With the application of the distinction to Roman law, however, abortion of the formed fetus was classified as homicide and merited capital punishment. In applying the distinction to English law, Bracton may have been the first to do for English law what Accursio did for Roman law.

But it should be pointed out that Bracton was preoccupied with classifying the abortion of a formed and animated fetus as homicide. He said nothing explicitly about abortion of the unformed fetus. There is no justification for the conclusion that no penalty was imposed on this kind of abortion. If the Roman (civil) law was used as a model, there is reason for believing that the contrary is true.

It is clear that during Bracton's era English common law classified abortion of the animated fetus as homicide. Presumably, this was understood in the traditional sense, namely, forty/ninety days after conception. This classification is confirmed by the anonymous judge whose commentary, published under the name *Fleta*, included steriliz-ing potions as well as abortifacients.[29]

At the end of the sixteenth century, English jurists began question-ing the capital sentence imposed on abortion. Eventually, this sentence disappeared from civil law. Sir Edward Coke argued that abortion would not constitute murder unless the child was born alive and then died as the result of the abortion.[30] Blackstone, the great eighteenth century jurist, followed Coke and said that abortion is not murder unless the fetus is delivered alive and then dies of the injuries inflicted.[31] Coke calls abortion a great "misprision" and says that "so horrible an offense should not go unpunished." Blackstone calls it a "very heinous misdemeanor." The expression seems contradictory if one understands "misdemeanor" in the modern sense of the term. To these eminent jurists, however, this was not some minor offense. It bordered on, but was not, a capital crime. And the penalty, though less than "life for life," might be quite severe, e.g., loss of a member, confiscation of property, or a life in prison.[32]

In spite of the historical testimony of Coke and Blackstone, the United States Supreme Court makes the claim that prior to the nineteenth century abortion of the quickened fetus went unpunished. The claim is based on a study by Cyril C. Means, Jr., who charges that Coke "invented" the crime of aborting a quickened fetus and that Blackstone uncritically followed him.[33] It is not within the scope of this article to offer a full critique of Means's hasty assertions, but his conclusions are based on very meager evidence. Consequently, one must turn to a more plausible interpretation that does less violence to historical truth. Abortion of the animated (quickened) fetus was classified as homicide centuries before Blackstone, Coke, or Bracton, and the classification was based on the judgment that the human soul was infused at the time of formation. Neither Coke nor Blackstone "invented" this. If they "invented" anything, it was the requirement that the fetus be alive after being aborted and then die from the injuries. This was not the basis for the original classification of homicide. Even for Coke and Blackstone this may have been more for evidentiary than for classification purposes. Practically speaking, what they did was to reduce the penalty for causing the abortion of a fetus that was formed and therefore animated (quickened), but dead at birth. The problem with this position is that the death before or at birth may have been attributable to the severity of the violence. In that event the requirement would seem to put a premium on greater violence.

More important from the viewpoint of our study is the fact that the position taken by Coke and Blackstone, apart from the above requirement, is consistent with the entire history of the subject. Means's inaccurate position that abortion of the "quickened" fetus went unpunished prior to the nineteenth century requires a complete rewriting of actual history.

Another development found in Blackstone was the association of "quickening" with the time when the fetus began to stir in the womb.[34] The term initially seems to have been the translation of the Latin term *fetus animatus*, referring to the fetus in whom the human soul was already infused. As we have seen, this was initially associated with the formation of the fetus and took place forty/ninety days after conception. "Quickening," in the sense in which Blackstone used it, occurred much later, not until the fourteenth to sixteenth week; so it had nothing to do with either the common estimate of the infusion time of the human soul or the time when the fetus was thought to become a human being. But it did replace the common time estimate in English law, as well as in early statutory law in this country. The understanding of "quickening" in Blackstone seemed to serve evidentiary purposes rather than the original purpose of the term, which was to indicate the beginning of human life.

Although Coke and Blackstone discuss the abortion issue, they say nothing explicitly about abortion before "quickening." Their concern seemed to be chiefly with the relation of abortion to murder and, hence, to capital punishment. Coming to any conclusion about abortion before quickening from what they said would be risky. *Roe v.*

Wade acquired this risk in drawing the conclusion from their silence that there was no penal law against abortion prior to "quickening."

Whatever may have been the development regarding the notion of quickening in English common law, the whole distinction would soon give way to a more sophisticated understanding of conception and fetal development.[35] This new thinking, both philosophical and scientific in origin, began with the discovery of ovulation and, eventually, of the ovum and fertilization, and led to immediate animation as a conclusion. In other words, both philosophers and physicians began to hold that human life was present virtually from the time of conception. It was easy to argue delayed animation when one thought that semen gradually turned into blood and then into flesh and bone and eventually into a human form. But with the discovery of fertilization, and particularly with the discovery of the genetic makeup of the fertilized ovum, it became quite clear that something new was present from the very time of fertilization. Delayed animation made less and less sense, and both philosophers and physicians began to argue in favor of very early, if not immediate, animation with a human soul. The distinction between formed and unformed fetuses gradually began to lose any meaning and eventually disappeared from both civil and ecclesiastical penal law. Today it is safe to say that the arguments for immediate animation are better than those for animation at any later date, although we should never expect the physical sciences to find the human soul. In summary, we can accurately assert the following:

1. Early Jews condemned abortion as immoral even though they believed that the fetus did not become a human being until birth. They also imposed legal penalties on abortion.
2. Later Jews imposed capital punishment on abortion after formation (homicide) at a time when the Aristotelian opinion about the beginnings of human life was not accepted by all Jews.
3. Even though the controversy about the beginnings of human life was never definitively settled, abortion continued to be generally condemned as immoral throughout the Christian era.
4. Throughout the Christian era, even after the Aristotelian opinion was generally accepted, penances continued to be imposed for abortions before formation.
5. Though the church, in the Christian era, never defined the beginning of human life, abortion after forty or ninety days was treated as homicide in the penitential discipline of the church.
6. Despite the fact that the fetus was not considered a human being until birth, Roman civil law from the end of the second century penalized abortion.

7. In the later Roman law, abortion after formation was punished as homicide even though the Aristotelian opinion on which this was based was still not definitive.

In full view of all the available evidence, one must conclude that the position taken by the Supreme Court—that one cannot legislate against abortion unless and until one can show that the fetus is a human being—has no historical precedent.

Notes

1. The Court admitted that the state might have "interests" in protecting potential life in the fetus, but these would be overridden by the woman's right to privacy. The latter would be "compelling" reasons for giving some protection to the fetus after viability, although later decisions seemed to void such reasons. And, even if they had not, the health of the mother would easily become a general overriding reason.

2. Roe v. Wade, 410 U.S. 113, 159 (1973).

3. Aristotle, "On the Generation of Animals," Book 2, 3, in W.D. Ross, ed., *The Works of Aristotle* (Oxford: Clarendon Press, 1912), vol. 5, 736. See also, Aristotle, "On the History of Animals," Book 3, 7, in Ross, op. cit., vol. 4, 583 (1910). *Roe*, 410 U.S. at 134, states that there was agreement that the fetus prior to formation was part of the mother. This was not true of Aristotle and his followers.

4. This thinking prevailed in Stoic philosophy, and was the basis for Roman law, but with the modification mentioned in text accompanying notes 22–24, infra.

5. See John R. Connery, *Abortion: The Development of the Roman Catholic Perspective* (Chicago: Loyola Univ. Press, 1977), 52.

6. J.A. Kleist, trans., Didache 18, in Johannes Quasten and Joseph C. Plumpe, *Ancient Christian Writers* (Westminster, Md.: The Newman Press, 1948). See also Epistle of Barnabas, in Kleist, op. cit., 64.

7. J.P. Audet, *La Didachè, Instructions des Apôtres* (Paris: 1958), 188–89.

8. The first legislation against abortion is found in a council held at Elvira (c. A.D. 305) in Spain (Canon 63, Mansi, ed., *Amplissima Collectio Conciliorum*, vol. 1, 16). Because of its severity (a lifetime penance), it did not survive. Shortly after, the Council of Ancyra (A.D. 314) imposed a ten-year penance for abortion (Canon 21, Mansi, op. cit., vol. 2, 514). This became the common canonical penance, although a seven-year penance was also established.

9. The distinction, although found in the early Fathers, seems to have appeared first in penitential practice in the penitential books which came from Ireland and England, but it remained part of penitential discipline for many centuries.

10. Absolution began to be imparted immediately after confession at the end of the first millenium or the beginning of the second millenium.

11. Special "excommunication" was introduced into church discipline in the twelfth or thirteenth century.

12. *Roe*, 410 U.S. at 160–161.

13. The general conclusion that in the mind of the church the soul is infused before birth can be inferred from the condemnation by Innocent XI (1679) of the proposition that it is probable that the fetus is without a rational soul as long as it remains in the uterus and that it begins to have one only when it is born. Adolph Schoenmetzer, S.J., Henry Denziger, *Enchiridion Synbolorum* (New York: Herder, 1963), 461.

14. Tertullian, *Apology*, trans. T.R. Glover, Loeb Classical Reprint (London: 1966), 49.

15. *Roe*, 410 U.S. at 160.

16. Testimony of Dr. Jerome Lejeune, Professor of Fundamental Genetics, Medical College of Paris, France, April 23, 1981. *Hearing before The Subcomm. on Separation of Powers of the Sen. Comm. on the Judiciary on S. 158*, 97th Cong., 1st Sess. (Committee Print 1982), pp. 9–10.

17. 410 U.S. at 140–41.

18. 410 U.S. at 129.

19. S.P. Scott, ed. *Corpus Iuris Civilis*, 17 vols. (New York: AMS Press Inc., 1973), vol. 1, 326, *Opinions of Julius Paulus*, Book V, Title 23, para. 8; *Corpus Iuris Civilis*, op. cit., Digests or Pandects of Justinian, Book 48, Title 19, para. 38, sec. 5.

20. *Corpus Iuris Civilis*, op. cit., vol. 10, 328, Digests or Pandects, Book 47, Title 11, para. 4. It is referred to as the law *Divus*. In the Digest, *Corpus Iuris Civilis*, op. cit., vol. 11, 61, Book 48, Title 8, para.8, no mention is made of the husband.

21. Paolo Zacchia, an early seventeenth century physician, said that it is most difficult to detect a pregnancy during the first four months, but easier afterwards. Paolo Zacchia, *Questionum Medico-legalium*, Book 1, Title 1, Part 1 (Lyons: 1701).

22. *Roe*, 410 U.S. at 130, makes the claim that the concern of these laws was for the rights of the husband. This is true of the original Divus decree, but it is certainly not the whole truth. Cyril Means states that the U.S. abortion laws of the nineteenth century were aimed at the protection of the mother rather than the fetus. Means, *The Phoenix of Abortional Freedom: Is A Penumbral Or Ninth Amendment Right About To Rise From The Nineteenth Century Legislative Ashes of Fourteenth Century Common Law Liberty?* 17 N. Y. L. Forum 335, 382–391 (1971). Again, this is not the whole truth. Historically, abortion laws from Exodus to the present, while concerned with the welfare of the mother, punished abortion even when no harm was done to the mother.

23. *Corpus Iuris Civilis*, op. cit., vol. 6, 43–53, Digest, Book 25, Title 4, para. 1, sec. 1.

24. *Corpus Iuris Civilis*, op. cit., vol. 2, 228, Digest, Book 1, Title 5, Para. 7; Book 26.

25. Accursio, *Glossa in Divus*, in *Corpus Iuris Civilis*, Digest, Book 47, Title 11, para. 4. ("exilium"). See Accursio, *Digestum novum Pandectarum* (Lyons: 1557), p. 949.

26. Raymond of Penaforte, *Summa de penitentia et matrimonio* 2, 1, 6 (Rome: 1603).

27. 2 George Woodbine, ed., Bracton, *De legibus et consuetudinibus Angliae*, trans. Samuel E. Thorne (Cambridge, Mass.: Harvard Univ. Press, 1968), 341.

28. The distinction will be found in the seventh century penitentials of Theodore of Canterbury. H. Wasserschleben, *Die Bussordnungen der abendlandischen Kirche* (Graz: 1958), 155.

29. 2 H.G. Richardson and G.O. Sayles, eds., *Fleta* (London: Selden Society, 1955), 60–61.

30. Edward Coke, *Third Part of the Institutes of the Laws of England*, chap. 7.

31. 4 William Blackstone, *Commentaries on the Laws of England* (Chicago: Univ. of Chicago Press, 1979), p. 198. For the meaning of *misprision*, see 4 Blackstone, op. cit., p. 119 ff.

32. Coke, op. cit., p. 36, 39–40.

33. Means, op. cit., 346.

34. 1 Blackstone, op. cit., p. 125–126.

35. Delayed animation began to be questioned seriously in the early seventeenth century. *See* Connery, op. cit., 168 ff. For a full discussion of the born-alive rule and the quickening doctrine under the common law, *see* Forsythe, *Homicide of the Unborn Child: The Born Alive Rule and Other Legal Anachronisms*, 21 Val. U.L. Rev. No. 3 (to be published, 1987), and Horan, Forsythe, and Grant, *Two Ships Passing in the Night: An Interpretavist Review of the White-Stevens Colloquy on* Roe v. Wade, 6 St. L.Pub. L. rev. 43, 91-106 (1987).

JOSEPH W. DELLAPENNA

Abortion and the Law: Blackmun's Distortion of the Historical Record

HISTORY HAS ALWAYS had many uses. It has been shaped to fit preconceptions, or to express ill-considered modern prejudices. It has been called upon to justify varied and contradictory claims. History has even sometimes been used in the search for truth. No wonder then that history is presently out of fashion as an important mode of legal analysis, or as Henry Ford said, "history is bunk."[1] And yet, where else is one to begin in understanding a 200-year-old Constitution or a 115-year-old amendment?[2]

There are additional reasons why the history of abortion fascinates those who study and debate the merits of the question. The very suddenness of the dramatic turnaround in public opinion and legal institutions itself demands an historical explanation—which, it is hoped, will help to bring about a new consensus on what has proven to be one of the most intractable and yet intense issues to agitate our own and other societies.[3] Finally, many suspect that understanding the story of abortion as a social question will teach important lessons about the proper relationship between law or social policy and prevalent morality.[4]

So compelling are the reasons to consider the history of abortion that nearly everyone who writes or speaks about abortion includes at least a summary version of the history. As with nearly everything else relating to abortion, these histories generally divide into two hostile camps, between which there appears to be little communication. Unfortunately, there appears to be little communication between them. The competing versions exhibit the characteristics of a poor historical methodology.

Largely due to the imprimatur of the Supreme Court, the more widely known and most widely discussed versions have been those of the prochoice camp. This is reason enough to reconsider carefully the interpretation of abortion history in *Roe v. Wade*.[5] This version is important because it undergirds the Supreme Court's appraisal of the interests to be considered in a court's decision as to whether an abortion statute is constitutional. It also determines how the constitutional balance will be struck.[6] An attempt must be made to portray accurately the history of abortion, both to bring about a reconsideration of *Roe v. Wade* and to avoid making further fundamental mistakes based on erroneous historical premises.

I. Justice Blackmun's History of Abortion

JUSTICE BLACKMUN DEVOTED more than half of his majority opinion in *Roe v. Wade* to the history of abortion.[7] In the course of his analysis, Justice Blackmun concluded that "it now appear[s] doubtful that abortion was ever established as a common law crime."[8] For his opponents, it is relatively easy to demonstrate that leading scholars of the common law, beginning as early as the thirteenth century, condemned abortion as a crime.[9] Nonlawyers will probably conclude that abortion was a crime at common law. To a contemporary lawyer, however trained in the common law, Blackmun's conclusion seems reasonable. To lawyers, the law is what courts do in fact. If no judicial decisions can be found for punishing such a crime, then there was no crime. In fact, virtually no precedents can be found. Thus, the challenge is to explain why abortion should be considered a crime. Generally, this challenge has been ignored by opponents of legalized abortion; they have been content to rely on the secondary, scholarly sources while usually ignoring the lack of clear judicial precedent for treating abortion as a crime.[10]

Justice Blackmun's own attempt to reconstruct the history of abortion is a curious rendition of various attitudes expressed about abortion from ancient times to the present. He made little or no attempt to discover underlying causes for the changes that he noted, and he did not attempt to verify whether the purported abortion techniques were or could be used in the manner asserted. Rather, Justice Blackmun presumed that relatively safe and popular abortion techniques have always been available; however, he also assumed that these techniques were mysteriously unavailable in the nineteenth century.[11]

Besides being strangely unconcerned about the technical realities of abortion at various points in history, Justice Blackmun's rendition of history was very selective in what he chose to report or stress. Thus, Justice Blackmun filled three pages discussing the role of the Hippocratic oath in ancient times.[12] This oath prohibits physicians from administering a pessary—or a vaginal suppository ostensibly laced with drugs capable of inducing abortion.[13] He concluded that the oath was merely "a Pythagorean manifesto and not the expression of an absolute standard of medical morality."[14] Having apparently discredited the oath, he said not one word about the centuries from medieval to modern times when the oath was accepted throughout Europe and America as the "absolute standard of medical morality." Indeed, he entirely disregarded any historical experiences with abortion outside England or America—leaving the distinct impression that other cultures never moved beyond the mixed, ancient attitudes. Nor did Justice Blackmun consider why the Hippocratic oath addressed only pessaries.[15]

Justice Blackmun's rendition of the Anglo-American experience with abortion is equally eclectic and impressionistic. He began by accepting the classic statement of the early common law that abortion before "quickening" was no crime.[16] However, he then proceeded to raise substantial doubts about the contrary claim that abortions after quickening were crimes (at least misdemeanors) at common law by stressing the lack of actual judicial precedent.[17] Justice Blackmun even went so far as to suggest that Sir Edward Coke's famous statement that abortion after quickening was "a great misprision, and no murder" was an intentional misstatement of the law designed to foist his own peculiar views on an unsuspecting nation.[18] He did not explain how this was accomplished if Coke's views were unpopular; nor did he evaluate why this dictum was accepted by people for two centuries.

He presented the enactment of English statutes prohibiting abortion as a clear break with an uncertain past. The various statutes enacted from 1803 to 1861, progressively tightened restrictions on abortion. Cursorily, Justice Blackmun introduced these changes with no attempt to inquire as to the reasons for them.[19] Conversely, he gave more attention to twentieth century statutory and other changes whereby abortions became more permitted under English law; again there was no attempt to explain or justify the changes.[20]

Justice Blackmun's approach to retelling the American experience was markedly different in that he did attempt to explain why changes occurred. After briefly discussing some of the significant changes in American laws relating to abortion, Blackmun engaged in a prolonged discussion of the medical profession's changing attitudes toward abortion.[21] He discovered that the American Medical Association (AMA) was at the forefront of the antiabortion movement in the

nineteenth century and that both the AMA and the American Public
Health Association were in the forefront of the abortion reform
movement after 1967. Despite his own quotations of nineteenth
century AMA documents that the issue at stake was the protection of
the unborn human life, Justice Blackmun concluded that these
nineteenth century laws were designed to protect the health of the
mother from the dangerous abortion techniques then in use, not to
protect prenatal life.[22]

In summing up, Justice Blackmun asserted that abortion was not a
crime in the United States before the early nineteenth century, that
the early laws did not punish abortion before quickening, and that
abortion generally did not become illegal throughout the United
States until after the Civil War.[23] He even appeared to suggest that the
process of declaring most abortions serious crimes was not completed
until after 1950.[24]

Thus, Justice Blackmun painted a picture of abortion as a socially
and legally acceptable procedure in England and America until the
recent and brief aberration of the late nineteenth century and early
twentieth century abortion statutes. One might easily conclude that
England, the United States and other nations were simply coming to
their senses and reverting to the wisdom of earlier ages by repealing or
otherwise eliminating laws restricting access to abortion. The entire
process could be seen as another example of the rise and fall of
Comstockery, albeit with more justification in the concerns about
maternal health.

Careful reading of Justice Blackmun's history of abortion shows
that there was never a consensus in favor of abortion. Given the
changes in laws relating to abortion, one searches in vain for
explanations as to why. Justice Blackmun only offered a discussion of
attitudinal changes among professional groups; he made no effort to
consider why these attitudes changed. He ignored the proffered
explanation of desire to protect unborn humans in favor of a view of a
desire to protect the life or health of mothers, apparently without
considering why this became a concern in the nineteenth century.[25]
There is a notable lack of inquiry into the actual incidence or
techniques of abortion at any relevant time.

In short, Justice Blackmun provided no method to compare the
reality of abortion and the consequent historical attitudes to the
reality and attitudes of today.[26] This may explain his failure to
articulate clearly his own conclusions regarding the significance of the
history he told, and his consequent inability to relate his subsequent
analysis explicitly back to the history he examined.[27]

II. Other Prochoice Histories of Abortion

JUSTICE BLACKMUN DID not devise his version of history from the original sources. Rather, he relied on the work of Cyril Means, a law professor and legal counsel for the National Association for the Repeal of Abortion Laws (NARAL), now the National Abortion Rights Action League.[28] According to Means, abortion was never a crime at common law. Statements to the contrary in the seventeenth and eighteenth century cases were explained as mistaken statements or deliberate distortions by misguided persons intent on incorporating their personal morality into law.[29] Means then asserted that the nineteenth century statutes, which prohibited some (and later, all) forms of abortion, were merely attempts to protect the health of mothers, as at that time abortions were very dangerous, with one-third or more resulting in maternal death.[30] Abortions gradually became safer and by 1940 an early abortion was apparently safer than childbirth.[31] Means argued that developing technology rendered the nineteenth century abortion laws unnecessary to protect maternal health and thus unconstitutional; they no longer served any rational purpose.[32]

The only significant difference between Means's arguments and the rendition offered by Justice Blackmun was the justice's additional discussion of attitudes in the medical profession in both ancient and modern times.[33] The significant questions *not* asked in Justice Blackmun's opinion are all presaged by similar gaps in Means's articles. Justice Blackmun clearly drew his appraisal of the interests involved in the abortion laws from Means's arguments.[34] Strangely then, Justice Blackmun expressly repudiated the Means thesis in the companion case to *Roe v. Wade*.[35]

This contradiction may explain the oddly tentative tone of Justice Blackmun's version of history, which consisted mostly of rambling ruminations merely expressing theories and doubts and reaching no particular conclusions. But these contradictions have hardly been noticed by defenders of *Roe v. Wade*, who embraced Means's thesis through the medium of Blackmun's opinion.[36]

After *Roe v. Wade*'s version of abortion history evoked scathing criticism, the Ford and Rockefeller Foundations funded a major study of the subject by historian James Mohr. Mohr produced a more sophisticated version of the Means-Blackmun thesis. As a result, Mohr's version of the history has largely displaced the earlier works in prochoice writings on abortion.[37]

Mohr made two major methodological decisions which greatly eased his task of supporting the view that nineteenth century abortion laws

were aberrational. First, by beginning with 1800, he absolved himself
from having to resolve the controversies over the correct interpretation of the sparse and uncertain English materials.[38] This also
permitted Mohr to begin his history with a relatively advanced state of
abortion technology as the baseline of his evaluation of why attitudes
toward abortion changed.

Mohr's second major decision was to use current understanding of
the abortion process to evaluate historical attitudes toward, and laws
about, abortion. Thus, he willingly claimed that people really did not
disapprove of early abortions, even though he described the people at
the time as not understanding that the procedures, which we now
think of as being abortions, were abortions at all.[39]

One further quirk in Mohr's analysis was his willingness to accept
the technological claims of abortionists at face value. Thus he
described a number of herbal remedies for "obstructed menses"
without ever discussing the effects of ingesting any of the substances;
in each case the remedies would have been suicidal.[40] Mohr's own
expressed conclusions that abortions were not particularly dangerous
"by medical standards of the day" is contradicted on the next page by
his acknowledgment that this applied only to operative techniques,
not to widely used pharmaceutical or injury techniques.[41]

Mohr believed that abortion was not illegal until the mid-nineteenth
century.[42] He attributed the hardening of attitudes toward abortion in
the nineteenth century to several causes: concern about maternal
health;[43] distress over falling birthrates among the middle and upper
classes;[44] and a "moral prejudice" in favor of preserving what
physicians had come to think of as human life before birth.[45] But as a
central consideration, Mohr identifies the prohibition of abortion as
serving to promote the professional dominance of the newly organized AMA over its less qualified and less organized competitors in the
delivery of health care services.[46] Although Mohr never clearly
identifies these competitors, they were mostly midwives and woman
physicians.

The common thread in these versions of abortion history begins
with the claim that abortion was neither illegal nor even much
frowned upon prior to 1800. By this view, the laws prohibiting
abortion after the mid-nineteenth century were not only an aberration, but were also rooted in unworthy causes. The only reasonably
acceptable purpose for antiabortion laws was to protect maternal
health. By this theory, if abortion became safer than childbearing, the
laws prohibiting abortion became wholly irrational and unworthy of
continued vitality.

III. Prolife Versions of Abortion History

DESPITE A CERTAIN seductive appeal of the several prochoice theories, each of them depends upon a clear disregard and even distortion of numerous facts about abortion in history. Some of these defects are obvious to all but the most casual or favorably predisposed reader. First, casting aspersions on the motives of those who first announced the criminality of abortion does not alter the fact that there is respectable authority for the criminality of abortion before the nineteenth century.[47] Second, the claim that the only purpose of the nineteenth century statutes was to protect the life of the mother or to advance the organizational interests of the AMA ignores the far more common statements in legislatures, courts, and the press that the purpose of these laws was to protect the life of the fetus: a concern most strongly felt after critical discoveries in embryology.[48] Finally, even if one assumes that the prochoice versions of history are correct, no one has explained why a law passed for one purpose cannot acquire new purposes as knowledge changes.[49]

There are additional, more subtle matters not taken into account by the Means-Blackmun-Mohr theses of abortion history. None of them seriously examined the technologies available during the various historical periods of social and legal response to abortion. Neither did they consider what the real effects of abortions were during the period when, according to them, the practice of abortion was both popular and safe.[50] Thus, their theories cannot begin to consider what links exist between variations in attitudes toward abortion and changes in the available technology, or any other relevant social or cultural trends. They consider the process of shifting attitudes as merely changes of fashion, taste, arbitrary prejudice, or self-serving manipulation.[51]

Given the concerns disregarded or distorted in the prochoice versions of history, it was to be expected that a diametrically opposed history would emerge. This prolife version is most clearly and succinctly presented in the work of Professor Robert Byrn.[52] According-ing to this school, abortion has always been considered a heinous crime except in barbaric societies. Christian societies especially abhorred abortion. In particular, Byrn sought to prove that the sparse and often obscure common law materials demonstrated that abortion in England, at least after quickening, was treated as a serious crime. He treated the quickening rule itself as resulting from problems in proving that the child was alive, or had been killed by the abortion.[53] In the prolife view, the nineteenth century statutes were intended to clarify and reemphasize the criminality of abortion, and to eliminate the quickening rule.[54] Byrn thus saw twentieth century reforms as a capitulation to savagery and immorality, and explicable only by substitution of a "quality of life" ethic, more attuned to Nazism, for the traditional Judeo-Christian "sanctity of life" ethic.[55]

The problems with this view are several.[56] Before the nineteenth century, authoritative pronouncements from any source are sparse. It is almost impossible to find evidence of someone actually punished for an abortion before 1800. Finally, the nineteenth century abortion statutes never treated abortion as the equivalent of murder. Either fetuses were not seen as fully human, or the "sanctity of life" ethic was never as fully accepted as its proponents claim, an opinion supported by other evidence, such as the continued use of the death penalty or societal indifference to many life-endangering situations.

IV. What Actually Happened?

ANY BENEFICIAL AND informative history of abortion must account for all the facts and cogently answer all pertinent questions about the experience of abortion. The following summary of my own findings, published in greater detail elsewhere, will focus on the English and American experience with abortion.[57]

Anglo-American law relative to abortion has gone through four phases. These stages were shaped, in part, by the evolution of social and legal institutions in England and the United States and, in major part, by developments in the medical technology for performing abortions. These phases were:

I.	1200–1600:	Abortion relegated to the ecclesiastical courts.
II.	1600–1800:	Jurisdiction over abortion captured by the royal courts.
III.	1800–1960:	Statutory prohibition of abortion.
IV.	1960-present:	Legalization of abortion.

The precise dates of these phases vary from jurisdiction to jurisdiction, but for everywhere in the common law world these are close approximations.[58]

A. THE EARLY PERIOD

FROM 1200 TO 1600, jurisdiction over abortion was usually relegated to ecclesiastical courts, as were other matters which today pass without comment as the proper subject of secular law.[59] When occasional abortion cases did come before royal courts, the acts were considered wrong, but offenders went unpunished. Ecclesiastical court records during this period are equally devoid of actual punishments for abortion. Even secondary sources, legal or medical treatises or doctrinal pronouncements by church leaders, treated abortion more hypothetically than as a real problem. This is the key to understanding the seeming paradox between a universal condemnation of abortion and a failure to punish the act itself.[60]

During this period, techniques to induce abortions were either magical, and hence punishable as witchcraft (whether they were successful or not), or extremely crude invasions of the woman's body, likely to be fatal to the woman as well as to the fetus.[61] In the few cases where an abortionist was punished, it was for killing the mother. In fact, there is no evidence of voluntary abortion during this time. Abortions, if they occurred, seem to have resulted from assaults upon women rather than by their choice.[62] Even then, abortion prosecutions were hampered by ignorance of medical knowledge about the gestation process.[63] The net result of these circumstances was that abortion was rare and the law did not have to deal with it because hanging the abortionist for killing the mother was sufficient punishment for the few cases that did arise.

If abortions were rare in early times, then one should ask about the fate of unwanted children. The answer is infanticide. This conclusion is well supported by the legal, ecclesiastical, and medical literature of the times.[64] The killing of small infants remained a common occurrence throughout Western Europe into the nineteenth century. In contrast to the sparse attention given to abortion by legal institutions during this time, much attention was devoted to infanticide; and over the centuries new approaches were devised in an effort to eradicate the practice, but with only temporary, if any, success. This extended to the creation of legal presumptions that any dead infant had been killed by its parents or that a parent who concealed the death of a child had killed it.[65]

Some lawyers even argued that there was a legal right to "suppress" an unwanted child.[66] Ironically, the first movement in Europe which might be called feminist was a seventeenth century anti-infanticide crusade in France. It could be called "feminist" since girl babies were principal targets of infanticide; boys outnumbered girls by as much as four to one in medieval baptisms.[67] And the close link between midwives and infanticide, and later abortion, made the profession vulnerable to attacks by the competing medical profession.[68]

The second phase of abortion laws lasted from 1601 to about 1803. Its major feature was the displacement of ecclesiastical jurisdiction over abortion by that of the common law courts.[69] This transition was not as sectarian as it now appears. It was part of the general assertion of parliamentary supremacy over all aspects of life and society. As close allies of Parliament, the common law courts were prime beneficiaries of this movement. Among the other areas of jurisdiction which passed from ecclesiastical or other noncommon law courts to common law courts, were control over informal contracts, libel and slander, and attempts and conspiracies. The inclusion of abortion was hardly noticed, because until the end of this period the technology and the practices remained virtually unchanged. Thus, laws developed in the common law courts to displace those of the church courts were, for all purposes, the same as before. These included occasional denunciations of the criminality of the act, or rare cases leading to punishment for the death of the mother.[70]

B. THE NINETEENTH CENTURY

A THIRD PHASE opened with the enactment of Lord Ellenborough's Act in 1803.[71] This was the first comprehensive Crimes against the Person Act in English law. It included the first statutory prohibition of abortion in English or American law, prohibiting all abortions by drugs or poisons and providing for the death penalty if the woman was "quick with child." Recognizing the extraordinary conservatism of Lord Ellenborough, there is almost no chance that his act was intended to be in any degree innovative.[72] Further acts followed to extend the scope of statutorily prohibited abortions gradually until, by 1861, all abortions by any means and for practically any purpose were criminal.[73]

A similiar course was followed by legislatures in the United States, beginning with Connecticut in 1821.[74] By 1860, eighty-five percent of the population lived in the seventy percent of states prohibiting abortion. Contemporaneous with this new legislation was a dramatic upsurge in trials and appeals of persons charged with committing abortions.[75]

Why was this new legal activity necessary? Why was legislation necessary if abortion was already a common law crime? The evidence is fairly clear that around 1750 a new technique, the first major technological innovation for inducing abortion in English or American history, was introduced into England. This technique involved inserting objects into the womb to induce labor; and the technique's safety was improved when performed by surgeons or midwives.[76] It remained extremely dangerous and produced three potentially fatal problems: insertion could open the womb to infection; the procedure could cause enough pain to induce shock, and the object could puncture the uterine wall. Still, the procedure was no less dangerous than other surgery, in which about one of every three patients could expect to die.[77] This abortion technique was far less dangerous and painful than either the use of "noxious potions" or "injury techniques."[78]

The effect of this technical breakthrough was dramatic and swift. Abortions quickly replaced infanticide as the method of choice for disposing of unwanted children. Medical and other literature, and legal activity, attest to this fact. New legislation was enacted to make clear that abortions by whatever means, and not just abortions by traditional means, were criminal. The statutes also served to remove various technical limitations, i.e., to make the prohibitions apply to even the earliest abortions.[79] The laws were also solemn reaffirmations of social policy to counteract the widespread departure from traditional mores.[80]

But today, many people wonder why abortion was so wrong. Why was so much effort expended to prevent its introduction, once it became more or less feasible? Historical sources identify two reasons: the high death rate of women who chose to undergo abortions and the even more alarming consequences for fetuses who were aborted.[81] Generally, the major emphasis was placed on the latter, since it was about the time these laws were enacted that the basic discoveries of embryology occurred and the theory that a new human life began at conception gained general acceptance.[82] The coupling of these concerns also explained the otherwise anomalous fact that, out of all the voluntary surgeries possible at the time, only abortions were prohibited.[83] If protection of the patients' health were the only concern, then one would be hard put to justify such a limited law at a time when neither anesthesia nor antiseptics nor antibiotics were known and the already mentioned fatalities were a common result from all surgeries.

As long as both concerns supported the criminalization of abortion, the laws prohibiting abortions were not seriously challenged. By 1940, however, the development of anesthesia, antiseptics, and antibiotics had made early abortions safer than carrying the child to term and giving birth.[84] Development of greater employment opportunities for women and the necessity of child care created greater incentives for women to want abortions; simultaneously, the improved technology made the procedure safe and relatively painless.[85] Under these circumstances the elimination of prohibitions on abortion may well have been inevitable. This elimination, by repeal in England in 1967 and by Supreme Court decision in the United States in 1973, ushered in the present phase of almost complete freedom for women to abort, restricted only by their ability to pay and their opportunity to find a willing physician.[86]

If abortion freedom was inevitable in the latter part of the twentieth century, then so was continued opposition from those who believed that the abortus is a living person. They believe the fetus is entitled to societal protection like any other person or more so, given the innocence of the fetus of any possible grounds with which society normally justifies the taking of a life.[87] Just as medical advances made abortion feasible, technology has played a dramatic role in bolstering antiabortion persistence. Steady growth of embryological knowledge only reinforces the notion that, at some point long before birth, there is a human being present in the womb.[88] Doctors who specialize in embryology or fetology treat the fetus as an individual quite separate from the mother, even performing surgery inside the womb.[89] These doctors cannot in good conscience contend that the fetus is merely an expendable part of the mother. Doctor Bernard Nathanson, a former abortionist, became one of the leading examples of this transformation when he became a fetologist and later repented of his role in taking 60,000 unborn lives.[90]

V. Lessons for the Future

OUR OVERVIEW OF abortion history can be summarized in a few sentences. Prior to 1800, official pronouncements and recorded opinion on or about abortion were sparse, but the available documents were unanimous in condemning the practice. Before 1780, little evidence exists that people were actually punished for performing abortions. Since Justice Blackmun, Means, and Mohr share the popular belief that peoples in other places or other times had mysterious, magical techniques for accomplishing relatively safe and easy abortions, each concluded that no one really much cared about abortion before 1780. Their analyses are fatally flawed by their uncritical acceptance of the myth of free availability.[91]

In fact, abortion before 1780 was tantamount to suicide. Infanticide was the preferred technique for disposing of unwanted children. The introduction of new techniques relatively safe for the mother produced a measured upsurge in both medical and legal concern about, and experience with, abortion. During the same historical period, new knowledge established that a human being begins at the moment of conception. Thus, two distinct strands of developing medical technology lay behind the nineteenth century movement to reaffirm, strengthen, and broaden the previous, largely theoretical prohibitions of abortion.

As long as the two strands of technology converged to support the proscription of abortion, prohibition was easy to decree and not too difficult to enforce. Since 1820, the knowledge and technology for dealing with the fetus as a separate person has continued to grow, reinforcing the policy of prohibition. But, as ever greater refinements in surgical techniques made abortion considerably safer than child-bearing, this strand of medical technology undercut the policy of prohibition. These disparate strands could only lead to the sort of moral unraveling which bedevils societies around the world.

Supposedly, Justice Blackmun's opinion in *Roe v. Wade* eschewed judgment as to what he saw as the essentially technical question of when life begins. His opinion was intended to preclude the states from second-guessing the technical judgment of physicians performing abortions.[92] Nonetheless, the Supreme Court has increasingly found itself forced into the role of medical review board. Some would argue that this is an inappropriate role for the Court. However, the history of abortion amply demonstrates that without careful attention to the technological underpinnings of the controversy, no real resolution is possible.[93] The majority opinion in *Roe v. Wade* was condemned as incoherent when it was written because it lacked technological (medical) sophistication. Justice Blackmun's theories were set to collide with themselves whenever they were carefully scrutinized.

Technical developments since have forced such careful scrutiny.[94] If *Roe v. Wade* is overturned, the opinion replacing it must avoid these problems by expressing knowledgeable understanding and greater sophistication about the technological aspects of the abortion prob-lem. If this is too demanding for the Court, then it is all the more reason for it to defer to the research capabilities and legislative judgments of the states or Congress.[95]

Greater attention to the technological aspects of the abortion controversary does not assure one that the ensuing analysis will reach the correct result.[96] One must still determine the appropriate values to be applied to the technological facts for society to determine the appropriate response to available abortion technology.[97] History places the technological facts in a context of values. That is precisely how Justice Blackmun attempted to use history in *Roe v. Wade* when he sought to identify the "interests" the state seeks by its abortion law to juxtapose against the privacy interests of the mother. His attempt failed because he distorted history and because he made the intellec-tual leap from an erroneous factual conclusion that abortion laws were not enacted to protect the life of the fetus, to a normative conclusion that these laws could not serve such a purpose. The entire opinion in *Roe v. Wade* is based on these two errors. Once they are seen as errors, the entire opinion falls. While the Court might write other opinions upholding the constitutionality of abortion, they must present more definitive analysis of the technical facts and the moral values.[98]

The study of history, especially a technologically sensitive history, shows us that abortion law is simply another chapter in the struggle by society to protect its children from abuse by their parents.[99] The point is worth emphasizing: abortion is not merely similiar to infanticide, it is infanticide. This is more than merely a rhetorical flourish. History demonstrates that abortion was a direct replacement of the prior practice of infanticide, and infanticide is merely the most egregious form of child abuse. One should no more applaud a woman's right to privacy in making the abortion decision than one would acclaim a woman's right to privacy in deciding to abuse her three-year-old physically and irreparably. To emphasize this point, some cases have confronted the Supreme Court with the argument that the right to "terminate a pregnancy" is not complete unless it includes the right to terminate the life of the fetus even if ending the pregnancy would not ordinarily endanger the child's life.[100]

Another anomoly is that abortions induced through assault upon a woman could be prosecuted as homicide when, at the same time, abortions deliberately induced by a physician are no crime at all.[101] There is also a further anomaly arising from the maternal duty to protect fetal health, a breach of which is actionable as a tort after the child is born alive, although there is no impediment to the willful destruction of her child through abortion.[102]

In a proper technological and historical context none of this should be surprising. Only by exposing and facing such technologically based contradictions and by pressing the Court to consider the social and moral implications of capitulating to technologically based developments, will the Court be made to confront, and thus to reconsider, its decision of *Roe v. Wade*.[103]

The vulnerability of the Court to such an approach is suggested by its decision in *Simopoulos v. Virginia*, where the Court did not defer to the individual medical judgment of the attending physician whose conduct in his abortion practice was shocking.[104] Decisions concerning life and death are simply too important to be left solely to the judgment of physicians.

Viewed in the context of the history of infanticide, attempts to suppress abortion are neither aberrations nor based on unworthy motives. Rather, the crusade against abortion is integral to, and the highest expression of, a crusade against child abuse and in favor of feminism. If the abortion controversy is placed in an accurate historical context, then those who are uncommitted can be persuaded that this issue deserves their attention and support. Only by viewing abortion in this context can we hope to bring the controversy to an appropriate conclusion.

Notes

1. Oxford Dictionary of Quotations 209 (2d ed. 1955). Curiously, Mr. Ford was testifying as a witness in his libel suit against the Chicago Tribune in July, 1919, when he made his oft-quoted remark. *See also* Brest, *The Misconceived Quest for the Original Understanding,* 60 B.U.L. Rev. 204 (1980); Tushnet, *Following the Rules Laid Down: A Critique of Interpretivism and Neutral Principles,* 96 Harv. L. Rev. 781 (1983).

2. This is conceded by even the strongest critics of the historic method of constitutional interpretation, Brest, *supra* note 1 at 234–238. *See also* Berger, *Mark Tushnet's Critique of Interpretivism,* 51 Geo. Wash. L. Rev. 532 (1983). *See generally* A. Bickel, The Least Dangerous Branch (1962); J. Ely, Democracy and Distrust (1980); and M. Perry, The Constitution, the Courts, and Human Rights (1982).

3. These qualities are illustrated and analyzed in F. Frohock, Abortion (1983), where interviews with representatives of various points of view are quoted and discussed at length.

4. *See generally* Frohock, *supra* note 3; Dellapenna, *Nor Piety Nor Wit: The Supreme Court on Abortion,* 67 Col. Hum. Rts. L. Rev. 379 (1975); and Wellington, *Common Law Rules and Constitutional Double Standards: Some Notes on Adjudication,* 83 Yale L.J. 221 (1973).

5. 410 U.S. 113, 129–152 (1973).

6. *Id.* at 147–152, 156–166.

7. *Id.* at 129–152, 156–162.

8. *Id.* at 136.

9. 2 H. Bracton, The Laws and Customs of England 279 (Twiss *ed.* 1879), quoted in *Roe v. Wade,* 410 U.S. at 134 n. 23. *See also* Fleta, Book I, C. 23 (Seldon Soc. 1955); and E. Coke, Third Institute of the Laws of England 50–51 (1644). See generally Dellapenna, *The History of Abortion: Technology, Morality, and Law,* 40 U. Pitt. L. Rev. 359, 366–367, 379–389 (1979).

10. See, e.g., Byrn, *An American Tragedy: The Supreme Court on Abortion,* 41 Fordham L. Rev. 807, 814–825 (1973).

11. 410 U.S. at 130, 148–150.

12. *Id.* at 130–132.

13. G. Devereux, A Study of Abortion in Primitive Societies 37 (1955); F. Taussig, Abortion Spontaneous and Induced 355–356 (1936).

14. 410 U.S. at 132, *quoting* L. Edelstein, The Hippocratic Oath 64 (1943).

15. Hippocrates himself is recorded as having recommended as a technique

for inducing abortion that a woman jump in the air and kick her heels against her hips a magical seven times. Taussig, *supra* note 13 at 33. There is some controversy over whether the attribution to Hippocrates is accurate.

16. Roe v. Wade, 410 U.S. at 132–133.

17. 410 U.S. at 134–136.

18. *Id.* at 135 n. 26.

19. *Id.* at 136.

20. *Id.* at 136–138.

21. *Id.* at 138–146.

22. *Id.* at 141–142, 148–152, 156–162.

23. *Id.* at 139–140.

24. *Id.* at 139.

25. *Id.* at 141–142, 148–150.

26. For an extended discussion of these problems *see* Dellapenna, *supra* note 9, at 361–365.

27. Dellapenna, *supra* note 4, at 381.

28. Means, *The Law of New York Concerning Abortion and the Status of the Foetus, 1664–1968: A Case of Cessation of Constitutionality,* 14 N.Y.L.F. 411 (1968) (hereafter cited as Means I), cited three times by Justice Blackmun; Means, *The Phoenix of Abortion Freedom: Is A Penumbral or Ninth Amendment Right about to Arise from the Nineteenth-Century Legislative Ashes of a Fourteenth-Century Common-Law Liberty?,* 17 N.Y.L.F. 335 (1971) (hereafter cited as Means II), cited four times by Justice Blackmun. Justice Blackmun also relied heavily on a book by the founding president of the National Abortion Rights Action League, citing it seven times. L. Lader, Abortion (1966).

29. Means II, *supra* note 28, at 346, 359–360.

30. *Id.* at 382–392.

31. Means I, *supra* note 28, at 436, 511–512; and Means II, *supra* note 28, at 391–392. *See also* Dellapenna, *supra* note 9, at 411–413. There is considerable controversy over this claim that abortion is safer for the mother than giving birth. Hilgers, *The Medical Hazards of Legally Induced Abortion,* in Abortion and Social Justice 57–85 (T. Hilgers & D. Horan, eds. 1972); and Hilgers & O'Hara, *Abortion Related Maternal Mortalilty: an In-depth Analysis,* in New Perspectives on Human Abortion 69–91 (T. Hilgers, D. Horan & D. Mall eds. 1981). The differences in maternal risk between pregnancy and abortion are so miniscule as to be inappropriate as a basis for constitutional decision. I therefore do not quarrel with this claim that abortion is slightly safer.

32. Means I, *supra* note 28, at 418, 453, 511–515; Means II *supra* note 28, at 382–384.

33. 410 U.S. at 130–132, 141–146.

34. *Id.* at 147–152.

35. Doe v. Bolton, 410 U.S. 179, 190–191 (1973).

36. *See, e.g.,* The Law and Politics of Abortion xvii–xviii (C. Schneider & M. Vinovkis eds. 1980); and E. Rubin, Abortion, Politics and the Courts 9–13 (1982).

37. J. Mohr, Abortion in America (1978). *See generally* The Law and Politics of Abortion, *supra* note 36, at xvi–xvii; Frohock, *supra* note 3, at 59–60; Rubin, *supra* note 36, at vii, 9–15; and White, *The Concept of Person, the Law and the Use of Fetus in*

Biomedicine, in Abortion and the Status of the Fetus 119, 123–127 (W. Bondeson, H. Engelhardt, S. Spicker & D. Winship eds. 1983). Even prolife authors tend to accept, in general, Mohr's book as the ultimate authority on abortion history. *See, e.g.,* L. Wardle & M. Wood, A Lawyer Looks at Abortion 27–31 (1982). *See also* C. Francome, Abortion Freedom 29–31 (1984). For criticism of *Roe's* version of the history of abortion, see Byrn, *supra* note 10, at 814–839; Dellapenna, *supra* note 9.

38. Mohr, *supra* note 37, at 3.

39. *Id.* at 3–19.

40. Dellapenna, *supra* note 9, at 371–375. *See* Mohr, *supra* note 37, at 11–14.

41. Mohr, *supra* note 37, at 18.

42. Mohr, *supra* note 37, at 3–6.

43. *Id.* at 25–32. Given Mohr's views about the relative safety of abortion at the time, he necessarily discounts this as a purpose of the prohibitory legislation, *Id.* at 32–40.

44. *Id.* at 85–118, 128, 167–168.

45. *Id.* at 35–36, 175–176, 182–196.

46. *Id.* at 32–37, 147–182. *See generally* P. Starr, The Social Transformation of American Medicine (1982). Interestingly, Starr did not consider abortion to be a significant factor in the rise of an organized profession of medicine; he never mentions abortion in this context.

47. Dellapenna, *supra* note 9, at 366–368, 379–382, 386–389.

48. *Id.* at 401–405. *See* Dougherty v. People, 1 Colo. 514 (1872); State v. Moore, 25 Iowa 128 (1868); People v. Sessions, 58 Mich. 594, 26 N.W. 291 (1886); State v. Gedicke, 43 N.J.L. 86 (1881); and State v. Howard, 32 Vt. 380 (1859).

49. Dellapenna, *supra* note 9, at 365; Dellapenna, *supra* note 4, at 382 n. 22.

50. Stated most clearly in Mohr, *supra* note 37, at 3–19.

51. Consider *Roe v. Wade* in this light, 410 U.S. at 148–152, 156–162. Means, of course, offers a rational basis for the law's protection of maternal health, but suggests no reason why this should suddenly become a concern in the nineteenth century. *See also* Mohr, *supra* note 37, at 32–37, 147–225.

52. Byrn, *supra* note 10, at 814–839. *See also* G. Grisez, Abortion: The Myths, the Realities, and the Arguments 117–266 (1970); and Quay, *Justifiable Abortion—Medical and Legal Foundations,* 49 Geo. L.J. 173 (Part I) (1960), 49 Geo. L. J. 395 (Part II) (1961).

53. Byrn, *supra* note 10, at 815–824. *See also* Grisez, *supra* note 52, at 130–155; R. Huser, The Crime of Abortion in Canon Law 16–36 (1942).

54. Byrn, *supra* note 10, at 824–833.

55. *Id.* at 833–834; and Grisez, *supra* note 52, at 202–203. See also *Biomedical Ethics and the Shadow of Nazism,* 6 Hastings Center Rep., Spec. Supp.(Aug. 1976); D. Callahan, Abortion: Law, Choice and Morality 307–346 (1970); Byrn, *Abortion on Demand: Whose Morality?,* 46 Notre Dame Law. 5, 25–26 (1970); and Friedman, *Interference with Human Life: Some Jurisprudential Reflections,* 70 Colum. L. Rev. 1058 (1970).

56. Dellapenna, *supra* note 9, at 366–367, 379–384, 387–389, 393–395, 404–406.

57. Dellapenna, *supra* note 9.

58. These dates would be for much of the rest of the world as well. *See* Francome, *supra* note 37, at 29–30, 128–157; and Isaacs, *Reproductive Rights 1983: an International Survey*, 14 Col. Hum. Rts. L. Rev. 311 (1983).

59. For a discussion of ecclesiastical courts, *see* Dellapenna, *supra* note 9, at 367–368, 377–378, 383. Other matters relegated to ecclesiastical courts were such topics as informal contracts, marriage, wills, and the slander of ordinary people, as well as other topics without which modern secular law would be seriously defective. *See generally* 1 W. Holdsworth, A History of English Law 65–77, 580–632 (1903–1973) (hereafter Holdsworth); 3 Holdsworth 296, 408–428, 534–536; 15 Holdsworth 198–208; T. Plucknett, A Concise History of the Common Law 301-3-5, 483–498, 657–670, 727–746 (5th ed. 1956); 1 F. Pollock & F. Maitland, The History of English Law before the Time of Edward I 88–114 (2d ed. 1898); and Means II, *supra* note 28, at 350–352. Judgments from the church courts were enforced by the king's sheriff, 1 Holdsworth, 614–621, 630–632; 1 Pollock & Maitland, *supra*, at 461–463; and Means I, *supra* note 28, at 439 n. 64.

60. For cases where abortions were not punished by the royal courts, *see* The Twinslayer's Case, Y.B. Mich. 1 Edw. 3, f. 23, pl. 28 (1327), translated in Means II, *supra* note 28, at 337, 338 n. 4; The Abortionist's Case, Fitzherbert, Graunde Abridgement, tit. Corone, f. 268r, pl. 263 (1st ed. 1516) [Y.B. Mich. 22 Edw. 3 (1348)], translated in Means II, *supra* at 339. *See also* Byrn, *supra* note 10, at 817–819; and Dellapenna, *supra* note 9, at 366–370. For records of ecclesiastical court cases, *see* Dellapenna, *supra* note 9, at 383; Means I, *supra* note 28, at 439 n. 63; Means II, *supra* note 28, at 346–347. *Compare* 6 Holdsworth, *supra* note 59, at 196–208. *See also* Dellapenna, *supra* note 9, at 371 n. 68.

61. For descriptions of typical "magical techniques," see Dellapenna, *supra* note 9, at 372–373. For the connection to witchcraft, *see* T. Forbes, The Midwife and the Witch (1966). These invasive techniques involved "noxious potions" which brought about the abortion by so weakening the woman's body that she was unable to sustain the pregnancy. The alternative techniques involved blows to the woman's body with the same effect. These techniques were so commonly fatal that Devereux, *supra* note 13, at 28, 149–150, described abortion in primitive cultures as being tantamount to suicide. *See generally* J. Bates & E. Zawadzki, Criminal Abortion 14–23, 85–91 (1964); Devereux, *supra* note 13; Taussig, *supra* note 13, at 31–45, 352–357; and Dellapenna, *supra* note 9, at 373–376. Every item Mohr, *supra* note 37, at 11–14, lists as a herbal agent for abortion in 1800 is a dangerous toxic potion.

62. This was true in both the Twinslayer's Case, and the Abortionist's Case, *supra* note 60. *See also* Dellapenna, *supra* note 9, at 376–379.

63. Dellapenna, *supra* note 9, at 377–378.

64. *See* D. Bakan, The Slaughter of Innocents (1971); G. Payne, The Child in Human Progress (1976); M. Piers, Infanticide: Past and Present (1974); The History of Childhood (de Mause ed. 1974); Dellapenna, *supra* note 9, at 395–400; Langer, *Infanticide: a Historical Survey*, 2 Hist. of Childhood Q. 353 (1974); Rosenblum & Budde, *Historical and Cultural Considerations of Infanticide*, in Infanticide (D. Horan & M. Delahoyde eds. 1982); and Shorter, *Infanticide in the*

Past, 1 Hist. of Childhood Q. 178 (1973). The rates of deaths among children caused by adults is even more shocking if one adds in the widespread abandonment and neglect of children, Dellapenna, *supra* note 9, at 395 n. 231, 397 n. 239. Even wetnurses doubled as child-disposal services, *id.* at 397 n. 240; and Rosenblum & Budde, *supra* at 4–5. For the extension of infanticide into the nineteenth century, *see* Krause, *Some Implications of Recent Work of Historical Demography,* 1 Comp. Stud. in Soc'y & Hist. 164, 177 (1959). *See also* Dellapenna, *supra* note 9, at 397 n. 239. Even in the nineteenth century dead babies were reportedly a common sight in the streets of London, I. Pinchbeck & M. Hewitt, Children in English Society 302 (1969); de Mause, *supra* note 64, at 244–245; and Rolph, *A Backward Glance at the Age of "Obscenity,"* 32 Encounter 23 (June 1969). *See also* Dellapenna, *supra* note 9, at 395–397.

65. "An Act to Prevent the Destroying and Murdering of Bastard Children," 21 Jac. 1, ch. 27, 3 (1623), prohibited concealing the death of a child to conceal its birth. When copied by the American colonies and states, the presumption of murder was generally attached to only one or the other type of concealment. *See* Dellapenna, *supra* note 9, at 397–399.

66. In France, at least, de Mause, *supra* note 64, at 282.

67. *Id.* at 25–28, 284–287.

68. As early as the seventeenth century, midwives were made to swear not to kill, hurt, or dismember the children whose birth they assisted, de Mause, *supra* note 64 at 306. *See also* Forbes, *supra* note 61 at 144–147; and Horan & Marzen, *Abortion and Midwifery: a Footnote in Legal History,* in New Perspectives on Human Abortion, *supra* note 31, at 199–204.

69. Common law jurisdiction over abortion was signalled by the decision in Sim's Case, 75 Eng. Rep. 1075 (K.B. 1601), where the court in what might be dictum announced that if there is an assault on a pregnant woman which results in the birth of a baby who subsequently dies from the assault, the culprit is guilty of murder. *See generally* Dellapenna, *supra* note 9, at 379–389.

70. 1 W. Blackstone, Commentaries on the Laws of England 129–130 (1765); 4 W. Blackstone, Commentaries 198 (1765); E. Coke, *supra* note 9, at 50–51; M. Hale, History of Pleas of the Crown 429–433 (1736); and W. Hawkins, Treatise of the Pleas of the Crown 80 (1716).

71. 43 Geo. 3, c. 58 (1803). *See generally* Dellapenna, *supra* note 9, at 389–407.

72. He was the judge who approved a demand for trial by battle, Ashford v. Thornton, 106 Eng. Rep. 149 (K.B. 1818). *See* Dellapenna, *supra* note 9 at 391–392.

73. Offenses against the Person Act, 24 & 25 Vict. c. 100, §58, 59 (1861).

74. Conn. Stat. tit. 22, §14 (1821). *See* Dellapenna, *supra* note 9, at 389 n. 195. These statutes are collected in Quay, *supra* note 52, at 477–520.

75. There are reported cases in 1327, 1349, 1601, and 1670. *See supra* notes 80 & 70, and Hale, *supra* note 70, at 429–430. There were two cases in England between 1781 and 1803, and prosecutions and appeals became common in both England and the United States in the next few decades. Dellapenna, *supra* note 9, at 393–394. *See also* Mohr, *supra* note 31, at 46–85, on the great upsurge in abortion in the nineteenth century.

76. First clearly reported in Margaret Tinckler's Case (1781), 1 E. East, A

Treatise of the Pleas of the Crown 354–356 (1806). There is a newspaper report of such a practice as early as 1732. *See* Dellapenna, *supra* note 9, at 394–395. For a discussion of techniques and consequences, see Bates & Zewadzki, *supra* note 61 at 85–87; Means II, *supra* note 28, at 382–392.

77. Dellapenna, *supra* note 9, at 400, 412; Means II, *supra* note 28, at 384–386.

78. Operative techniques appear to have become the method of choice and have remained such to today. One study (now 29 years old) found that 90% of abortions were with operative techniques, 9% with pharmaceutical techniques, and less than 1% with injury techniques. *See* P. Gebhardt et al., Pregnancy, Birth and Abortion 193–196 (1958).

79. *See generally* Grisez, *supra* note 52, at 188–194, 220–222; Mohr, *supra* note 37, at 200–225; and Quay, *supra* note 52, at 435–438, 447–520.

80. Dellapenna, *supra* note 9, at 395.

81. State v. Murphy, 27 N.J. L. 112, 114–115 (1858). *See also* the cases cited at note 48, *supra.*

82. *See* Dellapenna, *supra* note 9, at 402–406. *See generally,* A. Meyer, The Rise of Embryology (1939); J. Needham, A History of Embryology (1959); Callahan, *supra* note 55, at 410–461; Grisez, *supra* note 52, at 177–181; Means I, *supra* note 28, at 414–416.

83. A point stressed by Mohr, *supra* note 37, at 28–31, in rejecting Means's claim that protection of maternal health was the sole or even primary purpose of the abortion statutes. See also Dellapenna, *supra* note 9, at 400–401.

84. *Roe,* 410 U.S. at 149. *See also* Dellapenna, *supra* note 9, at 413 n. 339. While this is open to some dispute, *see* note *supra.*

85. Dellapenna, *supra* note 9, at 411–414.

86. *See* The Abortion Act of 1967, 15 & 16 Eliz. 2, c. 87 1967) (repeal of abortion prohibitions); Roe v. Wade, 410 U.S. 113 (1973) (legalizing abortion); for funding cases, *see* Harris v. McRae, 448 U.S. 297 (1980); Poelker v. Doe, 432 U.S. 519 (1977); Maher v. Roe, 432 U.S. 464 (1977); Beal v. Doe, 432 U.S. 438 (1977); and Singleton v. Wulff, 428 U.S. 106 (1976). *See also* Greco v. Orange Memorial Hospital, 423 U.S. 1000 (1975). The consistent deference of the Supreme Court to the opinions and concerns of the medical profession is one of the most peculiar features of *Roe v. Wade* and its progeny. *See* Thornburgh v. American College of Obstetricians and Gynecologists, 106 S. Ct. 2169 (1986); Planned Parenthood of Kansas City v. Ashcroft, 462 U.S. 476 (1983); City of Akron v. Akron Center for Reproductive Health, Inc., 462 U.S. 416 (1983); Colautti v. Franklin, 439 U.S. 379 (1979); Planned Parenthood of Central Missouri v. Danforth, 428 U.S. 52 (1976); Singleton v. Wulff, 428 U.S. 106 (1976); Connecticut v. Menillo, 423 U.S. 9 (1975); Doe v. Bolton, 410 U.S. 179, 192–193, 196–201 (1973); and Roe v. Wade, 410 U.S. 113, 130–132, 141–146, 149–150, 159, 162–166 (1973). *But see* Diamond v. Charles, 106 S. Ct. 1697 (1986); Simopoulos v. Virginia, 462 U.S. 506 (1983).

87. The Supreme Court has itself suggested that the very powerlessness of a class is all the more reason for the Court to interpose its protection for the class. United States v. Carolene Products Co., 304 U.S. 144, 152 n. 4 (1938).

88. Dellapenna, *supra* note 9, at 414–416. *See also* Lenow, *The Fetus as a Patient: Emerging Rights as a Person?* 9 Am. J. L. & Med. 1 (1983); Milby, *The New Biology and*

the Question of Personhood: Implications for Abortion, 9 Am. J.L. & Med. 31 (1983); Munir, *Perinatal Rights*, 24 Med. Sci. L. 31 (1984); Parness, *Social Commentary: Values and Legal Personhood*, 83 W. Va. L. Rev. 487 (1981); Ross, *Abortion and the Death of the Fetus*, 11 Philos. & Public Aff. 232 (1982); Sneideman, *Abortion: A Public Health and Social Policy Perspective*, 7 N.Y.U. Rev. L. & Soc. Change 187 (1978); Zaitchik, *Viability and the Morality of Abortion*, 10 Philos. & Public Affairs 18 (1981); Note, *The Fetus under Section 1983: Still Struggling for Recognition*, 34 Syr. L. Rev. 1029 (1983); and Annot. 64 ALR Fed. 886 (1983). *See generally* Defining Human Life (M. Shaw & A. Doudera eds. 1983).

89. Blakeslee, *Fetus Returned to Womb Following Surgery*, N.Y. Times, Oct. 7, 1986, at C1, col. 5.

90. Nathanson, *Deeper into Abortion*, 291 N. Eng. J. Med. 1189 (1974). *See also* B. Nathanson, Aborting America (1979); and B. Nathanson, The Abortion Papers (1983).

91. Devereux, *supra* note 13, at 40–42, 171–358. *See also* B. Malinowski, The Sexual Life of Savages in North-Western Melanesia 168–169 (3d ed. 1932); and Dellapenna, *supra* note 9, at 372–375.

92. 410 U.S. at 159, 162–166; Doe v. Bolton, 410 U.S. 179 1973).

93. As recognized and discussed at length in Justice O'Connor's dissent, Akron v. Akron Center for Reproductive Health, Inc., 462 U.S. 416, 452–475 (1983). For the Court's involvement as a medical review board, *see Thornburgh*, 106 S. Ct. 2169, *Simopoulos*, 462 U.S. 506, Planned Parenthood v. Ashcroft, 462 U.S. 476 (1983);Colautti v. Franklin, 439 U.S. 379 (1979); Planned Parenthood v. Danforth, 428 U.S. 52 (1976).

94. *See Akron*, 462 U.S. at 455–458 (O'Connor, J., dissenting).

95. This was argued in *Roe v. Wade*, 410 U.S. at 221–223 (White & Rehnquist, J.J., dissenting). *See also* Dellapenna, *supra* note 4, at 412–413; Sony Corp. of America v. Universal City Studios, Inc., 464 U.S. 417, 430–431 (1984).

96. E.g., Note, *Current Technology Affecting Supreme Court Abortion Jurisprudence*, 27 N.Y.L.S. L. Rev. 1237 (1982).

97. Dellapenna, *supra* note 4, at 389–398.

98. Even the defenders of *Roe v. Wade* invariably begin by apologizing for Justice Blackmun's opinion, which they then ignore. *See, e.g.*, Heyman & Barzelay, *The Forest and the Trees: Roe v. Wade and Its Critics*, 53 B.U. L. Rev. 765 (1973); Perry, *Abortion, the Public Morals, and the Police Power: the Ethical Function of Substantive Due Process*, 23 U.C.L.A. L. Rev. 689, 690–692 (1976); and Tribe, *Forward: Toward a Model of Roles in the Due Process of Life and Law*, 87 Harv. L. Rev. 1, 2–5 (1973). For a view upholding abortion on other constitutional grounds, *see* Regan, *Rewriting* Roe v. Wade, 77 Mich. L. Rev. 1569 (1979).

99. *See also* Ney, *Infant Abortions and Child Abuse: Cause and Effect*, in The Psychological Aspects of Abortion 25–38 (D. Mall & W. Watts eds. 1979).

100. *Thornburgh*, 106 S. Ct. at 2177–2185; *Akron*, 462 U.S. at 426–431, 444–452; Planned Parenthood v. Danforth, 428 U.S. 52, 75–79, 95–99 (1976). The problem of the "live-birth" abortion has received considerable attention recently, with several doctors accused of murder for killing babies after they are born. At least one has been convicted, Phila Inq., Sept. 29, 1983, p. 14A, col. 2. *See generally*, Kleiman, *When Abortion Becomes Birth*, N. Y. Times, Feb. 15, 1984

at B1, col. 1; and Jeffries & Edmonds, *Abortion: the Dreaded Complication*, Phil. Inq. Today Magazine, Aug. 2, 1981, at 14.

101. People v. Watson, 30 Cal. 3d 290, 179 Cal. Rptr. 43, 637 P. 2d 279 (1981); People v. Apodaca, 76 Cal. App. 3d 479, 142 Cal. Rptr. 830 (1978); People v. Smith, 57 Cal. App. 3d 751, 129 Cal. Rptr. 498 (1976). Most courts still require the fetus to be born alive before it is homicide, Charles v. Carey, 627 F. 2d 772, 790–791 (7th Cir. 1980); People v. Greer, 79 Ill. 2d 103, 402 N.E. 2d 203 (1980); Hollis v. Commonwealth, 652 S.W. 2d 61 (Ky. 1983); State v. Brown, 378 So. 2d 916 (La.1980); State v. Gyles, 313 So. 2d 799 (La. 1975); State v. A.W.S., 182 N.J. Super. 278, 440 A.2d 1144 (1981); State v. Anderson, 135 N.J. Super. 423, 343 A. 2d 505 (1975); State v. Willis, 98 N.M. 771, 652 P. 2d 1222 (1982); State v. Willis, 98 N.M. 771, 652 P 2d 1222 (1982); State v. Dickinson, 28 Oh. St. 2d 65, 275 N.C. 2d 599 (1971); State v. Amaro, 448 A. 2d 1257 (R.I. 1983); and State v. Larsen, 578 P. 2d 1280 (Utah 1978). Just how tenuous this distinction can be is shown by People v. Bolar, 109 Ill. App. 3d 384, 440 N.E. 2d 639 (1982), where a reckless homicide charge was upheld because the baby's heart beat a few times after birth. One federal court has found a fetus to be a person for purposes of a Section 1983 action, Douglas v. Town of Hartford, 524 F. Supp. 1267 (D. Conn. 1982).

102. For the mother's duty to fetal health, *see* Beal, *"Can I Sue Mommy?" An Analysis of a Woman's Tort Liability for Prenatal Injuries to her Child Born Alive*, 21 San Diego L. Rev. 325 (1984); Shaw, *Conditional Prospective Rights of the Fetus*, 5 J. Legal Med. 63 (1984); and Note, *A Maternal Duty to Protect Fetal Health*, 58 Ind. L.J. 531 (1983). Physicians find themselves in somewhat the same situation as a result of the new tort called "wrongful life." See Note, *Damages: Recovery of Damages in Actions for Wrongful Birth, Wrongful Life and Wrongful Conception*, 23 Washburn L.J. 309 (1984); and Note, *Wrongful Life: The Tort that Nobody Wants*, 23 Santa Clara L. Rev. 847 (1983).

103. This seems to be the point of Justice O'Connor's dissent in Akron, 462 U.S. at 452. *Cf. Symposium on Technology and the Law*, 18 Gonzaga L. Rev. 429 (1983).

104. 462 U.S. 506 (1983).

M A R T I N   A R B A G I

Roe and the Hippocratic Oath

HISTORY AND MEDICINE can be regarded scientifically as following certain rules of procedure. For an evaluation of the evidence considered in *Roe v. Wade*, we must consider the scientific aspect of historical inquiry. Some sciences deal in empirical evidence. A chemist, when asked what happens as an electric current is passed through water, can confidently and verifiably reply that the liquid is broken down into two gasses: hydrogen and oxygen. Some scientists do not study the provable phenomena but, based on educated conjecture, make evaluations of important phenomena. Astronomers cannot directly observe the interior of the sun; but they *believe* they know what is happening: the fusion of hydrogen atoms into those of helium under inconceivable temperatures and pressures. This explanation is merely a working hypothesis based upon inferences drawn from observations of the sun's surface from millions of miles away.

Ancient historians resemble astronomers more than chemists. Lacking verification of some crucial facts or critical events, the historian of antiquity can offer only a working hypothesis of what existing data indicate probably happened. Our understanding of Graeco-Roman attitudes toward abortion is not completely verifiable; instead, it is based on partial evidence, reasoned conjecture, and judicious interpretation.

I. Edelstein's Analysis of the Oath

VIRTUALLY NOTHING IS known about Hippocrates except that he was a Greek physician, probably born on the Aegean island of Cos between 475 and 450 B.C., possibly died at the city of Larissa in northeastern Greece between 400 and 370 B.C., and frequently travelled during his lifetime. By the Middle Ages Hippocrates had become "the embodiment of the ideal physician" and, because of this reputation, a large body of writings has been attributed to him. His authorship is questionable; and historians of ancient medicine now believe that he did not write most the works in the Hippocratic corpus.[1] Until recently, the Hippocratic oath has been held in awe by physicians as a timeless statement of medical ethics. Although the oath is falling into disuse, many medical schools administer a modified version of it to their graduates.

In 1943, Ludwig Edelstein, a classicist and distinguished historian of Graeco-Roman medicine, published a short monograph on the Hippocratic oath contending that the oath, like most of the Hippocratic corpus, had not really been authored by the great physician.[2] Who, then, composed it? Edelstein hypothesized that the oath was a statement or manifesto of Pythagorean ethics. Pythagoras, a Greek mathematician and philosopher living about 500 B.C., is known as the discoverer of a geometrical theorem. He also founded a religious sect that briefly flourished in a southern Italian region populated by Greeks. Pythagoras's followers believed in reincarnation and probably regarded all animal life as sacred; consequently, strictly observant sect members were most likely vegetarian. Pythagoreans worshipped the traditional pagan gods, especially Apollo; but unlike virtually all other pagans, they did not offer bloody animal sacrifices. Pythagoreanism also attracted many medical doctors as well as mathematicians.[3]

Considering the Hippocratic oath as a Pythagorean manifesto solves a number of historical difficulties. The oath appears to be an initiation into a brotherhood of physicians. Earlier commentators believed that brotherhoods called Asclepiads existed in antiquity. At first, the Asclepiads were family-dominated; later, they admitted outsiders by an adoption or initiation ceremony—vestiges of which survive in the oath. It is true that many trades in classical times had rudimentary professional associations which the Romans called *collegia*. But the notion that doctors also had such associations or brotherhoods, as Edelstein asserted, was based upon flimsy evidence. If one accepts the Pythagorean authorship of the oath, the difficulty is cleared up because the sect was organized as a group of semi-secret clubs in southern Italy. Even after the clubs disappeared, the bond between individual Pythagorean teachers and their students was considered to be as close as that between parent and child. Earlier commentators believed that the oath's prohibition of surgery is due to the fact that, by Hippocrates's day, medicine and surgery had become two different professions. According to Edelstein, this belief was based on weak evidence. Before A.D. 175, ancient physicians practiced surgery; however, we know that although Pythagorean doctors had no fundamental objections to surgery, it was not valued as highly as other treatments such as diet or drugs, and they themselves would not perform surgery. Conceivably, this was connected with the sect's general avoidance of bloody animal sacrifices. In any case, a second difficulty with the oath has been neatly solved.[4] Our main concern here is the Hippocratic oath's absolute prohibition of abortion. To quote Professor Edelstein's translation:

> I will neither give a deadly drug to anybody if asked for it, nor will I make a suggestion to this effect. Similarly, I will not give to a woman an abortive remedy [pesson phtheorion]. In purity and holiness I will guard my life and my art.[5]

Edelstein attached great importance to this double prohibition. It was his contention that "[i]n no other stratum of Greek opinion were such views held in the same spirit of uncompromising austerity" as among the Pythagoreans.[6] This, combined with the religious nature of the injunction, Pythagoreans' singularly advanced position on what we now call "human rights," which also condemned infanticide and argued for the equality of slaves and women, and with other evidence, made it likely that the Hippocratic oath,

> [f]ar from being the expression of the common Greek attitude toward medicine or of the natural duties of the physician...rather reflects opinions which were peculiarly those of a small and isolated group."[7]

Because Dr. Edelstein's monograph was published in 1943, at the height of World War II, it was not widely reviewed outside the United States. Within the United States, learned journals accorded it a favorable reception. But two independent reviewers found one defect in an otherwise praiseworthy contribution to Graeco-Roman medicine. One critic, Edwin L. Minar, remarked that "[i]n a few instances, the author seems to attempt to prove too much."[8]

H.N. Couch used somewhat stronger language:

> Without challenging the claim that the Oath is derived from the scientific and ethical principles of the Pythagoreans, one is at times troubled by a tendency to overargue the case; the reader feels that he is being forced to accept a predetermined conclusion when alternate explanations might have some validity."[9]

Such statements came as no surprise to those who knew Edelstein's work. After his death in 1965, friendly biographers said of him that his constant deviation from accepted views put him under suspicion of "being a *frondeur* [i.e. one who enjoys controversy for its own sake] for whom opposition was vital. Such an impression was enhanced by his presentation of his arguments as cogent demonstrations with inescapable results."[10]

The biographers concluded that this statement was an erroneous view of Edelstein because his unswerving devotion to historical truth would never have allowed him to become merely a controversial figure.

Nonetheless, we are left with the impression of a great scholar whose enthusiasm for his own views occasionally led him to some degree of exaggeration. For example, Professor Edelstein called the Pythagoreans "a small and isolated group." However, those familiar with the history of classical philosophy will testify that the sect had an influence far disproportionate to the number of its adherents. Pythagoreanism had a profound effect upon the formation of Plato's theories.[11] Even if one concedes that the sect had no further direct influence—a dubious proposition—its doctrines would have continued indirectly to affect the evolution of Greek and Roman philosophy through Platonism and Neoplatonism.[12] Although the Pythagorean clubs of southern Italy were suppressed between 460 and 400 B.C., the sect's doctrines continued to be taught. In the first century B.C., a Neopythagorean school appeared in Alexandria, which was a Greek and Jewish rather than an Egyptian city. From Alexandria, Neopythagoreanism exerted considerable influence upon the thought of late antiquity, on Judaism through the hellenized Jewish philosopher Philo, and on Christianity through Clement of Alexandria.[13]

In his eagerness to strengthen his proof, Professor Edelstein unduly minimized Pythagorean involvement in the mainstream of Graeco-Roman thought. His penchant for overargument led him at least once into the realm of the absurd. Edelstein flatly stated that "[a]ncient religion...remained indifferent to foeticide." Yet, Pythagoreanism was an "ancient religion" and *it* prohibited abortion.[14]

II. Blackmun's Misplaced Reliance on Edelstein

IN ITS 1973, *Roe v. Wade* decision, the Supreme Court of the United States declared that for all practical purposes abortion on demand was legal. The opinion of the Court was delivered by Justice Harry Blackmun. If one can believe *The Brethren*, a gossipy history of the Supreme Court, Justice Blackmun considers himself an expert on medical affairs and history.[15] So it is not surprising that Blackmun, early in his opinion, declared that we have inquired, and in this opinion place some emphasis upon, medical and medical-legal history and what that history reveals about man's attitudes toward the abortive procedure.[16]

Blackmun's survey began with the ancient classical, or Graeco-Roman, world. Though brief, the portion of *Roe v. Wade* dealing with the history of abortion in antiquity falls into two parts: a general overview of Greek and Roman attitudes toward abortion, and a section dealing specifically with the Hippocratic oath. In neither section did Blackmun cite any primary sources. Though he cited a number of other secondary works as window-dressing, Blackmun relied almost exclusively on Edelstein's monograph for both sections and occasionally quoted or paraphrased it without credit. He started on a correct and scholarly note: the views of the ancients on abortion "are not capable of precise determination."[17] Then scholarship and judicious historical interpretation disappear. Quoting Professor Edelstein, Blackmun asserted that among the Greeks and Romans abortion "was resorted to without scruple."[18] To be sure, Soranus of Ephesus, "the greatest of the ancient gynaecologists," approved of abortion when the mother's life was in danger but otherwise "appears to have been generally opposed to Rome's prevailing free-abortion practices."[19] But Soranus, according to Blackmun, was merely the exception to the rule:

> Greek and Roman law afforded little protection to the unborn. If abortion was prosecuted in some places, it seems to have been based on a concept of a violation of the father's right to his offspring. Ancient religion did not bar abortion.[20]

What of the Hippocratic oath? It condemned abortion absolutely.

The late Dr. Edelstein provided us with a theory: "Most Greek thinkers...commended abortion, at least prior to viability...the Oath [therefore] originated in a group representing only a small segment of Greek opinion."[21] And so the oath's opposition to abortion was dismissed. Its "apparent rigidity" must be understood "in historical context." Only subsequently, with the triumph of Christianity in late antiquity, did the oath become a universally accepted expression of medical ethics.[22]

Unfortunately for American jurisprudence, Blackmun overlooked three problems with his ponderous reliance upon Professor Edelstein's work. First, Blackmun used Edelstein's monograph not only for that portion of *Roe v. Wade* dealing with the Hippocratic oath, but also for the general survey of classical attitudes toward abortion. But Edelstein's monograph does not primarily concern abortion. Though Greek and Roman attitudes toward the procedure played an important role in Edelstein's attempt to prove his hypothesis, his focus remained first and foremost upon the Hippocratic oath and its authorship.

Second, by 1973 the monograph was already thirty years old. Usually, this is not a major weakness; in the field of classical history, large quantities of new evidence rarely come to light. Most scholarly research consists of the reexamination of data that have long been available. Consequently, many studies published decades ago are not obsolete and remain perfectly valid. However, there *is* a constant trickle of new evidence—mostly provided by archaeologists. As we shall see, evidence published in the 1960s may modify Edelstein's theory on abortion in classical antiquity.

Third, Dr. Edelstein's penchant for overargument and his zeal for his own unorthodox hypotheses caused him to depict the proofs for them as "inescapable." We have already seen two examples of this. Furthermore, Edelstein's thesis itself raises new problems in the very act of laying old ones to rest. An obvious example: how can Pythagoras be said to have written the oath when he prohibited his disciples from taking oaths? This prohibition was observed by both Pythagoreans and Neopythagoreans.[23]

Barring major discoveries of relevant new evidence, Edelstein's theory on the authorship of the oath must remain just that: a theory whose absolute *truth* can never be demonstrated, though its probability, or lack thereof, can be asserted. Justice Blackmun paid lip-service to this; but the rhetorical thrust of that portion of *Roe v. Wade* devoted to the classical world shows that, in practice, he elevated Edelstein's hypothesis to the status of absolute fact.

III. The Hippocratic Corpus and Ancient Attitudes on Abortion: New Evidence

Is EDELSTEIN'S WORK correct and worthy of recitation in such important circumstances? *Roe v. Wade* was decided in January, 1973. Justice Blackmun spent much of 1972 doing research for the opinion.[24] The magisterial work of Enzo Nardi, *Procurato aborto nel mondo greco romano*, appeared in 1971, but it was not cited by Blackmun.[25] Possibly, it was not available in the United States nor had it been translated into English. Professor Nardi's work contained much to contradict Blackmun's preconceived conclusions. Nardi's methodology was to collect every extant passage from Greek and Latin writers, from earliest times through the early Middle Ages, that had anything to do with abortion. He quoted from physicians, poets, philosophers, playwrights, lawyers, historians, canonists, theologians, scientists, pagans, Jews and Christians. These passages were reprinted in the original Greek or Latin with a facing Italian translation and a commentary. Massive footnotes provided encyclopedic references to most previous scholarship on the subject.

What were Nardi's conclusions? He thought that evidence for the period before 500 B.C. is too skimpy and unreliable to prove anything. From 500 B.C. onwards, it must be concluded that the Greeks practiced abortion somewhat more freely than did Western society until quite recently. Nonetheless, opposition always existed. Before 300 B.C., it was minimal; from 300 B.C. onward, Nardi believed that there was a growing and broadly based opposition to abortion. It was not confined to Pythagorean or Christian circles. Even before the triumph of Christianity in the fourth century A.D., this increasing opposition had led to a gradual hardening of legal attitudes in the Roman Empire.

The impartiality and depth of Professor Nardi's scholarship are unexceptionable and for our purposes it is important to evaluate a representative sample of the sources he discussed. Though the chronological purview of Nardi's book extends through late antiquity and into the early Middle Ages, our sample will be restricted to the period from 400 B.C. to A.D. 100. None of the sources is Christian.

A. PSEUDO-LYSIAS

THE ANCIENT ATHENIANS did not have a class of professional lawyers. They believed that any well-informed citizen ought to know enough of the law to be aware when his rights were breached and to prosecute the violator(s) of those rights. As law became more complex, this position was modified. By the middle of the fifth century B.C. there arose a group of men at Athens, and in other Greek city-states where the situation was similar, who were called sophists, rhetoricians, or orators. They wrote, for a fee, speeches to be delivered in court by others.

Lysias (ca. 460 [or 445]-380 B.C.) was a sophist. Many of his orations were preserved; unfortunately, the one we wish to examine has disappeared. It was, however, referred to by a number of ancient sources, one of whom actually quoted a sentence from it. The title of this speech was *On Abortion* (*Peri tes Ambloseos*) or perhaps *Against Antigenes on an Indictment* [or *Accusation*] *of Abortion*. It appears that a certain Antigenes was prosecuting his wife on a charge of homicide for having undergone an abortion. The abortion seems to have been performed late enough in the pregnancy that the sex of the child was obvious, for one of the points Antigenes appears to have made to the jury was that his wife had deprived him of a son. Lysias' speech was written for Antigenes's wife—or more accurately, her brother, since there is some question as to whether a woman could speak in an Athenian court. The line of defense taken was that homicide could not have been committed against the unborn child since he had not been alive to begin with.

Although the date of the speech, about 400 B.C., seems reasonably certain, its authorship is not. Even in antiquity, several of the sources referring to the speech question its authenticity. For our purpose it does not matter whether or not Lysias actually wrote it so long as the approximate date is correct.[26] Other criticisms are more relevant.

Some scholars, including Edelstein, alleged that the reason why Antigenes was prosecuting his wife was not because of the abortion but because she had undergone the procedure without his consent and deprived him of a male child. Closely related to this is the objection that, given the absence of a public prosecutor at Athens, no charges would have been brought against "Ms. Antigenes" had she had her abortion with her husband's consent. To both of these criticisms the reply must be made that the charge was *homicide (phonos)*, and *not* "a violation of the father's right to his offspring"—male or female. Antigenes doubtless used the fact that his boy had been killed to win the sympathy of the all-male jury; one does not need to be a feminist to deplore the misogyny of the ancient Greeks. Without a public prosecutor in Athens, *any* homicide went unpunished if no citizen, usually a member of the victim's family, could be found to prosecute the murderer.[27]

The evidence, indicating that before 300 B.C. the attitude of the Greeks toward abortion was lenient, should not be minimized, although one text, frequently cited to prove this, actually demonstrated no such thing.[28] Nonetheless, some felt that the procedure was immoral, even criminal, and the echo of their voices can still be heard but, deplorably, not in *Roe v. Wade*.

B. THE HELLENISTIC JEWISH COMMUNITY

IT WAS NOT until the Hellenistic period that vocal opposition to abortion became substantial and broadly based. The distinction between the Hellenic and Hellenistic phases of classical civilization is normally placed at 323 B.C., Alexander the Great's death, or 322 B.C., Aristotle's death. The difference between the Hellenic and Hellenistic eras is to a great extent one of cultural diffusion. Until the time of Alexander the Great, Hellenic civilization was confined to Greece proper, Macedonia and Thrace, the islands of the Aegean sea, Sicily and southern Italy, the west coast of Asia Minor, the periphery of the Black Sea, and a few other outposts such as the city of Cyrene in what is now Libya. Alexander, a hellenized Macedonian from just north of Greece, overran a vast area of the Near and Middle East extending to what is now Afghanistan (then called Bactria) and northwestern India. This Greek civilization was diffused from the Indus river to Sicily. As other ethnic groups became hellenized, assimilated to the Greeks, all that was required was that one speak *koine*, the simplified form of classical Greek that served as the common speech of the Hellenistic world.

In the cosmopolitan Hellenistic world, Jews played a role that was by no means unimportant. The Diaspora, a Greek word meaning "dispersion," was composed of Jews who had left their homeland to seek opportunity elsewhere. The largest of these Diasporic communities was in Alexandria, where thirty to forty percent of the inhabitants were Jews. Although they could never become completely hellenized without abandoning their ancestral religion, they exhibited a high degree of linguistic and cultural assimilation. Many second- and third-generation Jews of the Diaspora felt far more comfortable with *koine* Greek than with Hebrew or Aramaic.[29] There is no reason why a Hellenized Jew such as Philo ought not be considered a Greek.

The Septuagint, a Greek translation of the Hebrew Old Testament written in Alexandria between 300 and 250 B.C., was prepared for the benefit of the Jewish community members who had forgotten Hebrew and spoke Greek as their native language. The Septuagint exhibits certain important differences from the Hebrew Old Testament. One of these is on the matter of abortion. It has sometimes been alleged that the Hebrew Old Testament has nothing to say on abortion. This is not entirely true. A modern English translation of Exodus 21:22–25 states:

> If, when men come to blows, they hurt a woman who is pregnant and she suffers a miscarriage [i.e., an involuntary abortion], though she does not die of it, the man responsible must pay the compensation demanded of him by the woman's master [husband]; he shall hand it over, after arbitration. But should she die, you shall give life for life, eye for eye, tooth for tooth, hand for hand, foot for foot, burn for burn, wound for wound, stripe for stripe.[30]

Compare the English translation of the Septuagint version of Exodus, 21:22–25:

> And if two men fight and smite a woman with child, and her child be born [dead and] imperfectly formed, he [i.e., the man responsible] shall be forced to pay a penalty: as the woman's husband may lay upon him, he

shall pay with a valuation. But if it [the child] be [dead but otherwise] perfectly formed, he [the responsible one] shall give life for life, eye for eye, tooth for tooth, hand for hand, foot for foot, burn for burn, wound for wound, stripe for stripe.[31]

In the Septuagint the emphasis has been moved from injury to the *mother* to injury to the *child*. A man who caused an accidental abortion had, at the very least, to pay a substantial fine if the child were found to be "imperfectly formed" (μὴ ἐξεικονισμένον) (me exeikonismenon) which probably means that the pregnancy was terminated early enough that the fetus did not have fully human shape. But, if the child were "perfectly formed" (ἐξεικονισμένον) (exeikonismenon), probably meaning that the pregnancy was terminated at a stage late enough that the fetus was obviously and recognizably of human shape, the offense was treated as a homicide. Whether or not this represents a hardening of Jewish attitudes toward abortion from the time the Hebrew Exodus was written, or whether the translator of the Septuagint had access to manuscripts now lost to us, can no longer be determined. But there can be no question that Hellenistic Jewry took this passage to mean a nearly absolute ban on abortion.[32]

Ludwig Edelstein, himself a Jew, was aware of this opposition.[33] Why did he ignore this source when writing his monograph? Simply answered, it was not his topic. His monograph was on the Hippocratic oath, not on abortion. And the oath was a *pagan* one, as shown by the first clause, where the taker swears "by Apollo [the] Physician . . . and all the gods and godesses." Since this pagan invocation precludes Jewish authorship, there was no need for Edelstein to consider Judaic opposition to abortion. Yet, the Jewish community was an important part of the Graeco-Roman world after Alexander the Great. Justice Blackmun blindly and uncritically used Edelstein's work as a general survey of classical attitudes toward abortion, a purpose for which it was never intended, and overlooked the Hellenistic Jewish community. *Roe v. Wade* is a much weaker decision because of Blackmun's failure to assemble current scholarly opinion.

C. TWO TEMPLE DESCRIPTIONS

STILL, IT MUST be conceded that a stronger case could be argued if one could uncover religious opposition to abortion that was purely pagan, yet not Pythagorean, in origin. Evidence for such opposition exists. In 1963 and 1969, two Greek inscriptions uncovered at pagan temples were published. The first can be dated to about 130 B.C. and comes from a temple of Dionysius in the Greek town of Philadelphia in Lydia,

Western Asia Minor. The inscription invites all, men or women, slave or free, into the temple, presumably to worship. But only those are permitted to enter who have employed, or counselled or helped anyone to employ "neither philters, nor abortifacients, nor contraceptives, nor any other type of infanticide" (<μὴ>φίλτρον, μὴ φθορεῖον, μὴ <ἀτ>οκεῖον, μ<ὴ ἄλλο τι παιδο>φόνον) (*philtron, me phthoreion, me <at>okeion, m<e allo ti paido> phonon.*). Malefactors who have done any of these things are excluded from the temple forever. Was this inscription unique? Did it merely represent an isolated local tradition? By no means! Another Greek inscription has been discovered in Ptolemais, in Upper (southern) Egypt. It dates from the first century B.C., about 100 years after the inscription at Philadelphia. The Egyptian inscription is very mutilated. What does remain shows that a woman who had undergone an abortion, or perhaps merely attempted an abortion, for the meaning of the word ἔκτρωσμος is ambiguous, is barred from entering the temple for forty days.[34] Would Professor Edelstein have modified his hypothesis had he been aware of these inscriptions? We have no way of knowing. But it ought to have occurred to Justice Blackmun that some new evidence might have turned up in the thirty years between 1943 and 1973. Apparently, it did not occur to him; and *Roe v. Wade* suffered another blow to its scholarly integrity.

D. CICERO'S *ON BEHALF OF CLUENTIUS (PRO CLUENTIO)*

MARCUS TULLIUS CICERO (106–43 B.C.) was antiquity's greatest trial lawyer. His defense attorney speech, given in 66 B.C. at the trial of Aulus Cluentius, provides us with an interesting clue to both Roman and Greek abortion attitudes. Cluentius' case was sordid. It seems that the charges against him were trumped up by the prosecuting attorney, Oppianicus, because Cluentius had earlier in his career prosecuted Oppianicus' father. Much of Cicero's time was spent in proving that Oppianicus senior had been legitimately prosecuted by Cluentius. One of the charges against the elder Oppianicus had been that he had bribed a woman to have an abortion in order to change the outcome of a lucrative will. Speaking to the jury, Cicero recalled a case which occurred during his travels in Asia. "A certain woman of Miletus," a Greek town in Western Asia Minor, was pregnant at the time of her husband's death. The dying husband wrote a will making the unborn child his primary heir. Cicero did not mention whether the child's sex would have made any difference under the will, so we can assume it had no bearing on the events. Tentative heirs were provided for if the child did not survive. These exchangeable heirs bribed the widow to have an abortion; presumably, the estate was a substantial one and well worth the risk. When the crime was discovered, she was condemned to death. "And rightly so," continues Cicero,

> for she [i.e., the widow] had cheated the father of his hope, his name of memory, his clan of its support [*subsidium*], his [immediate] family of an heir, and the state [i.e., Miletus] of a citizen-to-be."[35]

Like the case of Lysias some 350 years earlier, objections have been made that this does not demonstrate an anti-abortion sentiment in the classical world. Many of the protests are similar. As with the case of Lysias, Edelstein stated the widow was put to death *not* because of the abortion, *but* "because the father's right to his offspring had been violated by the mother's action."[36] The fact that the husband was dead at the time of the actual abortion robs this argument of some persuasive force.

A second question is related to the first; the widow was killed for testamentary fraud and not for the abortion. We understand little about Greek law, but it is unlikely that testamentary fraud was a capital offense. As noted in the quote above, there were a variety of reasons for the execution. One of the charges levied against the widow was that she had deprived her husband's clan of its *subsidium* (numerical support). Most of the ancients, including the Jews, wanted their immediate and extended families to "be fruitful and multiply" so the line would not die out. In addition, the fact that Miletus considered the unborn child a *designatum . . . civum* (citizen to be) suggests that the fetus was thought of as a person.

A final group of critics pointed out that Cicero was referring to a local law and not to a measure applicable throughout Roman dominions. Cicero's entire life was spent in the last decades of the Roman Republic. Though Rome acquired substantial foreign sovereignty in the republican period, these territories were allowed to live under their own local laws. The idea of a uniform code of laws for the entire Roman state did not arise until the imperial period was well under way. The only evidence this quoted passage provides, so say the critics, is that abortion was a capital offense in Miletus but *not* throughout the Roman state.

We must carefully reevaluate Cicero's quote. *On Behalf of Cluentius*, an actual speech, was delivered in court before a jury. Cicero was trying to shock them with the alleged misdeeds of the elder Oppianicus. Would he have wasted his valuable time describing an incident if he thought the jury would disregard the event as trivial? Of course not! Cicero, a shrewd courtroom tactician, knew that a substantial number of jurors would be horrified that the prosecuting attorney's father had once bribed a woman to undergo an abortion even if such a deed were not an indictable offense. Cicero was not relying solely on the abortion to shock the jurors, because the list of Oppianicus senior's crimes was a long one, nor were there any unambiguous indications that abortion was against Roman (as opposed to Milesian) law. Still, the clear implication is that it was a reprehensible deed and that there *ought* to be a law against it. But if one believes the reasoning in *Roe v. Wade*, the deed and judgment were a simple matter of "a concept of a violation of the father's right to his offspring."[37]

E. THE TESTIMONY OF JUVENAL

OTHER EVIDENCE ON abortion exists as we turn from a great jurist to the renowned Roman satirist Juvenal. He probably penned most of his writings between A.D. 100 and 130. Though he seems to have mellowed somewhat with age, his satires are a scathing indictment of the follies, vices, and foibles of contemporary Roman society. Were Juvenal alive today, he would be considered a right-wing extremist, albeit a brilliant one, for he blamed many of Rome's troubles on foreigners, homosexuals, and "liberated" women.

Juvenal mentioned abortion several times. In his *Sixth Satire*, he railed against women who have love affairs with sterile men "because there is no need for an abortion."[38] Later in the *Satire*, he described the low birth rate among the upper classes of his day:

> ...but when did you discover
> Labor pains in a golden bed? There are potent prescriptions,
> Fine professional skills, to be hired for inducing abortions.
> Killing mankind [*homines*] in the womb. Rejoice, unfortunate husband,
> Give her the dose yourself, whatever it is; never let her
> Carry until quickening time, or go to full term and deliver.... [39]

These and one or two other passages in Juvenal have been cited *ad nauseam* to show the prevalence of abortion among at least the social elite of the Roman Empire. But Juvenal was a satirical writer and used the traditional weapons of the genre, including hyperbole and caricature. He began his *Sixth Satire* with a diatribe aimed at a friend who was engaged to be married. Why get married, argued Juvenal, when good sturdy rope was so cheap and there were so many convenient places in Rome to hang oneself?

Today, we still understand the humor; and so must have Juvenal's audience. But a modern, academic sociologist using this passage to prove that a high percentage of Roman males committed suicide just before marriage would be laughed out of his profession. Why do scholars take a different view of the passages on abortion? There is a substantial grain of truth to Juvenal's assertions, but he exaggerated beyond proportion in order to write effective satire.[40]

Another point should be made. Just as did Cicero, but for different reasons, Juvenal was trying to shock his audience; it is unlikely he would have tried to horrify his audience with an act they regarded as neither immoral nor shocking. Reason asserts that the Roman society of Juvenal's time contained substantial numbers of people who regarded abortion as an abhorrent and reprehensible deed. These people *may* have been a minority in A.D. 100, but the evidence indicates they were a minority that had been growing steadily for four centuries. Unfortunately, we could never know this from a reading of the *Roe v. Wade* decision.

IV. Edelstein, Hippocrates, and Justice Blackmun: Reappraisal and Rebuttal

DESPITE THE ABOVE stated objections, Ludwig Edelstein's assertion on the authorship of the Hippocratic oath was a viable hypothesis. However, it must be restated in a more cautious and less encompassing fashion. Recall that this essay examined only one aspect of Edelstein's proof. The oath's prohibition of surgery and its initiatory tone still point to a Pythagorean source. To use the oath's prohibition of euthanasia as proof of Pythagorean origin is suspect. While Romans seem to have had a lenient view of suicide, we know considerably less about the Greeks' attitudes toward the act.

Interestingly, specific examples of suicide, whether physician assisted or otherwise, cited in Edelstein's monograph, were preponderantly drawn from Roman, not Hellenic or Hellenistic, sources.[41] Since the original language of the Hippocratic oath is Greek, not Latin, it is certain that the author was not Roman. Consequently, Edelstein ought to have been more cautious in using evidence on suicide and euthanasia drawn from the Roman period. More importantly, his allegations that "[a]bortion was practiced in Greek times no less than the Roman era, and that it was resorted to without scruple," with its implied premise that *all* Greeks and *all* Romans at *all* times approved the procedure, is still indefensible. It was over-argument by Edelstein. Similarly, we have seen how Edelstein oversimplified the data provided by Lysias's *On Abortion* and Cicero's *On Behalf of Cluentius* by asserting that in each case, the "abortion was prosecuted...because the father's right to his offspring had been violated by the mother's action." Much more scientific and scholarly was Edelstein's statement that "[in] no other stratum of Greek opinion were such [antiabortion] views held in the same spirit of uncompromising austerity" as among the Pythagoreans, particularly if one adds the words "before 300 B.C." to the sentence.

In 450 B.C. most Greeks probably did not regard abortion as either repellent or distasteful. We know little about what the Romans thought at this time. But, by A.D. 100, antiabortion sentiment had gained ground to the point where it had become the prevailing attitude of at the very least a substantial minority, possibly a majority, of Greeks and Romans.[42] Although Christianity had no impact on this trend, one could plausibly argue that the rise of prolife sentiments may have been due in part to the influence of the Hellenized and Romanized Jewish Diaspora.

Edelstein dated the composition of the Hippocratic oath between 400 and 300 B.C.[43] Except among the Pythagoreans, antiabortion feeling was weak at this time, though it did exist in some quarters. Consequently, Edelstein's argument concerning abortion can be used in support of his hypothesis, provided it is restated in a more conservative and specific manner. One should not regard with condescension the fact that the Pythagoreans were the first pagans in classical antiquity to systematically oppose abortion. They were quite influential in the evolution of Greek religious, ethical, philosophical, and scientific thought. We have also seen that the Pythagorean attitude toward what we refer to as human rights was far in advance of its time. Also, Pythagorean affirmation of the equality of women was a rarity among Greeks and Romans.[44]

Justice Blackmun was inept in his attempt to understand history and he compounded his inadequacies with several naive and sloppy mistakes when he researched and wrote that portion of *Roe v. Wade* evaluating the ancient world. He did not consult any primary sources, even though most of them were available in English translations. Instead, he relied exclusively on a single secondary monograph, the main topic of which was not even abortion. Incredibly, he ignored the possibility that new evidence might have appeared in the thirty-year interval since the initial publication of Edelstein's essay. The monograph was highly technical and written for Edelstein's fellow classicists, who were knowledgeable enough to recognize and compensate for his occasional exaggerations and unwarranted generalizations. They understood that his assertions that "ancient religion" was "indifferent" to abortion really meant, "Most pagans in classical antiquity, especially before the Hellenistic period, were indifferent to abortion."

Justice Blackmun was apparently unaware of his misreading of historical studies. Moreover, as the essays by Professors Joseph Dellapenna and John Connery show, this kind of third-rate historical scholarship pervades much more of *Roe v. Wade* than just the section on antiquity. In reply to the objection that the decision ought to be judged on legal and not historical grounds, one must cite Blackmun's own wish to "place some emphasis upon... history and what history reveals about man's attitude toward the abortive procedure." As a historical document, *Roe v. Wade* makes a decisive comment on modern American society. Certainly we cannot be proud of the judgment history will make of us based on Blackmun's decision.

This leads to a final analogy. The above-stated conclusion on *Roe v. Wade* is both cogent and inescapable. With careful selection of evidence, virtually anything can be justified by appeals to historical fact. The following analogy speaks for itself. Let us assume a lawsuit seeking to reinstate slavery in the United States is heard before the Supreme Court. Of course, no one would be forced to own slaves; it would be a matter of personal choice. The majority opinion declares that history and what history reveals about man's attitude toward slavery will receive proper emphasis. The decision notes that laws banning or restricting slavery are of recent origin. Laws proscribing slavery were not of ancient nor common law beginnings. Instead, they were derived from changes occurring in the latter half of the nineteenth century. The Court announces that slavery was practiced by both the Greeks and Romans, and that it was resorted to without scruple. Ancient religions did not bar slavery.

There was opposition, but it originated among the Pythagoreans, as well as among the Stoics in the Hellenistic and Roman periods. These were small and isolated groups. No other stratum of Greek or Roman opinion held such views with the same spirit of uncompromising austerity. In fact, most Greek thinkers commended slavery. The apparent rigidity of the Pythagorean and Stoic opposition to slavery can thus be explained in historical context.[45] With the end of antiquity, a decided change took place. Christianity considered slavery unethical, at least in theory, but opposition to slavery was confined primarily to ecclesiastical circles. Slavery in mediaeval Western Europe declined, but it never disappeared. Even the common law recognized slavery. After 1500, slavery revived and in America it became an integral part of the American tradition. The commonly held view that the American Civil War was fought to abolish slavery is a misinterpretation of history. Actually, conflicts over tariff policy and geographical sectionalism were the primary causes of the war. President Lincoln promulgated his Emancipation Proclamation as a wartime punitive measure against the Confederacy, not because he had a commitment to human rights.

Given the division of opinion, the Court concludes, all official bans on slavery, including federal, state, and local laws, must be regarded as an unconstitutional imposition of private religious or ethical beliefs upon the general public. Therefore, all such laws must be immediately repealed.

An absurd analogy? Those who agree with *Roe v. Wade* and are consistent with Justice Blackmun's reasoning must agree with the cogency of the analogical reasoning. Most people recognize the analogy as patently absurd. Unfortunately, since the 1973 *Roe v. Wade* opinion, we are burdened with an illogical and historically flawed United States Supreme Court decision. It is time to correct the record.

Notes

1. A suitable compromise to the question of the authenticity of the Hippocratic corpus is accepted by W.H.S. Jones in his "General Introduction" to [The Works of] *Hippocrates, with an English Translation*, The Loeb Classical Library (Cambridge: Harvard University Press, 1923), xxix. According to Jones, the works attributed to Hippocrates represent an archive or library of his school. Much more recently, Edwin B. Levine has states in *Hippocrates* (New York: Twayne Publishers, 1971), 20, that Jones's conclusion "needs no important modification though it was made more than forty-five years ago."

2. Ludwig Edelstein, *The Hippocratic Oath: Text, Translation, and Interpretation*, Supplements to *The Bulletin of the History of Medicine*, no. 1 (Baltimore: The Johns Hopkins Press, 1943). The original edition is now rather hard to get. I have used the more accessible (and unaltered) reprint in *Ancient Medicine: Selected Papers of Ludwig Edelstein*, ed. Owsei and C. Lilian Temkin (Baltimore: The Johns Hopkins Press, 1967), 3–63, hereafter cited as "Edelstein, *Oath*." The pagination of the reprint differs slightly from that of the original, but this is a small inconvenience which is compensated for by the wider availability of the former.

3. Edelstein, *Oath*, 53–54.

4. There is a vast scholarly literature on Pythagoras and his school. Here, as elsewhere in these notes, I have confined myself mostly to what has been published in English. The following four books are representative of those appearing since 1960. Peter Gorman, *Pythagoras: A Life* (London: Routledge & Kegan Paul, 1979) is the newest and most frankly "popular" of the four. Though aimed at an educated general audience, it provides a good bibliography for those wishing further to explore the subject. More scholarly are three other books, two with the same title: C.J. de Vogel, *Pythagoras and Early Pythagoreanism* (Assen, Netherlands: Van Gorcum & Co., 1962); J.A. Philip, *Pythagoras and Early Pythagoreanism* (Toronto: University of Toronto Press, 1966); and Walter Burkert, *Lore and Science in Ancient Pythagoreanism*, trans. Edwin L. Minar, Jr. (Cambridge: Harvard University Press, 1972). A shorter account of

Pythagoras and his school can be found in John Burnet's classic *Early Greek Philosophy*, 4th ed. (London: The Macmillan Co., 1930), chap. II, §§32–54, chap. VII, passim. Nothing written by Pythagoras himself survives, but a selection from the writings of later Pythagoreans, plus what philosophers of other schools said of Pythagoreanism, can be found in English translation in Milton C. Nahm, *Selections from Early Greek Philosophy*, 3rd ed. (New York: Appleton-Century-Crofts, 1947), 68–83. On the attraction Pythagoreanism had for medical doctors, see de Vogel, *Pythagoras and Early Pythagoreanism*, chap. X. He notes that all three biographies of Pythagoras which have come down to us state that he practiced medicine. See also Jones, "General Introduction," xi: "The first philosophers to take a serious interest in medicine were the Pythagoreans." In this period, the distinction we now make between a philosopher and a scientist did not exist.

Edelstein, *Oath*, 40–41, points out that the belief that doctors were initiated into brotherhoods can be traced back no further than the writings of Galen, a physician who lived around A.D. 130–200. Galen, a figure from the late classical period, does not use the Hippocratic oath to support this view, leaving modern scholars with the strong suspicion that at the time there existed another commonly accepted explanation for the initiatory tone of the oath.

The Pythagorean clubs are often referred to as "brotherhoods" or "fraternities." This is misleading, for women were admitted to membership on an equal basis with men.

See also Edelstein, *Oath*, 26–30, 32, 43–47.

5. Edelstein, *Oath*, 5 (Greek text), 6 (English translation). At the 1981 annual meeting of the American Philological Association, Edwin B. Levine challenged the conventional translation of πεσσόν φϑηόριον/*pesson phtheorion*. Levine believes that "the Oath does not refer to abortion at all." *Abstracts of Papers Read at the 1981 Meeting*, American Philological Association, 17. To my knowledge, no other scholar has supported this interpretation, nor has the full text of Professor Levine's paper been published.

6. Although the prohibitions on physician-assisted suicide and abortion do not occur until the fourth paragraph of the Oath, Edelstein examined them first in his monograph. Edelstein, *Oath*, 9–20.

7. Edelstein, *Oath*, 39.

8. Review by Edwin L. Minar, Jr. of Connecticut College, in *The American Journal of Philology* 66 (1945): 108.

9. Review by H.N. Couch of Brown University in *Classical Philology* 39 (1944): 260.

10. Owsei and C. Lilian Temkin, "Editors' Introduction," in *Ancient Medicine*, ix.

11. G.M.A. Grube's classic study, *Plato's Thought* (1935; reprint ed., London: Methuen, 1980), 4: "The Pythagoreans also quite clearly had a great influence on Plato, as [also] probably on Socrates . . ." This is merely one of dozens of similar authorities. See also de Vogel, *Pythagoras and Early Pythagoreanism*, 197–98.

12. R.T. Wallsi, *Neoplatonism* (London: Gerald Duckworth & Co., 1972), 32, observes that doctrines of late Pythagoreanism (or Neopythagoreanism,

though Wallis notes that adherents of the school would have rejected the preface "Neo-") "are not easily distinguished from those of Middle Platonism and some of its representatives like Numenius of Apamea [second century A.D.] are indifferently assigned by our sources to both schools."

13. For a good summary of the influence of Pythagoreanism on Greek and Roman science, religion, and philosophy, see Gorman, *Pythagoras: A Life*, chap. X, "The Heritage of Pythagoreanism." The Pythagorean clubs of southern Italy appear to have been suppressed because they became involved in political activities, but their precise intentions were unclear. See Kurt von Fritz, *Pythagorean Politics in South Italy* (New York: Columbia University Press, 1940) and Edwin L. Minar, Jr., *Early Pythagorean Politics in Practice and Theory*, Connecticut College Monographs, no. 2 (Baltimore: The Waverly Press, 1942). On Philo and (Neo-) Pythagoreanism, see Erwin Goodenough, *An Introduction to Philo Judaeus*, 2nd ed. (New York: Barnes & Noble, 1962), 110–11. Harry A. Wolfson, *Philo: Foundation of Religious Philosophy in Judaism, Christianity, and Islam*, 3rd ed. rev., vol. 1 (Cambridge: Harvard University Press, 1947, 107–8, tends to minimize the influence of Pythagoreanism on Philo. For the sect's influence on Clement, see Salvatore R.C. Lilla, *Clement of Alexandria* (Oxford: Oxford University Press, 1971), 195–96.

14. Edelstein, *Oath*, 16.

15. Robert Woodward and Scott Armstrong, *The Brethren* (New York: Simon & Schuster, 1979), 173, 174–75. Blackmun served for ten years as general counsel to the Mayo Clinic.

16. Roe v. Wade, 410 U.S. 113, 116–117 (1973).

17. 410 U.S. at 130.

18. 410 U.S. at 130, quoting Edelstein, *Oath*, at 13 (p. 10 of the original edition).

19. 410 U.S. at 130, paraphrasing Edelstein, *Oath*, at 14.

20. 410 U.S. at 130, paraphrasing Edelstein, *Oath*, at 15–16.

21. 410 U.S. at 131–132, paraphrasing Edelstein, *Oath*, at 18, 39.

22. 410 U.S. at 132.

23. Edelstein, *Oath*, 53.

24. Woodward & Armstrong, 165–89, 229–40.

25. Milan: A. Guiffre, 1971; hereafter cited as Nardi, *Aborto*.

26. Nardi, *Aborto*, 82–90 gives the sources that refer to the lost speech of Lysias, with full references (most will only be found in large universities with research libraries) and Italian translations. Unfortunately, the one sentence we have from the oration has nothing to do with the central issue, though it does seem to establish that "Ms. Antigenes" was defended by her brother rather than speaking on her own behalf: "Observe [,gentlemen of the jury,] how our adversary Antigenes has proceeded: after having launched a lawsuit against our mother, he pretended to marry our sister, all the while pressing his lawsuit to avoid paying a fine of a thousand drachmas..." The case was obviously an unsavory one. Perhaps Antigenes had married (apparently illegally) his wife to prevent her from testifying against him in a lawsuit he was pressing against her mother. An attorney experienced in criminal or divorce law could posit a dozen explanations for the sentence.

27. There is one other objection: The so-called speech of Lysias may not refer to an actual court case at all. It may simply be a dialogue between representatives of "prolife" and "prochoice" factions in Athens set as a fictional court case. Plato and Xenophon had popularized the dialogue as a literary form. Nardi does not pass judgment, nor does he cite any scholarly works advocating this thesis. However, in English this view is taken by Angela C.Darkow, *The Spurious Speeches in the Lysianic Corpus* (Bryn Mawr: Bryn Mawr College, 1917). Darkow proposed the hypothesis that none of Lysias's "speeches" were actually delivered in court. They are merely fictional dialogues or rhetorical exercises. Her theory has not, to my knowledge, found general acceptance.

28. This, of course, is Plato *Republic* 5. 461c cited by Edelstein, *Oath*, 18, n. 39, and by many others. But what is the *Republic*? It is Plato's vision of the ideal state. As such, it is also the first known example of a remarkably long-lived genre: the utopian fantasy. No utopian (more properly, eutopian or kallo-topian) fantasy can be used as a reliable index for the mores of its day. Would we use Sir Thomas More's *Utopia* to show what conditions were like in Henry VIII's England? Or Edward Bellamy's *Looking Backward* as a guide to nineteenth century America? Plato's ideal state is ruled by an oligarchy of "philosopher kings" who practice absolute communism, including the holding of wives and husbands in common. Was this typical of most Greek societies around 400 B.C.—or ever? The section of the *Republic* just before that on abortion (5. 451D-456E) contains the classic argument for women's equality (women were to be equals only among the elite which governed Plato's utopia—commoners were not affected). Can we argue on the basis of these paragraphs that women were generally conceded a status equal to men in ancient Greece? Hardly! Plato himself admits this (452A-B). He is here writing speculative fiction (the currently fashionable and more accurate term for "science-fiction"). As John Noonan has pointed out, "it is impossible to say with what seriousness Plato endorsed this suggestion." "An Almost Absolute Value in History," in *The Morality of Abortion* (Cambridge: Harvard University Press, 1970), 5.

29. Victor Tcherikover, *Hellenistic Civilization and the Jews* (New York: Jewish Publications Society of America, 1959), 347: "The Jews outside Palestine spoke, wrote, and generally thought in Greek."

30. The King James version is not very clear on this passage; this translation is from the Jerusalem Bible.

31. *The Septuagint Version of the Old Testament, with an English Translation* (Grand Rapids: Zondervan Publishing House, 1970). The translator's name is not given, but this appears to be an unaltered reprint of a much older edition, probably that of Thackeray (1917). That Graeco-Roman Jewry generally regarded this passage as a general ban on abortion is shown by Philo Judaeus, *De Specialibus Legibus* (*On the Special Laws*) 3. 19. 108-9. Just after his condemnation of abortion, Philo condemns infanticide (3. 20. 110-19).

32. If there did exist another manuscript tradition of Exodus, it must have been already lost by late antiquity, for St. Jerome, in his Vulgate translation of the Bible, made between A.D. 387 and 402, used essentially the same Hebrew text that we use today.

33. Edelstein, *Oath*, 16, n. 31, attributed antisuicide sentiment in late antiquity to "the influence of Jewish-Christian ideas." Again at 19, n. 45, opposition to abortion by the poet Phocylides was dismissed by Edelstein because this particular man was not the well-known Phocylides who wrote around 540 B.C., but "a Hellenistic Jew [who lived at] the beginning of the Christian era," either named Phocylides, or using this as a pen-name.

34. The full (surviving) texts of both inscriptions, as well as Italian translations and references to where the texts were originally published, are given in Nardi, *Aborto*, 193–94, 213–14. The publication of the Philadelphia inscription in 1963 was not its first. It was first printed in 1920, in Wilhelm Dittenberg, ed. *Sylloge Inscriptionum Graecarum*, III (Lepizig, S. Hirzel, 1920; reprinted, 1960), 985.20–21. At that time, the inscription attracted the attention of philologists because of the appearance of ἀτοκεῖον/*atokeion* ("contraceptive"), a word infrequently used in ancient Greek. In 1920, an alternative reading was given to the last few words of the inscription: "....μ<ὴ ἀρπαγμὸν, μὴ> φόνον/ ... m<e harpagmon, me>phonon [... no<r rate, nor> homicide]." A word of explanation about the inscription: Those portions of the inscription in triangular braces are missing in the original because of mutilations, but have been restored. A gap in an inscription (called a "lacuna"; plural, "lacunae") can often be restored by an epigrapher (one who specializes in the study of inscriptions) if it is short, and especially if the number of letters in the lacuna can be estimated. I have inserted the braces in the English translation at about the same places where they are inserted in the Greek original. One reading takes up 14 spaces; the other, 15—there is no letter "H" in Classical or Modern Greek, the sound being indicated by a diacritical mark appearing above what would in English be the second letter, and there would have been no punctuation on the inscription. Either reading is perfectly permissible.

Nardi, *Aborto*, 191–93, gives the text of a third inscription discovered on the Aegean island of Delos and probably dating to the second century B.C. It bars women from entering a temple for seven days after giving birth; forty days after undergoing an abortion. A distinction must be made here between *sin* and *ritual impurity*. The concept of ritual impurity is found in many primitive religions. One that survives is the restriction placed by Orthodox Judaism on menstruating women. This does not imply moral condemnation of a woman's menstrual cycle which, after all, is a perfectly natural process. The Delos inscription appears to be concerned more with ritual or cult impurity than with moral impurity (i.e., sin). This is indicated by the fact that women who have given birth are excluded from the temple. However, the exclusion is only for seven days, while it is forty days for an abortion. This may show that the builders of the temple had some awareness of the moral implications of abortion. Consequently, this inscription may, with some reservations, be mentioned with the others to show pagan religious opposition to abortion.

There can be little question that the Philadelphia inscription condemns both abortion and contraception as sins, and—if one accepts Nardi's reading— also infanticide. Note how not only the women how have indulged in these practices are excluded from the temple, but also those (regardless of gender) who have counselled or aided them. This is in keeping with the tone of the inscription, which seems to imply that the builders of the temple believed in the equality of men and women, slaves and freemen. The Pythagoreans also believed in this. It is possible, but improbable, that the builders of the temple were Pythagoreans. Temples were primarily places where sacrifices (usually bloody) were offered to the gods. While Pythagoreans, as we have seen, worshipped the traditional gods, they did not offer bloody animal sacrifices, and there is no evidence that they ever built temples. If the temple at Philadelphia had been dedicated to Apollo rather than Dionysius, the hypothesis of a Pythagorean builder(s) would be more plausible, since Apollo was honored by the sect above all other gods.

Although, in the text of the paper, I have largely followed Nardi's reasoning on the Ptolemais inscription, I can be more speculative in this footnote. Liddell and Scott's standard *Greek-English Lexicon* is clear on the meaning of ἔκτρωσμος /*ektrōsmos*. It means *attempted* abortion, not the act itself. It is tempting to speculate that the surviving portion of the inscription is merely a lesser penalty, and that women who attempted abortions and succeeded were condemned more severely— perhaps to be forever excluded from the temple, as at Philadelphia. Of course, this hypothesis can never be proven.

35. Cicero, *Pro Cluentio*, XI, 32. The translation is that of H. Grose Hodge, *Cicero: The Speeches*, The Loeb Classical Library (Cambridge: Harvard University Press, 1927), 255. I have eliminated one misleading word from Hodge's translation and substituted another which is closer to Cicero's probable meaning.

36. Edelstein, *Oath*, 15–16.

37. For a fuller commentary, see Nardi, *Aborto*, 214–28.

38. Juvenal, *Satire*, VI, line 368.

39. Ibid., ll. 594–600. The translation is by Rolfe Humphries, *The Satires of Juvenal* (Bloomington: University of Indiana Press, 1958), 87.

40. This observation is not original. Many others have pointed out the element of exaggeration inherent in all satire, including Juvenal's. See Nardi, *Aborto*, 316, n. 7. To Nardi's citations should be added the remark of Gilbert Highet, *Juvenal the Satirist* (Oxford: Oxford University Press, 1954), 101: "[This passage in Satire Six] strikes us with the same unreality as the account of the men's homosexual society in Satire Two, and its details are unconfirmed by other writers: so that it might all come from Juvenal's angry conviction that Roman women were hopelessly corrupt, and rather be inference and invention rather than true evidence. We have no way of checking. All we can say is that nothing Juvenal describes is impossible and that worse things are known from both ancient and modern times."

41. Edelstein, *Oath*, 11, n. 15. Edelstein mentions many Greek thinkers who approved suicide in theory. But most of his examples of persons who committed suicide are from the Roman period. Romans who killed themselves (Lucretia, Gaius Gracchus, Brutus, Cato the Younger, Marc Antony, Nero) are widely known, but there are few Greeks who did the same.

42. Nardi, *Aborto*, 318–19, protests against those (including Edelstein) who see the dominant opinion among pagans about A.D. 100 as being that the unborn child

was merely part of the mother's body. He points to the two passages from Juvenal just quoted as indicating the existence of a "consapevolezza popolare che l'aborto sia omicido"—"popular consensus that abortion is homicide." Note also Juvenal's condemnation of infanticide in the lines just after 600 in the Sixth Satire.

43. Edelstein, *Oath*, 55–60.

44. Edelstein, *Oath*, 34–35. The Pythagoreans also condemned homosexuality. When all is said and done, I must agree with E.D. Phillips, *Greek Medicine* (London: Thames & Hudson, 1973), 116, that Edelstein's "is at least a tenable theory, which explains the peculiarities of the Oath."

45. Neither the Pythagoreans nor the Stoics were isolated groups, though both had few members. The Stoics were quite influential among the upper-class intellectuals of the Roman Empire. To say that ancient religion did not bar slavery ignores not only Pythagoreanism and Stoicism (though admittedly the latter was not necessarily a "religion"), but also Jewish restrictions upon slavery. As with abortion, few challenged the institution of slavery before 300 B.C. With the rise of "Middle Stoicism" after 200 B.C., a steadily rising tide of antislavery sentiment could be detected among educated pagans, eventually leading to legislation under the Roman Empire mitigating the condition of slaves and to large-scale voluntary manumission. On this, see William Westerman, *The Slave Systems of Greek and Roman Antiquity* (Philadelphia: The American Philosophical Society, 1955), chap. 17.

PART III

Strategies for the Reversal of Roe v. Wade

William Bentley Ball

Case Tactics and Court Strategies for Reversing *Roe v. Wade*

THE LOGICAL POINT of departure in discussing litigation strategy is at least one step removed from a discussion of court-room tactics. In the case of abortion litigation, one should start with a consideration of the social and historical setting in which that litigation will be conducted. That setting has been marked by several recent developments of great consequence. Theistic religion and its derivative morality have been widely abandoned in individual lives. Arising in their stead have been a materialistic and hedonistic culture and a profound tendency to restrict liberties associated with a belief in God. This culture has acquired power and established its own legal regime, resulting in the gradual erosion of fundamental human rights. Denial of civil rights to the unborn is a prime embodiment of this very process.

It is not surprising that decisions of federal judges are influenced by America's materialistic, sensate culture. One must only ponder whether there is enough ethical integrity, as conceived in the great traditions of civility which are our inheritance, to assure that judges will respect life and liberty.

Courtroom arguments by attorneys, no matter how knowledgeable, acute and fervent, may be unable to overcome the pervasive effect of American culture. However, the good news is that the prolife movement *is* affecting that culture; and it is reaching past the biased media to men and women everywhere. As a result, the antiabortion forces can more ably move the courts to render life-affirming decisions.

The substance of *Roe v. Wade* can be strategically attacked through democratic and rational litigation processes. In his chapter, Michael

Pfeifer establishes that overrulings by the Supreme Court are fairly common. Justice Brandeis has clearly stated that, "in cases involving the federal constitution, where correction through legislative action is practically impossible, this Court has often overruled its earlier decisions."[1] Fifty years passed before *Brown v. Board of Education* overruled *Plessy v. Ferguson*. On the other end of the reversal spectrum, in the Second Flag Salute case, notably at the height of World War II, the Court overruled itself within three years.[2] It may be argued that these decisions did not involve the ousting of an already declared constitutional right. However, the case against abortion is stronger because it involves an attack upon a fraud, upon shoddy science, and upon a ruling which did not vindicate a constitutional right, but established a constitutional monstrosity. The prolife cause is aimed at reestablishing the most fundamental and appealing of all human rights.

Situations will continually arise in which there will be opportunities to restore the right to life. The crude campaign of misinformation by the major television networks will doubtless give coverage to those who will attack prolife moves as biased attempts to "bypass" or "circumvent" the bizarre decision in *Roe v. Wade*. Let them be assured that what we have in mind is not circumvention, but instead, a total erasure of legal access to abortion on demand. Nor is the court strategy a conspiracy: it is an open effort, in which all are encouraged to join. Broadly speaking, it will involve moves both to chip away at the props now thought to uphold *Roe* and to forthrightly destroy the entire artifice.

Efforts made in state legislatures and in the Congress to limit the reach and impact of the Supreme Court decision, and the efforts to defend these initiatives in the courts, are praiseworthy. However, those efforts have been aimed at proving the negative proposition that specific legislation, which reduces the impact or the availability of abortion, does not run counter to *Roe*. To achieve ultimate victory, a strategy for overruling *Roe v. Wade* must be a positive, offensive design.

The first planning step is recognition of the *theory* of the case. Contemplating litigation, whether one is suing or being sued, one must take time to think the case through to its ultimate implications in every respect. Constitutional lawyers have seen noble causes ruined by zealous and hasty action; the prolife movement must avoid those well-motivated but inadequately prepared and unskilled attorneys who, believing their cause to be self-evident and lacking preparatory diligence and experience, careen into the courts. Little in the courts can be considered self-evident. Nothing can be a substitute for patient deliberation, exhaustive research, and a grand design based upon the fruits of those labors.

No conscientious attorney can assure his client of victory at the outset of litigation. If, in preparing test litigation, attorneys have a responsible answer for every possible objection to their position, then a "closed circle" of argument can be made which the court will be unable to reject without itself committing basic error or palpable injustice. The same deliberative "think through" process must be employed whether one is initiating or defending a lawsuit; factors beyond our control such as time frame or unfortunate actions or omissions by a prolife client, may mean that the lawyer cannot manage to state that "closed circle" of argument.

A second step in planning is choosing the *forum*; that is, where will the case be brought? Undue emphasis may be placed on "forum shopping" or the attempt to get one's case before a judge who, if not prolife, is known to be fair-minded and diligent. Obviously, it is desirable to get one's case before as favorable a forum as possible, but the actual possibility of alternative options is exaggerated. Although, when a prolife client is sued, one may seek removal, on proper grounds, to a different court, it is more likely that there will be no choice. If the prolife party is suing, again there may be no choice; nonetheless, adequate thought should always be given to choice of forum. In such cases, the first question is whether to sue in federal or state court. There are no easily applied guidelines. Conservatives have condemned Supreme Court excesses under Chief Justice Earl Warren; many of their criticisms have merit. They similarly attack "the power of the federal judiciary," noting that great numbers of "liberals" were appointed to the federal bench by Presidents Carter, Johnson, and Kennedy and to a lesser extent by Presidents Nixon and Ford. This should not automatically lead one to opt for state courts because neither court system is immune to the current secularist culture.

Selection of the forum should not be based solely on the trial court; one must also consider the court to which the case will be appealed. Some appellate courts may have a distinct record of antilife bias. Even in selecting a court in which to bring suit, it may be impossible to determine which judges will decide the case.

Once the forum is determined, it is prudent to discover as much as possible about the background of the *judge* who will hear the case, read his opinions, and determine his mindset. Although this research may be tedious and without dramatic results, it is a factor in trial preparation which should not be overlooked. For example, if a judge's decisions, articles, or addresses show an inclination toward "strict construction," then the attorney's argument should appeal to that penchant. I once tried a case before a judge who had, in a previous litigation, jailed my client. My client's attorney in that case had had an ill-prepared defense, made emotional pleas to the court, and disregarded the decorum associated with the proper presentation of a case. Knowing the judge's sensitivity to that kind of conduct, I was especially careful to observe every amenity toward His Honor which he might possibly expect.

Another factor in determining case strategy is the decision of whether to *sue or be sued*. Generally, it is more blessed to sue than to be sued, primarily because plaintiffs can usually have better control of the time, place, parties, and issues. However, a defendant may benefit by appearing in the sympathetic role of underdog. The defense of unborn human life is an underdog's case. Society considers cases involving less volatile issues, such as discrimination in job promotion, of major significance. In the case of abortion, the issue is not mere discrimination, but rather, discrimination costing the unborn its very existence. Hence, the protector of unborn human life, and not his adversary, should be seen as an underdog deserving the court's sympathy. Public perception of that role obviously will depend in part upon media reporting.

Identities of *parties* to litigation is another important factor to consider in adequate case preparation. Sometimes, not all the initial parties in a lawsuit involving abortion issues are appropriate representatives of their argued position. Cases are brought where neither the plaintiffs nor defendants are prolife. For example, a state law regulating abortion may be challenged by abortionists who are represented by American Civil Liberties Union attorneys; the state's attorney general may be less than enthusiastic about defending the law. This could be a situation where prolife parties should seek intervenor's status to make them full parties in the case. Intervention strategies must be considered in the original "think out" of the litigation. In the *Akron Center* case, parents intervened to represent the interests of parents of minor daughters who might seek abortions. Despite the fact that they were not initial parties in the case, their presence in the case was important. They represented major interests and a group of issues which, without their presence as parties in the case, otherwise probably could not have been litigated.[3]

Parties are not the only significant individuals in the courtroom; *witnesses* must also be carefully chosen and prepared. It is unfortunate that in too many cases of constitutional importance, witnesses are not well prepared. Witnesses called to the stand are not mere names in a courtroom scenario. To the greatest extent possible they must be people who not only believe in the prolife interests they assert but who possess exact knowledge in the areas their testimony will cover. Attorneys must sufficiently prepare these people. Counsel's job is not to tell them what to say, but to help them articulate their thoughts and opinions. In order to discover any weaknesses, they must be questioned prior to the trial. That preparation should simulate the grueling courtroom experience as faithfully as possible. Prior to the trial it is necessary to contradict them, bait them, try to mislead them, smirk at their answers, tire them, and provoke them. When clients are on the witness stand, they must be satisfactorily prepared to confidently face the adversary.

Counsel must have a clear understanding of their role and take absolute *charge* of the case. Unhappily, all lawyers have met the kind of client who, having heard the advice of one attorney, turns to others so that he or she can pick and choose among various legal opinions. This turns the attorney/client relationship on its head. In effect, since the client is making a legal judgment as to which attorney's opinion is correct, he or she becomes the attorney. Attorneys should not accept a case they do not manage or wherein they will defer to clients' judgments as to law and strategy. Of course, the client may have very valuable contributions, even as to legal ideas. Likewise, even though counsel is the "boss" of the litigation, the client is free to question his or her conclusions and judgment. The client who persists in asking questions, argues, and insists on being "shown" exactly why it is that his or her attorney maintains a certain position can be of great benefit.

Naturally, prolife people need to be careful in their selection of legal counsel. There are as many differences and specialties among lawyers as there are among physicians. One would not go to an ophthalmologist for a snapped Achilles tendon; likewise, in a prolife case, one would not go to an attorney unfamiliar with constitutional litigation. It is very important to be wary of attorney enthusiasm unmatched by experience and diligence. A number of very important constitutional cases have been carried forward in the courts to disastrously bad rulings, therefore becoming disastrously bad precedents, by attorneys who imagined that their ardent belief in a cause was sufficient to win the day. Because their declamations had not been sustained by tedious, knowledgeable, painstaking preparation, they lacked substance and were unconvincing. Nevertheless, enthusiasm has an important role to play in the conduct of litigation. Granted that the assiduous homework has been done, enthusiasm for a cause will fuel resourcefulness in counsel and spell the difference between success and failure.

A word about *timing*. While concerns over timing may pertain to ripeness or mootness, the real question concerning timing in prolife litigation is: what chance will any prolife case have if it reaches the U.S. Supreme Court while the Court is composed of the present justices? It would be inappropriate to comment upon particular members of the Supreme Court, but it is hoped that our justices, who have inherited the bounty of America's "traditions of civility" and the supreme honor of protecting them, will eventually share in a growing revulsion at the evil which *Roe v. Wade* perpetuates. Whether or not the present justices are yet on the bench when the next abortion cases come to the high court, it is entirely desirable to be litigating abortion issues, and related prolife issues, as thoroughly and as soon as possible.

Once the preliminary case tactics have been decided, and prolife interests are represented by parties in a lawsuit, the *court strategies*, the actual unfolding of the case at trial, assume paramount significance.

Assuming we are now in court, how should the litigation be prepared? An important first stage is *discovery*, that is, the serving of interrogatories, requests for documents, and the taking of an opponent's depositions. Comprehensive knowledge of an adversary's case prior to the beginning of trial is essential. Discovery enables lawyers to prepare for effective cross-examination, produce evidence, and evaluate other evidence. Exposure of every flawed crevice in the other side's case needs to be done in advance of the trial. If discovery proceedings are omitted, the attorney may be going into court with just half a case. For example, opponents' statistics and scientific studies should not be taken for granted. Counsel should evaluate the credibility of the authors, those funding the studies, the sponsors, and how the studies were published. Discovery is conducted with an eye to calling these opposition parties to the stand as "hostile witnesses," and cross-examining them as part of the case. Defending human life means not simply defending but also attacking.

Two other aspects of the litigation are immediately important: *"pleadings"* and *"record."* Pleadings consist mainly of the complaint of the plaintiff and the responsive pleadings of the defendant. If we represent the plaintiff, our complaint must be drafted with the greatest care, because whatever is written in the complaint is binding; it will be the lasting bridge across which the litigation will pass in all the events and developments as it unfolds over the years. The complaint is a concrete expression of the case's theory, arising from that initial "think out." If we represent the defendant, we must give thought to whether we should raise so-called "affirmative defenses" in our answer; and whether we should counter claim, raising claims against the plaintiff, or whether we should answer at all, instead filing some form of motion or preliminary objection. Defects in complaints and answers frequently result in ultimate failure and that failure is tragic because it can be traced to inadequate preparation and "thinking out" of the case. Whether a complaint or answer is filed, it is vital to assure that every needed legal issue is raised in the pleadings.

Broadly speaking, there are two kinds of record, a stipulated record and a record based on live testimony. In constitutional litigation it is invariably vital that a record consisting of live testimony be made—a true trial record. A stipulated record is made where the attorneys agree as to the facts of the case; those facts are simply typed and treated by the court as adjudicated facts. Stipulated records in any prolife case should be treated with extreme caution. For example, back in the 1960s I represented Amish parents in Wisconsin who were being criminally prosecuted for failure to enroll their children in high school. Undertaking the case, I found that during the prior term the Supreme Court refused to hear an identical case begun in Kansas. I obtained the record in that case and found it to be simply a stipulated record. The lawyers did not present live testimony and basically offered a recital of the dry facts. I refused, in the Wisconsin case, to enter into any stipulation of fact; instead, I insisted on proceeding to a trial with live testimony and related exhibits presented in court. The case eventually reached the Supreme Court of the United States, which held in favor of my Amish clients.

The interesting feature of the case, from the viewpoint of the record, was the fact that the Supreme Court, in numerous passages of its opinion, referred to the testimony of particular witnesses whom we had presented and to exhibits we introduced as evidence. During its prior term, the Court expressed no interest in a case involving a stipulated record. This contrast is instructive to those preparing prolife cases. One of the major instances of failure in prolife cases is in the area of evidence. For example, Justice Blackmun, in the *Danforth* case, referred to the parental consent issue in these words: "It is difficult, however, to conclude that providing a parent with absolute power to overrule a determination made by the physician and his minor patient, to terminate the patient's pregnancy, will serve to strengthen the family unit." From the viewpoint of evidence, we must then ask: was evidence presented as to the physician's financial interest? the minor's vulnerability? Was there expert testimony on how the family unit was strengthened or weakened?

No area of vitally important litigation can be found where evidence is more needed than in the prolife area. Prolife counsel has to attack the *Roe* presumptions, its pseudoscience, and its dated notions by unmasking a whole battery of hard evidence and using expert testimony. We must let our witnesses be fully subject to cross-examination. The presence of intensive expert testimony will result in a record in which either the opposition will have provided no parallel expert testimony or in which it has put on its own experts. If the former, prolife counsel will have accomplished an important eviden-

tiary objective by default. If the latter, counsel will have the opportunity to force these experts "to the wall" under cross-examination.

Finally, a critical factor relating to litigation is the *media*. While
attorneys are betraying the traditions of their profession by advertising, and attorneys in litigation are more and more prone to try their
cases on the steps of the courthouse before the news cameras, it is to
be hoped that the prolife bar would concentrate its energies inside the
courtroom rather than outside. But, prolife cases do indeed need
media coverage: the assistance of people who will get our side, our
witnesses, our story into the media. Judges read the press and watch
television. They are creatures of the culture which the media helps
form. Often the prolife cause in court either is a media nonevent or
prompts a telecast leading off with: "Claiming violation of their
constitutional rights, fifteen women today appeared in federal court to
attack the state's new legislation restricting abortion. . . . "

We are aware of the mordant affliction the major media bear in
attempting to cope with their own biases. Further, having had our
own share of disappointments, we can understand the anguish the
major media news actors and their bosses must feel when they realize
that by airing their own bigotries, they are beginning to lose the
popular audience. The populace is at long last starting to ignore media
fictions. Do not despair for the media; some persons of honor and
professionalism are still employed in their ranks. To these, the prolife
organizations should give every news break possible concerning their
side in any litigation. Treat media people as though they were honest.
Give them news releases, in advance of trial or argument, straight-
forwardly explaining the case, containing copies of briefs, and
communicating usable human interest stories on witnesses.

Prolife clients must receive adequate counsel. When prolife lawyers
deliberately and expertly prepare the theory of their cases, choose the
forum, evaluate the judges, decide (where possible) on whether to sue
or be sued, appraise the parties to the litigation, assess the evidence
submitted, prepare the witnesses, take charge of the case, comprehensively expedite all the discovery work necessary, determine
pleadings, marshal the evidence in order to make the right record, and
effectively utilize the media—then the legal regime of a sensate,
material culture and its denial of human rights will be confronted and
defeated. Then, and only then, will the battle to protect the inviolable
rights of all human life be won.

Notes

1. Burnet v. Coronado Oil and Gas Co., 285 U.S. 393, 407 (1932) (Brandeis, J., dissenting).

2. West Virginia State Board of Education v. Barnette, 319 U.S. 624 (1943), *overruling*, Minersville School District v. Gobitis, 310 U.S. 586 (1940); Brown v. Board of Education, 347 U.S. 483 (1954); *overruling* Plessy v. Ferguson, 163 U.S. 537 (1896).

3. In future cases, it may be more difficult for prolife parties to intervene in abortion litigation. This point is discussed in the final chapter of this volume by Mr. Grant.

VICTOR G. ROSENBLUM AND
THOMAS J. MARZEN

Strategies for Reversing
Roe v. Wade through the Courts

ACCORDING TO U.S. SUPREME COURT Justice Sandra Day O'Connor, the legal theory embodied in *Roe v. Wade* "is on a collision course with itself."[1] Those seeking to reverse *Roe* must ensure that this "collision" occurs at the earliest possible time and with the greatest effect in protecting unborn human life. The collapse and reversal of *Roe* can be accomplished either by a direct frontal assault or by laying a siege and waiting for its inner erosion. In either case, some fundamental precept of the *Roe* doctrine must be destroyed before its edifice falls.

One practical consequence of *Roe* is that the state cannot effectively restrict or prohibit the practice of abortion. Thus, reversal of *Roe* can be achieved *only* to the extent that this limitation on state and/or local authority is also abolished.

Legal doctrines obstructing or restricting the exercise of state authority toward abortion revolve around three principles:

(1) The "right to privacy" doctrine is broad enough to encompass pregnancy termination;[2]
(2) the unborn child is not a constitutional "person"; thus, when formulating constitutional doctrine, the child has no "right to life" which must be balanced against the woman's right to have an abortion;[3] and,
(3) there is no state interest warranting significant restrictions on abortion practices.[4]

Any effective, practical, reversal strategy must focus on the dissolution of one or more of these doctrines.

Before established doctrines can be corrected, certain conditions must exist. First, *Roe* must be subject to legitimate historical, legal, and social criticism. Fortunately, *Roe's* central premises enjoy scant scholarly support. Second, the judiciary must either favor or be open to the possibility of reversal. In 1986, although the Supreme Court reaffirmed the *Roe* doctrine, it did so by a five-to-four majority, with the dissenters calling for reexamination and reversal of *Roe*.[5] A constructive reversal process can begin when one of the five justices in the pro-*Roe* majority is replaced with a judge who opposes *Roe*. Appointments to the Supreme Court in 1986 have accomplished part of the necessary change by solidifying the strength of the dissent to *Roe*.

Third, the opponents of abortion need to achieve and maintain enough legislative strength, especially in state legislatures, to pass legislation making reversal possible. Courts can reverse only if presented with a legal case or controversy requiring judicial resolution. Advocates of permissive abortion have pursued their purposes by attacking restrictive abortion laws they feel have denied women a constitutionally guaranteed "abortion privacy right." From the other side, at least since *Roe*, foes of abortion cannot claim that the state's failure to prohibit abortion violates the Constitution. Laws specifically designed to be challenged by advocates of permissive abortion must be enacted so that they can provide the opportunity for confronting some aspect of *Roe*. This scenario, emphasizing the continuing importance of prolife political strength in the state legislatures and in Congress, assumes that opponents of abortion will be able to pass legislation.

Fourth, any law designed to challenge or explore any aspect of *Roe* must be competently defended during the course of ensuing litigation. Prolife attorneys should, if possible, intervene in defense of the law. However, if intervention is denied, government attorneys should at least be willing to accept the assistance of prolife counsel. Vigorous litigation by government attorneys will depend on the political influence of prolifers within each particular jurisdiction.

Assume that these preconditions for reversal exist: five members of the Supreme Court are open to reversal, the proper scholarly preparation has been completed, political strength has been exercised, and appropriate legislation has been enacted and is waiting for a defense. Where does the process of reversal begin? Is the best strategy to seek an immediate holding that abolishes the abortion privacy right by way of a statute simply banning abortion? Should the plan begin by attempting to reverse *Roe's* holding that the unborn are not "persons" under the Fourteenth Amendment to the U.S. Constitution? Can the strategy best begin by seeking the expansion of a state's vested interest warranting the prohibition of abortion? Naturally, the

Supreme Court could choose to reverse itself in any of these three ways when it considers an abortion-related case. However, vindication of all three claims is essential to the ultimate and permanent demise of *Roe*.

As analyses of the *Roe* holdings will make clear, the most logical and potentially workable strategy for reversal is to focus on expanding the state's compelling interest in fetal life to encompass the woman's entire pregnancy. A simultaneous effort should also be undertaken to widen the state's interest in maternal health. Once these goals are achieved, the abortion privacy right would be drained of content, lose its significance, and could be directly attacked. With sufficiently compelling state interests, and without the protection currently given by the Constitution, judicial recognition of Fourteenth Amendment "personhood" could be sought for the unborn.

I. The Expansion of State Interests Warranting Restriction of Abortion

ROE'S FRAMEWORK RESULTED from the Court's assessment of the nature and strength of state interests which might potentially limit exercise of the abortion privacy right. In particular, the *Roe* Court found that the state's compelling interest in maternal health warranted limitations on abortion practices after the onset of the second trimester of pregnancy, and that a compelling interest in the protection of fetal life justified some restrictions after fetal viability.[6] In fact, later Court decisions conceded that interests in the protection of minors, parental rights, spousal rights, and population control warrant further restrictions on abortion practices.[7]

Plainly, any strategy assaulting this legal situation must upset the balance the Court established between the abortion privacy right and competing state interests. This involves dismantling the obstacles the Supreme Court erected against the assertion of compelling state interest—barriers confining the authority of the state to rigidly fixed stages or particular pregnancy circumstances.

A. EXPANSION OF AN INTEREST IN THE UNBORN

EVEN THOUGH THE Supreme Court held that the unborn were not constitutional "persons," it also decided that the unborn were the proper subjects of a valid state interest throughout gestation. When the unborn child reaches viability, this interest becomes sufficiently compelling to prohibit abortion—unless the abortion is performed to preserve the mother's life or health.[8] Under *Roe*, a state could ban abortion at any stage of pregnancy because of its interest in fetal life. However, the Court placed two conceptual hurdles in the path of such an outcome: the requirement that the fetus must be "viable" before the state can claim a compelling interest which would justify the prohibition of abortion, and the condition that "health" abortions are permitted even when the state asserts a compelling interest that could prohibit abortion. If these obstacles and their protective legal edifices are removed, the legal practice of abortion will topple.

Focusing our attention on this tactic has unique advantages. First, the fetus's biologically human nature would be an important factor in any controversy exploring *Roe* doctrines. State statutes raising critical biological issues would purport to control abortion practices on behalf of the unborn during the later stages of pregnancy. This is the most favorable psychological terrain for opponents of permissive abortion. Emphasis on the biologically human character of the fetus is essential to undercutting the social and legal claims justifying recognition of the abortion privacy right and it sets the groundwork for recognizing the constitutional personhood of the unborn.

Second, present opponents of *Roe* sitting on the Supreme Court prefer this approach. Justices O'Connor, Rehnquist, and White would find that the state maintains a compelling interest in the protection of fetal life at all stages of pregnancy without regard to "viability," thereby extending the state's authority to prohibit abortion for the entire gestational period.[9]

Third, the "viability" and "health" criteria are conceptually weak and difficult for abortionists to defend; these criteria would invoke several unexplored legal issues which could be raised through legislation. Fourth, advancing medical technology is a strong prolife ally. Viability, the ability to sustain a child's life outside the womb, depends on sophisticated medical technology, and new discoveries and techniques mean that fetal life can be sustained at earlier stages than ever before. Also, science continues to minimize the number of circumstances that justify abortion for maternal health reasons.

Taken together, these considerations suggest that undercutting the "viability" criterion and inducing the Court to define "health" in a restrictive manner represent a beneficial strategy in reversing *Roe*. Prolifers should also encourage sympathetic legislators to implement practical steps. For instance, legislators should favor research grant appropriations which improve prenatal care and methods for sustaining the fetus apart from the mother's body.

Understanding the potential for medico-technological research and practice in undercutting the *Roe* doctrine is critical. The Supreme Court's pro-*Roe* majority held that utilization of the dilatation and evacuation (D&E) abortion method narrowed the state's interest in maternal health—such abortions cannot be regulated to the same degree as more dangerous procedures.[10] By similar reasoning and under *Roe's* own principles, development and implementation of technology reducing the age of viability would lead to an expansion of the state's interest in protecting fetal life. Justice O'Connor outlined the manner in which scientific developments undercut *Roe* doctrine:

> In 1973, viability before 28 weeks was considered unusual. The fourteenth edition of L. Hellman & J. Prichard, *Williams Obstetrics*, on which the Court relied in *Roe* for its understanding of viability, stated that "[a]ttainment of a [fetal] weight of 1,000 g [or a fetal age of approximately 28 weeks gestation] is . . . widely used as the criterion of viability." *Id.*, at 493. However, recent studies have demonstrated increasingly earlier fetal viability. It is certainly reasonable to believe that fetal viability in the first trimester of pregnancy may be possible in the not too distant future. Indeed, the Court has explicitly acknowledged that *Roe* left the point of viability "flexible for anticipated advancements in medical skill." . . . "[W]e recognized in *Roe* that viability was a matter of medical judgment, skill and technical ability, and we preserved the flexibility of the term." The *Roe* framework, then, is clearly on a collision course with itself. As the medical risks of various abortion procedures decrease, the point at which the State may regulate for reasons of maternal health is moved further forward to actual child birth. As medical science becomes better able to provide for the separate existence of the fetus, the point of viability is moved further back toward conception.[11]

Legislation augmenting a medical basis for reversal must be enacted in a way which will compel the courts to consider also the essential legal issues. "Viability" could be further defined and thus weakened. For example, a law establishing the application of stringent medical care and a homicide code for all children born alive as the result of an abortion would challenge the postbirth application of the viability concept and underscore its arbitrary character.[12] Other themes could be suggested and elaborated; however, the main intention is the passage of legislation offering an opportunity for a willing Supreme Court to begin the reversal process by discarding "viability" as a valid criterion for the onset of a compelling state interest in protecting life.

Another critically important objective is to limit the scope of criteria which may justify an abortion on grounds of "maternal health." The concept of "health," as defined by the Supreme Court in *Doe v. Bolton*, includes all medical, psychological, social, familial, and economic factors which might potentially inspire a decision to procure an abortion.[13] As such, "health" abortion is indistinguishable from elective abortion. Thus, until a more narrow definition of "health" is obtained, it may not be possible to limit effectively the number of abortions performed.

It has been argued that the concept of "health" abortion which must be permitted after viability *is* distinguishable from "health" abortions as defined in *Doe v. Bolton*.[14] It is essential to prove that this argument is correct. An initial step would be the enactment of legislation banning sex-selection abortion after viability and, if such a law could be sustained, the "health" exception would be implicitly limited to more physical and less vaguely psychosocial factors.[15] Further legislation could then be built on precedents generated by these laws, the goal being limitation of the "health" concept to the most narrow set of possible circumstances.

Reversal strategy, which begins by weakening "viability" and "health" abortion arguments, is calculated to attack the framework of the abortion privacy doctrine at its most vulnerable point. This approach offers the greatest potential for a complete repudiation of *Roe*, and generates a climate for the full recognition of fetal "personhood."

B. MATERNAL HEALTH

IN *ROE*, THE Supreme Court held that the state maintained a compelling interest in maternal health. This interest begins at approximately the onset of the second trimester of pregnancy, and becomes "compelling" when the rate of maternal mortality arising from abortion exceeds the rate of maternal mortality arising from childbirth.[16] In 1973, medical practice said this occurred at about the thirteenth week or at the beginning of the second trimester of pregnancy.[17] The Court perceived a "compelling interest" and held that the state could require that abortions after the onset of the second trimester must be performed in situations minimizing maternal health risks.

A decade later, the Court ruled that performance of second trimester D&E abortions could not be confined to hospitals.[18] D&E abortion, a refined technique involving fetal dismemberment, was said to be safer than childbirth, even in the second trimester. Thus, under *Roe*'s rationale, there was no compelling interest justifying regulation on behalf of maternal health.[19] Yet, it is unclear whether or not the Court relied on the relative maternal mortality test of *Roe* in reaching its decisions on D&E procedures. The Court seemed to hold that a compelling interest justifying state regulation on behalf of maternal health arose only when the manner in which abortion is performed violated "accepted medical practice." Since "accepted medical practice" allowed abortions outside hospitals in the second trimester, the Court found that there was not a compelling interest justifying a requirement that abortions be performed in hospitals.[20]

"Accepted medical practices" must change before barriers to reversal can be broken down; whether or not an abortion is "acceptable" is determined by the views and customary practices of the very people who perform abortions. They are unwilling to increase the state's authority to regulate abortion. A possible long-term approach to meeting this dilemma is the development of new sources for abortion data. This can be achieved by enacting statutes creating neutral, governmentally sponsored research agencies with the authority to investigate independently incidents of abortion-related morbidity or mortality.

Another approach is to enact legislation requiring detailed reporting on incidents of mortality arising from childbirth and abortion.[21] New statutes launching government-funded programs can significantly reduce maternal mortality related to childbirth and pregnancy. If pregnancy and childbirth are rendered safer than abortion, then the state maintains a compelling interest in maternal health under the old *Roe* formula. The claim that certain abortion practices should not be regulated simply because they are medically acceptable to abortion practitioners would no longer be valid.

Both approaches would yield objective data on abortion and would tend to negate the strong policy argument for permissive abortion based on its relative safety. Justices O'Connor, Rehnquist, and White would hold that a "compelling interest" in maternal health exists sufficiently to warrant government restrictions on abortion at any time in pregnancy.[22] Their position seems to have little to do with relative rates of mortality or definitions of "accepted medical practice." Instead, their argument seems to rest on the premise that since abortion imposes some risk, however minimal, the state may assert a "compelling interest" which warrants regulation. Accumulation of favorable statistical data would help vindicate this position and therefore ought to be regarded as an important legislative priority.

C. SECONDARY INTERESTS: PROTECTION OF THE MINOR, PARENTAL RIGHTS, SPOUSAL AND PARENTAL INTERESTS, DEMOGRAPHIC AND EUGENIC CONDITIONS

SINCE *ROE*, CASE law has recognized that the state maintains interests in certain circumstances which might warrant the regulation and restriction of abortion: when the woman is a minor, when she is married, or when legitimate demographic considerations are relevant.[23] Can prolife forces jeopardize fundamental aspects of the *Roe* doctrine by asserting or expanding these "circumstantial interests"?

The extent to which the state can currently mandate parental involvement in a minor's abortion is well defined. Parental consent can only be required if a judicial alternative to consent is provided. A procedure by which the minor can obtain court permission in lieu of parental consent would be provided if the minor is sufficiently "mature" to consent to the abortion on her own or the abortion is deemed in her "best interest."[24] Likewise, parental notification can be required only if an alternative judicial procedure is provided that permits the minor to procure an abortion without parental notification: if the minor is sufficiently mature to make the abortion decision on her own or if notification of the parents is not in the minor's best interest.[25] Under either scheme, court proceedings must be expedient and confidential; the minor must be accorded all necessary assistance to ensure that she can effectively utilize the court procedures.[26]

Parental notice and consent statutes are incidentally supported by a state's interest in protecting parents' right to custody and control of their minor child; however, the major supporting justification is the presumptive incompetence of minors and their consequent need to have parental assistance in making decisions.[27] Unfortunately, it is doubtful that extension of this rationale could threaten any of *Roe*'s core principles. The inherent legitimacy of legalized abortion cannot be effectively attacked in the context of the special case of the individual who may simply need third-party assistance in making the abortion decision.

The actual degree to which the state may require spousal or parental involvement is less well defined. Under present law, it is clear that the state cannot require blanket spousal consent prior to abortion. Although the state maintains an interest in encouraging "spousal consultation," it cannot lend the husband a "veto power" over abortion that it does not possess itself.[28] Following this rationale, the only time the state could impose any spousal (or paternal) *consent* requirement is after fetal viability, when the state itself can proscribe abortion unless it is performed to preserve maternal life or health. Protection of the formal integrity of the marital relationship *and* the husband's procreative rights comprise a "compelling interest" and would justify such a law.[29] The state would probably not require that an unmarried father must be provided with similar notice because without a marriage there is no interest in the integrity of marriage. Although the law presumes that the husband is the father of any child conceived from marriage, no such presumption would benefit an unwed father; he would be unable to prove that his procreative rights are at stake in a particular proposed abortion.

Like parental consent and notice laws, spousal notice laws could provide a significant opportunity to reduce the incidence of abortion. But whether a spouse is involved or has notice of his wife's abortion decision raises no issues central to the *Roe* doctrine. The state's interests in marital equity and in preserving some modicum of the husband's right to have children, interests necessarily confined within the marital relationship, lack the scope to lead any effective assault on the framework of *Roe*. Thus, issues of parental or spousal involvement are too remote to be useful to the legal strategy to reverse *Roe*.

In a similiar vein, the state's interest in "population control" is too far removed from any reason sufficient to warrant restrictions on abortion practices. Although the population could experience such a decline that a compelling interest might warrant restriction of abortion, it is highly unlikely that present demographic trends would command immediate suppression of what is now acknowledged to be a fundamental right. Even if such a claim could be substantiated, it would do little to dismantle *Roe*. A plan to reverse *Roe* by asserting some interest in population expansion or control is no strategy at all.[30]

An inevitable conclusion is that state interests in the minor's or married woman's abortion, or in demographic or eugenic considerations, provide scant help in assaulting any principle critical to the survival of *Roe*. Particular issues raised by special, circumstantial interests are too remote from the core of the *Roe* doctrine to be of any use in a reversal strategy.

II. Abolition of the Abortion Privacy Right

ROE'S CORNERSTONE DOCTRINE asserts that there exists a fundamental "right of privacy" which is "broad enough to encompass a woman's decision whether or not to terminate her pregnancy."[31] Elimination of this abortion privacy right is essential. If it did not exist, the state would be free to regulate and prohibit abortion to the extent it chose to do so. As the Supreme Court has acknowledged, the state maintains valid, sometimes compelling interests in the protection of unborn human life and in maternal health. If abortion were not protected as a fundamental right, then these interests, even if not "compelling" at all stages of pregnancy and even if the fetus were not a "person," would be sufficient to warrant governmental regulation and prohibition.

As documented in the chapter authored by Horan and Balch, the

Court's holding that there is an abortion privacy right does not seem to rest on any strict form of legal or logical analysis.[32] It is built on an intuition, rooted in preconceptions of the Court majority and its sense of the social milieu, that abortion is outside the proper sphere of government concern. Abortion involves sex, family, religion, and what goes on inside the reproductive organs of a woman's body, and the state should not intrude in such private matters. A patchwork quilt of medical, legal, and historical authorities was assembled to buttress the Court's intuition, and the fabric of the Constitution was stretched to clothe it.

If the true origins of the abortion privacy right lie in the Court's perception of a preferred *social* policy, then scholarly refutation alone will probably not be adequate to assure its repudiation. Regardless of the legitimacy of its historical and legal parentage, the abortion privacy right now has a life of its own. Developing case law has given it form and it is currently sustained by the common assumptions of our social consciousness after more than a decade of permissive abortion. Abortion has become a normative solution to any "problem" pregnancy; the more abortion becomes an institutionalized, customary, and common practice, the more credible the *Roe* Court's premise that permissive abortion is "implicit in the concept of ordered liberty" will seem.[33] Apart from legal and historical scholarship, those who wish to see the abortion right expunged from our law must persistently maintain and nurture an attitude of resistance to permissive abortion in American culture. This is the critical role that prolife activists and educators must play in the reversal process.

Common social practices, usually because they cause some verifiable social harm, are often subjected to governmental control. Thus, accumulation of supportive data can demonstrate any medical, demographic, eugenic, psychological, economic, or other social deficits caused by abortion, which can then be brought to the attention of the judiciary. This is also essential to counterbalance the social and cultural acceptance of the practice. Abortion advocates have understood the full import of this aspect of the controversy. They have applied significant private and government resources to the development of favorable statistical data, the result being that almost all reported data assume the medical and social desirability of permissive abortion. The *Roe* decision itself is replete with uncontroverted data offered by abortion advocates. The result is a central matrix of binding information that comfortably fits permissive abortion.[34] Plainly, this situation needs to be corrected.

Whatever the social deficits or ethical issues raised by abortion, as long as pregnant women are subjected to social and economic discrimination, or are unable to secure necessary public or private assistance in caring for the child and themselves, abortion will be regarded as a necessary evil. Abortion represents an immediate, cheap, relatively uncomplicated solution to women trapped in these circumstances; it is naive to assume that women would be ethically sensitive and then choose a more costly and complicated alternative. This fact of American life is essential to understanding the degree to which sensitivity to the perceived and real difficulties confronted by pregnant women contributed to judicial creation of the abortion privacy right. Immediately after the Supreme Court declared the existence of this right, it continued by way of explanation:

> The detriment that the State would impose upon the pregnant woman by denying this choice altogether is apparent. Specific and direct harm medically diagnosable even in early pregnancy may be involved. Maternity, or additional offspring, may force upon a woman a distressful life and future. Psychological harm may be imminent. Mental and physical health may be taxed by child care. There is also the distress, for all concerned, associated with the unwanted child, and there is the problem of bringing a child into a family already unable, psychologically and otherwise, to care for it. In other cases, as in this one, the additional difficulties and continuing stigma of unwed motherhood may be involved. All these are factors the woman and her responsible physician necessarily will consider in consultation.[35]

Except for a brief reference to possible physical problems caused by pregnancy, the Court's predominant concern was the social, psychological, and economic "detriments" and "stigmas" attached to pregnancy. From this perspective, a fully convincing case for abolition of the *Roe* doctrine can be made only in the context of a social and legal milieu in which these stigmas and detriments are alleviated or erased. There is a cause and effect relationship between the abolition of the abortion right and the development and enforcement of laws forbidding pregnancy discrimination and providing economic and social support to pregnant women. Private charitable assistance to women given through alternatives to proabortion agencies is not enough. Alternative assistance as a substantial legal argument negating the assertion that there is a "need" for legally guaranteed abortion must be made a matter of public record. In order to balance the claim that abortion practices should be legally and socially deinstitutionalized, alternative assistance to pregnant women must also be formally institutionalized in society as a matter of legal right.

In this regard, the prolife cause can be allied with "progressive" and "feminist" causes which relieve women of socially conditioned penalties and burdens arising from their childbearing capacity—penalties and burdens not suffered by men. The prolife cause is essentially feminist in character because it affirms the woman in the exercise of her sexually distinguishing characteristic—the capacity to bear and give birth to children. Jack Nicholson's personal opposition to abortion arose from his illegitimacy, "I don't have a right to any other view. My only emotion is gratitude for my life." The actor commented that his mother and grandmother raised him and "if they had been of less character, I never would have gotten to live. It's a feminist narrative in the very purest form."[36]

In sum, demolition of *Roe's* cornerstone doctrine depends initially on the development of legal and historical scholarship rebutting the existencè of any constitutional basis or tradition for recognition of an abortion privacy right, a task already on its way to completion. Secondary tasks, the development of statistical data demonstrating the social and medical harm caused by abortion, have barely begun, and the creation of social, economic, and legal policies assisting the pregnant woman to carry her child to term and thereafter are even further behind. Antiabortion forces should publicly pressure legislators to provide substantial grants-in-aid for: supportive development of adequate statistical data, elimination of pregnancy discrimination and discrimination against working and single mothers, and the provision of financial assistance for pregnant women and the agencies serving them. Precisely because the *Roe* doctrine is so firmly and obviously rooted in the problems public policies would address, they are legally relevant to *Roe's* reversal.

Assuming the best possible foundation for abolition of the abortion privacy right has been prepared, specific legal strategies most likely to bring about this result should be considered. The abortion privacy right is amorphous and multifaceted; it is an expansive and elusive target. From this perspective, a law simply banning abortion in the manner of many pre-*Roe* statutes might seem to be the best approach. Such a law permits a frontal and basic assault on the *Roe* doctrine; moreover, it offers the hope of quick and final abolition of the abortion privacy right in a manner calculated to secure the earliest possible legal protection for the unborn. Nevertheless, there are at least two reasons why this strategy is probably not the wisest course. The first simply recognizes the practical reality that in the near future there probably will not be a majority of justices on the Supreme Court willing to repudiate precipitously the abortion privacy right. At least three current anti-*Roe* justices would reverse on the basis of finding compelling interests that warrant regulation of abortion throughout pregnancy.[37] But it is unclear how many justices are ready to hold that there exists no abortion privacy right at all—which is probably what would be required to uphold a statute simply prohibiting all, or almost all, abortions.[38]

The second reason relates both to the conservatism of the American judicial order and to the role of the judiciary in protecting individual "rights" against incursions by legislative majorities. These inter-related factors militate against the prompt and direct repudiation of the abortion privacy right suggested by a law that simply bans abortion. On one hand, the American legal system depends heavily on the presumption that prior court decisions represent firm ground on which subsequent case law can be built. Expressed most directly through the doctrine of *stare decisis* ("let the decision stand"), this presumption does not impose any absolute obstacle to reversal; however, it powerfully influences the courts to avoid direct or quick reversal of prior decisions. The reversal of a prior decision by the Supreme Court has usually been preceded by an initial process of erosion emptying the decision of substantive content. Only when the decision is practically a vacant shell caused by the passage of time has the Court been willing to announce the obvious—that the prior decision is reversed. There is little reason to believe that the Court would proceed any differently with *Roe*.

On the other hand, *Roe* significantly expanded the "rights" of women and a unique role of the American judiciary is to protect and articulate individual rights. This makes it unwilling to assert forth-rightly that a recognized "right" is suddenly no "right" at all. The courts would be more inclined gradually to deprive it of significance than directly to proclaim its demise.

It appears probable that repudiation of the abortion privacy right would come in a series of steps which would completely empty it of content, rather than from a law simply banning all abortions. There is danger in a premature and precipitous frontal assault on the abortion privacy right suggested by a statute that simply bans all abortions. It could result in a reformulation or recapitulation of the "right" by a newly constituted Supreme Court majority; this would seriously delay and damage the prospect for full repudiation of the *Roe* doctrine.

Until the Court has been tested to determine its willingness to hold that no abortion privacy right exists, it would be imprudent to confront the Court with a general prohibition on abortion. A wiser strategy is to match the natural rhythms of the reversal process by confronting the Court with a series of specific, carefully considered issues calculated to open life-sapping wounds in the *Roe* doctrine.

This more cautious method does not necessarily mean that reversal would come more slowly than by way of a confrontational statute that defiantly dares the Court to reverse; it could reverse any time it decides on abortion-related issues. A careful step-by-step approach appears advisable because any form of crude confrontation with the Court may invoke an angry response that does great harm to the ultimate prospects for reversal.

The most fruitful path toward repudiation of the abortion privacy right begins with a consideration of issues emphasizing the biologically human character of the unborn. Statutes regulating the manner in which abortion may be performed at or around viability (rather than whether it can be performed at all), or exploring the meaning of fetal viability, would require the judiciary to confront the most salient legal and ethical matters relating to abortion. This strategy would be conducted in a manner coinciding neatly with a strategy calculated to expand the state's compelling interest in fetal life to include all of pregnancy.

The abortion privacy right proceeds from a web of case law and social policy generally supporting reproductive, procreative, and familial freedom from governmental interference. Abortion must be sorted out from such private matters; emphasis on the biologically human character of the unborn accomplishes just that. In particular, it distinguishes abortion from contraceptive forms of birth control. It is one thing for the state to invade the "sacred precincts of the marital chamber" to determine whether a crime has been committed by use of a condom or diaphragm; it is quite another thing for the state to inquire into medical practices that result in the death of a biologically human being.[39]

Further, this emphasis demystifies the supposedly unknown quantity that is the object of every abortion—the unborn child. The idea that abortion is simply a matter of choice, perhaps even a quasi-religious matter somehow implicating the free exercise and establishment clauses of the First Amendment,[40] is rooted largely in a conception of the unborn child as a kind of empty shell with no objective or intrinsic character into which others—parents, religious authorities, society—arbitrarily interject meaning and value. Emphasis on issues relating to the biological nature of the unborn tends to dispel this simple, naive thinking. Thus, emphasis on the expansion of a compelling interest in the unborn becomes not only the most useful initial strategy for attacking the framework of *Roe*, but also the one most calculated to pierce the heart of the abortion privacy right.

Repudiation of the abortion privacy right will not come about merely by making the judiciary aware of the "facts of fetal development"; they have been before the courts since the beginning and have had no dissuading power. Nor will the judiciary, which prides itself on emotional detachment, be swayed by sensational expositions of fetal remains. Emphasizing the biologically human character of the unborn means focusing attention on the technical, legal and medical problems and dilemmas involving the unborn created by *Roe* and its aftermath. Laws properly raising such matters must be carefully crafted and based on scientifically verifiable information, and ensuing litigation should be studiously dispassionate. *Roe* will not wither from the heat of prolife rhetoric or moral conviction; it will collapse when the cold steel of judicial logic cuts through its inner contradictions. The biologically human nature of the unborn should form the *context* rather than the *subject matter* of the reversal strategy. This strategy will provide the greatest potential for eventual repudiation of the abortion privacy right.

III. Fetal Personhood

THE MOST FUNDAMENTAL evil of *Roe v. Wade*, the recognition of a fundamental right to procure abortion as an aspect of the right of privacy, must be repudiated before *Roe* can be reversed. Also, recognition of constitutional personhood for the unborn, the highest expression of prolife principle, must be enshrined in law. Either of these goals might be achieved any time the Supreme Court is compelled to decide on an abortion-related issue. Even the most trivial case could be the occasion for reversal or for the triumph of prolife principle. There appear to be only three essential prerequisites: statutes that confront the judiciary with abortion-related issues must continue to be enacted; these statutes must be competently and vigorously defended; and the membership of the Supreme Court has to be altered so at least five justices are reasonably open to the possibility of reversing *Roe*.

In turn, these prerequisites dictate three political priorities to those seeking judicial reversal of *Roe*: achievement and maintenance of sufficient legislative strength, particularly in state legislatures, to continue enacting abortion related laws; achievement and maintenance of sufficient political strength to assure that statutes enacted will be properly defended; assurance that the president of the United States is committed to the appointment of United States Supreme Court justices who would favor reversal of *Roe*.

Achievement of these three goals would make judicial reversal possible, but would not guarantee its occurrence. Complete and prudent strategy that promptly and effectively reverses *Roe* must also include an array of additional components designed to undercut its legal, historical, and social foundations and to attack, weaken, and finally topple its logical framework.

IV. Conclusion

Thus, an assault on *Roe's* doctrinal foundations should proceed from several directions:

(1) Legal and historical scholarship, demonstrating that there is no rational basis for the claim that an abortion right is embedded in the fabric of the Constitution, must be completed and developed.

(2) Competent data should be gathered to demonstrate the medical, social, and economic deficits created by widespread abortion.

(3) Educational efforts to resist the institutionalization and acceptance of abortion as a normative practice should continue and be expanded.

(4) Medical research should be directed toward maximizing the survival and prospects for extremely premature infants, toward development of artificial life support technology for the human fetus, and toward reduction of maternal mortality and morbidity arising from pregnancy and childbirth.

(5) Programs eliminating discrimination against pregnant women and mothers and providing social and economic support for abortion alternatives should be enforced and greatly expanded.

(6) Governmental resources should be enlisted to provide generous financial support for data-gathering, research, alternatives assistance and educational programs, and for enforcement of antidiscrimination laws.

Assault on *Roe's* legal framework should begin by enacting carefully drafted statutes which prompt the judiciary to consider expansion of an interest in the unborn, to include all stages of gestation, and limit the definitional scope of abortions allegedly performed for maternal health. Prolifers should seek assurance that the issues raised by the enacted legislation will be litigated with vigor and great care. Subsequent tactics must be dictated by the nature of the precedents resulting from that litigation. These considerations and recommendations form the groundwork and initial tactics in a strategy to overturn *Roe v. Wade.*

Roe v. Wade does not stand astride our nation as an immortal monument to immutable truth. It can be overturned by the judiciary that formed its structure. Political, legal, and scholarly resources of the prolife movement must be uniformly directed toward the realization of a coherent strategy to accomplish the complete destruction of *Roe v. Wade* and its pernicious doctrines. Its shattered remains will be forever expelled from our law and the disgrace of its memory will be a lasting memorial to the countless number of human lives it has cost.

Notes

1. Akron v. Akron Center for Reproductive Health, 462 U.S. 416, 458 (1983) (O'Connor, J., dissenting).
2. Roe v. Wade, 410 U.S. 113, 153 (1973).
3. *Id.* at 158.
4. *Id.* at 164.
5. Thornburgh v. American College of Obstetricians and Gynecologists, 106 S. Ct. 2169 (1986).
6. 410 U.S. at 164, 165.
7. Planned Parenthood of Central Missouri v. Danforth, 428 U.S. 52, 76 (1976); Bellotti v. Baird (I), 428 U.S. 132 (1976); Bellotti v. Baird (II), 443 U.S. 622 (1979) (protection of minors and parental rights); Planned Parenthood v. Danforth, 428 U.S. 52, 67 (1976); Scheinberg v. Smith, 659 F. 2d 476 (5th Cir. 1981) (spousal rights); Maher v. Roe, 432 U.S. 464, 470 (1977) (population control).
8. 410 U.S. at 163–164.
9. Akron, 462 U.S. at 461 (O'Connor, J., dissenting).
10. *Id.* at 437.
11. *Id.* at 457–458 (O'Connor, J., dissenting).
12. Illinois and Pennsylvania have adopted separate approaches to this problem. Section 6 (2) (b) of Illinois Public Act No. 83–1128 (1984) amending the Illinois Abortion Law of 1975, is as follows:

Subsequent to the abortion, if a child is born alive, the physician required by Section 6 (2) (a) to be in attendance shall exercise the same degree of professional skill, care and diligence to preserve the life and health of the child as would be required of a physician providing immediate medical care to a child born alive in the course of a pregnancy termination which was not an abortion. Any such physician who intentionally, knowingly or recklessly violates Section 6 (2) (b) commits a Class 3 felony. Ill. Rev. Stat. ch. 38, §81–26 (2) (b).

The Pennsylvania Abortion Control Act, 18 Pa. Cons. Stat. Ann. Sec. 3212 (Purdon 1983), is as follows:

(a) Status of fetus.—The law of this Commonwealth shall not be construed to imply that any human being born alive in the course of or as a result of an abortion or pregnancy termination, no matter what may be that human being's chance of survival, is not a person under the Constitution and laws of this Commonwealth.
(b) Care required.—All physicians and licensed medical personnel attending a child who is born alive during the course of an abortion or premature delivery, or after being carried to term, shall provide such child that type and degree of care and

treatment which, in the good faith judgment of the physician, is commonly and customarily provided to any other person under similar conditions and circumstances. Any individual who knowingly violates the provisions of this subsection commits a felony of the third degree.

(c) Obligation of physician.—Whenever the physician or any other person is prevented by lack of parental or guardian consent from fulfilling his obligations under subsection (b) he shall nonetheless fulfill said obligations and immediately notify the juvenile court of the facts of the case. The juvenile court shall immediately institute an inquiry and, if it finds that the lack of parental or guardian consent is preventing treatment required under subsection (b), it shall immediately grant injunctive relief to require such treatment.

The Illinois approach simply establishes that the child born alive as the result of abortion is an "individual" under its criminal code. Hence, whatever standards apply to the treatment of children who are not born as the result of abortion would logically also apply to the aborted child; identical standards also apply to children who are born "non-viable," whether or not they are born as the result of abortion. Pennsylvania accomplishes the same result by adopting an explicit equal protection standard for all infants. The Illinois law was the subject of litigation in Charles v. Carey, 627 F. 2d 772 (7th Cir. 1980), and was stricken because it was deemed unconstitutional for failure to include a definition of "born alive." *Id.* at 790–791. An amended law which remedies this insufficiency is subject to present litigation in Keith v. Daley, 84 C 5602 (N.D. Ill., filed July 2, 1984).

13. 410 U.S. 179, 192 (1973).

14. Professor Lynn Wardle has cogently argued that the definition of "health" employed in *Doe v. Bolton* is not coexistent with the "health" exception demanded by the Supreme Court in *Roe v. Wade* for any restrictions on postviability abortions. *See* L. Wardle, *The Abortion Privacy Doctrine: A Compendium and Critique of Federal Court Abortion Cases*, 61 (1981).

15. *E.g.*, Section 6(8) the Illinois Public Act No. 83–1128 (1984), amending the Illinois Abortion Law of 1975, is as follows:

No person shall intentionally perform an abortion with knowledge that the pregnant woman is seeking the abortion solely on account of the sex of the fetus. Nothing in Section 6(8) shall be construed to proscribe the performance of an abortion on account of the sex of the fetus because of a genetic disorder linked to that sex. If the application of Section 6(8) to the period of pregnancy prior to viability is held invalid, then such invalidity shall not affect its application to the period of pregnancy subsequent to viability.

Ill. Rev. Stat. ch. 38, §81–26 (8) (1984).

16. 410 U.S. at 163.

17. *Id.*

18. *Akron*, 462 U.S. at 437.

19. *Id.*

20. *Id.*

21. *E.g.*, the Pennsylvania Abortion Law at 18 Pa. Cons. Stat. Ann. Sec. 3214(g) (Purdon 1983) is as follows:

Report of maternal death.—After 30 days' public notice, the department shall henceforth require that all reports of maternal deaths occurring within the Commonwealth arising from pregnancy, childbirth or intentional abortion in every case state the cause of death, the duration of the woman's pregnancy when her death occurred and whether or not the woman was under the care of a physician during her pregnancy prior to her death and shall issue such regulations as are necessary to assure that such information is reported, conducting its own investigation if necessary in order to ascertain such data. A woman shall be deemed to have been under the care of a physician prior to her death for the purpose of this chapter when she had either been examined or treated by a physician, not including any examination or treatment in connection with emergency care for complications of her pregnancy or complications of her abortion, preceding the woman's death at any time which is both 21 or more days after the time she became pregnant and within 60 days prior to her death. Known incidents of maternal mortality of nonresident women arising from induced abortion performed in this Commonwealth shall be included as incidents of maternal mortality arising from induced abortions. Incidents of maternal mortality arising from continued pregnancy or childbirth and occurring after induced abortion has been attempted but not completed, including deaths occurring after induced abortion has been attempted but not completed as a result of ectopic pregnancy, shall be included as incidents of maternal mortality arising from induced abortion. The department shall annually compile a statistical report for the General Assembly based upon the data gathered under this subsection, and all such statistical reports shall be available for public inspection and copying.

22. *Akron*, 462 U.S. at 460 (O'Connor, J., joined by White, J., and Rehnquist, J., dissenting).

23. *See* authorities cited *supra* note 7.

24. Planned Parenthood v. Ashcroft, 462 U.S. 476, 491 (1983).

25. H.L. v. Matheson, 450 U.S. 398, 409 (1981).

26. Indiana Planned Parenthood v. Pearson, 716 F.2d 1127, 1134–39 (7th Cir. 1983); Planned Parenthood League of Massachusetts v. Bellotti, 641 F.2d 1006, 1011 (1st Cir. 1981).

27. *See* Bellotti v. Baird (II), 443 U.S. 622, 637 (1979).

28. *Danforth*, 428 U.S. at 69.

29. Scheinberg v. Smith, 659 F.2d at 485.

30. Restrictions on abortion enacted to further demographic or eugenic considerations are distinguishable from the restrictions on sex-selective abortions suggested in this article as a possible useful tactic toward reversal. Sex-selective restrictions would be enacted to test the parameters of the "health" exception to postviability abortions rather than to develop any general principle that would warrant a general prohibition on abortion.

31. 410 U.S. at 153.

32. *Id.* at 152–3. *See* Horan, Roe v. Wade: *No Justification in History, Law or Logic*.

33. *Id.*

34. *See, e.g.,* the Court's summary of American law, in *Roe*, 410 U.S. at 138.

35. *Id.* at 153.

36. Rolling Stone, March 29, 1984, at 17.

37. *Akron*, 462 U.S. at 459.

38. Only Justice Rehnquist would have apparently held that there exists no abortion right. *Roe*, 410 U.S. at 171 (Rehnquist, J., dissenting). Justice White might hold that there exists a right to "health" abortion. *Doe*, 410 U.S. at 221

(White, J., dissenting). Justice O'Connor's criticism of the *Roe* doctrine is rooted in her belief that there exist state interests sufficiently compelling to justify prohibition of abortion; she has nowhere stated that abortion is not a constitutionally protected activity. *See Akron*, 462 U.S. at 452 (O'Connor, J., dissenting).

39. *Cf.* Griswold v. Connecticut, 381 U.S. 479, 485 (1965).

40. *See* Harris v. McRae, 448 U.S. 297, 318 (1980); *Thornburgh v. American College of Obstetricians & Gynecologists*, 106 S. Ct. 2169 (1986)(Stevens, J., concurring.)

Lynn D. Wardle

Judicial Appointments to the Lower Federal Courts: The Ultimate Arbiters of the Abortion Doctrine

I. Introduction: The Importance of Judicial Appointments for the Prospect of Repudiating *Roe v. Wade*

RECENTLY, THERE HAS been a revived interest in the possibility of overturning *Roe v. Wade* through judicial action. Individuals and organizations opposed to the ethic of abortion on demand have been openly discussing the prospects of filling vacancies on the Supreme Court of the United States with persons receptive to arguments that *Roe v. Wade* should be repudiated for several obvious reasons.[1]

First, the Supreme Court single-handedly created the constitutional right of abortion on demand, and subsequently expanded that doctrine by invalidating laws which:

—required spousal consent before married women obtain abortions;[2]

—made parental consent a prerequisite before unmarried minor women obtain abortions;[3]

—prohibited dangerous and inhumane saline amniocentesis abortions;[4]

—established adequate medical attention for viable fetuses;[5]

—insured parental notice and participation in the abortion decision of their minor daughter;[6]

—required late-pregnancy abortions to be performed in hospitals;[7]

—demanded disclosure to pregnant women of vital facts pertaining to the humanity of the fetus prior to abortion;[8]

—established "cooling off" laws protecting a period of deliberation and consideration for women prior to the performance of abortion.[9]

For the sake of constitutional doctrine and judicial integrity, it would be preferable for the Court itself to correct these abuses.

Second, the Supreme Court, being the *only* government department which, by itself, could modify or reverse *Roe v. Wade*, is in the most feasible position to effect change in the rule of abortion on demand. Since *Roe* was announced as a matter of constitutional interpretation, the only way in which the other branches of government could directly overturn the *Roe* interpretation of constitutional law would be to amend the Constitution, but the constitutionally required procedures for proposal and ratification of constitutional amendments were and are intentionally designed to be discouragingly difficult.[10]

Recent events have demonstrated the difficulty in getting Congress to even propose a constitutional amendment to reverse *Roe v. Wade*. In fact, revival of interest in the possibility of judicial reversal of *Roe v. Wade* is probably attributable, at least in part, to the Senate's failure to pass the Human Life Federalism Amendment in 1983.[11] Previously, many dedicated prolife workers had harbored a sincere belief that they could convince at least one house of Congress to pass a Human Life Amendment, especially a moderate proposal simply to reverse abortion on demand. If such a proposal were brought to the floor, it could be debated, openly considered and possibly enough momentum built for eventual passage. However, that belief was predicated upon a naive assumption that a congressional majority would consider the merits of the issue, i.e., the merits of abortion on demand as a constitutionally mandated rule of law. Instead, in June 1983, when the Hatch-Eagleton proposal finally came up for a vote on the Senate floor, it became apparent that many politicians would evade consideration of the controversial abortion issue and, instead, would base their votes entirely upon political assessments of the strength and potential support of special interest groups lobbying for or against the proposition. Unfortunately, there are too many members of Congress who were courted by well-organized and well-financed proabortion special interest groups for the prolife cause to successfully compete at the same level on similar terms.

Third, Chief Justice Burger's resignation, the elevation of Justice William Rehnquist to replace him as chief justice, and the appointment of Antonin Scalia to be the newest associate justice, have demonstrated how profoundly one vacancy can alter the makeup of the

Court. Chief Justice Burger was seventy-seven years old when he resigned, reminding us that because of the age of the present members of the Supreme Court, there could be several vacancies on the Court within a relatively short time. Four members of the current Court are over seventy-seven: Justice William J. Brennan, Jr., Justice Thurgood Marshall, Justice Harry A. Blackmun, and Justice Lewis F. Powell, Jr.[12] Each of these justices voted with the prochoice majority in *Roe*. The remaining justices are under seventy years of age: Justice Byron R. White (69), Chief Justice William H. Rehnquist (61), Justice John Paul Stevens (66), Justice Sandra Day O'Connor (56), and Justice Antonin Scalia (50).[13] President Reagan already has filled two of the nine seats on the Court, and it is possible that he will have the opportunity to fill other vacancies.

Fourth, the impact which a change in the Supreme Court could have on the future of the *Roe* doctrine was clearly demonstrated when the Supreme Court decided *Akron* (in 1983) and *Thornburgh* (in 1986). Reagan appointee Sandra Day O'Connor, replacing Justice Potter Stewart (who had a mixed voting record on abortion), dissented from the prochoice majority decision in both cases. Her compelling and widely acclaimed criticism in *Akron* challenged the fundamental premises of *Roe v. Wade*.[14] One additional Reagan appointee, replacing any member of the proabortion majority, could bring an end to abortion on demand as a constitutional doctrine.[15]

Thus, the way in which vacancies on the U.S. Supreme Court are filled, and by whom, is of enormous significance to the future direction of constitutional law, including abortion doctrine. But, concern over judicial selection should not be limited to nominees for appointment to the Supreme Court. Citizens concerned about judge-made rules, such as the *Roe* doctrine of abortion on demand, must give judicious consideration to the quality, character, and judicial philosophy of judges presiding over the federal district courts and federal courts of appeals. While there is only one Supreme Court with nine justices, there are thirteen circuit courts of appeals with 168 federal court of appeals judges and ninety-one federal judicial districts with 568 federal district judges.[16]

II. The Significance of Selecting Judges to Fill Vacancies on the Federal District Courts and Federal Courts of Appeals

THE IMPORTANCE OF federal district courts and courts of appeals is often overlooked because they are obliged by principles of stare decisis and appellate review to follow the decisions of the Supreme Court.

However, federal district judges and court of appeals judges profoundly influence the development of judicial doctrines. More importantly,
since most federal court cases are not heard by the Supreme Court, the
lower federal courts control the practical applications of the law, and
generally, they exercise broad latitude in applying the principles
enunciated in Supreme Court rulings.

Since the Supreme Court hears comparatively few cases, the vast
majority of federal cases are ultimately decided by the district courts
and courts of appeals. A district judge has the final word in almost
ninety percent of the cases filed in federal district courts because less
than twelve percent of cases decided by the federal district courts are
ever appealed.[17] Usually, parties do not appeal because they agree to
some mutually satisfactory compromise or settlement, or they cannot
afford the cost of the appeal, or the likelihood of success does not
justify the additional expense and effort. Consequently, most decisions of a district judge are final and dispositive—as if he or she were a
one-person Supreme Court. Even when an appeal is taken, the
decision of the lower court is affirmed outright in more than seventy-
five percent of the cases.[18] Thus, in over ninety-five percent of the
cases brought in federal court, the district court resolution will be the
ultimate result in the suit.

Judges on the federal courts of appeals have an equally profound
impact on the cases argued before them. Every federal appellate judge
helps to dispose of about 500 appeals annually.[19] However, more than
one-half of these cases are consolidated or disposed of without hearing
or submission.[20] The remainder are decided by panels usually consisting of three judges; in most cases the three-appellate-judge panels
function as mini-Supreme Courts. Each federal appellate court judge
sat as a member of a panel to fully consider and decide an average of
230 cases on appeal in 1983.[21] Their decisions are dispositive and final
in those cases, because only one percent of the cases heard by federal
courts of appeals will ever be considered on the merits by the Supreme
Court.[22] Again, the cost of appeal and the likelihood of failure
discourage many appeals. Moreover, the Supreme Court accepts for
review only about seven percent of the cases in which appeals or
petitions for review are filed.[23] Furthermore, the Supreme Court
summarily disposes of nearly half of the cases it has accepted for
review, and only issues complete opinions in approximately 160 cases
per year.[24] In the 1982 term, sixteen percent of these written opinions
involved appeals from state court decisions.[25] That means that the
Supreme Court will hear and issue opinions in approximately 130
cases per year from *all* the federal circuits together. Thus, the
mathematical average number of cases decided by all the panels in any

one circuit that will be fully reviewed by the Supreme Court in any given year is approximately ten cases per circuit.[26] Restated, in all but a handful of cases each year, the decision reached by one federal district judge, or in a few cases the decision of two (or three) federal circuit judges, will be the final ruling on the matter in issue.

Since the lower federal courts have the final word in almost all cases, it is important to realize the latitude exercised by lower court judges. The principles enunciated in the opinions of the Supreme Court are usually general, and their decisions are always made in the context of a concrete factual situation. Thus, the discretionary powers of lower courts determine how the general principles enunciated in Supreme Court decisions should apply in other cases, and how differences between the facts of their case and facts of the Supreme Court case affect the application of the rule announced by the Supreme Court.

The process of applying precedent is very dynamic. Being "bound" by Supreme Court precedents does not mean the lower courts are forced to reach a particular conclusion or are precluded from reaching a specific result. Professor Karl Llewellyn elucidated this point when he explained to law students:

> What I wish to sink deep into your minds about the doctrine of precedent, therefore, is that it is two-headed. It is Janus-faced. That it is not one doctrine, nor one line of doctrine, but two, and two which, *applied at the same time to the same precedent, are contradictory of each other*. That there is one doctrine for getting rid of precedents deemed troublesome and one doctrine for making use of precedents that seemed helpful. That these two doctrines exist side by side.... You do not see how it is possible to avoid the past mistakes of courts, and yet to make use of every happy insight for which a judge in writing may have found expression. Indeed it seems to me that here we may have part of the answer to the problem as to whether precedent is not as bad as good—supporting a weak judge with the labors of strong predecessors, but binding a strong judge by the errors of the weak. For look again at this matter of *difficulty* of the doctrine. The strict view—that view that cuts the past away—is *hard* to use. An ignorant, an unskilful judge will find it hard to use: the past will bind him. But the skilful judge—he whom we would make free—*is* thus made free. He has the knife in hand; and he can free himself.[27]

It is apparent that the judicial philosophy and analytical skill of judges serving in the lower federal courts have a tremendous impact upon how the Supreme Court doctrines are applied.

Moreover, lower courts significantly shape the posture and define the context of Supreme Court cases. The district court is the court in which *the facts* are determined. The factual findings made by the district court are binding upon the courts of appeals and Supreme Court, except in unusual cases where the appellate tribunal determines that those findings are contrary to the clear weight of the evidence or are based on legal error. In addition, lower courts also shape the issues by determining what points to ignore, what questions to underscore, what legal doctrines to rely upon, and what arguments to address. To a significant extent, the Supreme Court is at the mercy of the lower courts for the facts and the issues which it reviews.

The lower courts' analysis and philosophy also influence the Supreme Court. When a particular case is heard by the Supreme Court, the legal analysis of the lower courts is often persuasive. This is particularly true if a controversial issue is involved; the Supreme Court prefers to defer to the credible analysis of the lower court when possible. Moreover, Supreme Court justices pay attention to the overall acceptance or rejection by the lower courts of the doctrines the Supreme Court has enunciated. If the lower court experience has been negative, i.e., if judges have struggled with the doctrine, if the Supreme Court ruling has proven difficult to apply, if the lower courts consistently criticize the doctrine, then the Supreme Court may be willing to modify or abandon a prior decision.

III. The Lower Federal Courts Are Composed Presently of Judges Supportive of *Roe v. Wade*

UNTIL RECENTLY, THE prevailing opinions and attitudes of the federal district and court of appeals judges made it unlikely that any significant change in the *Roe* rule of abortion on demand would be initiated by or seriously enforced by the lower federal courts. The decisions of the lower federal courts applying *Roe v. Wade* during the last thirteen years overwhelmingly have supported the rule of abortion on demand and have carried that doctrine to excessive extremes. Even if the Supreme Court of the United States had modified or overturned *Roe v. Wade*, it is probable that the effect of that decision would have been thwarted by district court and court of appeals judges broadly distinguishing or restrictively interpreting that decision.

The lower federal courts have been dominated by judges who support the rule of abortion on demand. Of the 629 active judges now sitting on the federal district courts and federal courts of appeals, excluding senior judges and judges on the Federal Circuit, more than 550 have been appointed since *Roe v. Wade* was decided.[28] If commitment to the basic humanitarian principles embodied in the Constitution, or respect for the constitutionally protected authority of a state to pass laws restricting abortion, had been a significant consideration in the appointment of federal judges during the past thirteen years, evolution of the doctrine of abortion privacy in the lower court would have taken a profoundly different direction.

During the twelve years after *Roe v. Wade* was decided, former President Jimmy Carter has had the most significant impact on the judicial philosophy of the federal courts. He appointed over half of the federal judges seated between January 22, 1973 and August 1, 1984.[29] During his presidential campaign, Carter promised he would select "all federal judges . . . strictly on the basis of merit, without any consideration of political aspects or influence."[30]

Soon after taking office, he created the Circuit Judge Nominating Commission; unfortunately, the partisanship of the federal judicial nominating commissions provoked controversy and criticism. One exhaustive study concluded that "the Circuit Judge Nominating Commission may simply represent a form of merit selection of Democrats by Democrats. . . . Partisan influences seem to have permeated the pre- and post-commission stages: namely, the selection of panelists and the selection of nominees from the list of candidates [submitted by the commissions]."[31] President Carter appointed 87% of the members of that commission from the Democratic party; and 79% of the candidates recommended by the Circuit Judge Nominating Commission to fill judicial vacancies on the federal courts of appeals were Democrats. Likewise, 76% of the nominees for district judge vacancies selected by district judge nominating commissions were Democrats.[32] President Carter's actual judicial *appointments* were even *more* partisan than his commissions' recommendations. *The National Law Journal* reported that, as of October 1980, 97.8% of the federal judges appointed by President Carter had been Democrats, and it further revealed that President Carter was more partisan in his judicial appointments that any other president in over fifty years.[33] And it is well known that during the Carter presidency the Democratic party became aggressively proabortion.[34]

The ideological bias of President Carter's judicial appointees is even more disturbing than their partisanship. In fact, fifty percent of the Circuit Judge Nominating Commission panelists rated themselves as either liberal or very liberal; only seven percent regarded themselves as conservatives. Some members of the judicial nominating commissions were so radical that they were even criticized by their copanelists for their "overt feminist politics." Expectedly, feminist-packed commissions were very concerned about the applicants' views on abortion. Forty-one percent of the members of President Carter's Circuit Judge Nominating Commission who were polled remembered that questions had been asked about candidates' positions on abortion during interviews with potential nominees.[35]

One of President Carter's principal objectives in making judicial appointments was "to develop a mechanism which would allow him to place a larger number of women and members of minority groups on the bench." Indeed, three presidential advisors considered the implementation of affirmative action to be the primary purpose of Executive Order 12,057.[36] In his first executive order dealing with judicial appointments, President Carter instructed his Circuit Judge Nominating Commission that prospective nominees should "possess, and have demonstrated, outstanding legal ability and commitment to equal justice under law."[37] Carter's standard was a clear signal to the judicial nominating commission to seek out and recommend people with a particular ideological point of view. One scholar wrote: "The standard is clearly an exhortation to find and recommend candidates who have demonstrated a particular philosophical orientation by their actions on or off the bench...It has a technical political meaning with implications for attempting to predict judicial decision-making. It is, like much political language, a kind of code. It allows elected officials to sponsor the appointment of judges who share their social philosophy and simultaneously permits them to deny that they are doing that."[38]

President Carter definitely "affected the ideological profile of the lower federal courts" and "left more of an imprint on the federal bench than any President before him."[39] A study of the voting records of Carter appointees to U.S. Courts of Appeals revealed not only that they were significantly more liberal than judges appointed by Republican presidents, but they apparently were more liberal than judges appointed by other Democratic presidents as well.[40]

Due in part to the Carter appointees, the federal district courts and federal courts of appeals have become increasingly supportive of the *Roe* doctrine since *Roe v. Wade* and have made some radically proabortion decisions. This may be why there have been so few dissents-in-principle in the lower court abortion opinions. In fact, until recently there had been only two or three concurring or dissenting lower federal court opinions since *Roe* was decided in which federal judges have questioned the wisdom of the *Roe* doctrine of abortion privacy.[41] None of the lower federal court judges have had the courage or the disposition to suggest, as did Justice O'Connor, that *Roe v. Wade* is "clearly on a collision course with itself," or that the Supreme Court abortion decisions have been "inconsistent...with the Court's approach to fundamental rights in other areas."[42]

The failure of lower federal court judges to criticize, limit, or discuss the problems in the doctrine of abortion on demand stands in stark contrast to the pre-*Roe* division of opinion. In the three years prior to *Roe*, lower federal courts rendered formal opinions in a dozen cases involving challenges to restrictive abortion laws. [43] Even though some of those "test cases" were brought by proabortion litigants in specially selected courts, the federal judges who considered those cases were split almost evenly upon the issue. Since then there has been an almost complete turnover in the personnel occupying the lower federal courts, and the new judges have enthusiastically extended the *Roe* doctrine of abortion on demand to abusive extremes. Indeed, on certain issues, such as abortion funding, the lower courts have been so aggressive in applying the *Roe* decision that the proabortion Supreme Court has had to restrain them. [44]

For all of the foregoing reasons, even if a majority of the members of the Supreme Court were persuaded that the constitutional doctrine of abortion on demand should be abolished, and even if the Supreme Court were to explicitly overrule *Roe v. Wade*, the impact of such a decision could be effectively thwarted for years by federal district court and court of appeals judges broadly distinguishing or restrictively applying the new Supreme Court decision. If judges occupying lower federal court benches do not hold a judicial philosophy that recognizes the worth in law of all humanity or respects the role of state legislatures in our federal system, they might distinguish or confine a Supreme Court decision reversing *Roe v. Wade* as a "derelict upon the waters of the law." Even if the proabortion philosophy among the majority of justices on the Supreme Court were to change, federal courts overall would continue to be sympathetic to the abortion cause until the current judicial philosophy of district judges and court of appeals judges is changed through education of the legal profession and through the judicial appointment process.

IV. How Judges Are Appointed to the Federal District Courts and the Federal Courts of Appeals

THUS, IT IS important to understand the appointment process for the federal district courts and courts of appeals. To ensure an independent judiciary, the drafters of the Constitution provided that federal judges, "both of the supreme and inferior Courts," would hold office during good behavior, could be removed only by congressional impeachment, and could not have their compensation reduced while they were in office. Article Two of the Constitution further provides that the president shall:

> nominate, and by and with the Advice and Consent of the Senate, shall appoint...Judges of the supreme Court, and all other Officers of the United States whose Appointments are not herein provided for, and which shall be established by Law; but the Congress may by Law vest the Appointment of such inferior Officers, as they think proper, in the President alone, in the Courts of Law, or in the Heads of Departments.[45]

Thus, the Constitution distinguishes among three categories of federal officers, including judicial officers, and provides two different methods for their appointment: "Judges of the [S]upreme Court" and "all other Officers of the United States" are nominated by the president and appointed by the president with advice and consent of the Senate. However, "inferior officers" are to be appointed as Congress determines by "the President alone," by the "Courts of Laws," or by the "Heads of Departments."

It is not clear from the text whether district judges and circuit judges are "other Officers of the United States," to be appointed by the president with the advice and consent of the Senate, or whether they are "inferior officers," to be appointed as Congress determines by either the president alone or by the courts of law. The question has never been judicially resolved.[46]

However, this constitutional ambiguity has not been a significant problem. "For most of our history, as Professor Chase has noted, it was simply assumed that federal judges were 'other officers.' In practice, Presidents began appointing lower court judges with the advice and consent of the Senate."[47] Today, President Reagan shares this view of the proper judicial appointment process.[48]

Since 1891 the appointment of federal judges has largely been regulated by legislation authorizing the creation of new judgeships. In 1948, when Congress rewrote the Judicial Code, it specifically provided that all circuit and district judges should be appointed by the president with senatorial consent. The relevant sections of the federal code today provide that "The President shall appoint, by and with the advice and consent of the Senate, circuit judges [and district judges]..."[49]

Thus, neither the Constitution nor any federal statute provides specific direction concerning the judicial appointment process. There is a great deal of discretion involved, and the precise allocation of powers and the particular procedures followed depends upon the personalities involved. The power, prestige, and philosophy of the president, his White House advisors, the attorney general, the Senate as a whole, the Senate Judiciary Committee and its chairman, interested senators, and special interest groups all affect the process of judicial appointment.

Historically, several factors have been significantly influential in the judicial appointment process. The relative role and influence of the president and the Senate in selecting federal judges is the most critical variable in the judicial appointments process. And the jurisdiction of the court has affected the relative influence of the White House and Senate in filling the judicial vacancy. The Senate traditionally has wielded enormous influence over appointments to the federal district courts.[50] The "local" interest of a senator's home state in filling the vacancies is obvious, and if both senators oppose the nomination it would be very awkward for the president to override their objections. Thus, for reasons of historical practice and out of respect for local interests, individual senators have always had a profound influence in the appointment of district court judges.

Historically, senators have also been very influential in selecting persons to fill circuit court vacancies. "Indeed, many critics contended that Senators actually nominated circuit judges, with the advice and consent of the President."[51] But, inasmuch as each circuit contains at least three states, no single senator or pair of senators from a state can claim an exclusive interest in filling judicial vacancies on a circuit court of appeals. Thus, the president has always had room to appoint his favorites to circuit court vacancies because, if the senators of one state in the circuit oppose the nomination, he can usually find a senator from some other state in the circuit to support the nomination.[52]

On December 13, 1976, President-elect Jimmy Carter and his attorney general-designate, Griffin Bell, met with the chairman of the Senate Judiciary Committee, Senator James Eastland, and worked out a new division of responsibility and allocation of roles between the administration and the Senate concerning judicial appointments. Although this agreement was never officially reduced to writing, its key elements apparently were: the president would retain control over Supreme Court nominations; the Senate would defer to the president's nominations to fill circuit court judgeships, provided he involved representatives of each affected jurisdiction in the selection process, attempted to place a judge from each jurisdiction on its circuit court, and attempted to secure the approval of senators of a state regarding nominees from their states; and, the president would defer to the senators' privilege of recommending persons for nomination to district court judgeships.[53] President Reagan has adhered essentially to this allocation of responsibility in filling judicial vacancies; the White House takes the initiative and has the greater influence in filling Supreme Court and circuit court vacancies, while the senators take the initiative and have the "understood" right to select nominees to fill district court vacancies.[54]

Another important variable in the judicial appointment process is the practice of "senatorial courtesy." Essentially, the Senate will not consent to a nominee's appointment if a senator from the state where the judge is to hold office objects to the appointment.[55] Since the mid-fifties, a privilege for "senatorial courtesy" has largely been exercised through the "blue slip" system. "Under this arrangement, a memorandum on a blue slip of paper is sent by the Senate Judiciary Committee formally inviting Senators from a nominee's home state to disclose opinions and information concerning the nominations. On it, the following statement appears: 'Under a rule of the Committee, unless a reply is received from you within a week from this date, it will be assumed that the senator has no objection to this nomination.'"[56] In practice, however, the Judiciary Committee contradicts these instructions; the Senate Judiciary Committee has never scheduled hearings on a judicial nominee in the absence of a returned blue slip. "Thus, as a practical matter, failure to return a blue slip [effectively] resulted in an automatic one-person veto over nominees."[57]

In 1979, when Senator Edward M. Kennedy became chairman of the Senate Judiciary Committee, the practice changed in theory and somewhat in practice. He decided and announced that the committee would no longer allow these slips to be used by individual senators as a unilateral veto of a particular nominee. The committee would reserve to itself the right independently to review and override a senator's failure to return the blue slip. But the reform announced by Senator Kennedy, while symbolically significant, did not appreciably change the practices in the Senate.[58]

In 1981, the Republicans won control of the Senate. Senator Strom Thurmond became chairman of the Senate Judiciary Committee, and it appears that he adhered to the "blue slip" system as well as to the symbolic reforms instituted by Senator Kennedy.[59]

Several other agencies or institutions have significantly influenced judicial appointments. It has been customary for the president to delegate to the attorney general and the Department of Justice an advisory responsibility regarding judicial appointments; traditionally, the attorney general has delegated this assignment to the deputy attorney general. He asks the Federal Bureau of Investigation to investigate every nominee and report all information—including unsubstantiated rumors and innuendos. The role of the Department of Justice primarily depends upon the personality, priorities, and prestige of the attorney general. The Department of Justice can perform a ministerial function, or it can serve as an active source of recommendations and rejections of potential appointees. It has been estimated that approximately twenty percent of judicial appointments were initially promoted by the Justice Department during the Eisenhower and Kennedy administrations. It also appears that, with the possible exception of the Nixon administration, the Department of Justice has assumed an increasingly active role in the process of appointing judges to the lower federal courts.[60]

Another institution playing a significant role in the judicial appointment process is the American Bar Association (ABA) and its Standing Committee on Federal Judiciary. Since 1948, the Senate Judiciary Committee has requested the ABA to express its opinion on the qualification of every official judicial nominee.[61] The ABA rates judicial nominees as Exceptionally Well Qualified, Well Qualified, Qualified, Not Qualified, or Not Qualified By Reason Of Age to fill the judicial office; then the Standing Committee chairman passes this "informal report" to the Department of Justice. If the proposed nominee is formally nominated, the ABA will submit a "formal report" on the candidate to the Department of Justice and to the Senate Judiciary Committee.[62] In evaluating judicial nominees, the ABA is primarily concerned with their professional qualifications, i.e., education, experience, trial experience, professional reputation, temperament, and so on. It is no secret that superficial investigation and "good ole boy" or "clubhouse" considerations often influence a rating. It has been suggested that the ABA is more influential in the judicial appointment process during Republican administrations when Republicans control the Senate Judiciary Committee.[63]

Personal advisors to the president also play a role in the process of filling judicial vacancies and can effectively veto any nomination. One writer described the role of a White House staff this way: "The President often relied on his staff for a final evaluation of the candidate. Again, the candidate's prior political activity and affiliation could improve or diminish the likelihood of nomination. If the staff recommended the President nominate the candidate, the President would submit his or her name to the Senate."[64]

During the last decade, judicial nominating commissions have played an increasingly important role in the judicial appointment process. Before 1975, judicial nominating commissions had rarely been used.[65] As governor of Georgia, Carter had established a nominating commission to assist him in the selection of the state judges.[66] Within a month after his inauguration, President Carter established, by executive order, the United States Circuit Judge Nominating Commission. The Circuit Judge Nominating Commission, consisting of thirteen panels (one for each of the present circuits, excluding the Federal Circuit, plus one additional panel for the large Ninth Circuit), was given responsibilities to recruit, screen, and recommend a limited number of persons "whom the panel[s] consider best qualified to fill the vacancy or vacancies."[67] During the Carter presidency, senators from thirty states created judicial nomination commissions to assist them in selecting nominees to fill district court vacancies as well.[68] In the case of circuit court vacancies, the nominating commission panels were instructed by the president to submit their list of final nominees directly to him, through the Department of Justice.[69] In the case of the district judge nominating commissions, the role of the commissions varied.[70]

President Reagan abolished the Circuit Judge Nominating Commission. Under his administration, the Department of Justice has actively undertaken the responsibility of identifying qualified and acceptable candidates to fill vacancies on the U.S. Courts of Appeals. Senators may recommend particular individuals to fill vacancies in circuits affecting their states; but the Reagan administration's overall view, consistent with the Carter pattern, is that the selection of nominees to fill circuit court vacancies is the prerogative of the president.[71] However, in the Reagan administration, the recommendation of nominees to fill district court vacancies has remained the prerogative of the senator(s) of the affected state. Many senators appoint judicial nominating commissions to assist them. The role and responsibility that judicial nominating commissions have in the process of appointing federal district judges depends entirely upon the wishes of the particular senator.

V. The Propriety of Inquiring about Judicial Candidates' Views Regarding Abortion

SINCE RONALD REAGAN took office, more than 200 judicial vacancies on the federal courts have been filled; and, undoubtedly, prolife organizations have attempted to influence judicial appointments in particular cases. However, there has been no overall, organized, appropriate effort by any responsible prolife organization to monitor judicial appointment opportunities, or appropriately to influence the selection of new judges to fill vacancies on the federal district courts and federal courts of appeals.

This oversight may be the greatest "missed opportunity" in the history of the prolife movement in America. President Reagan took office committed to appointing federal judges who recognize the basic worth of all human life and who believe in the constitutional allocation of decision-making power to elected state representatives. The 1980 Republican Party platform emphasized these very points and declared:

Under Mr. Carter, many appointments to federal judgeships have been particularly disappointing. By his partisan nominations, he has violated his explicit campaign promise of 1976 and has blatantly disregarded the public interest. We pledge to reverse the deplorable trend, through the appointment of women and men who respect and reflect the values of the American people, and whose judicial philosophy is characterized by the highest regard for protecting the rights of law-abiding citizens, and is consistent with the belief in the decentralization of the federal government and efforts to return decision making power to state and local elected officials. *We will work for the appointment of judges at all levels of the judiciary who respect traditional family values and the sanctity of innocent human life.*[72]

Again, in 1984, the Republican Party platform reiterated this position. After reaffirming support for "the fundamental individual right to life" of the unborn, it declared, "we applaud President Reagan's fine record of judicial appointments, and we reaffirm our support for the appointment of judges at all levels of the judiciary who respect traditional family values and the sanctity of innocent human life."[73]

The 1984 Democratic Party platform recognized the importance of judicial appointments for achieving legal and public policy objectives in the United States when it declared: "Our next president will likely have the opportunity to shape [the Supreme Court], not just for his own term—or even for his own lifetime —but for the rest of ours, and for our children's too." It further warned specifically that because of the president's power to appoint justices, the right to "reproductive freedom . . . could easily disappear during a second Reagan term."[74] Walter Mondale, the Democratic Party candidate, campaigned vigorously using the argument that, "[t]his election is not about Republicans sending hecklers to my rallies. It is about Jerry Falwell picking justices for the Supreme Court."[75]

Both political parties recognized the importance of appointing federal judges holding philosophies sympathetic to the party platform in order to secure political objectives in law and public policy; yet, Mondale managed to take the "high ground" in the public debate by implying that the way judges would be selected by Reagan would be improper. In view of Mondale's second-in-command service in the Carter administration, which compiled a record of blatant partisanship in judicial appointments, this was a remarkable accomplishment. But it does point out that inquiring into the personal philosophy of judicial nominees is a delicate matter, and may offend popular notions about the independence and integrity of the judicial branch. Using judicial appointments as "political payoffs" to distrusted special interest groups is an inappropriate way to elect federal judges.

However, the propriety of inquiring about a judicial candidate's social philosophy is well established in principle and in practice. Fifteen years ago, Professor Charles Black observed: "In a world that knows that a man's social philosophy shapes his judicial behavior, that philosophy is a factor in his fitness [for judicial office]."[76] In this vein, a 1977 memorandum from the Department of Justice informed members of judicial nominating commissions that:

> [A] person's general sense of values and outlook on society are significant factors for the panel to take into consideration, as they will bear on the soundness of the decisions he will make as a judge.... Since a judge is charged with doing "justice under law," a person's instincts for justice and injustice may properly influence his decisions as a judge, and the panel should consider these qualities.[77]

Interviews with members of the Circuit Judge Nominating Commission and the nominees they selected revealed that a majority of the members of both groups felt comfortable with questions probing judicial candidates' social philosophies. A sixty-two percent majority of panel members and sixty percent of the candidates believed it was appropriate to ask applicants questions about their personal views on social issues. Reasons offered by both groups were similar. One panel member stated that an applicant's positions were not important, "but the answers themselves were invaluable in providing insight into the applicant's character." Many candidates supported this reasoning, reiterating that panels were "entitled to know the 'whole person'." Another candidate remarked: "I think anyone aspiring to be a circuit judge should be able to handle this sort of question, and I think one's general view of life and society is fair game." It was also suggested that such questions were proper because a "panel should try to determine where ... [an applicant] stands on major issues facing our society and whether his positions are consistent with the President's." Several believed that "personal values are relevant" and "some inquiry helps [a] panel discover [an applicant's] psychological make-up."[78]

Having served on a judicial nominating commission which recommended nominees to fill a federal district court vacancy, I believe that there are two significant limitations on the extent to which the attitudes of judicial candidates regarding abortion or the constitutionalizing of abortion on demand can or should be effectively examined. First, nominating commissions are usually acting under time constraints; and it is not feasible for them to investigate thoroughly the philosophical history of applicants for the vacancy. Only persons who have been outspoken publicly have a readily accessible history. Individual members of the commission have time to ask only one or two questions during the formal interviews. The applicants, trying to appear and sound judicial, are usually noncommittal on controversial subjects. The most effective inquiry into a judicial nominee's philosophy relating to abortion and appropriate state regulation of abortion practices must occur at other stages of the judicial appointment process. Competent, qualified attorneys who are committed to the constitutional allocation of powers and who respect the value of all life should be encouraged to apply for judicial vacancies. Responsible individuals should openly inquire about the background, social philosophy, and professional history of all candidates recommended by nominating commissions or senators *before* a political or presidential decision to nominate one of them is made.

Second, eliciting a candidate's philosophy concerning abortion must be done with sensitivity and care. Most attorney-members of judicial nominating commissions are preoccupied with the professional qualifications of potential judges, and some are disconcerted by the thought that other factors, especially those which seem to smack of philosophical censorship, might be disqualifying factors. Heavy-handed "litmus test" questions about abortion seldom elicit meaningful responses and may alienate people. However, respectful and frank questions to determine the extent to which a candidate is committed to respecting the equal worth under law of all living humans, how he or she views the constitutional allocation of authority to the states to resolve such controversial social issues, and whether he or she has the analytical skill properly to distinguish and limit bad precedents are appropriate and should be asked. The legal community needs to be educated that abortion is a civil rights consideration for judicial fitness.

As Professor Laurence Tribe has written:

> It is perfectly appropriate to inquire into a judicial candidate's attitude toward *Roe*, and would in fact be bizarre *not* to, but the questions must address *principled* views about the decision and the legal doctrines relating to it—not mere aversion to, or mere endorsement of, its result. Regardless of *where* a nominee stands on an issue, a candidate for our highest court owes us an account of *why*. And that explanation must be based on principles and precedents, not prejudices or even good-faith preconceptions. There is nothing necessarily improper in an objection to *Roe v. Wade* based on a judgment that the Supreme Court gave insufficient weight to the value of fetal life, or on a protest that the court gave too much deference to mainstream medical opinion....[79]

VI. Conclusion

PROFESSOR LAURENCE TRIBE recently wrote a provocative little book encouraging the Senate to undertake more aggressive procedures in screening nominees for the Supreme Court.[80] Much of what Professor Tribe has written in the book is thoughtful and the specific encouragement he gives the Senate to take an active, principled investigatory approach to exercising the "advice and consent" responsibility would fit comfortably with the spirit and recommendations of this chapter concerning judicial appointments to the lower federal courts.

Professor Tribe generally endorses the propriety of inquiry about judicial nominees' views about abortion. He attempts to be even-handed, although he declares (with convenient loss of pre-1973 memory) that anyone who would reject *Roe v. Wade* because the right to abortion on demand is not explicitly stated in the Constitution should not be confirmed;[81] more disturbingly, questions about the proper role of the federal judicial branch, respect for the constitutional allocation of powers to the states, and judicial self-restraint are noticeably lacking from his list of permissible questions about abortion.[82]

But there is a darker side to Professor Tribe's call for greater political activism in the judicial appointment process. The partisanship of his tract is disturbing.[83] Indeed, he openly indicates that he was motivated to write his book, at least in part, because of the results of the 1984 reelection of President Reagan and the prospect of more Reagan appointments to the Supreme Court.[84] He begins the book with a chapter that essentially calls for the aged liberal justices to remain on the bench as long as they can.[85] He devotes a whole chapter to legitimating Senate toughness in the appointment process, lauding past confrontations with the president over nominations.[86]

Recently, we have had a chance to see how some senators are putting into practice Professor Tribe's call for more aggressive scrutiny of conservative judicial nominees. The result—the "Rehnquisition" of President Reagan's nominee to replace retiring Chief Justice Burger—was appalling. Encouraged by the popular professor's open support for tough inquisition of judicial nominees, opponents of the Rehnquist nomination engaged in a campaign of character assassination and personal vilification. Senators unhappy with Rehnquist's philosophy (which has been openly published in his judicial opinions for fifteen years and hardly needed a detective to ferret out) undertook a shabby search for dirt. For weeks the country witnessed the cheap spectacle of politicians parading out any potentially em-

barassing fact or rumor about the nominee (from family disagreements to traffic tickets to antiquated real estate titles) amid apocalyp-
tic cries of anguish, breast-beatings, and condemnations—all in the
hopes that something might stir public opinion against the nominee so
that the opponents could generate enough raw political clout to block
the nomination. In practice, the Tribe approach obviously is not the
high road he describes so eloquently in his book. Rather, it is nothing
more than a return to Neanderthal tactics and political gutter-fighting
beneath the smokescreen of intellectual respectability conveniently
provided by Professor Tribe.[87]

What I propose bears no resemblance to the practices employed by
opponents of the Rehnquist nomination. It is to the everlasting credit
of prolife advocates that, during six years of Republican hegemony in
the Senate and President Reagan in the White House, they have not
stooped to the thuggish tactics of "Rehnquisition." It is to the shame of
prochoice advocates that they have. And it is regrettable that
Professor Tribe has not been outspoken in condemnation of "Rehnquisition," since his book undoubtedly must share a large part of the
blame for encouraging and lending credibility to that sinister, reac-
tionary tactic.

The federal judiciary has been directly involved, and will be for the
next generation, in the development, expansion, modification, or
repeal of the *Roe* doctrine of abortion. Opponents of abortion on
demand should make a systematic, responsible effort to examine the
basic judicial philosophy of all candidates who seek positions on the
federal district courts and federal courts of appeals. Qualified lawyers
who respect constitutional values and allocations of power should be
encouraged to apply to fill judicial vacancies. Otherwise, it is unlikely
that any appreciable change will occur in the abortion-accommodating
philosophy of the federal courts. The future of the abortion doctrine
will largely be determined by the federal court system. Prolife citizens
cannot shrink from their participatory responsibilities in the judicial
selection process if they hope to see the doctrine of constitutionalized
abortion on demand repudiated during their lifetime.

Notes

1. 410 U.S. 113 (1973).
2. Planned Parenthood v. Danforth, 428 U.S. 52 (1976).
3. *Id.*
4. *Id.*
5. Colautti v. Franklin, 439 U.S. 379 (1979); Thornburgh v. American
College of Obstetricians and Gynecologists, 106 S.Ct. 2169 (1986).

6. Bellotti v. Baird, 443 U.S. 622 (1979); Planned Parenthood Association v. Ashcroft, 462 U.S. 476 (1983). *But see* H.L. v. Matheson, 450 U.S. 398 (1981) (law requiring parental notice upheld).

7. Doe v. Bolton, 410 U.S. 179 (1973); Akron v. Akron Center for Reproductive Health, 462 U.S. 416 (1983).

8. Akron v. Akron Center for Reproductive Health, 462 U.S. 416 (1983). In June, 1986, the Supreme Court also invalidated informed consent provisions requiring disclosure of the medical risks of the abortion to the woman, and disclosure of public and private childbirth and child support assistance programs. *Thornburgh*, 106 S.Ct. at 2180.

9. *Akron*, 462 U.S. at 416. The Supreme Court has agreed to consider the constitutionality of a 24-hour parental consultation period in Hartigan v. Zbaraz, No. 85–673 (appeal noted October 14, 1985).

10. The Constitution provides that an amendment to the Constitution may only be proposed in two ways—by a two-thirds vote of each house of Congress, or upon petition of two-thirds of the states. U.S. Const., art. V. It further provides that, once proposed, a constitutional amendment can only be ratified in two ways—by the positive vote of the legislatures in three-fourths of the states or by the vote of conventions of three-fourths of the states.

11. S. J. Res. 3, cosponsored by Senator Orrin Hatch, R-Utah, and Senator Thomas Eagleton, D-Missouri.

12. Judges of the United States 68 (The Bicentennial Committee of the Judicial Conference of the United States, 2d ed. 1983).

13. *Id.* (Ages are given as of July 1, 1986.)

14. *Akron*, 462 U.S. at 452. Justice O'Connor also wrote a devastating criticism of the abortion doctrine in *Thornburgh*, calling it "a major distortion in the Court's constitutional jurisprudence." *Thornburgh*, 106 S.Ct. at 2206, *infra* at 321 (O'Connor, J., dissenting).

15. The 5–4 decision in *Thornburgh*, in June 1986, demonstrated how close the Court already is to rejecting *Roe v. Wade*. All of the dissenting opinions urged the reexamination, if not the repudiation, of the *Roe* doctrine.

16. 28 U.S.C.A. §133 (1986 Supp.). The numbers of federal appellate and district judges mentioned in the text is the number of authorized judgeships. Before July 1984, there were only 144 judges sitting on the federal courts of appeals and 508 federal district judges, but as part of a bankruptcy law passed by Congress in late June and signed by President Reagan on July 10, 1984, twenty-four new federal court of appeals judgeships and sixty-one new federal district judgeships were created. H.R. 5174 (Pub. L. 98–353) 201, 202, 98th Cong., 2d Sess. (1984). The other six district judges apparently are authorized by other authorities for extraterritorial endows (*e.g.* for the Virgin Islands, Guam, North Marianas, etc.). But the new legislation provided that no more that eleven of the new appellate court judgeships and no more than twenty-nine of the new district court judgeships could be filled before January 21, 1985—the date of the next presidential inauguration. *Id. See generally, Bankruptcy Overhaul Awaits Reagan Signature*, 42 Cong. Q. Wkly. Rep. 1665, 1666 (1984). Marian Ott of the Administrative Office of the U.S. Courts reported that, as of November 7, 1986, there were 575 district court judges authorized.

Telephone interview with Marrian Ott, Administrative Office of the U.S. Courts, Statistical Analysis and Reports (Nov. 7, 1986). *See further infra* note 28.

17. This figure was ascertained by dividing the number of appeals filed in the circuit courts in 1983 (30,786) by the number of cases terminated in the district courts in 1983 (259,221), which gives the approximate percentage of cases appealed (12%). Of course, this is not exact because some cases terminated in 1982 were appealed in 1983 and some terminated in 1983 were appealed in 1984. Statistical Analysis and Reports Division, Ad. Off. of the U.S. Courts, Federal Judicial Workload Statistics 2, 7, 15 (1984) (and hereinafter cited as "Federal Judicial Workload Statistics").

18. *Id.* at A-2, Table B-1. In 1983 less than 16% of the cases disposed of by hearing in the courts of appeals were reversed while 77% were affirmed outright. *Id.*

19. This figure was ascertained by dividing the number of cases terminated in the circuit courts in 1983 (29,780) by the number of circuit judges counted in 722 F.2d (178) and multiplying by three. Federal Judicial Workload Statistics, *supra* note 17, at 2, Table 2. Again the figure is low because the number of appellate judges used (178) includes senior judges.

20. *Id.* at A-2, Table B-1. Out of 29,780 appeals disposed of in 1983, a total of 4,099 were consolidated, and 12,014 were disposed of without hearing or submission. *Id.*

21. This figure was ascertained by dividing the number of cases disposed of after hearing or submission in 1983 (13,667), *id.*, by multiplying that figure (76.8) by three (the number of judges per panel).

22. This figure was ascertained by adding the number of cases disposed of by written opinion (182) and per curiam or memorandum decisions (119) and then dividing this figure (301) by the number of appeals filed in the circuit courts in 1983 (30,786). *See* note 19, *supra*, and *The Supreme Court, 1982 Term*, 97 Harv. L. Rev. 70, 299 at Table II (1983) (hereinafter "*1982 Term*").

23. The Supreme Court has a great deal of discretion to decide whether or not to review any particular case that is brought before it on appeal or on petition for writ of certiorari. 28 USC §1254 (1976); United States Supreme Court Rule 17 (1) (1984). In the 1982 term the Court disposed of 301 cases by full written opinion, per curiam or memorandum decision. It denied review or discussed or had petitions for review withdrawn in 3887 additional cases. *1982 Term, supra* note 22, at 303.

24. In 1982 the Court issued full written opinions in 162 cases and resolved 119 cases by per curiam or memorandum decision. *1982 Term*, 97 Harv. L. Rev. at 299, Table II. The Court issued 137 written opinions in the 1978 term, 149 in 1979, 138 in 1980, 167 in 1981 and 162 in 1982. *1982 Term*, 97 Harv. L. Rev. 303 (1983).

25. Of the 162 written opinions in the 1982 term, 29 involved cases which originated in state court. *Id.* at 299, 303.

26. This computation is based on thirteen federal courts of appeals, including the court of appeals for the Federal Circuit. The figure is only a mathematical average. In the larger circuit where a larger number of cases are heard, a greater number of them will be reviewed by the Supreme Court.

Similarly, small circuits are likely to have fewer than the average number of decisions examined by the Supreme Court each year.

27. K. Llewellyn, The Bramble Bush 68 (1951) (emphasis in original).

28. This figure reflects the composition of the federal courts as of the fall of 1983. I say "more than 550" judicial vacancies have been filled because the authoritative sources are conflicting. There are several different points in the process of judicial appointment from which the date of appointment can be measured (*e.g.* nomination by the President, Senate approval, President signs the appointment, the nominee takes the oath of office, or the time of entry on duty). Also, some judges who were appointed to the court of appeals had previously been appointed to the federal district court and with creation of the Eleventh Circuit, a number of judges were reappointed, who had previously been appointed. Counting the federal judges listed in the front of 792 F. 2d (1986), the figure is 568.

29. Judges of the United States, *supra* note 12, reveals that 330 judicial appointments were made from the time of *Roe v. Wade* until the time that Ronald Reagan took office in January 1981. Of these, it identifies 229 as Carter appointees. However, Leta Barner, an employee of the administrative office of the U.S. Courts, and Sheila Joy, a staff assistant in the office of the deputy attorney general, told me in telephone conversation on May 9, 1984, that President Carter had appointed 260 federal judges, and that President Reagan had appointed 122. Volume 573 of Federal Supplement identifies 253 federal district court or court of appeals judges as having been appointed during the Carter tenure. Sheldon Goldman reports that President Carter appointed 202 federal district judges and 56 judges to the courts of appeals. Goldman, *Carter's Judicial Appointments: A Lasting Legacy*, 64 Judicature 344, 345 (1981) (hereinafter cited as "Goldman"). The overall ratio of appointments by President Carter, however, is about the same in all the lists. Gerald Ford appointed approximately 60 federal judges, and Richard Nixon appointed approximately 40 in the time he remained in office after January 22, 1973. *See supra* note 12. By November 1986, however, President Reagan had made 299 appointments to federal benches, including 291 appointments to federal district courts and courts of appeals. Ten of these were appointments to appellate positions of persons Reagan previously had appointed to the district court. Telephone interview with Marian Ott, *supra* note 16. As of August 1984, Ronald Reagan had appointed approximately 150 federal judges.

30. L. Berkson & S. Carbon, The United States Circuit Judge Nominating Commission: Its Members, Procedures and Candidates 1 (1980).

31. Likewise, political science professor John Gottschall has written: "Carter's initial pledge of non-partisan judicial selection was reduced in practice to merit selection among Democrats...." Gottschall, *Carter's Judicial Appointments: The Influence of Affirmative Action and Merit Selection on Voting on the U.S. Courts of Appeals*, 67 Judicature 165, 173 (1983).

32. *Id.* at 49, 134. *See also* A. Neff, The United States District Judge Nominating Commissions: Their Members, Procedures and Candidates 119 (1981). While these figures are disproportionate when compared to the party affiliation of the U.S. population in general, perhaps they are not dispropor-

tionate when compared to the party affiliation of the members of the judicial nominating commissions, or when one considers the process of "self-exclusion" by which many otherwise interested Republican lawyers or judges may have declined to apply for appointment, believing that their party affiliation or judicial philosophy would effectively preclude their chance for selection.

33. Fein, *The Silent Minorities?*, Jan. 12, 1986, Nat'l L. J. 15. That party allegiance is ascendent in the appointment of federal judges is confirmed by statistics showing the percentage of federal judicial appointees who shared the party allegiance of the appointing president:

Cleveland	Dem.	97.3
B. Harrison	Rep.	87.0
McKinley	Rep.	95.7
T. Roosevelt	Rep.	95.8
Taft	Rep.	82.2
Wilson	Dem.	98.6
Harding	Rep.	97.7
Coolidge	Rep.	94.1
Hoover	Rep.	85.7
F.D. Roosevelt	Dem.	96.4
Truman	Dem.	93.1
Eisenhower	Rep.	95.1
Kennedy	Dem.	90.9
L.B. Johnson	Dem.	95.2
Nixon	Rep.	93.7
Ford	Rep.	81.2
Carter	Dem.	97.8*

*As of Oct. 1, 1980.

Id. But see Goldman, *supra* note 29 at 348, 350 (reports that only 94.1% of Carter's district court appointees and 89.3% of his appellate court appointees were Democrats).

34. In 1976, when Jimmy Carter was the nominee for president, the Democratic party platform plank on abortion read:

> We fully recognize the religious and ethical nature of the concerns which many Americans have on the subject of abortion. We feel, however, that it is undesirable to attempt to amend the U.S. Constitution to overturn the Supreme Court decision in this area.

Democratic Platform: "A Contract With the People," 32 Cong. Q. Almanac 885, 860 (1976). In 1980, when Jimmy Carter had served four years as president and was again the Democratic Party nominee for president, the Democratic platform plank on abortion read:

> *Reproductive Rights.* We fully recognize the religious and ethical concerns which many Americans have about abortion. We also recognize the belief of many Americans that a woman has a right to choose whether and when to have a child.

> The Democratic Party supports the 1973 Supreme Court decision on abortion rights as the law of the land and opposes any constitutional amendment to restrict or overturn that decision.

1980 Democratic Platform Text, 36 Cong. Q. Almanac 91-B, 96-B, (1980).

In 1984, when Jimmy Carter's protege, Walter Mondale, was the nominee of the Democratic party, the Democratic party platform plank on abortion read:

> *Reproductive Freedom.* The Democratic Party recognizes reproductive freedom as a fundamental human right. We therefore oppose government interference in the reproductive decisions of Americans, especially government interference which denies poor Americans their right to privacy by funding or advocating one or a limited number of reproductive choices only. We fully recognize the religious and ethical concerns which many Americans have about abortion. But we also recognize the belief of many Americans that a woman has a right to choose whether and when to have a child. The Democratic Party supports the 1973 Supreme Court decision on abortion rights as the law of the land and opposes any constitutional amendment to restrict or overturn that decision. We deplore violence and harassment against health providers and women seeking services, and will work to end such acts. We support a continuing federal interest in developing strong local family planning and family life education programs and medical research aimed at reducing the need for abortion.

Text of 1984 Democratic Party Platform, 42 Cong. Q. Weekly Rep. 1747, 1767 (1984).

35. L. Berkson & S. Carbon, *supra* note 30, at 46, 98, 162–163.

> *Ideological Bias.* Several commissioners believed that the political ideology of some of their colleagues had a negative impact on the panel. Generally, these commissioners thought that their panels needed "more conservatives." One stated that some of his colleagues were "too politically liberal to be objective about the applicants." Another claimed that the panel was "politically slanted" and did not contain "a good cross representation of the public." One of his colleagues stated that "ideological considerations controlled the vote of the majority." . . .
>
> Some commissioners believed that the ideological bias of other members led them to strongly favor minorities and women. One panelist . . . in apparent reference to interview questions about ERA, was disturbed by the "effort to commit applicants to a certain philosophy." A member of another panel was offended by the "overt feminist politics of women."

Id. at 162, 163.

36. L. Berkson & S. Carbon, *supra* note 30, at 27. The commitment to affirmative action and to merit selection of judges created a significant potential conflict. See *id.* at 34, 35.

37. Exec. Order No. 11,972, 42 Fed. Reg. 9659 (Feb. 14, 1977). Moreover, he instructed the panel to "make special efforts to seek out and identify qualified women and members of minority groups as potential nominees." Exec. Order No. 12,057, 43 Fed. Reg. 20949 (May, 11, 1978).

38. A. Neff, *supra* note 32, at 150.

39. Goldman, *supra* note 29, at 344.

40. Gottschall, *supra* note 31, at 168–171. Because of sample size the variations between Carter appointees and appointees of other Democratic presidents were not statistically significant.

41. The only cases of which I am aware in which the lower courts have suggested criticism of the fundamental premises of *Roe* are Rosen v. Louisiana

Board of Medical Examiners, 380 F. Supp. 875 (E.D. La. 1974) (Ainsworth, J. and Boyle, J., concurring); and Gary-Northwest Indiana Womens Services v. Bowen, 421 F. Supp. 734, 736 (N.D. Ind. 1976) (Sharp, J., concurring); Margaret S. v. Edwards, 794 F.2d 994,995 (5th Cir. 1986). *See generally*, L. Wardle, The Abortion Privacy Doctrine, 303, 304 (1980).

42. *Akron*, 462 U.S. at 458, 452. (O'Connor, J., dissenting).

43. *See Roe*, 410 U.S. at 154, 155.

44. The Supreme Court had to decide and issue formal opinions in five cases before the lower courts accepted a conclusion that states were not mandated by a federal, constitutional or statutory law to provide funding for nonthera-peutic abortion. *See* Beal v. Doe, 432 U.S. 438 (1977); Maher v. Roe, 432 U.S. 464 (1977); Poelker v. Doe, 432 U.S. 519 (1977); Harris v. McRae 448 U.S. 297 (1980); Williams v. Zbaraz, 448 U.S. 358 (1980).

45. U.S. Const. art. II, §2, cl. 2.

46. L. Berkson & S. Carbon, *supra* note 30, at 11. The Federalist reveals that the drafters of the Constitution, at least Alexander Hamilton, believed that the federal judges would be appointed by the president with the advice and consent of the Senate. The Federalist No. 66 (A. Hamilton).

47. H. Chase, Federal Judges: The Appointing Process 4 (1972); Shartel, *Federal Judges—Appointment, Supervision and Removal—Some Possibilities Under the Constitution*, 28 Mich. L. Rev. 485 (1930).

48. Statement by the President, July 10, 1984 (criticizing provision in the "Bankruptcy Amendments and Federal Judgeship Act of 1984" restricting his power to appoint new district judges and circuit judges until after the next presidential inauguration: "I believe that these provisions clearly violate my constitutional authority under the Appointments Clause of the Constitution to submit nominations to the Senate and to make appointments after receiving the Senate's advice and consent." *Id.* at 2).

49. 28 U.S.C. §§44 & 133 (Supp. 1984).

50. A. Neff, *supra* note 32, at 5.

51. L. Berkson & S. Carbon, *supra* note 30, at 2.

52. *Id.* at 13, 14.

53. A. Neff, *supra* note 32, at 32; L. Berkson & S. Carbon, *supra* note 30, at 23.

54. Telephone interview with Sheila Joy, staff assistant, Office of Deputy Attorney General (Aug. 23, 1984).

55. L. Berkson & S. Carbon, *supra* note 30 at 12, 13; A. Neff, *supra* note 32, at 3, 4.

56. A. Neff, *supra* note 32, at 16, 17; L. Berkson & S. Carbon, *supra* note 30, at 13.

57. L. Berkson & S. Carbon, *supra* note 30, at 13.

58. A. Neff, *supra* note 32, at 42. While Senator Kennedy chaired the Judiciary Committee, "for the first time in modern history...the Senate Judiciary Committee opposed a fellow senator of the president's party from the state of vacancy and rejected a nominee found qualified (at least initially) by the A.B.A." Goldman, *supra* note 29, at 353. But that only happened once and the overall impression of seasoned observers is that the practice of "senatorial courtesy" is still solidly intact.

59. Telephone interview with Stephen J. Markman, Chief Counsel, Subcommittee on the Constitution of the Senate Judiciary Committee (Aug. 27, 1984).

60. L. Berkson & S. Carbon, *supra* note 30, at 14; A. Neff, *supra* note 32, at 19.

61. L. Berkson & S. Carbon, *supra* note 30, at 14; A. Neff, *supra* note 32, at 11. During the Carter administration, "two other organizations began to play a role in selection analogous to that of the American Bar Association: the National Bar Association, a predominately black lawyer's organization; and the Federation of Women Lawyers. [During the Carter presidency] the Justice Department requested each group to evaluate candidates in terms of their commitment to equal justice under law and for the presence or absence of fixed biases against racial, religious, or sexual groups." *Id.* at 45. While the influence of these two groups does not appear to have been particularly strong, it appears that the access afforded these two organizations made them potentially influential in the informal stages preceding the formal nomination of particular candidates. *Id.*

62. A. Neff, *supra* note 32, at 11–16, 44.

63. L. Berkson & S. Carbon, *supra* note 30, at 3, 30, 151, and 156 nn. 86, 87. Another writer summarized some of the criticisms that were voiced concerning the participation of the ABA in the judicial appointment process during the 1946–1976 era as follows:

> However, the Standing Committee was accused of representing only a small segment of the bar—the predominately white, male, high-income, corporate practice stratum—while purporting to represent all segments. The Committee was criticized for its demographically limited composition. During the transitional period, it had no female members or members from racial minorities. The Committee was accused of evaluative bias arising from its economic and demographic composition. The Committee was criticized for the secrecy in which it conducted its work and because each investigation was conducted by a single unsupervised member. It was also suggested that the Committee, as a representative of a private interest group such as the ABA, should not have a formal and exclusive role in screening candidates, as it did throughout the transitional period. The Committee was accused of having an arbitrary standard concerning age and trial experience. It disapproved of nominees over the age of 60 or with less than fifteen years trial experience. The Committee was inevitably criticized for being wrong in some of its predictions of judicial competence or incompetence.

A. Neff, *supra* note 32, at 16. *See also, id.* at 44.

64. A. Neff, *supra* note 32, at 30. During the Carter administration, "on the advice of his staff, the President refused for one year to nominate any candidate from the commission in Virginia because they were all white males. In another case, it has been alleged that one candidate cleared every hurdle prior to nomination but was rejected by the President's legislative liaison." *Id.* at 41.

65. A. Neff, *supra* note 32, at 53–56 and *id.* at Corrections and Errata.

66. L. Berkson & S. Carbon, *supra* note 30, at 31.

67. Exec. Order No. 11,972, 42 Fed. Reg. 9659 (Feb. 4, 1977). This order was enhanced and superseded by Exec. Order No. 12,057, 43 Fed. Reg. 20949 (May 11, 1978). The original order required that five names be transmitted; the later order deleted the numerical requirement.

68. A. Neff, *supra* note 32, at 53.

69. *Department of Justice Supplemental Instructions*, April 22, 1977, in L. Berkson & S. Carbon, *supra* note 30, at 217, 218; *Department of Justice Supplemental Instructions*, Oct. 2, 1978, in L. Berkson & S. Carbon, *supra* note 30, at 221, 222.

70. A. Neff, *supra* note 32, at 57–59.

71. Telephone interview with Sheila Joy, staff assistant, Office of Deputy Attorney General (Aug. 24, 1984).

72. *1980 Republican Platform Text*, 36 Cong. Q. Almanac, 55-B, 74-B (1980) (emphasis added).

73. *Text of 1984 Republican Party Platform*, 42 Cong. Q. Wkly., Rep. 2096, 2111 (1984).

74. *Text of 1984 Democratic Party Platform*, 42 Cong. Q. Wkly., Rep. 1747, 1764 (1984).

75. Witt, *Shaping the Supreme Court for a Generation*, 42 Cong. Q. Wkly. Rep. 2452 (1984).

76. Black, *A Note on Senatorial Consideration of Supreme Court Nominees*, 79 Yale L. J. 657 (1970). For an excellent overview of the propriety of asking Supreme Court nominees about their position on controversial issues, see Rees, *Questions For Supreme Court Nominees at Confirmation Hearings: Excluding the Constitution*, 17 Ga. L. Rev. 913, 943 (1983).

77. *Department of Justice Supplemental Instructions*, April 22, 1977 in L. Berkson & S. Carbon, *supra* note 30, at 220.

78. L. Berkson & S. Carbon, *supra* note 30, at 97, 98.

79. L. Tribe, God Save This Honorable Court 98 (1985).

80. *Id.*

81. *Id.* at 98.

82. *Id.* at 97–101.

83. As another law professor noted, "it is tempting to write off [Tribe's] whole thesis on the ground that it would seem far less appealing to its author if the White House were in liberal hands and the Senate were dominated by conservative recalcitrants!" Bloom, *Senators, Save This Honorable Court*, 61 Notre Dame L. Rev. 289, 297 (1985).

84. L. Tribe, *Supra* note 79, at ix-xi.

85. *Id.* at xv-xix (Prologue: The Graying of the Court).

86. *Id.* at 77–92 (Chapter Five: The Myth of the Spineless Senate).

87. Now that the Democrats (the party of the "Rehnquisitors") control the Senate decisively, one cannot help but be concerned about what the Rehnquist ordeal portends for the future.

PART IV

Conclusion

EDWARD R. GRANT

Abortion and the Constitution: The Impact of *Thornburgh* on the Strategy to Reverse *Roe v. Wade*

THE JUNE 1986 decision of the Supreme Court in *Thornburgh v. American College of Obstetricians and Gynecologists* is an important benchmark in the unfolding history of constitutional doctrine concerning abortion.[1] The tenor of the Court's 5–4 split decision, marked by hostility toward all attempts at state regulation of abortion in the majority opinion, and the direct attack on the foundations of *Roe v. Wade* among the dissenters, demonstrate that even within the tribunal that authored *Roe*, the abortion question is far from settled.[2] Upon initial examination, therefore, *Thornburgh* appears to prove the validity of the thesis that *Roe v. Wade* can be successfully attacked and eventually reversed through the judicial process.

Deeper analysis of the *Thornburgh* case is necessary, however, to determine if this proof is indeed reliable. This analysis must proceed on two levels: the textual analysis of the opinion, and a contextual examination of the legislative and litigative strategy that brought forth the opinion. Through the first, textual analysis, *Thornburgh* must be carefully examined not only to discern the philosophy of the dissenting justices, which should now guide the formation of the reversal strategy, but also to determine just how far the majority of five justices has expanded *Roe v. Wade*. It is indeed possible that advocates for the unborn must first seek to undo the *Thornburgh* decision before they can take on the larger target of *Roe*. Through the second, contextual analysis, these same advocates must examine the drafting of the Pennsylvania statute at issue in *Thornburgh*, the litigation strategy adopted by the commonwealth in defending the statute, and the litigation strategies followed by other parties, particularly before the U.S. Supreme Court.

245

Thornburgh, is, indeed, a case study for those who seek to reverse *Roe v. Wade,* and the lessons to be drawn from this case study must be applied to the formulation and execution of future reversal strategies. This chapter seeks to apply those lessons to the fundamental strategy that has been set forth in the earlier chapters of this volume.

I. The Setting for *Thornburgh*

THORNBURGH REPRESENTS THE eighteenth time since *Roe v. Wade* in 1973 that the Supreme Court has addressed state or federal regulation of abortion.[3] In general, the Court has approved restrictions on the expenditure of public funds for abortion,[4] but has stricken regulations directed to the abortion procedure itself.[5] Exceptions to this pattern include the *Ashcroft* and *Simopoulos* decisions of 1983, where the Court upheld regulations concerning late-term abortions,[6] and a line of cases which has upheld the right of states to require parental involvement in the abortion decision of an unmarried, unemancipated minor child.[7]

In light of this background, the decision of the five-member majority to invalidate each of the provisions of the Pennsylvania Abortion Control Act presented to the Court in *Thornburgh* was in some sense predictable, but in another sense troubling. Justice Blackmun's opinion is marked by an exasperated hostility not only to the statutory provisions in question, but seemingly to the entire enterprise of state regulation of abortion. This in itself is not surprising, since Blackkmun is the author of *Roe,* and, in *Thornburgh,* the solicitor general of the United States filed an *amicus* brief strongly criticizing *Roe* and calling for its reversal.[8] What is disturbing is the majority's across-the-board rejection of Pennsylvania's regulatory scheme. In *Akron* and *Ashcroft,* the Court, through the voice of Justice Lewis Powell, had displayed a more nuanced position, and raised hope that greater accommodation for the interests of at least viable unborn children would be forthcoming. In *Thornburgh,* however, this nuanced position is absent from the writing of the majority.

Many variables may have brought about this change, but it is evident that these variables had their greatest impact upon Justice Powell. In *Akron,* Powell wrote for a six-member majority which invalidated provisions governing hospitalization for second-trimester abortions, informed consent prior to all abortions, and mandatory parental involvement for minors under the age of fifteen.[9] Yet, in the companion case of *Ashcroft,* Powell wrote for a five-member majority upholding provisions requiring that a second physician be in attendance during late-term abortions, that an unemancipated minor obtain the consent of her parents or the authorization of a judge prior to abortion, and that pathology reports be conducted on all abortions.[10] Powell emerged in these cases, therefore, as a "swing" vote on the abortion issue.

In *Thornburgh*, however, Powell joined the entrenched foes of abortion restrictions—Blackmun, Marshall, Brennan, and Stevens— to invalidate (1) a far milder informed consent regulation than that in *Akron*, (2) a series of late-term abortion regulations designed to preserve viable unborn children, and (3) requirements for the reporting of data on the performance of each abortion in the state.[11] Powell's vote in *Thornburgh* seems contrary to the opinion he wrote in *Ashcroft*. The optimism for prolife forces engendered by the narrow 5–4 split by the Court on the merits of *Roe v. Wade* may be offset somewhat by the loss in *Thornburgh* of an important "swing" vote from the center of the Court.

II. *Thornburgh* on Informed Consent

THE PENNSYLVANIA INFORMED consent provisions presented the Supreme Court with a scheme of regulation different from that invalidated in the *Akron* case three years earlier. Pennsylvania required that a woman be given the following information prior to an abortion: the name of the physician to perform the abortion; the potential for detrimental physical and psychological effects of abortion; the particular medical risks associated with the abortion procedure; the probable gestational age of the unborn child; the medical risks of carrying the child to term; the fact that medical assistance may be available for prenatal care, childbirth, and neonatal care; and the fact that the father of the child is liable to assist in the child's support.[12] In order to avoid some of the difficulties that had plagued the *Akron* statute, Pennsylvania segmented other, "more controversial," information, such as the facts of fetal development, and the availability of state and private agencies which can assist with pregnancy and child care. This information was to be made available to the woman through printed materials which she had the right, but not the obligation, to review.[13]

Pennsylvania's scheme of informational requirements, although enacted prior to the Supreme Court's decision in *Akron*, appeared to anticipate and follow the guidelines set forth by *Akron*. The *Akron* majority stated that information regarding the identity of the physician, the gestational age of the fetus, the availability of assistance during pregnancy and thereafter, and, most importantly, the particular risks of the abortion procedure to be employed, were within the bounds of permissible regulation.[14]

The *Thornburgh* Court, however, criticized the Pennsylvania scheme as an "undesired and uncomfortable straitjacket" that intrudes upon the discretion of the woman's physician.[15] The change in philosophy may be noted by a comparison between *Akron* and *Thornburgh* on the question of whether a physician may be required to give medically accurate information pertaining to the risks of the particular abortion procedure. In *Akron*, the Sixth Circuit had invalidated a provision which required physicians to inform each woman "of the particular risks associated with her own pregnancy and the abortion techniques to be employed"[16] as an interference with the physician's medical judgment. The Supreme Court, by Justice Powell, disagreed:

> The information required clearly is related to maternal health and to the State's legitimate purpose in requiring informed consent .... [W]e [have] construed "informed consent" to mean "the giving of information to the patient as to just what would be done and as to its consequences." We see no significant difference in Akron's requirement that the woman be told of the particular risks of her pregnancy and the abortion technique to be used.[17]

In *Thornburgh*, by contrast, a virtually identical provision is vilified as an attempt to foist "state medicine" upon the physician and the woman contemplating abortion.

> The requirements . . . that the woman be informed . . . of "detrimental physical and psychological effects" and of all "particular medical risks" compound the problem of medical attendance, increase the patient's anxiety, and intrude upon the physician's exercise of proper professional judgment. This type of compelled information is the antithesis of informed consent.[18]

Similar hostility is evident in the Court's treatment of other informational requirements in the Pennsylvania statute, including the name of the physician, the gestational age of the fetus, the risks of carrying the child to term, and the availability of public and private assistance to carry a pregnancy to term. The majority cited two criteria as being "equally decisive" in striking these provisions: that the proffered information is not designed to inform women, but to dissuade them from abortion altogether; and that the information may not be relevant for all women. These criteria, however, are internally inconsistent, and contrary to the doctrine of *Roe* that the woman's liberty includes the right to decide to bear children, as well as the right to abort. If, as the Court claims, some of this information will dissuade women from having abortions, how can the Court then claim that this information is not "relevant" to the woman's decisions? Why is accurate information that may lead some women to exercise their constitutional right to give birth automatically suspect? Furthermore, why is it necessary that *all* of the information listed in the statute be equally relevant to every woman considering abortion? Should not the Court instead have inquired whether each item of information would be relevant to *some* women in this situation?

As the dissenting opinions fully explain, the majority leaves us with the absurd doctrine that it is unconstitutional to inform a woman, prior to abortion, of the name of her physician, the risks of the procedure, and the alternatives that may be available to her. To reach this result, the majority has dispensed with any attempt to balance the state interest in ensuring the woman's informed consent against the abortion privacy right. These interests are substantial, given that abortion is, for the most part, a medically elective procedure performed at free-standing clinics primarily devoted to that purpose, and by physicians who are not known to the women involved. *Thornburgh* has ignored these substantial interests, however, to create a virtually absolute barrier to effective state regulation on informed consent.[19]

III. *Thornburgh* on Reporting Requirements and Postviability Regulations

THE SAME CONCLUSION can be drawn from the Court's treatment of the reporting requirements in the Pennsylvania law. The act required a report to be prepared for every abortion performed in the commonwealth, with the following information: name of the physician performing the abortion, and of the referring physician (if any); data on the woman's age, race, city and state of residence, number of prior pregnancies and last menstrual period; the probable gestational age of the fetus; the basis for the determination, where appropriate, that the fetus was not viable; and the method of payment for the abortion.[20] The report, described by the majority as "detailed," could be completed on a single-page printed form.[21] However, it was not the burden upon the physician that raised the Court's hostility to this provision. Rather, the Court concluded that the information required could not be relevant to any valid interest in the statistical study of abortion, and concluded that the detailed nature of the information would create a likelihood that women seeking abortion would lose their anonymity.[22] The majority went so far as to say that "[i]dentification is the obvious purpose of these extreme reporting requirements."[23]

As noted in Justice White's dissent, these findings of fact, labelled "obvious" by the majority, are nowhere to be found in the factual record of the case, or in the findings of the lower court. Indeed, the record was clear that the statute required the reports to remain absolutely confidential regarding the identity of the woman.[24] Furthermore, as Justice White observed, "[i]t is implausible that a particular patient could be identified on the basis of the combination of the general identifying information and the specific medical information in these reports by anyone who did not already know (at a minimum) that the woman had been pregnant and obtained an abortion."[25]

The legitimate legislative purpose in requiring such reports was acknowledged by the Court in *Danforth*, but was thoroughly ignored by the *Thornburgh* majority: the collection and dissemination of demographic information concerning abortion.[26] Currently, surveillance of abortion statistics is the province of public agencies in those states which choose to engage in this endeavor, the Centers for Disease Control of the federal Department of Health and Human Services, and umbrella organizations representing the providers and proponents of legalized abortion.[27] The raw data and primary sources necessary to conduct such surveillance are largely unavailable to private researchers not affiliated in some way with these entities. The Pennsylvania reports were designed to make such data and sources available to a wider scope of researchers, perhaps resulting in more varied, timely, and objective analyses of the data.[28] Furthermore, the information included in the reports is not beyond that necessary to complete valid demographic studies. The Abortion Surveillance report of the Centers for Disease Control includes data on the following: residence status, age, race, marital status, number of prior live births, type of procedure, weeks of gestation, and abortion mortality and morbidity.[29]

The final set of regulations invalidated in *Thornburgh* required that, for abortions performed after viability, a second physician be present, and that the method of abortion be used that would provide the best opportunity for the unborn child to survive, unless that method would present a "significantly greater medical risk to the woman's life or health."[30] The first of these provisions fell because the Court determined that there was no "emergency" exception which would waive the second physician requirement for abortions performed under emergency conditions. The regulation on method of abortion fell because the Court determined, by its interpretation of the phrase "significantly greater medical risk," that the woman would be forced to "trade-off" her own health interests for the benefit of the viable fetus.[31]

These holdings on postviability regulation, like the holdings on informed consent, run counter to the 1983 decisions. In *Ashcroft*, the

Court upheld a similar "second physician" requirement. Justice Powell's opinion indirectly criticized the practice of late-term abortions, as well as the philosophy that every abortion should result in a dead fetus. [32] The majority's effort in *Thornburgh* to distinguish *Ashcroft*, by Pennsylvania's alleged failure to provide an exception for emergency situations, is illogical and contrary to proper methods of statutory construction. In *Ashcroft*, the Court also faced a statute with no clear emergency exception. However, the Missouri statute qualified its second physician requirement by the phrase, "provided that it does not pose an increased risk to the life or health of the woman." [33] Justice Powell found the "emergency" exception implicit in this phrase. In *Thornburgh*, the Pennsylvania statute provided that the second-physician requirement did not apply if the physician determined that "the abortion was necessary to preserve maternal life or health." [34] This clearly could have been read, like the Missouri statute, to apply in emergency situations. To hold contrary is simply to misread the statute. Furthermore, the Court's objection that the language used is not "language of emergency" is almost nonsensical. Since the exception would apply in all cases of medical *necessity*, it would obviously apply in cases where the degree of necessity reached the level of *emergency*.

In response to the majority's tortured interpretation, Justice White cited the maxim that, "[w]here fairly possible, courts should construe a statute to avoid a danger of unconstitutionality." The Court's reading, White concluded, "is obviously based on an entirely different principle: that in cases involving abortion, a permissible reading of a statute is to be avoided at all costs." [35]

IV. Do the Facts Matter in Abortion Litigation?

A FINAL HOLDING of the Court that should not escape the attention of prolife litigators is the procedural ruling that, despite the lack of a full factual development through a trial, the case was ripe for adjudication in the Supreme Court. At the commencement of the *Thornburgh* case in 1982, the plaintiff doctors and abortion providers submitted voluminous affidavits to form a factual record for the preliminary injunction phase of the proceedings. During this phase, the Court would decide only whether to allow the statute to be enforced pending a full determination of the constitutional issues after trial. The response of the trial court, rather than to invite counter-affidavits, was to require the parties to enter into a factual stipulation that would be binding *only* during this preliminary phase. The parties were given two weeks to complete this task, a period that included the Thanksgiving holiday.

Adding to the pressure to "settle" on facts, the court ordered the parties not to contest *any* fact proffered by their opponents unless they were prepared to present live testimony on the point at the close of the two-week period—a formidable task, given the complexity of the medical and social issues involved in the case.[36]

The stipulation that resulted was a document suitable for its purpose, to guide the court in the preliminary injunction decision. It was not the equivalent of the full trial record which Professor Myers and Attorney Ball have, elsewhere in this volume, emphasized as being critical to the course of prolife litigation. However, it was to be the final record in the case. The district court denied the plaintiffs' motion for a preliminary injunction, and immediate appeal to the Third Circuit Court of Appeals ensued.[37] This appeal eventually resulted in the decision that was affirmed by the Supreme Court, a decision which went beyond the scope of the preliminary injunction motion to strike major portions of the Pennsylvania statute as presumptively unconstitutional. Among the issues addressed to the Supreme Court by the commonwealth was whether the Court of Appeals had acted too hastily in entering a final ruling on these provisions without the opportunity for a full factual record. The majority effectively held, in response, that on such matters, fuller development of the factual record will not be relevant to its deliberations.[38]

V. A Different View: The *Thornburgh* Dissents

WHEN VIEWED FROM the vantage point of the dissenting opinions, *Thornburgh* takes on a different hue. The force of the dissents, and the contrast with the majority, are best appreciated by reading all of the opinions, which are printed in the appendix to this volume. The dissents of Justices White and O'Connor capably refute every holding of the majority, and there is no need to digest their statements here. Nevertheless, it is important to analyze those themes in the dissenting opinions that are relevant to legal strategists seeking the reversal of *Roe*.

The first such theme is the question of whether *Thornburgh* has merely reaffirmed *Roe*, or has created new and impenetrable barriers to the regulation of abortion. Whereas the majority excoriates the Pennsylvania legislature for its history of abortion regulation enacted since *Roe v. Wade* (even going so far as to criticize Pennsylvania's abortion funding restrictions that are consistent with the Court's decisions in *Harris v. McRae* and *Williams v. Zbaraz*),[39] the dissents remind us that a certain level of state regulation of abortion was clearly contemplated by *Roe*. According to Chief Justice Burger, "[u]ndoubtedly, the Pennsylvania Legislature added the second-physician requirement on the mistaken assumption that this Court meant what it said in *Roe* concerning the 'compelling interest' of the states in potential life after viability."[40] Justice White observed that the Court's hostility has led it to change the rules set forth in *Roe*.

> The history of the state legislature's decade-long effort to pass a constitutional abortion statute is recounted as if it were evidence of some sinister conspiracy. In fact, of course, the legislature's past failure to predict the evolution of the right first recognized in *Roe v. Wade* is understandable and is in itself no ground for condemnation....The majority, however, seems to find it necessary to respond by changing the rules to invalidate what before would have seemed possible.[41]

For each holding and significant *dictum* of the majority opinion, White notes a corresponding reversal or abandonment of prior legal or constitutional doctrine.[42] Two conclusions can be drawn from this. First, *Thornburgh* has indeed created a new standard of abortion jurisprudence that must be "reversed" as part of the strategy to reverse *Roe*. Second, in future cases, counsel must anticipate the majority's propensity to ignore or modify precedent that supports the prolife position by careful framing of issues and arguments designed to make such evasive legal reasoning more difficult.

A second theme raised by the dissenting opinions is the continuation of the process, initiated in *Akron*, of elaborating the jurisprudential errors of *Roe*. Significantly, all of the dissenters go beyond the merits of the Pennsylvania statute to question whether the integrity of the Court and judicial process is harmed by further adherence to and expansion of *Roe*. As noted by Professor Myers, a key component of a reversal strategy is to test continually the Court's ability to apply the offensive precedent to a variety of factual circumstances. The jurisprudential axiom on which this strategy rests was stated by Chief Justice Burger in *Thornburgh*: "The soundness of our holdings must be tested by the decisions that purport to follow them."[43] Justices O'Connor and White build upon this axiom by demonstrating that the progeny of *Roe* have resulted not in an enduring and workable set of constitutional principles, but in blunt-edged hostility toward all abortion regulations, even those enacted to promote interests that the Court has previously recognized as "compelling." Furthermore, as Justice O'Connor pointed out, the wreckage left behind by the majority in *Thornburgh* includes not only the "doctrines" of prior abortion cases, but also important and noncontroversial maxims of legal reasoning.

[N]o legal rule or doctrine is safe from ad hoc nullification by this Court when an occasion for its application arises in a case involving state regulation of abortion. The permissible scope of abortion regulation is not the only constitutional issue on which this Court is divided, but— except when it comes to abortion—the Court has generally refused to let such disagreements, however longstanding or deeply felt, prevent it from evenhandedly applying uncontroversial legal doctrines to cases that come before it.... That the Court's unworkable scheme for constitutionalizing the regulation of abortion has had this institutionally debilitating effect should not be surprising, however, since the Court is not suited to the expansive role it claimed for itself in the series of cases that began with *Roe v. Wade.*[44]

Prolife advocates should be heartened by the forthright accusation from four justices, not that *Roe* was wrongly decided for substantive reasons, but that *Roe* is flawed as a matter of legal process. This was a central thesis of the brief filed by the solicitor general in *Thornburgh* (see appendix), and has also been noted by legal scholars such as Professor Mary Ann Glendon of Harvard.[45] Even a recent federal court of appeals panel has reflected this viewpoint.[46] This form of criticism has long posed the gravest threat to *Roe*, and since it is removed from the substance of the abortion debate, may be more likely to attract and hold the attention of sitting justices.[47]

The strategy to reverse *Roe*, of course, is not limited to such "neutral" jurisprudential issues. Another theme to consider in the *Thornburgh* dissents is the justices' treatment of the merits of *Roe* and the ethics of abortion. No current justice has indicated that he or she would find affirmative legal protection for the unborn under the Constitution. The firmest position against *Roe* is that of Justices White and Rehnquist, who state outright that *Roe* should be reversed and the abortion question returned to the states. Justice O'Connor apparently refuses to state a position on the reversal of *Roe* until a litigant brings the issue to the Court. Finally, former Chief Justice Burger, whose vote is effectively replaced by Justice Scalia, called for reexamination of *Roe*.

The strategy developed in the wake of *Akron* to attack *Roe* on substantive grounds holds up well in light of the dissents in *Thornburgh*, and should not require major restructuring. The dissenting justices apparently respect the tactic adopted by states such as Pennsylvania, of finding the permissible grounds of regulation in the prior decisions of the Court, and legislating aggressively on those grounds. They affirmatively reject the thesis of the majority that such cautious legislative efforts are evidence of bad faith.[48] Thus, efforts to legislate in areas such as parental involvement and protection of viable unborn children should continue to hold the support of this segment of the Court, and, perhaps, to win votes among the "center" of the Court.

VI. *Thornburgh* as a Case Study in Reversal Strategy

TWO STRATEGIC ASPECTS of the *Thornburgh* litigation that merit attention, in addition to the issue of factual development that has already been discussed, are the impact of the solicitor general's *amicus* brief calling for the reversal of *Roe v. Wade*, and the potential for participation by prolife parties as intervening defendants in this and future litigation. The latter issue was also raised by the Supreme Court's dismissal in 1986 of an abortion case from Illinois, *Diamond v. Charles.*

The brief of the solicitor general, reprinted in the appendix to this volume, was, from the outset, a risk-laden enterprise. The interests of the federal government were not implicated in the case, and the issue of whether *Roe* should be reversed had not been argued in the lower courts, nor was it raised on appeal by the Pennsylvania attorney general. The stakes were evident from the outset: (1) the brief might detract attention from the merits of the case and raise hostility toward statutory provisions that apparently fell within the parameters of prior Supreme Court decisions; or (2) the brief might encourage a wavering centrist justice to abandon *Roe* by focusing on the jurisprudential difficulties of that decision. It is not clear whether the brief had either of these effects, for no reference to it can be found in the majority, concurring, or dissenting opinions. What evidence can be inferred from the text and from history indicates that the brief had an ambiguous effect. In *Thornburgh*, two justices appeared to alter their position on the *Roe* doctrines. Chief Justice Burger, who had originally concurred in *Roe* and had voted to reaffirm that decision as recently as 1983 in *Akron*, dissented from the holdings in *Thornburgh* and went further to suggest that *Roe* be reexamined. Justice Powell, as we have seen, moved in a different direction, abandoning his position set forth in *Ashcroft* on postviability regulations, and joining a majority opinion far more absolute in doctrine than the opinion he authored for the Court in *Akron*. Whether the solicitor general's brief contributed to this shift in the Court cannot be determined.

One argument in favor of the decision to ask for reconsideration of *Roe* is evident from the language of the brief itself. The brief commences with a persuasive series of arguments in favor of the challenged provisions, and then uses these same arguments to demonstrate that the root problem is not the decisions of the court of appeals which invalidated the provisions, but the underlying doctrines of *Roe*. According to this thesis, "these cases . . . are not just wrong turns on a generally propitious journey but indications of an erroneous point of departure," namely, *Roe*.[49] Thus, it is impossible to fully confront the argument in constitutional adjudication on abortion without returning to *Roe* as the source of the problem. Although not all of the dissenting justices in *Thornburgh* joined the call for outright reversal of *Roe*, all concurred in the thesis that the errors of the *Thornburgh* majority are inherent in the flaws of *Roe*.

This thesis is compelling, and not only for the fact that it is supported by the solicitor general of the United States and four justices of the Supreme Court. Indeed, as this volume demonstrates, the effort to restrict abortion by small increments is intended to increase the Court's recognition that *Roe* was fatally flawed from the outset. Nevertheless, there is a difference between implicit suggestion of this outcome to the Court through careful litigation strategy, and explicit condemnation of *Roe* in documents presented to the Court by parties and *amicus*. This difference should be respected by prolife litigators and their allies in future litigation.

The Court is clearly aware of the arguments against *Roe*, and the dissenting opinions create a permanent record of those arguments that may be cited to the Court, where appropriate. Attention in litigation must now be focused on the critical short-term goal of presenting issues and arguments before the courts that are likely to result in favorable outcomes. The strategy to reverse *Roe* requires a momentum that can only be provided by a series of court victories recognizing the legitimacy of the state interest in protecting unborn life. Unless the composition of the Supreme Court were to change so that success in making a reversal argument could be reasonably assured, such arguments should remain muted, or in most cases, removed altogether. The argument to reverse *Roe* may be preserved in appropriate cases by adding it to the list of issues presented before the district court and the court of appeals in abortion litigation. However, the decision to include that argument in a jurisdictional statement or petition for certiorari before the U.S. Supreme Court should only be made when there is a strong probability of success.

The final strategic aspect of *Thornburgh* to be discussed is the role of prolife intervenors. For the near future, it is apparent that opponents of *Roe* will have to rely upon the work of state officials defending abortion statutes to carry out much of the reversal strategy. In *Thornburgh*, the district court denied, without opinion, the petition of several physicians, parents, and an abortion alternatives agency to intervene as defendants.[50] No appeal was taken from this ruling. However, in *Keith v. Daley*, a prolife lobbying organization sought intervention in similar litigation concerning the Illinois abortion law. The petition for intervention was denied by the district court, and appeal was taken to the U.S. Court of Appeals for the Seventh Circuit, which affirmed. The Seventh Circuit held that the prolife group did not have a requisite interest to justify intervention, and that even if such an interest did exist, it would be competently represented by the state attorney general.[51] The Supreme Court's decision in *Diamond v. Charles* also emphasizes the central role of state attorneys general in abortion litigation. In *Diamond*, the Court dismissed an appeal taken by two prolife physicians who had been granted leave to intervene at the commencement of the litigation to defend the Illinois abortion law. The Court concluded that the intervenors lacked standing to take the appeal in the absence of the state defendant, the attorney general of Illinois, who had declined to take an appeal.[52] Under *Diamond*, therefore, it is evident that even if prolife parties are granted leave to intervene, their "control" over the litigation process will be limited, and dependent upon fundamental decisions made by state parties.

Although state officials will henceforth play this key role in litigation, private parties and state legislatures will also have an impact on the strategy to reverse *Roe*. In addition to the issues already discussed in this chapter, there are several maxims that may be derived from the experience of *Thornburgh* to guide future efforts.

First, legislatures must be advised in the strongest of terms not to enact provisions that appear to argue with the Court's conclusions in the *Akron*, *Ashcroft* and *Thornburgh* cases. In specific terms, provisions regulating informed consent and requiring hospitalization for second trimester abortions are ill advised.

Second, *Thornburgh* emphasizes the need for the greatest care in the drafting of regulatory legislation on abortion. Ordinary canons of statutory construction cannot be applied, and thus, all of the necessary conditions set forth by the Court in areas such as parental involvement and postviability regulation must be explicitly set forth, even repeatedly, in statutes.

Third, no effort to legislate in this area should be initiated without consultation with those individuals and organizations that are engaged in the prolife effort to direct the litigation strategy to reverse *Roe v. Wade*. The Pennsylvania statute in the *Thornburgh* case, while based upon a model provided by Americans United for Life, departed in small but significant ways from the AUL model. Those points of departure, enacted to "move faster" in the effort the regulate abortion, were among the points seized upon by the Court to invalidate the statute.[53] The sovereignty of state legislatures, of course, must be given great deference. However, if those legislatures are to recapture their authority to regulate on the question of abortion, their cooperation in the painstaking and purposeful process of bringing the right issues before the courts at the proper moment must be solicited.

Fourth, state legislatures must, where possible, create a factual record of testimony and exhibits to comprise a legislative history that may be used to defend statutes in court. *Thornburgh* teaches that prolife litigators cannot depend on the opportunity to present their witnesses in court. Hence, as suggested earlier by Professor Myers, the opportunity of legislative hearings should be utilized to substantiate the valid state interests behind such initiatives as postviability regulations.

Conclusion

THE 1986 DECISIONS of the Supreme Court present new challenges, as well as new opportunities, to those working to bring about the reversal of *Roe v. Wade*. Among these developments are a slight adjustment in Supreme Court voting patterns on abortion, a higher level of defensiveness concerning *Roe* and a concomitant hostility to even mild forms of prolife legislation among the majority, and a new boldness in criticizing *Roe* from the dissenters. In addition, it will be more difficult in the future for prolife parties to intervene in and control the course of abortion litigation. These developments should not be surprising to those knowledgeable on the vagaries of abortion litigation in the past, and are clear evidence that the strategy to challenge *Roe* through careful legislation and litigation is having an impact upon the Court. The lesson of *Thornburgh* to all those involved is that a greater degree of caution and coordination is essential in all aspects of this strategy. The strategy cannot afford the premature or imprecise presentation of issues, because opportunities to address the Supreme Court are few and far between. The guidelines set forth elsewhere in this volume remain valid and, to a large degree, are vindicated by the evidence, presented in *Thornburgh*, of intense judicial controversy over an issue that was supposedly settled almost fifteen years ago in *Roe v. Wade*.[54]

Notes

1. Thornburgh v. American College of Obstetricians and Gynecologists, 106 S. Ct. 2169 (1986), *aff'g*, 737 F. 2d 283 (3d Cir. 1985). The full Supreme Court opinion in *Thornburgh*, including dissents, is printed in the appendix to this volume. *See also* article cited at n.54, *infra*.

2. Lauter, Supreme Court Review, Nat'l Law J., August 11, 1986, at S-3.

3. See Table of Abortion Decisions by United States Supreme Court in appendix to this volume.

4. *E.g.,* Maher v. Roe, 432 U.S. 464 (1977); Harris v. McRae, 448 U.S. 297 (1980); Williams v. Zbaraz, 448 U.S. 358 (1980).

5. *E.g.,* Planned Parenthood of Central Missouri v. Danforth, 428 U.S. 52 (1976) (striking state prohibition of saline amniocentesis abortion method); Colautti v. Franklin, 439 U.S. 379 (1979) (striking state regulation on method of abortion used in postviability procedures); Akron v. Akron Center for Reproductive Health, Inc., 462 U.S. 416 (1983) (striking informed consent requirements).

6. Planned Parenthood of Central Missouri v. Ashcroft, 462 U.S. 476 (1983) (upholding requirement that second physician be present during postviability abortions); Simopoulos v. Virginia, 462 U.S. 506 (1983) (upholding by 8-1 vote prosecution of physician for performing second-trimester abortion in unlicensed clinic).

7. Bellotti v. Baird II, 443 U.S. 622 (1979) (invalidating state parental consent law, but setting forth guidelines for valid state regulation); H.L. v. Matheson, 450 U.S. 398 (1981) (upholding parental notification law applied to unmarried, unemancipated minors); Ashcroft, 462 U.S. at 490–493 (upholding parental consent law modeled after *Bellotti II* standards).

8. The solicitor general serves as the primary advocate for the federal government before the U.S. Supreme Court. At the time of the filing of this brief, the office was held by Charles Fried, a former professor at Harvard Law School. Mr. Fried's predecessor, Rex E. Lee, filed a brief in the 1983 *Akron* and *Ashcroft* cases, arguing that the provisions under challenge should be upheld. Mr. Lee's brief called into question the constitutional analysis used in abortion cases following *Roe*, but did not directly call for reversal of *Roe*.

9. *Akron*, 462 U.S. at 431–452. Joining Justice Powell in this opinion were Chief Justice Burger and Justices Blackmun, Brennan, Marshall, and Stevens.

10. *Ashcroft*, 462 U.S. at 482–493. Chief Justice Burger joined in this opinion, and Justices O'Connor, White, and Rehnquist concurred in the judgment on the provisions cited in the text, but dissented from the Court's judgment that a second-trimester hospitalization requirement in the Missouri statute was unconstitutional.

11. 106 S. Ct. at 2177–2184. The majority's discussion of the informed consent issue may be found in this volume at pages 275-278.

12. 18 Pa. Con. Stat. §§3205, 3208 (1983).

13. 18 Pa. Con. Stat., §3208.

14. 462 U.S. at 445–447, and n. 37.

15. 106 S. Ct. at 2179, *infra* at 277.

16. 462 U.S. at 446, *quoting* Akron Codified Ordinances, ch. 1870.06 (C).

17. 462 U.S. at 446. The Court nonetheless refused to sever this provision from the remaining provisions of the Akron ordinance that were found to be invalid, including a requirement that this information be given to the woman personally by the "attending physician." 462 U.S. at 447–448.

18. 106 S. Ct. at 2180, *infra* at 278.

19. According to a professor of obstetrics and gynecology from the University of California at Los Angeles, approximately "two percent of all abortions in this country are done for some clinically identifiable entity—physical health problem, amniocentesis, and identified genetic disease or something of that kind." The remainder are elective, "performed on women who for various reasons do not wish to be pregnant at this time." *Constitutional Amendments Relating to Abortion: Hearings on S.J. Res. 17, S.J. Res. 18, S.J. Res. 19, and S.J. Res. 110 Before the Subcommittee on the Constitution of the Senate Committee on the Judiciary,* 97th Cong., 1st Sess. 158 (statement of Irvin M. Cushner, M.D., M.P.H., U.C.L.A., School of Public Health). The lack of contact between women and the physicians who perform abortions is described in the district court opinion in the *Akron* case. 479 F. Supp. 1172, 1181–1182 (N.D. Ohio, 1979).

20. 18 Pa. Con. Stat. §3214.

21. A form prepared for this purpose by the Illinois Department of Public Health contains most of the information required by the Pennsylvania law, on a single-sided page. Certification for Termination of Pregnancy, Illinois Department of Public Health, A.F.A. 036, Revised January 1981. (In possession of author.)

22. 106 S. Ct. at 2181–2182, *infra* at 278–280.

23. *Id.* at 2182, *infra* at 280.

24. *Id.* at 2202. Justice White's dissent commences on page 299 of this volume.

25. *Id.* at 2202, *infra* at 312.

26. *Id.* at 2201, *infra* at 311.

27. *See* Department of Health and Human Services, Centers for Disease Control, Abortion Surveillance (1986); Henshaw et al., *A Portrait of American Women Who Obtain Abortions,* 17 Family Planning Perspectives 90, 91 (1985) (all references for statistical information for this study are from government agencies or proabortion organizations such as Alan Guttmacher Institute).

28. *Id.* These studies appeared four years after the relevant periods that were studied.

29. Abortion Surveillance, *supra,* note 27.

30. 18 Pa. Con. Stat. §3210(b).

31. 106 S. Ct. at 2182–2184, *infra* at 280–282.

32. *Ashcroft,* 462 U.S. at 483–484, and n. 7.

33. Mo. Rev. Stat. §188.030.3; *Ashcroft,* 462 U.S. at 484, n. 8.

34. 18 Pa. Con. Stat. §3210(c); 106 S. Ct. at 2184.

35. 106 S. Ct. at 2205, *infra* at 316 (White, J., dissenting).

36. American College of Obstetricians and Gynecologists v. Thornburgh, No. 82–4336 (E.D. Pa., Nov. 18, 1982) (order to prepare stipulation of facts for preliminary injunction hearing, and to submit identity of witnesses within 12 days of order on facts not stipulated to).

37. A.C.O.G. v. Thornburgh, 552 F. Supp. 791 (E.D. Pa. 1982), *rev'd,* 737 F. 2d 283 (3d Cir. 1984), *aff'd,* 106 S. Ct. 2169 (1986).

38. 106 S. Ct. at 2177, *infra* at 273-274 (referring to facts in this case as "established or of no controlling relevance"). *Cf.* 106 S. Ct. at 2209, *infra* at 325 (O'Connor, J., dissenting) (denying that there was a "full record" from the courts below).

39. 448 U.S. 297 (1980); 448 U.S. 358 (1980).

40. 106 S. Ct. at 2191, *infra* at 297 (Burger, C.J., dissenting).

41. 106 S. Ct. at 2198, *infra* at 306 (White, J., dissenting).

42. 106 S. Ct. at 2198-2206, *infra* at 306-317 (White, J., dissenting).

43. *Id.* at 2192, *infra* at 298 (Burger, C.J., dissenting).

44. *Id.* at 2206-2207, *infra* at 321-322 (O'Connor, J., dissenting).

45. *See* M. Glendon, Story and Language in American Law (Forthcoming, 1987). Professor Glendon elaborated on her criticism of *Roe* in the annual Rosenthal Lectures delivered at Northwestern University School of Law, Chicago, on October 27, 1986.

46. Margaret S. v. Edwards, 794 F.2d 994, 994-005, and n. 3 (5th Cir. 1986). The court notes that the Supreme Court's decisions on abortion have been "subjected to exceptionally severe and sustained criticism . . . for the manner in which they interpret the Constitution." *Id.* at 994. While disclaiming any intent to add to this criticism, the court adds, "we do not believe it would be improper to do so." *Id.* at 996, n. 3. The panel's opinion in this case, written by Judge Patrick E. Higginbotham, was bluntly criticized by the special concurring opinion of Judge Jerre S. Williams. 794 F. 2d at 999-1000.

47. Analysis of *Roe* as a study in legal process began as early as 1973 with the landmark article of Dean John Hart Ely. Ely, *The Wages of Crying Wolf: A Comment on* Roe v. Wade, 82 Yale L.J. 920 (1973). *See also* sources discussed in the chapter by Horan and Balch in this volume.

48. 106 S. Ct. at 2191, *infra* at 297 (Burger, C.J., dissenting); 106 S. Ct. at 2198, *infra* at 306 (White, J., dissenting).

49. Brief of Solicitor General in Support of Appellants, *Thornburgh*, at 2; this volume at 338.

50. 552 F. Supp. at 794.

51. 764 F. 2d 1265 (7th Cir. 1985), *cert. denied*, 106 S. Ct. 383 (1985).

52. 106 S. Ct. 1697 (1986).

53. One example is the incorporation of the phrase "significantly greater medical risk" into the Pennsylvania act's maternal health exception to the regulation of methods employed in postviability abortions. *See Thornburgh*, 106 S. Ct. at 2183, *infra* at 281.

54. For a more detailed discussion of this controversy, see Horan, Forsythe & Grant, *Two Ships Passing in the Night: An Interpretativist Review of the White-Stevens Colloquy on* Roe v. Wade, 6 St.L. Pub.L.Rev. 43 (1987).

PART V
Appendices

Appendix One

Supreme Court Decisions on Abortion Since 1973: A Summary

Following is a brief summary of Supreme Court abortion decisions commencing with *Roe v. Wade*, giving the citation, date, holding, and author of the majority opinion. References in this volume to the cases may be obtained through the full table of cases which appears immediately before the index.

Roe v. Wade, 410 U.S. 113 (1973) (discussed in depth in several chapters of this volume). *Roe* invalidated a nineteenth-century Texas statute prohibiting abortion except in cases where necessary to preserve maternal life, on the basis that the right of privacy secured by the Due Process clause of the Fourteenth Amendment includes a fundamental right to decide whether or not to bring a pregnancy to term. (Blackmun)

Doe v. Bolton, 410 U.S. 179 (1973). Invalidated Georgia "reform" abortion statute that permitted abortion where continued pregnancy would endanger woman's life or health, including mental health, where the fetus would likely be born with a serious defect, or where pregnancy resulted from rape. Statute also required that abortion be performed in accredited hospital, and that two physicians confirm the performing physician's judgment of necessity for abortion. *Doe* is frequently cited for its definition of maternal "health" to include a broad range of factors, including general maternal "well-being," as a justification for legalized abortion during the last trimester of pregnancy. (Blackmun)

Bigelow v. Virginia, 421 U.S. 809 (1975). Invalidating state ban on advertising for abortion. (Blackmun)

Connecticut v. Menillo, 423 U.S. 9 (1975). Upholding Connecticut antiabortion statute as it applies to nonphysicians. (Unsigned)

Singleton v. Wulff, 428 U.S. 106 (1976). Held that physicians may challenge abortion funding restrictions on behalf of their female patients seeking abortions. Has thus had strong impact upon abortion litigation, allowing physicians to act as plaintiffs, instead of individual women, as in the case of *Roe v. Wade*. (Blackmun)

Planned Parenthood of Missouri v. Danforth, 428 U.S. 52 (1976). Upheld definition of "viability" under state statute, and requirement that woman sign consent form prior to abortion. Invalidated provisions requiring consent of spouse (if any) to abortion, requiring consent of parents for abortion performed on minor daughter, prohibiting use of saline amniocentesis abortion procedure, and requiring those performing abortions to exercise professional skill and care to preserve the life of the fetus. (Blackmun)

Bellotti v. Baird (I), 428 U.S. 132 (1976). Abstained from ruling on constitutionality of Massachusetts parental consent statute pertaining to abortion until resolution by state courts of how statute is to be construed. (Blackmun)

Beal v. Doe, 432 U.S. 438 (1977). First in series of 1977 abortion funding cases. Upheld, by 6–3 vote, Pennsylvania restriction on use of Medicaid funds for abortion to those that are "medically necessary" against challenge that this policy violates Title XIX of the Social Security Act. (Powell)

Maher v. Roe, 432 U.S. 464 (1977). Second in series of 1977 abortion funding cases. Upheld, by 6–3 vote, Connecticut regulation restricting use of Medicaid funds to those abortions that are "medically necessary." Regulation was challenged on constitutional grounds of due process and equal protection. Reasoned that state is free to use its power of funding to encourage childbirth over abortion. Also noted that "a woman has at least an equal right to choose to carry her fetus to term as to choose to abort it." (Powell)

Poelker v. Doe, 432 U.S. 519 (1977). Third in series of 1977 abortion funding cases. Upheld St. Louis policy against performance of abortion in public hospitals. (Unsigned)

Colautti v. Franklin, 439 U.S. 379 (1979). Invalidated, by 6–3 vote, Pennsylvania statute creating standard for determination of viability of unborn child, and requiring use of abortion technique providing the best opportunity for the fetus to be aborted alive in abortions after viability. (Blackmun)

Bellotti v. Baird (II), 443 U.S. 622 (1979). Invalidated Massachusetts statute requiring parental consent, and held that states requiring the consent of parents to abortions upon minors must afford minors an alternative opportunity for authorization of the abortion where the minor may demonstrate that either she is mature enough to make her own decision, or that the abortion would be in her best interests. (Powell)

Harris v. McRae, 448 U.S. 297 (1980). Upheld, by 5–4 vote, the Hyde Amendment, restricting use of federal funds for abortion to those necessary to preserve the life of the mother. In bitterly contested litigation in New York federal court, Hyde Amendment was challenged as a denial of due process, equal protection, freedom of religion, and as an establishment of Roman Catholic dogma in violation of the First Amendment. Perhaps the most significant Supreme Court holding on abortion outside of *Roe*. (Stewart)

Williams v. Zbaraz, 448 U.S. 358 (1980). Companion to *Harris v. McRae*, upheld Illinois statute prohibiting use of state funds for abortion except where necessary to preserve the life of the woman undergoing abortion. (Stewart)

H.L. v. Matheson, 450 U.S. 398 (1981). Upheld Utah statute requiring notification of parents prior to abortion performed on unemancipated minors. (Burger)

Akron v. Akron Center for Reproductive Health, 462 U.S. 416 (1983). Invalidated, by 6–3 vote, Akron ordinance requiring all second-trimester abortions to be performed in hospitals, requiring consent of parents for all abortions performed on minors under the age of fifteen, requiring detailed information on medical risks of abortion, fetal development, and abortion alternatives to be given to women prior to abortions, and requiring twenty-four-hour waiting period between giving of required information and performance of abortion. Significant dissenting opinion written by Justice O'Connor in her first abortion case. (Powell)

Planned Parenthood Assn. of Kansas City v. Ashcroft, 462 U.S. 476 (1983). Invalidated second-trimester hospitalization requirement, but upheld regulations pertaining to parental consent, the presence of a second physician at postviability abortions, and pathology reports. (Powell)

Simopoulos v. Virginia, 462 U.S. 506 (1983). Upheld, by 8–1 vote, conviction of physician for performing second trimester abortion in unlicensed clinic. (Powell)

Diamond v. Charles, 106 S. Ct. 1697 (1986). Dismissed appeal brought by two physicians from ruling striking down an Illinois abortion statute, holding that failure of state to join in the appeal left the Court with no standing to resolve the matter. (Blackmun)

Thornburgh v. American College of Obstetricians and Gynecologists, 106 S. Ct. 2169 (1986). Reprinted in this volume and analyzed in detail in chapter by Edward Grant. Invalidated provisions of Pennsylvania abortion control act concerning informed consent, informational reporting requirements, and performance of abortions after viability. Notable for hostility of majority of five justices to apparently mild forms of abortion regulation, and strong dissents from four justices calling for reexamination or reversal of *Roe v. Wade*. (Blackmun)

APPENDIX TWO

Supreme Court of the United States

No. 84-495

RICHARD THORNBURGH, ET AL., APPELLANTS V.
AMERICAN COLLEGE OF OBSTETRICIANS
AND GYNECOLOGISTS ET AL.

On Appeal from the United States Court of Appeals
for the Third Circuit

[June 11, 1986]

Justice Blackmun delivered the opinion of the Court.

This is an appeal from a judgment of the United States Court of Appeals for the Third Circuit reviewing the District Court's rulings upon a motion for a preliminary injunction. The Court of Appeals held unconstitutional several provisions of Pennsylvania's current Abortion Control Act, 1982 Pa. Laws, Act No. 138, now codified as 18 Pa. Cons. Stat. §3201 *et seq.* (1983) (Act).[1] Among the provisions ruled invalid by the Court of Appeals were portions of §3205, relating to "informed consent"; §3208, concerning "printed information"; §§3210 (b) and (c), having to do with postviability abortions; and §3211(a) and §§3214(a) and (h), regarding reporting requirements.[2]

84-495 OPINION

THORNBURGH v. AMERICAN COLL. OF OBST. & GYN.

The Abortion Control Act was approved by the Governor of the Commonwealth on June 11, 1982. By its own terms, however, see §7 of the Act, it was to become effective only 180 days thereafter, that is, on the following December 8. It had been offered as an amendment to a pending bill to regulate paramilitary training.

The 1982 Act was not the Commonwealth's first attempt, after this Court's 1973 decisions in *Roe v. Wade*, 410 U.S. 113, and *Doe v. Bolton*, 410 U.S. 179, to impose abortion restraints. The State's first post-1973 Abortion Control Act, 1974 Pa. Laws, Act. No. 209, was passed in 1974 over the Governor's veto. After extensive litigation, various provisions of the 1974 statute were ruled unconstitutional, including those relating to spousal or parental consent, to the choice of procedure for a postviability abortion, and to the proscription of abortion advertisements. See *Planned Parenthood Assn. v. Fitzpatrick*, 401 F. Supp. 554 (ED Pa. 1975), summarily aff'd in part *sub nom. Franklin v. Fitzgerald*, 428 U.S. 901 (1976), and summarily vacated in part, and remanded, *sub nom. Beal v. Franklin*, 428 U.S. 901 (1976), modified on remand (No. 74–2440)(ED Pa. 1977), aff'd *sub nom. Colautti v. Franklin*, 439 U.S. 379 (1979). See also *Doe v. Zimmerman*, 405 F. Supp. 534 (MD Pa. 1975).

In 1978, the Pennsylvania Legislature attempted to restrict access to abortion by limiting medical-assistance funding for the procedure. 1978 Pa. Laws, Act No. 16A (pp. 1506–1507) and Act No. 148. This effort, too, was successfully challenged in federal court, *Roe v. Casey*, 464 F. Supp. 487 (ED Pa. 1978), and that judgment was affirmed by the Third Circuit. 623 F. 2d 829 (1980).

In 1981, abortion legislation was proposed in the Pennsylvania House as an amendment to a pending Senate bill to outlaw "tough-guy competitions."[3] The suggested amendment, aimed at limiting abortions, was patterned after a model statute developed by a Chicago-based, nonprofit anti-abortion organization. See Note, Toward Constitutional Abortion Control Legislation: The Pennsylvania Approach, 87 Dick L. Rev. 373, 382, n. 84. (1983). The bill underwent further change in the legislative process but, when passed, was vetoed by the Governor. See 737 F. 2d 283, 288–289 (CA3 1984). Finally, the 1982 Act was formulated, enacted, and approved.

After the passage of the Act, but before its effective date, the present litigation was instituted in the United States District Court for the Eastern District of Pennsylvania. The plaintiffs, who are the appellees here, were the American College of Obstetricians and

Gynecologists, Pennsylvania Section; certain physicians licensed in Pennsylvania; clergymen; an individual who purchases from a Pennsylvania insurer health-care and disability insurance extending to abortions; and Pennsylvania abortion counselors and providers. Alleging that the Act violated the United States Constitution, the plaintiffs, pursuant to 42 U.S.C. §1983, sought declaratory and injunctive relief. The defendants named in the complaint were the Governor of the Commonwealth, other Commonwealth officials, and the District Attorney for Montgomery County, Pa.

The plaintiffs promptly filed a motion for a preliminary injunction. Forty-one affidavits accompanied the motion. The defendants, on their part, submitted what the Court of Appeals described as "an equally comprehensive opposing memorandum." 737 F. 2d 283, 289 (1984). The District Court then ordered the parties to submit a "stipulation of uncontested facts," as authorized by local rule. The parties produced a stipulation "solely for purposes of a determination on plaintiffs' motion for preliminary injunction," and "without prejudice to any party's right to controvert any facts or to prove any additional facts at any later proceeding in this action." App. 9–10.

Relying substantially on the opinions of the respective Courts of Appeals in *Akron Center for Reproductive Health, Inc. v. City of Akron*, 651 F. 2d 1198 (CA6 1981), later aff'd in part and rev'd in part, 462 U.S. 416 (1983), and in *Planned Parenthood Assn. of Kansas City v. Ashcroft*, 655 F. 2d 848 (CA8 1981), later aff'd in part and rev'd in part, 462 U.S. 476 (1983), the District Court concluded that, with one exception, see n. 1, *supra*, the plaintiffs had failed to establish a likelihood of success on the merits and thus were not entitled to preliminary injunctive relief. 552 F. Supp. 791 (1982).

Appellees appealed from the denial of the preliminary injunction, and appellants cross-appealed with respect to the single statutory provision as to which the District Court had allowed relief. The Third Circuit then granted appellees' motion to enjoin enforcement of the entire Act pending appeal. After expedited briefing and argument, the court withheld judgment pending the anticipated decisions by this Court in *Akron, supra, Ashcroft, supra*, and *Simopoulos v. Commonwealth*, 221 Va. 1059, 277 S. E. 2d 194 (1981), all of which had been accepted for review here, had been argued, and were under submission. Those three cases were decided by this Court on June 15, 1983. See *Akron v. Akron Center for Reproductive Health, Inc.*, 462 U.S. 416; *Planned Parenthood Assn. of Kansas City, Mo. Inc. v. Ashcroft*, 462 U.S. 476; *Simopoulos v. Virginia*, 462 U.S. 506. After reargument in light of those decisions, the Court of Appeals, with one judge concurring in part and dissenting in part, ruled that various provisions of the Act were unconstitutional. 737 F.

2d 283 (1984). Appellants' petition for rehearing en banc was denied, with four judges voting to grant the petition. *Id.*, at 316, 317. When a jurisdictional statement was filed here, we postponed further consideration of the question of our jurisdiction to the hearing on the merits. [   ] U.S.[   ] (1985).

II

We are confronted initially with the question whether we have appellate jurisdiction in this case. Appellants purport to have taken their appeal to this Court pursuant to 28 U.S.C. §1254(2).[4] It seems clear, and the parties appear to agree, see Brief for Appellants 21, that the judgment of the Court of Appeals was not a final judgment in the ordinary meaning of that term. The court did not hold the entire Act unconstitutional, but ruled, instead, that some provisions were invalid under *Akron, Ashcroft,* and *Simopoulos,* and that the validity of other provisions might depend on evidence adduced at the trial, see 737 F. 2d, at 299–300, or on procedural rules to be promulgated by the Supreme Court of Pennsylvania, see *id.*, at 296–297. It remanded these features of the case to the District Court. *Id.*, at 304.

Slaker v. O'Connor, 278 U.S. 188, 189–190 (1929), and *McLish v. Roff,* 141 U.S. 661, 665–666 (1891), surely suggest that, under these circumstances, we do not have appellate jurisdiction.[5] See also *South Carolina Electric & Gas Co. v. Flemming,* 351 U.S. 901 (1956). Although the authority of *Slaker* and *South Carolina Electric* has been questioned, the Court to date has found it unnecessary to put the issue to rest. See *Doran v. Salem Inn, Inc.,* 422 U.S. 922, 927 (1975); *City of Renton v. Playtime Theatres, Inc.,*[   ] U.S. [   ],[   ], n. 1 (1986) (slip op. 1, n. 1). In some cases raising this issue of the scope of appellate jurisdiction, the Court has found any finality requirement to have been satisfied in light of the facts. See, *e.g., New Orleans v. Dukes,* 427 U.S. 297, 302 (1976); *Chicago v. Atchison, T. & S.F.R. Co.,* 357 U.S. 77, 82–83 (1958). In other cases, the Court has avoided the issue by utilizing 28 U.S.C. §2103 and granting certiorari. See, *e.g.., Doran,* 422 U.S., at 927; *El Paso v. Simmons,* 379 U.S. 497, 503 (1965); see also *Escambia County v. McMillan,* 466 U.S. 48, 50, n. 4 (1984).

We have concluded that it is time that this undecided issue be resolved. We therefore hold, on the reasoning of *McLish v. Roff,* 141 U.S., at 665–668, that in a situation such as this one, where the judgment is not final, and where the case is remanded for further development of the facts, we have no appellate jurisdiction under §1254(2).

We nevertheless treat appellant's jurisdictional statement as a petition for certiorari, grant the writ, and move on to the merits.[6]

III

Appellants assert that the Court of Appeals erred in holding portions of the Act unconstitutional since the scope of its review of the District Court's denial of a preliminary injunction as to those sections should have been limited to determining whether the trial court abused its discretion in finding the presence or absence of irreparable harm and a probability that the plaintiffs would succeed on the merits. Such limited review normally is appropriate, see *Doran v. Salem Inn, Inc.,* 422 U.S., at 931–932; *Brown v. Choate,* 411 U.S. 452, 456–457 (1973), inasmuch as the primary purpose of a preliminary injunction is to preserve the relative positions of the parties. See *University of Texas v. Camenisch,* 451 U.S. 390, 395 (1981). Further, the necessity for an expeditious resolution often means that the injunction is issued on a procedure less stringent than that which prevails at the subsequent trial on the merits of the application for injunctive relief. See *United States Steel Corp. v. Fraternal Assn. of Steelhaulers,* 431 F. 2d 1046 (CA3 1970); see also *Mayo v. Lakeland Highlands Canning Co.,* 309 U.S. 310, 316 (1940).

This approach, however, is not inflexible. The Court on more than one occasion in this area has approved proceedings deviating from the stated norm. In *Youngstown Sheet & Tube Co. v. Sawyer,* 343 U.S. 579 (1952), the District Court has issued a preliminary injunction restraining the Secretary of Commerce from seizing the Nation's steel mills. The Court of Appeals stayed the injunction. This Court found that the case was ripe for review, despite the early stage of the litigation, and went on to address the merits. *Id.,* at 585. And in *Smith v. Vulcan Iron Works,* 165 U.S. 518 (1897), the District Court issued injunctions in two patent cases and referred them to a Master for accounting. The Court of Appeals reversed. This Court ruled that the Court of Appeals had acted properly in deciding the merits since review of interlocutory appeals was designed not only to permit the defendant to obtain immediate relief but also in certain cases to save the parties the expense of further litigation. *Id.,* at 525.

The Third Circuit's decision to address the constitutionality of the Pennsylvania Act finds further support in this Court's decisions that when the unconstitutionality of the particular state action under challenge is clear, a federal court need not abstain from addressing the constitutional issue pending state-court review. See, *e.g., Bailey v. Patterson,* 396 U.S. 31, 33 (1962); *Turner v. City of Memphis,* 369 U.S. 350, 353 (1962); *Zwickler v. Koota,* 398 U.S. 241, 251, n. 14. See also *Singleton v. Wulff,* 428 U.S. 106, 121 (1976). See generally Spann, Simple Justice, 73 Geo. L. J. 1041, 1055, n. 77 (1985).[7]

Thus, as these cases indicate, if a District Court's ruling rests solely on a premise as to the applicable rule of law, and the facts are established or of no controlling relevance, that ruling may be reviewed even though the appeal is from the entry of a preliminary injunction.[8] The Court of Appeals in this case properly recognized and applied these principles when it observed:

> "Thus, although this appeal arises from a ruling on a request for a preliminary injunction, we have before us an unusually complete factual and legal presentation from which to address the important constitutional issues at stake. The customary discretion accorded to a District Court's ruling on a preliminary injunction yields to our plenary scope of review as to the applicable law." 737 F. 2d, at 290.

That a court of appeals ordinarily will limit its review in a case of this kind to abuse of discretion is a rule of orderly judicial administration, not a limit on judicial power. With a full record before it on the issues now before us, and with the intervening decisions in *Akron*, *Ashcroft*, and *Simopoulos* at hand, the Court of Appeals was justified in proceeding to plenary review of those issues.

IV

This case, as it comes to us, concerns the constitutionality of six provisions of the Pennsylvania Act that the Court of Appeals struck down as facially invalid: §3205 ("informed consent"); §3208 ("printed information"); §§3214(a) and (h) (reporting requirements); §3211(a) (determination of viability); §3210(b) (degree of care required in postviability abortions); and §3210(c) (second-physician requirement). We have no reason to address the validity of the other sections of the Act challenged in the District Court.[9]

A

Less than three years ago, this Court, in *Akron*, *Ashcroft*, and *Simopoulos*, reviewed challenges to state and municipal legislation regulating the performance of abortions. In *Akron*, the Court specifically raffirmed *Roe v. Wade*, 410 U.S. 111 (1973). See 462 U.S., at 420, 426–431. Again today, we reaffirm the general principles laid down in *Roe* and in *Akron*.

In the years since this Court's decision in *Roe*, States and municipalities have adopted a number of measures seemingly designed to prevent a woman, with the advice of her physician, from exercising her freedom of choice. *Akron* is but one example. But the constitutional principles that led this Court to its decisions in 1973 still provide the compelling reason for recognizing the constitutional dimensions of a woman's right to decide whether to end her pregnancy. "[I]t should go without saying that the vitality of these constitutional principles cannot be allowed to yield simply because of disagreement with them." *Brown v. Board of Education*, 394 U.S. 294, 300 (1955). The States are not free, under the guise of protecting maternal health or potential life, to intimidate women into continuing pregnancies. Appellants claim that the statutory provisions before us today further legitimate compelling interests of the Commonwealth. Close analysis of those provisions, however, shows that they wholly subordinate constitutional privacy interests and concerns with maternal health in an effort to deter a woman from making a decision that, with her physician, is hers to make.

B

We turn to the challenged statutes:

1. Section 3205 ("informed consent") and §3208 (printed information). Section 3205 (a) requires that the woman give her "voluntary and informed consent" to an abortion. Failure to observe the provisions of §3205 subjects the physician to suspension or revocation of his license, and subjects any other person obligated to provide information relating to informed consent to criminal penalties. §3205(c). A requirement that the woman give what is truly a voluntary and informed consent, as a general proposition, is, of course, proper and is surely not unconstitutional. See *Danforth*, 428 U.S., at 67. But the State may not require the delivery of information designed "to influence the woman's informed choice between abortion or childbirth." *Akron*, 462 U.S., at 443–444.

Appellants refer to the Akron ordinance, Brief for Appellants 45, as did this Court in *Akron* itself, 462 U.S., at 445, as "a litany of information" and as "a parade of horribles" of dubious validity plainly designed to influence the woman's choice. They would distinguish the Akron situation, however, from the Pennsylvania one. Appellants assert that statutes "describing the general subject matter relevant to informed consent," *ibid.*, and stating "in general terms the information to be disclosed," *id.*, at 447, are permissible, and they further assert that the Pennsylvania statutes do no more than that.

We do not agree. We conclude that, like Akron's ordinance, §§3205 and 3208 fail the *Akron* measurement. The two sections prescribe in detail the method for securing "informed consent." Seven explicit kinds of information must be delivered to the woman at least 24 hours before her consent is given, and five of these must be presented by the woman's physician. The five are: (a) the name of the physician who will perform the abortion, (b) the "fact that there may be detrimental physical and psychological effects which are not accurately fore-seeable," (c) the "particular medical risks associated with the particular abortion procedure to be employed," (d) the probable gestational age, and (e) the "medical risks associated with carrying her child to term." The remaining two categories are (f) the "fact that medical assistance benefits may be available for prenatal care, childbirth and neonatal care," and (g) the "fact that the father is liable to assist" in the child's support, "even in instances where the father has offered to pay for the abortion." §§3205(a)(1) and (2). The woman also must be informed that materials printed and supplied by the Commonwealth that describe the fetus and that list agencies offering alternatives to abortion are available for her review. If she chooses to review the materials but is unable to read, the materials "shall be read to her," and any answer she seeks must be "provided her in her own language." §3205(a)(2)(iii). She must certify in writing, prior to the abortion, that all this has been done. §3205(a)(3). The printed materials "shall include the following statement":

> "There are many public and private agencies willing and able to help you to carry your child to term, and to assist you and your child after your child is born, whether you choose to keep your child or place her or him for adoption. The Commonwealth of Pennsylvania strongly urges you to contact them before making a final decision about abortion. The law requires that your physician or his agent give you the opportunity to call agencies like these before you under go an abortion." §3208(a)(1).

The materials must describe the "probable anatomical and physiological characteristics of the unborn child at two-week gestational increments from fertilization to full term, including any relevant information on the possibility of the unborn child's survival." §3208 (a)(2).

In *Akron*, this Court noted: "The validity of an informed consent requirement thus rests on the State's interest in protecting the health of the pregnant woman." 462 U.S., at 443. The Court went on to state:

> "This does not mean, however, that a State has unreviewable authority to decide what information a woman must be given before she chooses to have an abortion. It remains primarily the responsibility of the physician to ensure that appropriate information is conveyed to his patient, depending on her particular circumstances. *Danforth's* recognition of the State's interest in ensuring that this information be given will not justify abortion regulations designed to influence the woman's informed choice between abortion or childbirth." *id.*, at 443–444.

The informational requirements in the *Akron* ordinance were invalid for two "equally decisive" reasons. *Id.*, at 445. The first was that "much of the information required is designed not to inform the woman's consent but rather to persuade her to withhold it altogether." *Id.*, at 444. The second was that a rigid requirement that a specific body of information be given in all cases, irrespective of the particular needs of the patient, intrudes upon the discretion of the pregnant woman's physician and thereby imposes the "'undesired and uncomfortable straitjacket'" with which the Court in *Danforth*, 428 U.S., at 67, n. 8, was concerned.

These two reasons apply with equal and controlling force to the specific and intrusive informational prescriptions of the Pennsylvania statutes. The printed materials required by §§3205 and 3208 seem to us to be nothing less than an outright attempt to wedge the Commonwealth's message discouraging abortion into the privacy of the informed-consent dialogue between the woman and her physician. The mandated description of fetal characteristics at 2-week intervals, no matter how objective, is plainly over-inclusive. This is not medical information that is always relevant to the woman's decision, and it may serve only to confuse and punish her and heighten her anxiety, contrary to accepted medical practice.[10] Even the listing of agencies in the printed Pennsylvania form presents serious problems; it contains names of agencies that well may be out of step with the needs of the particular woman and thus places the physician in an awkward position and infringes upon his or her professional responsibilities. Forcing the physician or counselor to present the materials and the list to the woman makes him or her in effect an agent of the State in treating the woman and places his or her imprimatur upon both the materials and the list. See *Women's Medical Center of Providence, Inc. v. Roberts*, 530 F. Supp. 1136, 1154 (RI 1982). All this is, or comes close to being, state medicine imposed upon the woman, not the professional medical guidance she seeks, and it officially structures—as it obviously was intended to do—the dialogue between the woman and her physician.

The requirements of §§3205(a)(2)(i) and (ii) that the woman be advised that medical assistance benefits may be available, and that the father is responsible for financial assistance in the support of the child similarly are poorly disguised elements of discouragement for the abortion decision. Much of this would be nonmedical information beyond the physician's area of expertise and, for many patients, would be irrelevant and inappropriate. For a patient with a life-threatening pregnancy, the "information" in its very rendition may be cruel as well as destructive of the physician-patient relationship. As any experienced social worker or other counsellor knows, theoretical financial responsibility often does not equate with fulfillment. And a victim of rape should not have to hear gratuitous advice that an unidentified perpetrator is liable for support if she continues the pregnancy to term. Under the guise of informed consent, the Act requires the dissemination of information that is not relevant to such consent, and, thus, it advances no legitimate state interest.

The requirements of §§3205(a)(1)(ii) and (iii) that the woman be informed by the physician of "detrimental physical and psychological effects" and of all "particular medical risks" compound the problem of medical attendance, increase the patient's anxiety, and intrude upon the physician's exercise of proper professional judgment. This type of compelled information is the antithesis of informed consent. That the Commonwealth does not, and surely would not, compel similar disclosure of every possible peril of necessary surgery or of simple vaccination, reveals the antiabortion character of the statute and its real purpose. Pennsylvania, like Akron, "has gone far beyond merely describing the general subject matter relevant to informed consent." *Akron*, 462 U.S., at 445. In addition, the Commonwealth would require the physician to recite its litany "regardless of whether in his judgment the information is relevant to [the patient's] personal decision." *Ibid.* These statutory defects cannot be saved by any facts that might be forthcoming at a subsequent hearing. Section 3205's informational requirements therefore are facially unconstitutional."[11]

Appellants assert, however, that even if this be so, the remedy is to allow the remainder of §3205 to be severed and become effective. We rule otherwise. The radical dissection necessary for this would leave §3205 with little resemblance to that intended by the Pennsylvania Legislature. We rejected a similar suggestion as to the ordinance in *Akron*, 462 U.S., at 445, n. 37, despite the presence there of a broad severability clause. We reach the same conclusion here, where no such clause is present, and reject the plea for severance. See *Carter v. Carter Coal Co.*, 298 U.S. 238, 312–313 (1936).

2. Sections 3214(a) and (h) (reporting) and §3211(a) (determination of viability). Section 3214(a)(8), part of the general reporting section, incorporates §3211(a). Section 3211(a) requires the physician to report the basis for his determination "that a child is not viable." It applies only after the first trimester. The report required by §§3214(a) and (h) is detailed and must include, among other things, identification of the performing and referring physicians and of the facility or agency; information as to the woman's political subdivision and State of residence, age, race, marital status, and number of prior pregnancies; the date of her last menstrual period and the probable gestational

age; the basis for any judgment that a medical emergency existed; the basis for any determination of nonviability ; and the method of payment for the abortion. The report is to be signed by the attending physician. §3214(b).

Despite the fact that §3214(e)(2) provides that such reports "shall not be deemed public records," within the meaning of the Commonwealth's "Right-to-Know Law," Pa. Stat. Ann., Tit. 65, §66.1 *et seq.* (Purdon 1959 and Supp. 1985), each report "shall be made available for public inspection and copying within 15 days of receipt in a form which will not lead to the disclosure of the identity of any person filing a report." Similarly, the report of complications, required by §3214(h), "shall be open to public inspection and copying." A willful failure to file a report required under §3214 is "unprofessional conduct" and the noncomplying physician's license "shall be subject to suspension or revocation." §3214(i)(1).

The scope of the information required and its availability to the public belie any assertions by the Commonwealth that it is advancing any legitimate interest. In *Planned Parenthood of Central Mo. v. Danforth*, 428 U.S. 52, 80 (1976), we recognized that recordkeeping and reporting provisions "that are reasonably directed to the preservation of maternal health and that properly respect a patient's confidentiality and privacy are permissible." But the reports required under the Act before us today go well beyond the health-related interests that served to justify the Missouri reports under consideration in *Danforth*. Pennsylvania would require, as Missouri did not, information as to method of payment, as to the woman's personal history, and as to the bases for medical judgments. The Missouri reports were to be used "only for statistical purposes." See *id.*, at 87. They were to be maintained in confidence, with the sole exception of public health officers. In *Akron*, the Court explained its holding in *Danforth* when it said: "The decisive factor was that the State met its burden of demonstrating that these regulations furthered important health-related state concerns." 462 U.S., at 430.

The required Pennsylvania reports, on the other hand, while claimed not to be "public," are available nonetheless to the public for copying. Moreover, there is no limitation on the use to which the Commonwealth or the public copiers may put them. The elements that proved persuasive for the ruling in *Danforth* are absent here. The decision to terminate a pregnancy is an intensely private one that must be protected in a way that assures anonymity. Justice Stevens, in his opinion concurring in the judgment in *Bellotti v. Baird*, 443 U.S. 662 (1979), aptly observed:

"It is inherent in the right to make the abortion decision that the right may be exercised without public scrutiny and in defiance of the contrary opinion of the sovereign or other third parties." *Id.*, at 655.

A woman and her physician will necessarily be more reluctant to choose an abortion if there exists a possibility that her decision and her identity will become known publicly. Although the statute does not specifically require the reporting of the woman's name, the amount of information about her and the circumstances under which she had an abortion are so detailed that identification is likely. Identification is the obvious purpose of these extreme reporting requirements.[12] The "impermissible limits" that *Danforth* mentioned and that Missouri approached, see 428 U.S., at 81, have been exceeded here.

We note, as we reach this conclusion, that the Court consistently has refused to allow government to chill the exercise of constitutional rights by requiring disclosure of protected, but sometimes unpopular, activities. See, *e.g.*, *Lamont v. Postmaster General*, 381 U.S. 301 (1965) (invalidating Post Office requirement that addressee affirmatively request delivery of "communist" materials in order to receive them); *Talley v. California*, 362 U.S. 60, 64–65 (1960) (striking down municipal ban on unsigned handbills); *NAACP v. Alabama ex rel. Patterson*, 357 U.S. 449, 462–465 (1958) (invalidating compelled disclosure of NAACP membership list). Pennsylvania's reporting requirements raise the spectre of public exposure and harassment of women who choose to exercise their personal, intensely private, right, with their physician, to end a pregnancy. Thus, they pose an unacceptable danger of deterring the exercise of that right, and must be invalidated.

3. Section 3210(b) (degree of care for postviability abortions) and §3210(c) (second-physician requirement when the fetus is possibly viable). Section 3210(b)[13] sets forth two independent requirements for a postviability abortion. First, it demands the exercise of that degree of care "which such person would be required to exercise in order to preserve the life and health of any unborn child intended to be born and not aborted." Second, "the abortion technique employed shall be that which would provide the best opportunity for the unborn child to be aborted alive unless," in the physician's good-faith judgment, that technique "would present a significantly greater medical risk to the life or health of the pregnant woman." An intentional, knowing, or reckless violation of this standard is a felony of the third degree, and subjects the violator to the possibility of imprisonment for not more than seven years and to a fine of not more than $15,000. See 18 Pa. Cons. stat. §§1101(2) and 1103(3) (1983).

The Court of Appeals ruled that §3210(b) was unconstitutional because it required a "trade-off" between the woman's health and fetal survival, and failed to require that maternal health be the physician's paramount consideration. 737 F. 2d, at 300, citing *Colautti v. Franklin*, 439 U.S. 379, 397–401 (1979) (where Pennsylvania's 1974 Abortion Control Act was reviewed). In *Colautti*, this Court recognized the undesirability of any "'trade-off'" between the woman's health and additional percentage points of fetal survival." *Id.*, at 400.

Appellants do not take any real issue with this proposition. See Brief for Appellants 84–86. They argue instead, as did the District Court, see 552 F. Supp., at 806–807, that the statute's words "significantly greater medical risk" for the life or health of the woman do not mean some additional risk (in which case unconstitutionality apparently is conceded) but only a "meaningfully increased" risk. That interpretation, said the District Court, renders the statute constituional. *Id.*, at 807. The Court of Appeals disagreed, pointing out that such a reading is inconsistent with the statutory language and with the legislative intent reflected in that language; that the adverb "significantly" modifies the risk imposed on the woman; that the adverb is "patently not surplusage"; and that the language of the statute "is not susceptible to a construction that does not require the mother to bear an increased medical risk in order to save her viable fetus." 737 F. 2d, at 300. We agree with the Court of Appeals and therefore find the statute to be facially invalid.[14]

Section 3210(c)[15] requires that a second physician be present during an abortion performed when viability is possible. The second physician is to "take control of the child and ... provide immediate medical care for the child, taking all reasonable steps necessary, in his judgment, to preserve the child's life and health." Violation of this requirement is a felony of the third degree.

In *Planned Parenthood Assn. v. Ashcroft*, 462 U.S. 476 (1983), the Court, by a 5–4 vote, but not by a controlling single opinion, ruled that a Missouri statute requiring the presence of a second physician during an abortion performed after viability was constitutional. JUSTICE POWELL, joined by THE CHIEF JUSTICE, concluded that the State had a compelling interest in protecting the life of a viable fetus and that the second physician's presence provided assurance that the State's interest was protected more fully than with only one physician in attendance. *Id.*, at 482–486. [16] JUSTICE POWELL recognized that, to pass constitutional muster, the statute must contain an exception for the situation where the health of the mother was endangered by delay in the arrival of the second physician. Recognizing that there was "no clearly expressed exception" on the face of the Missouri statute for the emergency situation, JUSTICE POWELL found the exception implicit in the statutory requirement that action be taken to preserve the fetus "provided it does not pose an increased risk to the life or health of the woman." *Id.*, at 485, n. 8.

Like the Missouri statute, §3210(c) of the Pennsylvania statute contains no express exception for an emergency situation. While the Missouri statute, in the view of JUSTICE POWELL, was worded sufficiently to imply an emergency exception, Pennsylvania's statute contains no such comforting or helpful language and evinces no intent to protect a woman whose life my be at risk. Section 3210(a)[17] provides only a defense to criminal liability for a physician who concluded, in good faith, that a fetus was nonviable "or that the abortion was necessary to preserve maternal life or health." It does not relate to the second-physician requirement and its words are not words of emergency.

It is clear that the Pennsylvania Legislature knows how to provide a medical-emergency exception when it chooses to do so. It defined "[m]edical emergency" in general terms in §3203, and it specifically provided a medical-emergency exception with respect to informational requirements, §3205(b); for parental consent, §3206; for post-first trimester hospitalization, §3209; and for a public official's issuance of an order for an abortion without the express voluntary consent of the woman, §3215(f). We necessarily conclude that the legislature's failure to provide a medical-emergency exception in §3210(c) was intentional. All the factors are here for chilling the performance of a late abortion, which, more than one performed at an earlier date, perhaps tends to be under emergency conditions.

V

Constitutional rights do not always have easily ascertainable boundaries, and controversy over the meaning of our Nation's most majestic guarantees frequently has been turbulent. As judges, however, we are sworn to uphold the law even when its content gives rise to bitter dispute. See *Cooper v. Aaron*, 358 U.S. 1 (1958). We recognized at the very beginning of our opinion in *Roe*, 410 U.S., at 116, that abortion raises moral and spiritual questions over which honorable persons can disagree sincerely and profoundly. But those disagreements did not then and do not now relieve us of our duty to apply the Constitution faithfully.

Our cases long have recognized that the Constitution embodies a promise that a certain private sphere of individual liberty will be kept largely beyond the reach of government. See, *e.g., Carey* v. *Population Services International,* 431 U.S. 678 (1977); *Moore* v. *East Cleveland,* 431 U.S.

494 (1977); *Eisenstadt* v. *Barid*, 405 U.S. 438 (1972); *Griswold* v. *Connecticut*, 381 U.S. 479 (1965); *Pierce* v. *Society of Sisters*, 268 U.S. 510 (1925); *Meyer* v. *Nebraska*, 262 U.S. 390 (1923). See also *Whalen* v. *Roe*, 429 U.S. 589, 598–600 (1977). That promise extends to women as well as to men. Few decisions are more personal and intimate, more properly private, or more basic to individual dignity and autonomy, than a woman's decision—with the guidance of her physician and within the limits specified in *Roe*—whether to end her pregnancy. A woman's right to make that choice freely is fundamental. Any other result, in our view, would protect inadequately a central part of the sphere of liberty that our law guarantees equally to all.

The Court of Appeals correctly invalidated the specified provisions of Pennsylvania's 1982 Abortion Control Act. Its judgment is affirmed.

It is so ordered.

Notes

1. The District Court had held invalid and had enjoined preliminarily only the requirement of §3205(a)(2) that at least 24 hours must elapse between a woman's receipt of specified information and the performance of her abortion. 552 F. Supp. 791, 797–798, 811 (E D Pa. 1982).

2. The Court of Appeals also held §3215(e) invalid. That section requires health-care insurers to make available, at a lesser premium, policies expressly excluding coverage "for abortion services not necessary to avert the death of the woman or to terminate pregnancies caused by rape or incest." This ruling on §3215(e) is not before us.

3. A "tough-guy competition" is a physical contact bout between persons who lack professional experience and who attempt to render each other unconscious. See Note, 87 Dick. L. Rev. 373, 382, n. 84 (1983).

4. Section 1254 reads in pertinent part: "Cases in the courts of appeals may be reviewed by the Supreme Court by the following methods:

"(2) By appeal by a party relying on a State statute held by a court of appeals to be invalid as repugnant to the Constitution, treaties or laws of the United States...."

5. Appellants ask that *Slaker* be overruled. See Brief for Appellants 10, 22–25.

6. We continue, however, to refer to the parties as appellants and appellees, respectively.

7. This principle finds an analogy in an established doctrine of administrative law. In *SEC v. Chenery Corp.*, 318 U.S. 80 (1943), the Court ruled that a reviewing court could not affirm an agency on a principle the agency might not embrace. But the ruling in *Chenery* has not required courts to remand in futility. See *Illinois v. ICC*, 722 F. 2d 1341, 1348–1349 (CA7 1983); see also

Friendly, *Chenery* Revisited, Reflections on Reversal and Remand of Administrative Orders, 1969 Duke L. J. 199.

8. A different situation is presented, of course, when there is no disagreement as to the law, but the probability of success on the merits depends on facts that are likely to emerge at trial. See *Delaware & H.R. Co. v. United Transportation Union,* 146 U.S. App. D.C. 142, 159, 450 F. 2d 603, 620, cert. denied, 403 U.S. 911 (1971). See also *Airco, Inc., v. Energy Research & Development Admin.,* 528 F. 2d 1294, 1296 (CA7 1975); *California ex rel. Younger v. Tahoe Regional Planning Agency,* 516 F. 2d 215, 217 (CA9), cert. denied, 423 U.S. 868 (1975); *Natural Resources Defense Council, Inc. v. Grand Lodge,* 584 F. 2d 308, 314 (CA9 1978), cert. dism'd, 441 U.S. 937 (1979); *FTC v. Southwest Sunsites, Inc.,* 665 F. 2d 711, 717 (CA5), cert. denied, 456 U.S. 973 (1982).

9. *Not* before us are: §3203 (definition of "abortion"); §3205 (24-hour waiting period and physician-only counseling); §§3207(b) and 3214(f) (public disclosure of reports); §3209 (requirement of hospitalization for an abortion subsequent to the first trimester); §3210(a) (penalties for abortion after viability, and the "complete defense" thereto); §3215(c) (proscription of use of public funds for abortion services); and §3215(e) (compulsory availability of insurance excluding certain abortion services). Remanded for record development or otherwise not invalidated, therefore not before us, are: §3206 (parental consent—operation of statute enjoined until promulgation of rules by the Supreme Court of Pennsylvania assuring confidentiality and promptness of disposition); §3207(b)(abortion facilities and reports from them for public disclosure); and §§3214(c), (d), (f), and (g) (other reporting requirements—challenges either not made or withdrawn). On June 17, 1985, the District Court, after hearing, preliminarily enjoined the enforcement of §§3207(b) and 3214(f). Civil Action No. 82–4336 (ED Pa.). See n. 12, *infra.* The Supreme Court of Pennsylvania issued the suggested rules, mentioned above, on November 26, 1984, after the appeal in this case was docketed here. See Pennsylvania Orphan's Court Rules 16.1 to 16.8, reprinted in 20 Pa. Cons. Stat. following §794 (Supp. 1985). Appellants thereupon filed a motion with the District Court that the injunction against enforcement of §3206 be vacated. App. 53. That Court, however, denied the motion, concluding that it had no jurisdiction "to issue the order [appellants] seek" while the case was on appeal here. *Id.,* at 57, 61. We decline appellants' suggestion that we now examine this feature of the case in the light of the new rules, for we conclude that this development should be considered by the District Court in the first instance.

10. Following this Court's lead in *Akron,* federal courts consistently have stricken fetal-description requirements because of their inflammatory impact. See, *e.g., Planned Parenthood League of Massachusetts v. Bellotti,* 641 F. 2d 1006, 1021–1022 (CA1 1981); *Charles v. Carey,* 627 F. 2d 772, 784 (CA7 1980); *Planned Parenthood Assn. of Kansas City v. Ashcroft,* 655 F. 2d 848, 868 (CA8 1981); *Women's Medical Center of Providence, Inc. v. Roberts,* 530 F. Supp. 1136, 1152–1154 (RI 1982).

11. In their argument against this conclusion, appellants claim that the informational requirements must be held constitutional in the light of this Court's summary affirmance in *Franklin v. Fitzpatrick,* 428 U.S. 901 (1976), of the

judgment in *Planned Parenthood Assn. v. Fitzpatrick*, 401 F. Supp. 554 (ED Pa. 1975). That litigation concerned the Commonwealth's 1974 Abortion Control Act. Its informed-consent provision, however, did not contain such plainly unconstitutional informational requests as those in the current Act, or any physician-only counseling or 24-hour waiting-period requirements. The summary affirmance also preceded the decision in *Akron* and, to the extent, if any at all, it might be considered to be inconsistent with *Akron*, the latter, of course, controls.

12. Appellees advise us, see Brief for Appellees 38–39, that they sought in the District Court a preliminary injunction against the requirement that the facility identification report and the quarterly statistical report be made available for public inspection and copying, and that on June 17, 1985, after full hearing, the District Court entered a preliminary injunction against the enforcement of these public disclosure requirements. Appellees assert that the record of that hearing shows a continuous pattern of violence and harassment directed against the patients and staff of abortion clinics; that the District Court concluded that this would be increased by the public disclosure of facility names and quarterly statistical reports; and that public disclosure would impose a burden on the woman's right to an abortion by heightening her fear and anxiety, and by discouraging her physician from offering an abortion because, by so doing, he would avoid pressure from anti-abortion forces. That record, of course, is not now before us. We need place no reliance upon it and we draw no conclusion from it.

13. Section 3210(b) reads:

"Every person who performs or induces an abortion after an unborn child has been determined to be viable shall exercise that degree of professional skill, care and diligence which such person would be required to exercise in order to preserve the life and health of any unborn child intended to be born and not aborted and the abortion technique employed shall be that which provides the best opportunity for the unborn child to be aborted alive unless, in the good faith judgment of the physician, that method or technique would present a significantly greater medical risk to the life or health of the pregnant woman than would another available method or technique and the physician reports the basis for his judgment. The potential psychological or emotional impact on the mother of the unborn child's survival shall not be deemed a medical risk to the mother. Any person who intentionally, knowingly or recklessly violates the provisions of this subsection commits a felony of the third degree."

14. This makes it unnecessary for us to consider appellees' further argument that §3210(b) is void for vagueness.

15. Section 3210(c) reads:

"Any person who intends to perform an abortion the method chosen for which, in his good faith judgment, does not preclude the possibility of the child surviving the abortion, shall arrange for the attendance, in the same room in which the abortion is to be completed, of a second physician. Immediately after the complete expulsion or extraction of the child, the second physician shall take control of the child and shall provide immediate medical care for the child, taking all reasonable steps necessary, in his judgment, to preserve the child's life and health. Any person who intentionally, knowingly, or recklessly violates the provisions of this subsection commits a felony of the third degree."

16. JUSTICE O'CONNOR, joined by JUSTICES WHITE and REHNQUIST, stated somewhat categorically that the second-physician requirement was constitutional. 462 U.S., at 505.

17. Section 3210(a) reads:

"Any person who intentionally, knowingly or recklessly performs or induces an abortion when the fetus is viable commits a felony of the third degree. It shall be a complete defense to any charge brought against a physician for violating the requirements of this section that he had concluded in good faith, in his best medical judgment, that the unborn child was not viable at the time the abortion was performed or induced or that the abortion was necessary to preserve maternal life or health."

Supreme Court of the United States

No. 84–495

RICHARD THORNBURGH, ET AL., APPELLANTS V.
AMERICAN COLLEGE OF OBSTETRICIANS
AND GYNECOLOGISTS ET AL.

On Appeal from the United States Court of Appeals
for the Third Circuit

[June 11, 1986]

JUSTICE STEVENS, concurring.

The scope of the individual interest in liberty that is given protection by the Due Process Clause of the Fourteenth Amendment is a matter about which conscientious judges have long disagreed. Although I believe that that interest is significantly broader than JUSTICE WHITE does,[1] I have always had the highest respect for his views on this subject.[2] In this case, although our ultimate conclusions differ, it may be useful to emphasize some of our areas of agreement in order to ensure that the clarity of certain fundamental propositions not be obscured by his forceful rhetoric.

Let me begin with a reference to *Griswold v. Connecticut*, 381 U.S. 479 (1965), the case holding that a State may not totally forbid the use of birth control devices. Although the Court's opinion relied on a "right of marital privacy" within the "penumbra" of the Bill of Rights, *id.*, at 481–486, JUSTICE WHITE's concurring opinion went right to the heart of the issue. He wrote:

> "It would be unduly repetitious, and belaboring the obvious, to expound on the impact of this statute on the liberty guaranteed by the Fourteenth Amendment against arbitrary or capricious denials or on the nature of this liberty. Suffice it to say that this is not the first time this Court has had occasion to articulate that the liberty entitled to protection under the Fourteenth Amendment includes the right 'to marry, establish a home and bring up children,' *Meyer v. Nebraska*, 262 U.S. 390, 399, and 'the liberty . . . to direct the upbringing and education of children,' *Pierce v. Society of Sisters*, 268 U.S. 510, 534-535, and that these are among 'the basic civil rights of man.' *Skinner v. Oklahoma*, 316 U.S. 535, 541. These decisions affirm that there is a 'realm of family life which the state cannot enter' without substantial justification. *Prince v. Massachusetts*, 321 U.S. 158, 166. Surely the right invoked in this case, to be free of regulation of the intimacies of the marriage relationship, 'come[s] to this Court with a momentum for respect lacking when appeal is made to liberties which derive merely from shifting economic arrangements.' *Kovacs v. Cooper*, 336 U.S. 77, 95 (opinion of Frankfurter, J.)." *Id.*, at 502–503 (WHITE, J., concurring in the judgment).

He concluded that the statute could not be constitutionally applied to married persons, explaining:

> "I find nothing in this record justifying the sweeping scope of this statute, with its telling effect on the freedoms of married persons, and therefore conclude that it deprives such persons of liberty without due process of law." *Id.*, at 507.

That conclusion relied in part on the fact that the statute involved "sensitive areas of liberty"[3] and in part on the absence of any colorable justification for applying the statute to married couples.

In *Eisenstadt v. Baird*, 405 U.S. 438 (1972), JUSTICE WHITE concluded that a similar Massachusetts statute was invalid as applied to a person whom the record did not identify as either married or unmarried, *id.*, at 464–465, and in *Carey* v. *Population Services International*, 431 U.S. 678 (1977), he subscribed to this explanation of the holdings in *Griswold* and *Eisenstadt*:

"The fatal fallacy in [the appellants'] argument is that it overlooks the underlying premise of those decisions that the Constitution protects 'the right of the individual ... to be free from unwarranted governmental intrusion into ... the decision whether to bear or beget a child.' [*Eisenstadt v. Baird*, 405 U.S.] at 453. *Griswold* did state that by 'forbidding the *use* of contraceptives rather than regulating their manufacture or sale,' the Connecticut statute there had 'a maximum destructive impact' on privacy rights. 381 U.S., at 485. This intrusion into 'the sacred precincts of marital bedrooms' made that statute particularly 'repulsive.' *id.*, at 485–486. But subsequent decisions have made clear that the constitutional protection of individual autonomy in matters of childbearing is not dependent on that element. *Eisenstadt v. Baird*, holding that the protection is not limited to married couples, characterized the protected right as the '*decision* whether to bear or beget a child.' 405 U.S., at 453 (emphasis added). Similarly, *Roe* v. *Wade* held that the Constitution protects 'a woman's *decision* whether or not to terminate her pregnancy.' 410 U.S., at 153 (emphasis added). See also *Whalen v. Roe*, [429 U.S. 589,] 599–600, and n.26. These decisions put *Griswold* in proper perspective. *Griswold* may no longer be read as holding only that a State may not prohibit a married couple's use of contraceptives. Read in light of its progeny, the teaching of *Griswold* is that the Constitution protects individual decisions in matters of childbearing from unjustified intrusion by the State." 431 U.S., at 687; *id.*, at 702 (WHITE, J., concurring in pertinent part and concurring in result).

Thus, the aspect of liberty at stake in this case is the freedom from unwarranted governmental intrusion into individual decisions in matters of childbearing. As JUSTICE WHITE explained in *Griswold*, that aspect of liberty comes to this Court with a momentum for respect that is lacking when appeal is made to liberties which derive merely from shifting economic arrangements.

Like the birth control statutes involved in *Griswold* and *Baird*, the abortion statutes involved in *Roe* v. *Wade*, 410 U.S. 113 (1973), and in the case before us today apply equally to decisions made by married persons and by unmarried persons. Consistently with his views in those cases, JUSTICE WHITE agrees that "a woman's ability to choose an abortion is a species of 'liberty' that is subject to the general protections of the Due Process Clause." *Post*, at [302]. His agreement with that "indisputable" proposition, *ibid.*, is not qualified or limited to decisions made by pregnant women who are married and, indeed, it would be a strange form of liberty if it were so limited.

Up to this point in JUSTICE WHITE's analysis, his opinion is fully consistent with the accepted teachings of the Court and with the major premises of *Roe* v. *Wade*. For reasons that are not entirely clear, however, JUSTICE WHITE abruptly announces that the interest in "liberty" that is implicated by a decision not to bear a chld that is made a few days after conception is *less* fundamental than a comparable decision made before conception. *Post*, at [304]. There may, of course, be a significant difference in the strength of the countervailing state interest, but I fail to see how a decision on child-bearing becomes *less* important the day after conception than the day before. Indeed, if one decision is more "fundamental" to the individual's freedom than the other, surely it is the post-conception decision that is the more serious. Thus, it is difficult for me to understand how JUSTICE WHITE reaches the conclusion that restraints upon this aspect of a woman's liberty do not "call into play anything more than the most minimal judicial scrutiny." *Id.*, at [302].[4]

If JUSTICE WHITE were correct in regarding the post-conception decision of the question whether to bear a child as a relatively unimportant, second-class sort of interest, I might agree with his view that the individual should be required to conform her decision to the will of the majority. But if that decision commands the respect that is traditionally associated with the "sensitive areas of liberty" protected by the Constitution, as JUSTICE WHITE characterized reproductive decisions in *Griswold*, 381 U.S., at 503, no individual should be compelled to surrender the freedom to make the decision for herself simply because her "value preferences" are not shared by the majority.[5] In a sense, the basic question is whether the "abortion decision" should be made by the individual or by the majority "in the unrestrained imposition of its own, extraconstitutional value preferences." *Post*, at [304]. But surely JUSTICE WHITE is quite wrong in suggesting that the Court is imposing value preferences on anyone else. *Ibid.*[6]

JUSTICE WHITE is also surely wrong in suggesting that the governmental interest in protecting fetal life is equally compelling during the entire period from the moment of conception until the moment of birth. *Post*, at [305]. Again, I recognize that a powerful theological argument can be made for that position, but I believe our jurisdiction is limited to the evaluation of secular state interests.[7] I should think it obvious that the state's interest in the protection of an embryo—even if that interest if defined as "protecting those who will be citizens," *ibid.*—increases progessively and dramatically as the organism's capacity to feel pain, to experience pleasure, to survive, and to react to its surroundings increases day by day. The development of a fetus—and pregnancy itself—are not static conditions, and the assertion that the government's interest is static simply ignores this reality.

Nor is it an answer to argue that life itself is not a static condition, and that "there is no nonarbitrary line separating a fetus from a child, or indeed, an adult human being," *post*, at [304]. For, unless the religious view that a fetus is a "person" is adopted—a view JUSTICE WHITE refuses to embrace, *ibid.*—there is a fundamental and well-recognized difference between a fetus and a human being; indeed, if there is not such a difference, the permissibility of terminating the life of a fetus could scarcely be left to the will of the state legislatures.[8] And if distinctions may be drawn between a fetus and a human being in terms of the state interest in their protection—even though the fetus represents one of "those who will be citizens"—it seems to me quite odd to argue that distinctions may not also be drawn between the state interest in protecting the freshly fertilized egg and the state interest in protecting the 9-month-gestated, fully sentient fetus on the eve of birth. Recognition of this distinction is supported not only by logic, but also by history[9] and by our shared experiences.

Turning to JUSTICE WHITE's comments on *stare decisis*, he is of course correct in pointing out that the Court "has not hesitated to overrule decisions, or even whole lines of cases, where experience, scholarship, and reflection demonstrated that their fundamental premises were not to be found in the Constitution." *Post*, at [300]. But JUSTICE WHITE has not disavowed the "fundamental premises" on which the decision in *Roe* v. *Wade* rests. He has not disavowed the Court's prior approach to the interpretation of the word "liberty" or, more narrowly, the line of cases that culminated in the unequivocal holding, applied to unmarried persons and married persons alike, "that the Constitution protects individual decisions in matters of child-bearing from unjustified intrusion by the State." *Carey*, 431 U.S., at 687; *id.*, at 702 (WHITE, J., concurring in pertinent part).[10]

Nor does the fact that the doctrine of *stare decisis* is not an absolute bar to the reexamination of past interpretations of the Constitution mean that the values underlying that doctrine may be summarily put to one side. There is a strong public interest in stability, and in the orderly conduct of our affairs, that is served by a consistent course of constitutional adjudication. Acceptance of the fundamental premises that underlie the decision in *Roe v. Wade*, as well as the application of those premises in that case, places the responsibility for decision in matters of childbearing squarely in the private sector of our society.[11] The majority remains free to preach the evils of birth control and abortion and to persuade others to make correct decisions while the individual faced with the reality of a difficult choice having serious and personal consequences of major importance to her own future—

perhaps to the salvation of her own immortal soul—remains free to seek and to obtain sympathetic guidance from those who share her own value preferences.

In the final analysis, the holding in *Roe* v. *Wade* presumes that it is far better to permit some individuals to make incorrect decisions than to deny all individuals the right to make decisions that have a profound effect upon their destiny. Arguably a very primitive society would have been protected from evil by a rule against eating apples; a majority familiar with Adam's experience might favor such a rule. But the lawmakers who placed a special premium on the protection of individual liberty have recognized that certain values are more important than the will of a transient majority.[12]

Notes

1. Compare *e.g.*, his opinion for the Court in *Meachum v. Fano*, 427 U.S. 215 (1976), with my dissent in that case, *id.*, at 229.

2. See *e.g.*, Stevens, Judicial Restraint, 22 San Diego L. Rev. 437, 449–450 (1985).

3. "The nature of the right invaded is pertinent, to be sure, for statutes regulating sensitive areas of liberty do, under the cases of this Court, require 'strict scrutiny,' *Skinner v. Oklahoma*, 316 U.S. 535, 541, and 'must be viewed in the light of less drastic means for achieving the same basic purpose.' *Shelton v. Tucker*, 364 U.S. 479, 488. 'Where there is a significant encroachment upon personal liberty, the State may prevail only upon showing a subordinating interest which is compelling.' *Bates v. Little Rock*, 361 U.S. 516, 524. See also *McLaughlin v. Florida*, 379 U.S. 184. But such statutes, if reasonably necessary for the effectuation of a legitimate and substantial state interest, and not arbitrary or capricious in application, are not invalid under the Due Process Clause. *Zemel v. Rusk*, 381 U.S. 1." *Id.*, at 503–504.

4. At times JUSTICE WHITE's rhetoric conflicts with his own analysis. For instance, his emphasis on the lack of a decision by "the people . . . in 1787, 1791, 1868, or any time since," *post*, at [306], stands in sharp contrast to his earlier, forthright rejection of "the simplistic view that constitutional interpretation can possibly be limited to 'the plain meaning' of the Constitution's text or to the subjective intention of the Framers." *Post*, at [301]. Similarly, his statement that an abortion decision should be subject to "the will of the people," *post*, at 12, does not take us very far in determining *which* people—the majorities in state legislatures or the individuals confronted with unwanted pregnancies. In view of his agreement that the decision about abortion is "a species of liberty" protected by the Constitution, moreover, *post*, at [302], and in view of the fact that "liberty" plays a rather prominent role in our Constitution, his suggestion that the Court's evaluation of that interest represents the imposition of "extraconstitutional value preferences," *post*, at [304], seems to me inex-

plicable. This characterization of the Court's analysis as "extraconstitutional" also does not reflect JUSTICE WHITE's simultaneous recognition that "[t]he Constitution... is a document announcing fundamental principles in value-laden terms that leave ample scope for the exercise of normative judgment by those charged with interpreting and applying it." *Post*, at [302]. Finally, I fail to see how the fact that "men and women of good will and high commitment to constitutional government," *post*, at [304], are on both sides of the abortion issue helps to resolve the difficult constitutional question before us; I take it that the disputants in most constitutional controversies in our free society can be similarly characterized.

5. "What a person is, what he wants the determination of his life plan, of his concept of good, are the most intimate expressions of self-determination, and by asserting a person's responsibility for the results of this self-determination we give substance to the concept of liberty." C. Fried, Right and Wrong, 146–147 (1978).

6. JUSTICE WHITE's characterization of the governmental interest as "protecting those who will be citizens if their lives are not ended in the womb," *post*, at [305], reveals that his opinion may be influenced as much by his own value preferences as by his view about the proper allocation of decisionmaking responsibilities between the individual and the State. For if federal judges must allow the State to make the abortion decision, presumably the State is free to decide that a woman may *never* abort, may *sometimes* abort, or as in the People's Republic of China, must *always* abort if her family is already too large. In contrast, our cases represent a consistent view that the individual is primarily responsible for reproductive decisions, whether the State seeks to prohibit reproduction, *Skinner v. Oklahoma,* 316 U.S. 535 (1942), or to require it, *Roe* v. *Wade,* 410 U.S. 113 (1973).

7. The responsibility for nurturing the soul of the newly born, as well as the unborn, rests with individual parents, not with the State. No matter how important a sacrament such as baptism may be, a State surely could not punish a mother for refusing to baptize her child.

8. No member of this Court has ever suggested that a fetus is a "person" within the meaning of the Fourteenth Amendment.

9. See *Roe* v. *Wade, supra,* at 129–147.

10. He has, however, suggested that the concept of "liberty" is limited by two basic "definitions" of the values at stake. *Post*, at [303]. Like JUSTICE WHITE, I share Justice Harlan's concern about "judges... roaming at large in the constitutional field." *Ibid.;* see also Stevens, 22 San Diego L. Rev., at 449–450. But I am convinced that JUSTICE WHITE's use of "definitions" is an inadequate substitute for the difficult process of analysis and judgment that the guarantee of liberty requires, a process nowhere better expressed than by Justice Harlan: "Due process has not been reduced to any formula; its content cannot be determined by reference to any code. The best that can be said is that through the course of this Court's decisions it has represented the balance which our Nation, built upon postulates of respect for the liberty of the individual, has struck between that liberty and the demands of organized society. If the supplying of content to this Constitutional concept has of

necessity been a rational process, it certainly has not been one where judges have felt free to roam where unguided speculation might take them. The balance of which I speak is the balance struck by this country, having regard to what history teaches are the traditions from which it broke. That tradition is a living thing. A decision of this Court which radically departs from it could not long survive, while a decision which builds on what has survived is likely to be sound. No formula could serve as a substitute, in this area, for judgment and restraint.

*   *   *   *   *   *   *   *   *

"Each new claim to Constitutional protection must be considered against a background of Constitutional purposes, as they have been rationally perceived and historically developed. Though we exercise limited and sharply restrained judgment, yet there is no 'mechanical yardstick,' no 'mechanical answer.' The decision of an apparently novel claim must depend on grounds which follow closely on well-accepted principles and criteria. The new decision must take 'its place in relation to what went before and further [cut] a channel for what is to come.' *Irvine* v. *California*, 347 U.S. 128, 147 (dissenting opinion)." *Poe* v. *Ullman*, 367 U.S. 497, 542–544 (1961)(Harlan, J., dissenting).

11. "These cases do not deal with the individual's interest in protection from unwarranted public attention, comment, or exploitation. They deal, rather, with the individual's right to make certain unusually important decisions that will affect his own or his family's, destiny. The Court has referred to such decisions as implicating 'basic values,' as being 'fundamental,' and as being dignified by history and tradition. The character of the Court's language in these cases brings to mind the origins of the American heritage of freedom—the abiding interest in individual liberty that makes certain state intrusions on the citizen's right to decide how he will live his own life intolerable. Guided by history, our tradition of respect for the dignity of individual choice in matters of conscience and the restraints implicit in the federal system, federal judges have accepted the responsibility for recognition and protection of these rights in appropriate cases." *Fitzgerald* v. *Porter Memorial Hospital*, 523 F. 2d 716, 719–720 (CA7 1975) (footnotes omitted), cert. denied, 425 U.S. 916 (1976).

12. "The very purpose of a Bill of Rights was to withdraw certain subjects from the vicissitudes of political controversy, to place them beyond the reach of majorities and officials and to establish them as legal principles to be applied by the courts. One's right to life, liberty, and property, to free speech, a free press, freedom of worship and assembly, and other fundamental rights may not be submitted to vote; they depend on the outcome of no elections." *West Virginia State Board of Education* v. *Barnette*, 319 U.S. 624, 638 (1943).

Supreme Court of the United States

No. 84–495

RICHARD THORNBURGH, ET AL., APPELLANTS V.
AMERICAN COLLEGE OF OBSTETRICIANS
AND GYNECOLOGISTS ET AL.

On Appeal from the United States Court of Appeals
for the Third Circuit

[June 11, 1986]

CHIEF JUSTICE BURGER, dissenting.

I agree with much of JUSTICE WHITE's and JUSTICE O'CON-
NOR's dissents. In my concurrence in the companion case to *Roe* v.
Wade in 1973, I noted that

"I do not read the Court's holdings today as having the sweeping
consequences attributed to them by the dissenting Justices; the dissenting views discount the reality that the vast majority of physicians
observe the standards of their profession, and act only on the basis of
carefully deliberated medical judgments relating to life and health.
Plainly, the Court today rejects any claim that the Constitution requires
abortions on demand." *Doe* v. *Bolton*, 410 U.S. 179, 208 (1973).

Later, in *Maher* v. *Roe*, 432 U.S. 464, 481 (1977), I stated my view that

"[t]he Court's holdings in *Roe* . . . and *Doe* v. *Bolton* . . . simply require that a State not create an absolute barrier to a woman's decision to have an abortion."

I based my concurring statements in *Roe* and *Maher* on the principle expressed in the Court's opinion in *Roe* that the right to an abortion "is not unqualified and must be considered against important state interests in regulation." 410 U.S., at 154–155. In short, every member of the *Roe* Court rejected the idea of abortion on demand. The Court's opinion today, however, plainly undermines that important principle, and I regretfully conclude that some of the concerns of the dissenting Justices in *Roe*, as well as the concerns I expressed in my separate opinion, have now been realized.

The extent to which the Court has departed from the limitations expressed in *Roe* is readily apparent. In *Roe*, the Court emphasized

"that the State does have an important and legitimate interest in preserving and protecting the health of the pregnant woman. . . . " *Id.*, at 162.

Yet today the Court astonishingly goes so far as to say that the State may not even require that a woman contemplating an abortion be provided with accurate medical information concerning the risks inherent in the medical procedure which she is about to undergo and the availability of state-funded alternatives if she elects not to run those risks. Can anyone doubt that the State could impose a similar requirement with respect to other medical procedures? Can anyone doubt that doctors routinely give similar information concerning risks in countless procedures having far less impact on life and health, both physical and emotional than an abortion, and risk a malpractice lawsuit if they fail to do so?

Yet the Court concludes that the State cannot impose this simple information dispensing requirement in the abortion context where the decision is fraught with serious physical, psychological, and moral concerns of the highest order. Can it possibly be that the Court is saying that the Constitution *forbids* the communication of such critical information to a woman?[1] We have apparently already passed the point at which abortion is available merely on demand. If the statute at issue here is to be invalidated, the "demand" will not even have to be the result of an informed choice.

The Court in *Roe* further recognized that the State "has still *another* important and legitimate interest" which is "separate and distinct" from the interest in protecting maternal health, *i.e.*, an interest in "protecting the potentiality of human life." *Ibid.* The point at which these interests become "compelling" under *Roe* is at viability of the fetus. *Id.*, at 163. Today, however, the Court abandons that standard and renders the solemnly stated concerns of the 1973 *Roe* opinion for the interests of the States mere shallow rhetoric. The statute at issue in this case requires that a second physician be present during an abortion performed after viability, so that the second physician can "take control of the child and . . . provide immediate medical care . . . taking all reasonable steps necessary, in his judgment, to preserve the child's life and health." 18 Pa. Cons. Stat. §3210 (c).

Essentially this provision simply states that a viable fetus is to be cared for, not destroyed. No governmental power exists to say that a viable fetus should not have every protection required to preserve its life. Undoubtedly the Pennsylvania Legislature added the second physician requirement on the mistaken assumption that this Court meant what it said in *Roe* concerning the "compelling interest" of the states in potential life after viability.

The Court's opinion today is but the most recent indication of the distance traveled since *Roe*. Perhaps the first important road marker was the Court's holding in *Planned Parenthood of Missouri v. Danforth*, 428 U.S. 52 (1976), in which the Court held (over the dissent of JUSTICE WHITE joined by JUSTICE REHNQUIST and myself) that the State may not require that minors seeking an abortion first obtain parental consent. Parents, not judges or social worker's, have the inherent right and responsibility to advise their children in matters of this sensitivity and consequence. Can one imagine a surgeon performing an amputation or even an appendectomy on a 14-year-old girl without the consent of a parent or guardian except in an emergency situation?

Yet today the Court goes beyond *Danforth* by remanding for further consideration of the provisions of Pennsylvania's statute requiring that a minor seeking an abortion without parental consent petition the appropriate court for authorization. Even if I were to agree that the Constitution requires that the State may not provide that a minor receive parental consent before undergoing an abortion, I would certainly hold that judicial approval may be required. This is in keeping with the longstanding common law principle that courts may function in *loco parentis* when parents are unavailable or neglectful, even though courts are not very satisfactory substitutes when the issue is whether a 12-, 14-, or 16-year-old unmarried girl should have an abortion. In my view, no remand is necessary on this point because the statutory provision in question is constitutional.

In discovering constitutional infirmities in state regulations of abortion that are in accord with our history and tradition, we may have lured judges into "roaming at large in the constitutional field." *Griswold* v. *Connecticut*, 381 U.S. 479, 502 (1965) (Harlan, J., concurring). The soundness of our holdings must be tested by the decisions that purport to follow them. If *Danforth* and today's holding really mean what they seem to say, I agree we should reexamine *Roe*.

Notes

1. The Court's astounding rationale for this holding is that such information might have the effect of "discouraging abortion," *ante*, at [277], as though abortion is something to be advocated and encouraged. This is at odds not only with *Roe* but with our subsequent abortion decisions as well. As I stated in my opinion for the Court in *H. L.* v. *Matheson*, 450 U.S. 398 (1981), upholding a Utah statute requiring that a doctor notify the parents of a minor seeking an abortion: "The Constitution does not compel a state to fine-tune its statutes so as to encourage or facilitate abortions. To the contrary, state action 'encouraging childbirth except in the most urgent circumstances' is 'rationally related to the legitimate governmental objective of protecting potential life.'" *Id.*, at 413 (quoting *Harris* v. *McRae*, 448 U.S. 297 325 (1980).

Supreme Court of the United States

No. 84–495

RICHARD THORNBURGH, ET AL., APPELLANTS V.
AMERICAN COLLEGE OF OBSTETRICIANS
AND GYNECOLOGISTS ET AL.

On Appeal from the United States Court of Appeals
for the Third Circuit

[June 11, 1986]

JUSTICE WHITE, with whom JUSTICE REHNQUIST joins, dissenting.

Today the Court carries forward the "difficult and continuing venture in substantive due process," *Planned Parenthood of Missouri* v. *Danforth*, 428 U.S. 52 (1976) (WHITE, J., dissenting), that began with the decision in *Roe* v. *Wade*, 410 U.S. 113 (1973), and has led the Court further and further afield in the 13 years since that decision was handed down. I was in dissent in *Roe* v. *Wade* and am in dissent today. In Part I below, I state why I continue to believe that this venture has been fundamentally misguided since its inception. In Part II, I submit that even accepting *Roe* v. *Wade*, the concerns underlying that decision by no means command or justify the results reached today. Indeed, in my view, our precedents in this area, applied in a manner consistent with sound principles of constitutional adjudication, require reversal of the Court of Appeals on the ground that the provisions before us are facially constitutional.[1]

I

The rule of *stare decisis* is essential if case-by-case judicial decision-making is to be reconciled with the principle of the rule of law, for when governing legal standards are open to revision in every case, deciding cases becomes a mere exercise of judicial will, with arbitrary and unpredictable results. But *stare decisis* is not the only constraint upon judicial decisionmaking. Cases—like this one—that involve our assumed power to set aside on grounds of unconstitutionality a State or federal statute representing the democratically expressed will of the people call other considerations into play. Because the Constitution itself is ordained and established by the people of the United States, constitutional adjudication by this Court does not, in theory at any rate, frustrate the authority of the people to govern themselves through institutions of their own devising and in accordance with principles of their own choosing. But decisions that find in the Constitution principles or values that cannot fairly be read into that document usurp the people's authority, for such decisions represent choices that the people have never made and that they cannot disavow through corrective legislation. For this reason, it is essential that this Court maintain the power to restore authority to its proper possessors by correcting constitutional decisions that, on reconsideration, are found to be mistaken.

The Court has therefore adhered to the rule that *stare decisis* is not rigidly applied in cases involving constitutional issues, see *Glidden Co.* v. *Zdanok*, 370 U.S. 530, 543 (1962) (opinion of Harlan, J.), and has not hesitated to overrule decisions, or even whole lines of cases, where experience, scholarship, and reflection demonstrated that their fundamental premises were not to be found in the Constitution. *Stare decisis* did not stand in the way of the Justices who, in the late 1930s, swept away constitutional doctrines that had placed unwarranted restrictions on the power of the State and Federal Governments to enact social and economic legislation, see *United States* v. *Darby*, 312 U.S. 100 (1941); *West Coast Hotel Co.* v. *Parrish*, 300 U.S. 379 (1937). Nor did *stare decisis* deter a different set of Justices, some fifteen years later, from rejecting the theretofore prevailing view that the Fourteenth Amendment permitted the States to maintain the system of racial segregation. *Brown* v. *Board of Education,* 347 U.S. 483 (1954). In both instances, history has been far kinder to those who departed from precedent than to those who would have blindly followed the rule of *stare decisis.* And only last Term, the author of today's majority opinion reminded us once again that "when it has become apparent that a prior decision has departed from a proper understanding" of the Constitution, that decision must be overruled. *Garcia* v. *San Antonio Metropolitan Transit Authority* 105 S.Ct. 1005,1021 (1985).

In my view, the time has come to recognize that *Roe* v. *Wade,* no less than the cases overruled by the Court in the decisions I have just cited, "departs from a proper understanding" of the Constitution and to overrule it. I do not claim that the arguments in support of this proposition are new ones or that they were not considered by the Court in *Roe* or in the cases that suceeded it. Cf. *Akron* v. *Akron Center for Reproductive Health,* 462 U.S. 416, 419–420 (1983). But if an argument that a constitutional decision is erroneous must be novel in order to justify overruling that precedent, the Court's decisions in *Lochner* v. *New York,* 198 U.S. 45 (1905), and *Plessy* v. *Ferguson,* 163 U.S. 537 (1896), would remain the law, for the doctrines announced in those decisions were nowhere more eloquently or incisively criticized than in the dissenting opinions of Justices Holmes (in *Lochner*) and Harlan (in both cases). That the flaws in an opinion were evident at the time it was handed down is hardly a reason for adhering to it.

A

Roe v. *Wade* posits that a woman has a fundamental right to terminate her pregnancy, and that this right may be restricted only in the service of two compelling state interests: the interest in maternal health (which becomes compelling only at the stage in pregnancy at which an abortion becomes more hazardous than carrying the pregnancy to term) and the interest in protecting the life of the fetus (which becomes compelling only at the point of viability). A reader of the Constitution might be surprised to find that it encompassed these detailed rules, for the text obviously contains no .references to abortion, nor indeed, to pregnancy or reproduction generally; and, of course, it is highly doubtful that the authors of any of the provisions of the Constitution believed that they were giving protection to abortion. As its prior cases clearly show, however, this Court does not subscribe to the simplistic view that constitutional interpretation can possibly be limited to the "plain meaning" of the Constitution's text or to the subjective intention of the Framers. The Constitution is not a deed setting forth the precise metes and bounds of its subject matter;

rather, it is a document announcing fundamental principles in value-laden terms that leave ample scope for the exercise of normative judgment by those charged with interpreting and applying it. In particular, the Due Process Clause of the Fourteenth Amendment, which forbids the deprivation of "life, liberty, or property without due process of law," has been read by the majority of the Court to be broad enough to provide substantive protection against State infringement of a broad range of individual interests. See *Moore* v. *City of East Cleveland*, 431 U.S. 494, 541–552 (WHITE, J., dissenting).

In most instances, the substantive protection afforded the liberty or property of an individual by the Fourteenth Amendment is extremely limited: State action impinging on individual interests need only be rational to survive scrutiny under the Due Process Clause, and the determination of rationality is to be made with a heavy dose of deference to the policy choices of the legislature. Only "fundamental" rights are entitled to the added protection provided by strict judicial scrutiny of legislation that impinges upon them. See *id.*, at 499 (opinion of POWELL, J.); *id.*, at 537 (Stewart, J., joined by Rehnquist, J., dissenting); *id.*, at 547–549 (WHITE, J., dissenting). I can certainly agree with the proposition—which I deem indisputable—that a woman's ability to choose an abortion is a species of "liberty" that is subject to the general protections of the Due Process Clause. I cannot agree, however, that this liberty is so "fundamental" that restrictions upon it call into play anything more than the most minimal judicial scrutiny.

Fundamental liberties and interests are most clearly present when the Constitution provides specific textual recognition of their existence and importance. Thus, the Court is on relatively firm ground when it deems certain of the liberties set forth in the Bill of Rights to be fundamental and therefore finds them incorporated in the Fourteenth Amendment's guarantee that no State may deprive any person of liberty without due process of law. When the Court ventures further and defines as "fundamental" liberties that are nowhere mentioned in the Constitution (or that are present only in the so-called "penumbras" of specifically enumerated rights), it must, of necessity, act with more caution, lest it open itself to the accusation, that, in the name of identifying constitutional principles to which the people have consented in framing their Constitution, the Court has done nothing more than impose its own controversial choices of value upon the people.

Attempts to articulate the constraints that must operate upon the Court when it employs the Due Process Clause to protect liberties not specifically enumerated in the text of the Constitution have produced varying definitions of "fundamental liberties." One approach has been to limit the class of fundamental liberties to those interests that are "implicit in the concept of ordered liberty" such that "neither liberty nor justice would exist if [they] were sacrificed." *Palko* v. *Connecticut*, 302 U.S. 319, 325, 326 (1937); see *Moore* v. *City of East Cleveland, supra* at 537 (Stewart, J., joined by REHNQUIST, J., dissenting). Another, broader approach is to define fundamental liberties as those that are "deeply rooted in this Nation's history and tradition." *Id.*, at 503 (opinion of POWELL, J.); see also *Griswold* v. *Connecticut*, 381 U.S., at 501 (Harlan, J., concurring). These distillations of the possible approaches to the identification of unenumerated fundamental rights are not and do not purport to be precise legal tests or "mechanical yardstick[s]," *Poe* v. *Ullman*, 367 U.S., at 544 (1961) (Harlan, J., dissenting). Their utility lies in their effort to identify some source of constitutional value that reflects not the philosophical predilections of individual judges, but basic choices made by the people themselves in constituting their system of government—*"the balance struck by this country," id.*, at 542 (emphasis added)—and they seek to achieve this end through locating fundamental rights either in the traditions and consensus of our society as a whole or in the logical implications of a system that recognizes both individual liberty and democratic order. Whether either of these approaches can, as Justice Harlan hoped, prevent "judges from roaming at large in the constitutional field," *Griswold*, 381 U.S., at 502, is debatable. What for me is not subject to debate, however, is that either of the basic definitions of fundamental liberties, taken seriously, indicates the illegitimacy of the Court's decision in *Roe* v. *Wade.*

The Court has justified the recognition of a woman's fundamental right to terminate her pregnancy by invoking decisions upholding claims of personal autonomy in connection with the conduct of family life, the rearing of children, marital privacy and the use of contraceptives, and the preservation of the individual's capacity to procreate. See *Carey* v. *Population Services International*, 431 U.S. 678 (1977); *Moore* v. *City of East Cleveland, supra*; *Eisenstadt* v. *Baird*, 405 U.S. 438 (1972); *Griswold* v. *Connecticut, supra*; *Skinner* v. *Oklahoma*, 316 U.S. 535 (1942); *Pierce* v. *Society of Sisters*, 268 U.S. 510 (1925); *Meyer* v. *Nebraska*, 262 U.S. 390 (1923). Even if each of these cases was correctly decided and could be properly grounded in rights that are "implicit in the concept of ordered liberty" or "deeply rooted in this Nation's history and tradition," the issues in the cases cited differ from those at stake where abortion is concerned. As the Court appropriately recognized in *Roe* v. *Wade*, "[t]he pregnant woman cannot be isolated in her privacy," 410 U.S., at 159; the termination of a pregnancy typically involves the destruction of another entity: the fetus. However one answers the metaphysical or theological question whether it is a "person" as that term is used in the Constitution, one must at least recognize, first, that the fetus is an entity that bears in its cells all the genetic information that characterizes a member of the species *homo sapiens* and distinguishes an individual member of that species from all others, and second, that there is no nonarbitrary line separating a fetus from a child or, indeed, an adult human being. Given that the continued existence and development—that is to say, the *life*—of such an entity are so directly at stake in the woman's decision whether or not to terminate her pregnancy, that decision must be recognized as *sui generis*, different in kind from the others that the Court has protected under the rubric of personal or family privacy and autonomy.[2] Accordingly, the decisions cited by the Court both in *Roe* and in its opinion today as precedent for the fundamental nature of the liberty to choose abortion do not, even if all are accepted as valid, dictate the Court's classification.

If the woman's liberty to choose an abortion is fundamental, then, it is not because any of our precedents (aside from *Roe* itself) commands or justifies that result; it can only be because protection for this unique choice is itself "implicit in the concept of ordered liberty" or, perhaps, "deeply rooted in this Nation's history and tradition." It seems clear to me that it is neither. The Court's opinion in *Roe* itself convincingly refutes the notion that the abortion liberty is deeply rooted in the history or tradition of our people, as does the continuing and deep division of the people themselves over the question of abortion. As for the notion that choice in the matter of abortion is implicit in the concept of ordered liberty, it seems apparent to me that a free, egalitarian, and democratic society does not presuppose any particular rule or set of rules with respect to abortion. And again, the fact that many men and women of good will and high commitment to constitutional government place themselves on both sides of the abortion controversy strengthens my own conviction that the values animating the Constitution do not compel recognition of the abortion liberty as fundamental. In so denominating that liberty, the Court engages not in constitutional interpretation, but in the unrestrained imposition of its own, extraconstitutional value preferences.[3]

B

A second, equally basic error infects the Court's decision in *Roe v. Wade*. The detailed set of rules governing state restrictions on abortion that the Court first articulated in *Roe* and has since refined and elaborated presupposes not only that the woman's liberty to choose an abortion is fundamental, but also that the state's countervailing interest in protecting fetal life (or, as the Court would have it, "potential human life," 410 U.S., at 159) becomes "compelling" only at the point at which the fetus is viable. As JUSTICE O'CONNOR pointed out three years ago in her dissent in *Akron* v. *Akron Center for Reproductive Health*, 462 U.S. 416, 461 (1983), the Court's choice of viability as the point at which the state's interest becomes compelling is entirely arbitrary. The Court's "explanation" for the line it has drawn is that the state's interest becomes compelling at viability "because the fetus then presumably has the capacity of meaningful life outside the mother's womb." 410 U.S., at 163. As one critic of *Roe* has observed, this argument "mistakes a definition for a syllogism." Ely, *The Wages of Crying Wolf: A Comment on* Roe v. Wade, 82 Yale L. J. 920, 924 (1973).

The governmental interest at issue is in protecting those who will be citizens if their lives are not ended in the womb. The substantiality of this interest is in no way dependent on the probability that the fetus may be capable of surviving outside the womb at any given point in its development, as the possibility of fetal survival is contingent on the state of medical practice and technology, factors that are in essence morally and constitutionally irrelevant. The State's interest is in the fetus as an entity in itself, and the character of this entity does not change at the point of viability under conventional medical wisdom. Accordingly, the State's interest, if compelling after viability, is equally compelling before viability.[4]

C

Both the characterization of the abortion liberty as fundamental and the denigration of the State's interest in preserving the lives of nonviable fetuses are essential to the detailed set of constitutional rules devised by the Court to limit the States' power to regulate abortion. If either or both of these facets of *Roe* v. *Wade* were rejected, a broad range of limitations on abortion (including outright prohibition) that are now unavailable to the States would again become constitutional possibilities.

In my view, such a state of affairs would be highly desirable from the standpoint of the Constitution. Abortion is a hotly contested moral and political issue. Such issues, in our society, are to be resolved by the will of the people, either as expressed through legislation or through the general principles they have already incorporated into the Constitution they have adopted.[5] *Roe* v. *Wade* implies that the people have already resolved the debate by weaving into the Constitution the values and principles that answer the issue. As I have argued, I believe it is clear that the people have never—not in 1787, 1791, 1868, or at any time since—done any such thing. I would return the issue to the people by overruling *Roe* v. *Wade*.

II

As it has evolved in the decisions of this Court, the freedom recognized by the Court in *Roe* v. *Wade* and its progeny is essentially a negative one, based not on the notion that abortion is a good in itself, but only on the view that the legitimate goals that may be served by state coercion of private choices regarding abortion are, at least under some circumstances, outweighed by the damage to individual autonomy and privacy that such coercion entails. In other words, the evil of abortion does not justify the evil of forbidding it. Cf. *Stanley* v. *Georgia*, 394 U.S. 557 (1969). But precisely because *Roe* v. *Wade* is not premised on the notion that abortion is itself desirable (either as a matter of constitutional entitlement or of social policy), the decision does not command the States to fund or encourage abortion, or even to approve of it. Rather, we have recognized that the States may legitimately adopt a policy of encouraging normal childbirth rather than abortion so long as the measures through which that policy is implemented do not amount to direct compulsion of the woman's choice regarding abortion. *Harris* v. *McRae*, 448 U.S. 297 (1980); *Maher* v. *Roe*, 432 U.S. 464 (1977); *Beal* v. *Doe*, 432 U.S. 438 (1977). The provisions before the Court today quite obviously represent the State's effort to implement such a policy.

The majority's opinion evinces no deference toward the State's legitimate policy. Rather, the majority makes it clear from the outset that it simply disapproves of any attempt by Pennsylvania to legislate in this area. The history of the state legislature's decade-long effort to pass a constitutional abortion statute is recounted as if it were evidence of some sinister conspiracy. See *ante*, at [270]. In fact, of course, the legislature's past failure to predict the evolution of the right first recognized in *Roe* v. *Wade* is understandable and is in itself no ground for condemnation. Moreover, the legislature's willingness to pursue permissible policies through means that go to the limits allowed by existing precedents is no sign of *mens rea*. The majority, however, seems to find it necessary to respond by changing the rules to invalidate what before would have seemed permissible. The result is a decision that finds no justification in the Court's previous holdings, departs from sound principles of constitutional and statutory interpretation, and unduly limits the state's power to implement the legitimate (and in some circumstances compelling) policy of encouraging normal childbirth in preference to abortion.

A

The Court begins by striking down statutory provisions designed to ensure that the woman's choice of an abortion is fully informed—that is, that she is aware not only of the reasons for having an abortion, but also of the risks associated with an abortion and the availability of assistance that might make the alternative of normal childbirth more attractive than it might otherwise appear. At first blush, the Court's action seems extraordinary: after all, *Roe* v. *Wade* purports to be about freedom of choice, and statutory provisions requiring that a woman seeking an abortion be afforded information regarding her decision not only do not limit her ability to choose abortion, but would also appear to enhance her freedom of choice by helping to ensure that her decision whether or not to terminate her pregnancy is an informed one. Indeed, maximization of the patient's freedom of choice—not restriction of his or her liberty—is generally perceived to be the principal value justifying the imposition of disclosure requirements upon physicians:

> "The root premise is the concept, fundamental in American jurisprudence, that '[e]very human being of adult years and sound mind has a right to determine what shall be done with his own body....' True consent to what happens to one's self is the informed exercise of a choice, and that entails an opportunity to evaluate knowledgeably the options available and the risks attendant upon each. The average patient has little or no understanding of the medical arts, and ordinarily has only his physician to whom he can look for enlightenment with which to reach an intelligent decision. From these almost axiomatic considerations springs the need, and in turn the requirement, of a reasonable divulgence by physician to patient to make such a decision possible." *Canterbury* v. *Spence*, 150 U.S. App. D. C. 263, 271, 464 F. 2d 772, 780 (1972).

One searches the majority's opinion in vain for a convincing reason why the apparently laudable policy of promoting informed consent becomes unconstitutional when the subject is abortion. The majority purports to find support in *Akron* v. *Akron Center for Reproductive Health, Inc.* 462 U.S. 416 (1983). But *Akron* is not controlling. The informed consent provisions struck down in that case, as characterized by the majority, required the physician to advance tendentious statements concerning the unanswerable question of when human life begins, to offer merely speculative descriptions of the anatomical features of the fetus carried by the woman seeking the abortion, and to recite a "parade of horribles" suggesting that abortion is "a particularly dangerous procedure." *Id.*, at 444–445. I have no quarrel with the general proposition, for which I read *Akron* to stand, that a campaign of state-promulgated disinformation cannot be justified in the name of "informed consent" or "freedom of choice." But the Pennsylvania statute before us cannot be accused of sharing the flaws of the ordinance at issue in *Akron*. As the majority concedes, the statute does not, on its face, require that the patient be given any information that is false or unverifiable. Moreover, it is unquestionable that all of the information required would be relevant in many cases to a woman's decision whether or not to obtain an abortion.

Why, then, is the statute unconstitutional? The majority's argument, while primarily rhetorical, appears to offer three answers. First, the information that must be provided will in some cases be irrelevant to the woman's decision. This is true. Its pertinence to the question of the statute's constitutionality, however, is beyond me. Legislators are ordinarily entitled to proceed on the basis of rational generalizations about the subject matter of legislation, and the existence of particular cases in which a feature of a statute performs no function (or is even counterproductive) ordinarily does not render the statute unconstitutional or even constitutionally suspect. Only where the statute is subject to heightened scrutiny by virtue of its impingement on some fundamental right or its employment of a suspect classification does the inprecision of the "fit" between the statute's ends and means become potentially damning. Here, there is nothing to trigger such scrutiny, for the statute does not directly infringe the allegedly fundamental right at issue—the woman's right to choose an abortion. Indeed, I fail to see how providing a woman with accurate information—whether relevant or irrelevant—could ever be deemed to impair *any* constitutionally protected interest (even if, as the majority hypothesizes, the information may upset her). Thus, the majority's observation that the statute may require the provision of irrelevant information in some cases is itself an irrelevancy.

Second, the majority appears to reason that the informed consent provisions are invalid because the information they require may increase the woman's "anxiety" about the procedure and even "influence" her in her choice. Again, both observations are undoubtedly true; but they by no means cast the constitutionality of the provisions into question. It is in the very nature of informed consent provisions that they may produce some anxiety in the patient and influence her in her choice. This is in fact their reason for existence, and—provided that the information required is accurate and non-misleading—it is an entirely salutary reason. If information may reasonably affect the patient's choice, the patient should have that information; and, as one authority has observed, "the greater the likelihood that particular information will influence [the patient's] decision, the more essential the information arguably becomes for securing her informed consent." Appleton, Doctors, Patients and the Constitution, 63 Wash. U.L.Q. 183, 211 (1985). That the result of the provision of information may be that some women will forgo abortions by no means suggests that providing the information is unconstitutional, for the ostensible objective of *Roe* v. *Wade* is not maximizing the number of abortions, but maximizing choice. Moreover, our decisions in *Maher*, *Beal*, and *Harris* v. *McRae* all indicate that the State may encourage women to make their choice in favor of childbirth rather than abortion, and the provision of accurate information regarding abortion and its alternatives is a reasonable and fair means of achieving that objective.

Third, the majority concludes that the informed consent provisions are invalid because they "intrud[e] upon the discretion of the pregnant woman's physician," *ante*, at [277], violate "the privacy of the informed-consent dialogue between the woman and her physician," *ibid.*, and "officially structur[e]" that dialogue, *id.*, at [277]. The provisions thus constitute "state medicine" that "infringes upon [the physician's] professional responsibilities." *Ibid.* This is nonsensical. I can concede that the Constitution extends its protection to certain zones of personal autonomy and privacy, see *Griswold* v. *Connecticut*, 381 U.S. 479, 502 (1965) (WHITE, J., concurring in judgment), and I can understand, if not share, the notion that that protection may extend to a woman's decision regarding abortion. But I cannot concede the possibility that the Constitution provides more than minimal protection for the manner in which a physician practices his or her profession or the "dialogues" in which he or she chooses to participate in the course of treating patients. I had thought it clear that regulation of the practice of medicine, like regulation of other professions and of economic affairs generally, was a matter peculiarly within the competence of legislatures, and that such regulation was subject to review only for rationality. See, *e.g.*, *Williamson* v. *Lee Optical of Oklahoma, Inc.*, 348 U.S. 483 (1955).

Were the Court serious about the need for strict scrutiny of regulations that infringe on the "judgment" of medical professionals, "structure their relations with their patients, and amount to "state medicine," there is no telling how many state and federal statutes (not to mention principles of state tort law) governing the practice of medicine might be condemned. And of course, there would be no reason why a concern for professional freedom could be confined to the medical profession; nothing in the Constitution indicates a preference for the liberty of doctors over that of lawyers, accountants, bakers, or brickmakers. Accordingly, if the State may not "structure" the dialogue between doctor and patient, it should also follow that the State may not, for example, require attorneys to disclose to their clients information concerning the risks of representing the client in a particular proceeding. Of course, we upheld such disclosure requirements only last Term. See *Zauderer* v. *Office Disciplinary Counsel*, 471 U.S. [626] (1985).

The rationale for state efforts to regulate the practice of a profession or vocation is simple: the government is entitled not to trust members of a profession to police themselves, and accordingly the legislature may for the most part impose such restrictions on the practice of a profession or business as it may find necessary to the protection of the public. This is precisely the rationale for infringing the professional freedom of doctors by imposing disclosure requirements upon them: "Respect for the patient's right of self-determination on particular therapy demands a standard set by law for physicians rather than one which physicians may or may not impose upon themselves." *Canterbury* v. *Spence*, 464 F. 2d, at 784. Unless one is willing to recast entirely the law with respect to the legitimacy of state regulation of professional conduct, the obvious rationality of the policy of promoting informed patient choice on the subject of abortion must defeat any claim that the disclosure requirements imposed by Pennsylvania are invalid because they infringe on "professional freedom" or on the "physician-patient relationship."

I do not really believe that the Court's invocation of professional freedom signals a retreat from the principle that the Constitution is largely unconcerned with the substantive aspects of governmental regulation of professional and business relations. Clearly, the majority is uninterested in undermining the edifice of post-New Deal constitutional law by extending its holding to cases that do not concern the issue of abortion. But if one assumes, as I do, that the majority is unwilling to commit itself to the implications of that part of its rhetoric which smacks of economic due process rights for physicians, it becomes obvious that the talk of "infringement of professional responsibility" is mere window-dressing for a holding that must stand or fall on other grounds. And because the informed-consent provisions do not infringe the essential right at issue—the right of the woman to choose to have an abortion—the majority's conclusion that the provisions are unconstitutional is without foundation.

B

The majority's decision to strike down the reporting requirements of the statute is equally extraordinary. The requirements obviously serve legitimate purposes. The information contained in the reports is highly relevant to the State's efforts to enforce §3210(a) of the statute, which forbids abortion of viable fetuses except when necessary to the mother's health. The information concerning complications plainly serves the legitimate goal of advancing the state of medical knowledge concerning maternal and fetal health. See *Planned Parenthood of Central Mo. v. Danforth*, 428 U.S., at 80. Given that the subject of abortion is a matter of considerable public interest and debate (constrained to some extent, of course, by the preemptive effect of this Court's ill-conceived constitutional decisions), the collection and dissemination of demographic information concerning abortions is clearly a legitimate goal of public policy. Moreover, there is little reason to believe that the required reports, though fairly detailed, would impose an undue burden on physicians and impede the ability of their parents to obtain abortions, as all of the information required would necessarily be readily available to a physician who had performed an abortion. Accordingly, under this Court's prior decisions in this area, the reporting requirements are constitutional. *Planned Parenthood Assn. of Kansas City, Mo., Inc. v. Ashcroft*, 462 U.S. 476, 486–490 (1983) (opinion of POWELL, J.); *id.*, at 505 (opinion of O'CONNOR, J.); *Planned Parenthood of Central Missouri v. Danforth, supra*, 428 U.S. at 79-81.

Nonetheless, the majority strikes down the reporting requirements because it finds that notwithstanding the explicit statutory command that the reports be made public only in a manner ensuring anonymity, "the amount of information about [the patient] and the circumstances under which she had an abortion are so detailed that identification is likely," *ante* at [280], and the "[i]dentification is the obvious purpose of these extreme reporting requirements," *ibid.* Where these "findings" come from is mysterious, to say the least. The Court of Appeals did not make any such findings on the record before it, and the District Court expressly found that "the requirements of confidentiality in §3214(e) regarding the identity of both patient and physician prevent any invasion of privacy which could present a legally significant burden on the abortion decision." 552 F. Supp. 791, 804 (ED Pa. 1982). Rather than pointing to anything in the record that demonstrates that the District Court's conclusion is erroneous, the majority resorts to the handy, but mistaken, solution of substituting its own view of the facts and strikes down the statute.

I can accept the proposition that a statute whose purpose and effect are to allow harassment and intimidation of citizens for their constitutionally protected conduct is unconstitutional, but the majority's action in striking down the Pennsylvania statute on this basis is procedurally and substantively indefensible. First, it reflects a complete disregard for the principle, embodied in Rule 52(a), that an appellate court must defer to a trial court's findings of facts unless those findings are clearly erroneous. The Rule is expressly applicable to findings of fact that constitute the grounds for a district court's action granting or refusing a preliminary injunction, and, of course, the Rule limits this Court to the same degree as it does any other federal appellate court, see *United States* v. *General Dynamics Corp.*, 415 U.S. 486 (1974).

Second, the majority has seriously erred in purporting to make a final determination of fact, conclusive of the constitutionality of the statute, on a motion for preliminary injunction. In so doing, the Court overlooks the principle that although a district court's findings of fact on a motion for a preliminary injunction are entitled to deference on appeal from the grant or denial of preliminary relief, "the findings of fact ... made by a court granting a preliminary injunction are *not* binding at trial on the merits" because "a preliminary injunction is customarily granted on the basis of procedures that are less formal and evidence that is less complete than in a trial on the merits." *University of Texas* v. *Camenisch*, 451 U.S. 390, 395 (1981) (emphasis added). What *Camenisch* stated to be true customarily is also true in this case: the record on which the motion for preliminary injunction was decided in the trial court consisted solely of affidavits and a stipulation of undisputed facts, none of which provides a sufficient basis for a conclusive finding on the complex question of the motive and effect of the reporting requirements and the adequacy of the statute's protection of the anonymity of doctors and patients. Issuing what amounts to a final declaratory judgment on the constitutionality of the statute under these circumstances is highly inappropriate.

Finally, in addition to being procedurally flawed, the majority's holding is substantively suspect. The information contained in the reports identifies the patient on the basis of age, race, marital status, and "political subdivision" of residence; the remainder of the information included in the reports concerns the medical aspects of the abortion. It is implausible that a particular patient could be identified on the basis of the combination of the general identifying information and the specific medical information in these reports by anyone who did not already know (at a minimum) that the woman had been pregnant and obtained an abortion. Accordingly, the provisions pose little or no threat to the woman's privacy.

In sum, there is no basis here even for a preliminary injunction against the reporting provisions of the statute, much less for a final determination that the provisions are unconstitutional.

C

The majority resorts to linguistic nit-picking in striking down the provision requiring physicians aborting viable fetuses to use the method of abortion most likely to result in fetal survival unless that method would pose a "significantly greater medical risk to the life or health of the pregnant woman" than would other available methods. The majority concludes that the statute's use of the word "significantly" indicates that the statute represents an unlawful "trade-off" between the woman's health and the chance of fetal survival. Not only is this conclusion based on a wholly unreasonable interpretation of the statute, but the statute would also be constitutional even if it meant what the majority says it means.

The majority adopts the Court of Appeals' view that the statute's use of the term "significantly" renders it "not susceptible to a construction that does not require the mother to bear an increased medical risk in order to save her viable fetus." *Ante*, at [281] (quoting 737 F. 2d 283, 300 (CA3 1984)). The term "significant" in this context, however, is most naturally read as synonymous with the terms "meaningful," "cognizable," "appreciable," or "non-negligible." That is, the statute requires only that the risk be a real and identifiable one. Surely, if the State's interest in preserving the life of a viable fetus is, as *Roe* purported to recognize, a compelling one, the State is at the very least entitled to demand that that interest not be subordinated to a purported maternal health risk that is in fact wholly insubstantial. The statute, on its face, demands no more than this of a doctor performing an abortion of a viable fetus.

Even if the Pennsylvania statute is properly interpreted as requiring a pregnant woman seeking abortion of a viable fetus to endure a method of abortion chosen to protect the health of the fetus despite the existence of an alternative that in some substantial degree is more protective of her own health, I am not convinced that the statute is unconstitutional. The Court seems to read its earlier opinion in *Colautti* v. *Franklin*, 439 U.S. 379 (1979), as incorporating a *holding* that trade-offs between the health of the pregnant woman and the survival of her viable fetus are constitutionally impermissible under *Roe* v. *Wade*. Of course, *Colautti* held no such thing: the Court there stated only that it did not address the "serious ethical and constitutional difficulties" that such a trade-off would present. 439 U.S., at 400.⁶ Nothing in *Colautti* or any of the Court's previous abortion decisions compels the *per se* "trade-off" rule the Court adopts today.

The Court's ruling in this respect is not even *consistent* with its decision in *Roe* v. *Wade*. In *Roe*, the Court conceded that the State's interest in preserving the life of a viable fetus is a compelling one, and the Court has never disavowed that concession. The Court now holds that this compelling interest cannot justify *any* regulation that imposes a quantifiable medical risk upon the pregnant woman who seeks to abort a viable fetus: if attempting to save the fetus imposed any additional risk of injury to the woman, she must be permitted to kill it. This holding hardly accords with the usual understanding of the term "compelling interest," whcih we have used to describe those govern- mental interests that are so weighty as to justify substantial and ordinarily impermissible impositions on the individual—impositions that, I had thought, could include the infliction of some degree of risk of physical harm. The most obvious illustration of this principle may be found in the opinion of the elder Justice Harlan in *Jacobson* v. *Massachusetts*, 197 U.S. 11, 29 [   ] (1905): "The liberty secured by the Fourteenth Amendment . . . consists, in part, in the right of a person 'to live and work where he will,' *Allgeyer* v. *Lousiana*, 165 U.S. 578 [   ] (1897); and yet he may be compelled, by force if need be, against his will and without regard to his personal wishes or his pecuniary interests, . . . to take his place in the ranks of the army of his country and risk the chance of being shot down in its defense." The actual holding of *Jacobson* provides another illustration, more pertinent to this particular case: the Court there sustained a regulation requiring all adult citizens of Cambridge, Massachusetts to be vaccinated against smallpox, notwithstanding that exposure to vaccination carried with it a statistical possibility of serious illness and even death. If, as I believe these examples demonstrate, a compelling state interest may justify the imposition of some physical danger upon an individual, and if, as the Court has held, the State has a compelling interest in the preservation of the life of a viable fetus, I find the majority's unwillingness to tolerate the imposition of *any* nonnegligible risk of injury to a pregnant woman in order to protect the life of her viable fetus in the course of an abortion baffling.

The Court's ruling today that any trade-off between the woman's health and fetal survival is impermissible is not only inconsistent with *Roe*'s recognition of a compelling state interest in viable fetal life; it directly contradicts one of the essential holdings of *Roe*—that is, that the State may forbid *all* post-viability abortions except when *necessary* to protect the life or health of the pregnant woman. As is evident, this holding itself involves a trade-off between maternal health and protection of the fetus, for it plainly permits the State to forbid a postviability abortion even when such an abortion may be statistically safer than carrying the pregnancy to term, provided that the abortion is not medically necessary.[7] The trade-off contained in the Pennsylvania statute, even as interpreted by the majority, is no different in kind: the State has simply required that when an abortion of some kind is medically necessary, it shall be conducted so as to spare the fetus (to the greatest degree possible) unless a method less protective of the fetus is itself to some degree medically necessary for the woman. That this choice may involve the imposition of some risk on the woman undergoing the abortion should be no more troublesome than that a prohibition on nonnecessary postviability abortions may involve the imposition of some risk on women who are thereby forced to continue their pregnancies to term; yet for some reason, the Court concludes that whereas the trade-offs it devises are compelled by the Constitution, the essentially indistinguishable trade-off the State has attempted is foreclosed. This cannot be the law.

The framework of rights and interests devised by the Court in *Roe* v. *Wade* indicates that just as a State may prohibit a post-viability abortion unless it is necessary to protect the life or health of the woman, the State may require that postviability abortions be conducted using the method most protective of the fetus unless a less protective method is necessary to protect the life or health of the woman. Under this standard, the Pennsylvania statute—which does not require the woman to accept any significant health risks to protect the fetus—is plainly constitutional.

D

The Court strikes down the statute's second-physician requirement because, in its view, the existence of a medical emergency requiring an immediate abortion to save the life of the pregnant woman would not be a defense to a prosecution under the statute. The Court does not question the proposition, established in the *Ashcroft* case, that a second-physician requirement accompanied by an exception for emergencies is a permissible means of vindicating the compelling state interest in protecting the lives of viable fetuses. Accordingly, the majority's ruling on this issue does not on its face involve a substantial departure from the Court's previous decisions.

What is disturbing about the Court's opinion on this point is not the general principle on which it rests, but the manner in which that principle is applied. The Court brushes aside the fact that the section of the statute in which the second-physician requirement is imposed states that "[i]t shall be a complete defense to *any* charge brought against a physician for violating the requirements *of this section* that he had concluded, in good faith, in his best medical judgment, . . . that the abortion was necessary to preserve maternal life or health" (emphasis added). 18 Pa. Cons. Stat. §3210(a) (1982). This language is obviously susceptible of the construction the State advances: namely, that it is a defense to a charge of violating the second-physician requirement that the physician performing the abortion believed that performing an abortion in the absence of a second physician was necessary to the life or health of the mother.

The Court's rejection of this construction is based on its conclusion that the statutory language "does not relate to the second-physician requirement" and that "its words are not words of emergency." *Ante*, at [282]. This reasoning eludes me. The defense of medical necessity "relates" to any charge that a doctor has violated one of the requirements of the section in which it appears, and the second-physician requirement is imposed by that section. The defense thus quite evidently "relates" to the second-physician requirement. True, the "words" of the defense are not "words of emergency," but words of necessity. Why this should make a difference is unclear: a defense of medical necessity is fully as protective of the interests of the pregnant woman as a defense of "emergency." The Court falls back, *ibid.*, on the notion that the legislature "knows how to provide a medical-emergency exception when it chooses to do so." No doubt. But the legislature obviously also "knows how" to provide a medical necessity exception, and it has done so. Why this exception is insufficient is unexplained and inexplicable.

The Court's rejection of a perfectly plausible reading of the statute flies in the face of the principle—which until today I had thought applicable to abortion statutes as well as to other legislative enactments—that "[w]here fairly possible, courts should construe a statute to avoid a danger of unconstitutionality." *Planned Parenthood Assn.* v. *Ashcroft*, 462 U.S., at 493. The Court's reading is obviously based on an entirely different principle: that in cases involving abortion, a permissible reading of a statute is to be avoided at all costs. Not sharing this viewpoint, I cannot accept the majority's conclusion that the statute does not provide for the equivalent of a defense of emergency.[8]

E

Finally, the majority refuses to vacate the preliminary injunction entered against the enforcement of the parental notice and consent provisions of the statute. See *ante*, at [274, 284 n.9]. The reason offered is that the propriety of the injunction depends upon the adequacy of the rules, recently promulgated by the Pennsylvania Supreme Court, setting forth procedures by which a minor desiring an abortion may speedily and confidentially obtain either judicial approval of her decision to obtain an abortion or a judicial determination that she herself is capable of an informed consent to the procedure. The Court concludes that review of the rules is best carried out in the first instance in the District Court.

The Court's decision in *Ashcroft*, however, compels the conclusion that the Third Circuit erred in directing that the operation of the parental notice and consent provisions be enjoined pending promulgation of the required rules; accordingly, the injunction should be vacated irrespective of the adequacy of those rules. As the Court of Appeals apparently recognized, the Pennsylvania statute, on its face, is substantively identical to that upheld by the Court in *Ashcroft*; thus, the sole basis for the injunction ordered by the Court of Appeals was the absence of procedural rules implementing the statute. What the Court of Appeals failed to recognized was that this Court denied relief to the plaintiffs challenging the statute in *Ashcroft* despite the same purported defect: in that case, as in this, the State Supreme Court had not yet promulgated rules establishing the expedited procedures called for by the statute. Nonetheless, as JUSTICE POWELL's opinion explained, the plaintiffs were not entitled to any relief against enforcement of the statutory scheme, as "[t]here is no reason to believe that [the State] will not expedite any appeal consistent with the mandate in our prior opinions." 462 U.S., at 491, n. 16 [   ]. Similarly, there was no reason here for the Court of Appeals to believe that Pennsylvania would not provide for the adequate, expedited procedures contemplated by the statute; thus, its entry of an injunction against enforcement of the statute was erroneous.

III

The decision today appears symptomatic of the Court's own insecurity over its handiwork in *Roe* v. *Wade* and the cases following that decision. Aware that in *Roe* it essentially created something out of nothing and that there are many in this country who hold that decision to be basically illegitimate, the Court responds defensively. Perceiving, in a statute implementing the State's legitimate policy of preferring child-birth to abortion, a threat to criticism of the decision in *Roe* v. *Wade*, the majority indiscriminately strikes down statutory provisions that in no way contravene the right recognized in *Roe*. I do not share the warped point of view of the majority, nor can I follow the tortuous path the majority treads in proceeding to strike down the statute before us. I dissent.

Notes

1. I shall, for the most part, leave to one side the Court's somewhat extraordinary procedural rulings. I do not strongly disagree with the Court's decision to read a finality requirement into 28 U.S.C. §1254(2), although I would have thought it incumbent on the Court to explain why the Court of Appeals' judgment as to the statutory provisions before us today, which represents a definitive ruling on their constitutionality, is not sufficiently "final" to satisfy the jurisdictional statute as interpreted by the Court.

As for the Court's ruling that it is permissible for an appellate court to resolve an appeal from the grant or the denial of a preliminary injunction by issuing a final judgment as to the constitutionality of a statute, I do not disagree that this may, in rare cases, be an appropriate course of action where the constitutional issues are clear. I would stress that this is by no means the preferred course of action in the run of cases, and I assume that the majority's opinion is not to the contrary. I do disagree quite strongly with the majority's opinion of this principle here, as I believe, contrary to the majority, that it is quite evident that the statute before us is constitutional in its face. I also believe, as will become evident, that at least one of the Court's rulings is exceedingly inappropriate in view of the preliminary posture of this case even if the majority's legal premises are accepted.

2. That the abortion decision, like the decisions protected in *Griswold*, *Eisenstadt*, and *Carey*, concerns childbearing (or, more generally, family life) in no sense necessitates a holding that the liberty to choose abortion is "fundamental." That the decision involves the destruction of the fetus renders it different in kind from the decision not to conceive in the first place. This difference does not go merely to the weight of the state interest in regulating abortion; it affects as well the characterization of the liberty interest itself. For if the liberty to make certain decisions with respect to contraception without governmental constraint is "fundamental," it is not only because those decisions are "serious" and "important" to the individual, see *ante*, at [290] (STEVENS, J., concurring), but also because some value of privacy or individual autonomy that is somehow implicit in the scheme of ordered liberties established by the Constitution supports a judgment that such decisions are none of government's business. The same cannot be said where, as here, the individual is not "isolated in her privacy."

My point can be illustrated by drawing on a related area in which fundamental liberty interests have been found: childrearing. The Court's decisions in *Moore* v. *East Cleveland*, *Pierce* v. *Society of Sisters*, and *Meyer* v. *Nebraska* can be read for the proposition that parents have a fundamental liberty to make decisions with respect to the upbringing of their children. But no one would suggest that this fundamental liberty extends to assaults committed upon children by their parents. It is not the case that parents have a fundamental liberty to engage in such activities and that the State may intrude to prevent them only because it has a compelling interest in the well-being of children; rather, such activities, by their very nature, should be viewed as outside the scope of the fundamental liberty interest.

3. JUSTICE STEVENS asserts, *ante*, at [290], that I am "quite wrong in suggesting that the Court is imposing value preferences on anyone else" when it denominates the liberty to choose abortion as "fundamental" (in contradistinction to such other, nonfundamental liberties as the liberty to use dangerous drugs or to operate a business without governmental interference) and thereby disempowers state electoral majorities from legislating in this area. I can only respond that I cannot conceive of a definition of the phrase "imposing value preferences" that does not encompass the Court's action.

JUSTICE STEVENS also suggests that it is the legislative majority that has engaged in "the unrestrained imposition of its own, extraconstitutional value choices" when a state legislature restricts the availability of abortion. *Ibid.* But a legislature, unlike a court, has the inherent power to do so unless its choices are constitutionally *forbidden*, which, in my view, is not the case here.

4. Contrary to JUSTICE STEVENS' suggestion, *ante*, at [290], this is no more a "theological" position than is the Court's own judgment that viability is the point at which the state interest becomes compelling. (Interestingly, JUSTICE STEVENS omits any real effort to defend this judgment.) The point is that the specific interest the Court has recognized as compelling after the point of viability—that is, the interest in protecting "potential human life"—is present as well before viability, and the point of viability seems to bear no discernible relationship to the strength of that interest. Thus, there is no basis for concluding that the essential character of the state interest becomes transformed at the point of viability.

Further, it is self-evident that neither the legislative decision to assert a state interest in fetal life before viability nor the judicial decision to recognize that interest as compelling constitutes an impermissible "religious" decision merely because it coincides with the belief of one or more religions. Certainly the fact that the prohibition of murder coincides with one of the Ten Commandments does not render a State's interest in its murder statutes less than compelling, nor are legislative and judicial decisions concerning the use of the death penalty tainted by their correspondence to varying religious views on that subject. The simple, and perhaps unfortunate, fact of the matter is that in determining whether to assert an interest in fetal life, a State cannot avoid taking a position that will correspond to some religious beliefs and contradict others. The same is true to some extent with respect to the choice this Court faces in characterizing an asserted state interest in fetal life, for denying that such an interest is a "compelling" one necessarily entails a negative resolution of the "religious" issue of the humanity of the fetus, whereas accepting the State's interest as compelling reflects at least tolerance for a state decision that is congruent with the equally "religious" position that human life begins at conception. Faced with such a decision, the most appropriate course of action for the Court is to defer to a legislative resolution of the issue: in other words, if a state legislature asserts an interest in protecting fetal life, I can see no satisfactory basis for *denying* that it is compelling.

5. JUSTICE STEVENS, see *ante*, at [290 n.4], finds a contradiction between my recognition that constitutional analysis requires more than mere textual analysis or a search for the specific intent of the Framers, *supra* at [290 n.4], and

my assertion that it is ultimately the will of the people that is the source of whatever values are incorporated in the Constitution. The fallacy of JUSTICE STEVENS' argument is glaring. The rejection of what has been characterized as "clause-bound" interpretivism, J. Ely, Democracy and Distrust 12 (1980), does not necessarily carry with it a rejection of the notion that constitutional adjudication is a search for values and principles that are implicit (and explicit) in the structure of rights and institutions that the people have themselves created. The implications of those values for the resolution of particular issues will in many if not most cases not have been explicitly considered when the values themselves were chosen—indeed, there will be some cases in which those who framed the provisions incorporating certain principles into the Constitution will be found to have been incorrect in their assessment of the consequences of their decision. See, *e.g.*, *Brown* v. *Board of Education*, 347 U.S. 483 [   ] (1953). Nonetheless, the hallmark of a correct decision of constitutional law is that it rests on principles selected by the people through their Constitution, and not merely on the personal philosophies, be they libertarian or authoritarian, of the judges of the majority. While constitutional adjudication involves judgments of value, it remains the case that some values are indeed "extraconstitutional," in that they have no roots in the Constitution that the people have chosen. The Court's decision in *Lochner* v. *New York*, 198 U.S. 45 (1905), was wrong because it rested on the Court's belief that the liberty to engage in a trade or occupation without governmental regulation was somehow fundamental—an assessment of value that was unsupported by the Constitution. I believe that *Roe* v. *Wade*—and today's decision as well— rests on similarly extraconstitutional assessments of the value of the liberty to choose an abortion.

6. Interestingly, the Court's statement seems to have assumed that the Court would have had the same authority over "ethical questions" as "constitutional issues" had it chosen to reach them—an illuminating revelation of the state of the Court's jurisprudence in this area.

7. Surely it cannot be argued that any abortion that is safer than delivery is medically necessary, since under such a definition an abortion would be medically necessary in all pregnancies.

8. Even if I were to accept the majority's conclusion that the medical necessity defense of §3210(a) is not specifically applicable to charges brought under §3210(c), I would not strike down the statute. Under Pennsylvania criminal law, justification is a defense, see 18 Pa. Cons. Stat. §502 (1982), and, under the general rule of justification, conduct is deemed justified if "the actor believes [it] to be necessary to avoid a harm or evil to . . . another," and "the harm or evil sought to be avoided by such conduct is greater than that sought to be prevented by the law defining the offense charged." §503(a)(1). I have little doubt that a Pennsylvania court applying this statute would find noncompliance with the second-physician rule justified where necessary to save the life of the pregnant woman.

Supreme Court of the United States

No. 84–495

RICHARD THORNBURGH, ET AL., APPELLANTS V.
AMERICAN COLLEGE OF OBSTETRICIANS
AND GYNECOLOGISTS ET AL.

On Appeal from the United States Court of Appeals
for the Third Circuit

[June 11, 1986]

JUSTICE O'CONNOR, with whom JUSTICE REHNQUIST joins, dissenting.

This Court's abortion decisions have already worked a major distortion in the Court's constitutional jurisprudence. See *Akron* v. *Akron Center for Reproductive Health, Inc.*, 462 U.S. 416, 452 (1983) (O'CONNOR, J., dissenting). Today's decision goes further, and makes it painfully clear that no legal rule or doctrine is safe from ad hoc nullification by this Court when an occasion for its application arises in a cases involving state regulation of abortion. The permissible scope of abortion regulation is not the only constitutional issue on which this Court is divided, but—except when it comes to abortion—the Court has generally refused to let such disagreements, however long-standing or deeply felt, prevent it from evenhandedly applying uncontroversial legal doctrines to cases that come before it. See *Heckler* v. *Chaney*, 470 U.S. [821], [   ] (1985), (BRENNAN, J., concurring) (differences over the validity of the death penalty under the Eighth Amendment should not influence the Court's consideration of a question of statutory administrative law). That the Court's unworkable scheme for constitutionalizing the regulation of abortion has had this institutionally debilitating effect should not be surprising, however, since the Court is not suited to the expansive role it has claimed for itself in the series of cases that began with *Roe* v. *Wade*, 410 U.S. 113 (1973).

The Court today holds that "[t]he Court of Appeals correctly invalidated the specified provisions of Pennsylvania's 1982 Abortion Control Act." *Ante,* at [283]. In so doing, the Court prematurely decides serious constitutional questions on an inadequate record, in contravention of settled principles of constitutional adjudication and procedural fairness. The constitutionality of the challenged provisions was not properly before the Court of Appeals, and is not properly before this Court. There has been no trial on the merits, and appellants have had no opportunity to develop facts that might have a bearing on the constitutionality of the statute. The only question properly before the Court is whether or not a preliminary injunction should have been issued to restrain enforcement of the challenged provisions pending trial on the merits. This Court's decisions in *Akron* v. *Akron Center for Reproductive Health, supra, Planned Parenthood Assn. of Kansas City, Mo., Inc.* v. *Ashcroft*, 462 U.S. 476 (1983), and *Simopoulos* v. *Virginia*, 462 U.S. 506 (1983), do not establish a likelihood that appellees would succeed on the merits of their constitutional claims sufficient to warrant overturning the District Court's denial of a preliminary injunction. Under the approach to abortion regulation outlined in my dissenting opinion in *Akron*, to which I adhere, it is even clearer that no preliminary injunction should have issued. I therefore dissent.

I

The only issue before the District Court in this case was whether to grant appellees' motion for a preliminary injunction against enforcement of Pennsylvania's Abortion Control Act. The limited record before the District Court consisted of affidavits submitted by appellees, the parties' memoranda of law, the Act itself, including the findings of the Pennsylvania Legislature, and a stipulation of uncontested facts. As the District Judge noted, this stipulation "was entered into solely for the purpose of the motion for preliminary injunction." 552 F. Supp. 791, 794, n. 1 (ED Pa. 1982). Indeed, the parties expressly provided that the stipulation should be "without prejudice to any party's right to controvert any facts or to prove any additional facts at any later proceeding in this action." App. 9a-10a. In light of the stipulation of uncontested facts, no testimony or evidence was submitted at the hearing on the motion for a preliminary injunction.

In these circumstances, the District Judge's consideration of the motion before him was governed by the black-letter law recapitulated in *University of Texas* v. *Camenisch*, 451 U.S. 390, 395 (1981):

> "The purpose of a preliminary injunction is merely to preserve the relative positions of the parties until a trial on the merits can be held. Given this limited purpose, and given the haste that is often necessary if those positions are to be preserved, a preliminary injunction is customarily granted on the basis of procedures that are less formal and evidence that is less complete than in a trial on the merits. A party thus is not required to prove his case in full at a preliminary injunction hearing, and the findings of fact and conclusions of law made by a court granting a preliminary injunction are not binding at trial on the merits. In light of these considerations, it is generally inappropriate for a federal court at the preliminary injunction stage to give a final judgment on the merits.
>
> "Should an expedited decision on the merits be appropriate, Rule 65(a)(2) of the Federal Rules of Civil Procedure provides a means of securing one. That Rule permits a court to 'order the trial of the action on the merits to be advanced and consolidated with the hearing of the application.' Before such an order may issue, however, the courts have commonly required that 'the parties should normally receive clear and unambiguous notice [of the court's intent to consolidate the trial and the hearing] either before the hearing commences or at a time which will still afford the parties a full opportunity to present their respective cases'" (citations omitted).

The District Judge scrupulously adhered to these settled principles. He granted the preliminary injunction as to one provision of the Act, and denied preliminary relief as to all the other challenged provisions. Having seen no occasion to issue a Rule 65 order, he properly refrained from rendering final judgment on the merits by declaratory judgment or otherwise. That the District Judge understood the preliminary nature of the proceedings, and ruled accordingly, is incontrovertible:

> "I have applied the traditional criteria applicable to a motion for preliminary injunction: likelihood of success on the merits, irreparable harm if the relief is not granted, possibility of harm to the non-moving party, and where relevant, harm to the public. Given the importance of

the right involved in this litigation, I have assumed that if the plaintiffs were able to show likelihood of success on the merits, then the irreparable harm requirement would be met. I conclude that in only one instance, the 24-hour waiting period, did the plaintiffs carry their burden of demonstrating likelihood of success on the merits.

*   *   *   *   *   *   *

"My adjudication is limited to the plaintiff's request for a *preliminary* injunction. It is circumscribed by the record produced by the parties and the arguments advanced in the briefs on this motion. After applying the criteria for a preliminary injunction, I conclude that the only portion of the Act which the plaintiffs have demonstrated should be preliminarily enjoined is the 24-hour waiting period. In all other respects, the plaintiffs have failed to show a right to a preliminary injunction pending the outcome of the trial on the merits." 552 F. Supp., at 811 (emphasis in original).

The District Judge correctly discerned that "[t]he traditional standard for granting a preliminary injunction requires a plaintiff to show that in the absence of its issuance he will suffer irreparable injury and also that he is likely to prevail on the merits." *Doran* v. *Salem Inn, Inc.,* 422 U.S. 922, 931 (1975). Unsurprisingly, the likelihood of success on the merits emerged, in the District Judge's view, as the most important factor in determining whether an injunction should issue in this case. In sum, when the District Judge denied appellees' motion for a preliminary injunction, he faithfully applied uncontroversial criteria for ruling on such motions and rendered a decision that "was not in any sense intended as a final decision as to the constitutionality of the challenged statute." *Brown* v. *Chote,* 411 U.S. 452, 456 (1973).

When the appeal was taken to the Court of Appeals for the Third Circuit, that court's review should have been limited to determining whether the District Court had abused its discretion in denying *preliminary* relief. *Doran, supra,* 422 U.S. at 931–932; *Brown, supra,* 411 U.S. at 457. If the Court of Appeals concluded that the District Court had committed legal errors that infected its assessment of the likelihood that appellees would succeed on the merits, the Court of Appeals should then have addressed the remaining factors that make up the preliminary injunction inquiry. If it concluded that denial of the preliminary injunction was an abuse of discretion, it should have entered judgment providing for entry of a preliminary injunction. What it should *not* have done, and what it did do, was to issue a final, binding declaration on the merits of appellees' constitutional claims.

The Court concedes that a court of appeals should ordinarily review the denial of a preliminary injunction under an abuse of discretion standard, and it concedes that a court of appeals should ordinarily confine itself to assessing the "probability that the plaintiffs would succeed on the merits." *Ante*, at [273]. But the Court purports to find an exception to this rule in the decisions in *Youngstown Sheet & Tube Co.* v. *Sawyer*, 343 U.S. 579 (1952), and *Smith* v. *Vulcan Iron Works*, 165 U.S. 518 (1897). It asserts that these cases indicate that "if a District Court's ruling rests solely on a premise as to the applicable rule of law, and the facts are established or of no controlling relevance, that ruling may be reviewed even though the appeal is from the entry of a preliminary injunction." *Ante*, at [273-74]. The Court then announces that the requirement that appellate review proceed under the deferential abuse of discretion standard is "a rule of orderly judicial administration, not a limit on judicial power." *Ibid.*, at [274]. Postulating that the Court of Appeals had a "full record before it on the issues now before us," *ibid.*, at [274], the Court concludes that this "full record," and the fact that this Court's decisions in *Akron*, *Ashcroft*, and *Simopoulos* were handed down during the pendency of the appeal, justified the Court of Appeals "in proceeding to plenary review of those issues." *Ibid.*

This analysis mischaracterizes the proceedings in the District Court and is unsupported by precedent or logic. No one doubts that the legal premises on which the District Judge proceeded were reviewable. But the fact is that the District Judge did not make the final, definitive "ruling" on the merits the Court imputes to him. The only "ruling" the Court of Appeals had before it with respect to the merits was a determination of "likelihood of success" based on facts which were stipulated *only* for purposes of the preliminary injunction motion, and on arguments framed with a view toward only those facts. Nor was there a "full record" upon which the Court of Appeals could decide the merits. The Court falls into precisely the error pointed out in *Camenisch*, 451 U.S., at 394, where this Court unanimously rejected the proposition that determinations on the propriety of preliminary relief are "tantamount to decisions on the underlying merits," because that view "improperly equates 'likelihood of success' with 'success', and, what is more important, . . . ignores the significant procedural differences between preliminary and permanent injunctions."

The Court of Appeals was convinced that the District Judge, in reliance on the decisions of the Courts of Appeals that were later reviewed in *Akron* and *Ashcroft*, had taken a view of the applicable law which this Court's decisions in those cases demonstrated to be erroneous. Citing *Apple Computer, Inc.* v. *Franklin Computer Corp.*, 714 F. 2d 1240, 1242 (CA3 1983), cert. dism'd under this Court's Rule 53, 464

U.S. 1033 (1984), the Court of Appeals stated that "[t]he customary discretion accorded to a district court's ruling on a preliminary injunction yields to our plenary scope of review as to the applicable law." 737 F. 2d 283, 290 (1984). *Apple Computer*, in turn, relied on Judge Friendly's opinion for the Second Circuit in *Donovan v. Bierwirth*, 680 F. 2d 263, 269 (1982), cert. denied, 459 U.S. 1069 (1982): "Despite oft repeated statements that the issuance of a preliminary injunction rests in the discretion of the trial judge whose decisions will be reversed only for 'abuse', a court of appeals must reverse if the district court has proceeded on the basis of an erroneous view of the applicable law, or of the standards governing the granting or denial of interlocutory relief" (citations omitted).

Donovan's reasoning, however, goes only to the *standard* of appellate review, not to the *extent* of the issues to be reviewed. Whether or not *Donovan's* approach is sound, it is clear that a district court does not have discretion to rule on the basis of a misapprehension of controlling law. But even assuming *arguendo* that, where a court of appeals detects such an error, it may then engage in *de novo* review of the determination whether a preliminary injunction should issue, see *id.*, at 270, such discretion does not ordinarily extend to deciding the merits of the controversy with finality. Judge Friendly did no such thing in *Donovan*, see 680 F. 2d, at 276, nor did the Third Circuit in *Apple Computer*, see 714 F. 2d, at 1242.

What is at issue here is a matter of legal principle. As JUSTICE BLACKMUN has observed on a previous occasion, "[t]he distinction between the preliminary and final injunction stages of a proceeding is more than mere formalism. The time pressures involved in a request for a preliminary injunction require courts to make determinations without the aid of full briefing or factual development, and make all such determinations necessarily provisional." *Firefighters v. Stotts*, 467 U.S. 561, 603–604, n. 7 (1984) (dissenting opinion). The holding of the Court today thus comes at the expense of the basic principle underlying the framework set out in *Camenisch* for ruling on a motion for a preliminary injunction: that fairness to the parties and reliable adjudication of disputes require final, binding rulings on the merits of a controversy to be made only after each side has had an opportunity to establish its version of the disputed facts or to establish that the facts are not in dispute.

Equally neglected by the Court is a second principle, closely related to the first:

> "Ordinarily an appellate court does not give consideration to issues not raised below. For our procedural scheme contemplates that parties shall come to issue in the trial forum vested with authority to determine

questions of fact. This is essential in order that parties may have the opportunity to offer all the evidence they believe relevant to the issues which the trial tribunal is alone competent to decide; it is equally essential in order that litigants may not be surprised on appeal by final decision there of issues upon which they have had no opportunity to introduce evidence." *Hormel v. Helvering*, 312 U.S. 552, 556 (1941).

See also *Singleton v. Wulff*, 428 U.S. 106, 120–121 (1976); cf. *Fountain v. Filson*, 336 U.S. 681, 683 (1949) (*per curiam*) (reversing a summary judgment order "made on appeal on a new issue as to which the opposite party had no opportunity to present a defense before the trial court"). The cases on which the Court relies simply do not support the short shrift the Court gives these basic principles.

In *Youngstown Sheet & Tube Co.*, President Truman, invoking an immediate threat to the national defense precipitated by a threatened nationwide strike in the steel industry, ordered the Secretary of Commerce to seize the steel mills and keep them running. 343 U.S., at 583. The steel companies sought a declaratory judgment, a preliminary injunction, and a permanent injunction against the seizure, on the grounds that the President had no authority to order it. *Ibid.* Although the District Court had before it only "motions for temporary injunctions" when it ruled, 103 F. Supp. 569, 572 (DC 1952), "in the light of the facts presented, the District Court saw no reason for delaying decision of the constitutional validity of the orders." *Youngstown Sheet & Tube Co.*, *supra*, 343 U.S. at 585. Indeed, the District Court had "com[e] to a fixed conclusion ... that defendant's acts are illegal.... Nothing that could be submitted at such trial on the facts would alter the legal conclusion I have reached." 103 F. Supp., at 576.

Thus, the District Court's preliminary injunction in *Youngstown Sheet & Tube Co.* rested on what amounted to a declaratory judgment that the orders were constitutionally invalid. That in itself was a pronounced departure from normal practice, although one that this Court found proper in the highly unusual circumstances presented in *Youngstown Sheet & Tube Co.*, where time was manifestly of the essence [1], and there was no contention that the Government had been deprived of an opportunity to present facts that could have altered the resolution of the constitutional question. To the contrary, when "[p]laintiffs moved for a preliminary injunction before answer or hearing, [d]efendant opposed the motion, filing uncontroverted affidavits of Government officials describing the facts underlying the President's order." 343 U.S., at 678 (Vinson, C.J., dissenting).

Neither of the foregoing justifications for the District Court's unusual decision to reach the merits in *Youngstown Sheet & Tube* is present here. No emergency remotely comparable to the one in

Youngstown Sheet & Tube confronted the Court of Appeals, which granted appellees' motion to enjoin enforcement of the entire Act pending appeal, and withheld judgment until after this Court had ruled in *Akron* and its companion cases. 737 F. 2d, 290. Appellants conceded in the Court of Appeals that several provisions of the Abortion Act were unconstitutional in the wake of those decisions, but appellants did not concede that the provisions on which the Court of Appeals dispositively ruled were unconstitutional. Nor is there any suggestion that appellants conceded in the Court of Appeals that there were no factual issues that could have a bearing on the constitutionality of these provisions. Consequently, even if a preliminary injunction should have issued, the proper course would have been to remand for final determination of the merits.

Indeed, since *Youngstown Sheet & Tube Co.* was decided this Court has expressly reaffirmed that "a state statute should not be declared unconstitutional by a district court if a preliminary injunction is granted a plaintiff to protect his interests during the ensuing litigation." *Withrow v. Larkin*, 421 U.S. 35, 43 (1975). See *Mayo v. Lakeland Highlands Canning Co.*, 309 U.S. 310 (1940). If it is improper for a district court to enter such a declaratory judgment when it grants a preliminary injunction, then *a fortiori* it is improper for a court of appeals to do so when the district court has only appraised the likelihood of success on the merits. What happened here is even more extreme: the Court of Appeals, reviewing the *denial* of a preliminary injunction, held in the first instance that nothing that could be submitted at a trial on the merits would alter *its* conclusion that "most of the provisions attacked by appellants are unconstitutional as a matter of law." 737 F. 2d, at 287. Nothing in *Youngstown Sheet & Tube Co.* remotely suggests that it was proper for the Court of Appeals to take this extraordinary step. "*Camenisch* makes clear that a determination of a party's entitlement to a preliminary injunction is a separate issue from the determination of the merits of the party's underlying legal claim, and that a reviewing court should not confuse the two." *Stotts*, 467 U.S. at 603 (BLACKMUN, J., dissenting).

The Court strays even further afield when it invokes *Smith v. Vulcan Irons Works* in defense of the Court of Appeals' decision to reach and resolve the merits despite the fact that the District Court had not done so and without giving the parties "the benefit . . . of a full opportunity to present their cases." *Camenisch*, 451 U.S., at 396. The trial court in *Smith*, "upon a bill in equity for the infringement of a patent for an invention . . . entered an interlocutory decree, *adjudging that the patent was invalid and had been infringed*, granting an injunction, and referring the case to a master to take an account of profits and damages." 165 U.S., at 518 (emphasis added). The defendant challenged the trial court's alleged "error in holding that the patent was invalid, and that it has been infringed." *Ibid*. The Circuit Court of Appeals reversed the decree, rejecting the plaintiff's contention that it could rule only on "whether an injunction should be awarded." *Ibid*. This Court held that under the plain language of the statute conferring jurisdiction on the Circuit Court of Appeals, an appeal was authorized "from the whole of such interlocutory order or decree, and not from that part of it only which grants or continues an injunction," and consequently the statute conferred "authority to consider and decide the case upon its merits." *Id*., at 525. The trial court, of course, had already done precisely that, deciding the issue of liability after the parties had joined issue on the merits, while referring the matter of damages to a master. Reliance on *Smith* in this case is therefore misplaced, for, to repeat, the District Court did not decide—and could not properly have decided—the merits of appellees' constitutional claims when it refused to grant a preliminary injunction.

The Court also seeks comfort in an analogy to the rule that a federal court need not abstain, pending state-court review, from reviewing a constitutional challenge to the validity of a state statute that is not fairly subject to an interpretation that will avoid the constitutional question. *Zwickler v. Koota*, 389 U.S. 241, 251, and n. 14 (1967). When a federal district court declines to abstain, however, it does not in so doing decide the merits of the constitutional question even if the parties have not had a full opportunity to air them. The court simply proceeds to decide the case in accordance with the normal procedural requirements that safeguard the parties' right to be heard. A refusal to abstain therefore infringes neither the principle that final judgment should follow a full opportunity to be heard on the factual and legal merits of the case, nor the principle that "parties shall come to issue in the trial form." *Hormel*, 312 U.S., at 556. The same cannot be said of what the Court of Appeals did here.

Whatever the exceptions which would justify a district court in finally resolving an issue on the merits at the preliminary injunction stage, no such exception was applicable here. Nor is this a case in which the Court of Appeals was justified in resolving an issue not passed on in the district court because proper resolution was beyond any doubt or grave injustice might result from failure to do so. See *Singleton v. Wulff*, 428 U.S., at 121. The Court of Appeals not only decided to stand in the shoes of the District Court by ruling on an issue not passed upon below—it ruled on an issue on which, absent extraordinary circumstances, the District Court could not have ruled without "'clear and unambiguous notice'" that would "'afford the parties a full opportunity to present their respective cases.'" *Camenisch, supra*, 451 U.S. at 395. The Court attempts to veil the impropriety of its decision to affirm on the merits despite the procedural posture of this case by implying that the challenged provisions are patently unconstitutional. But this claim too is unsupported in this Court's decisions concerning state regulation of abortion.

The discretionary exception the Court fashions today will also prove vexatious to administer. Parties now face the risk that a final ruling on the merits will be entered against them by a court of appeals when an appeal is taken from the grant or denial of a motion for a preliminary injunction, although the district court made only an initial assessment of the likelihood that the moving party would succeed on the merits. It is predictable that parties will respond by attempting to turn preliminary injunction proceedings into contests over summary judgment or full-scale trials on the merits. That tendency will make the preliminary injunction less useful in serving its intended function of preserving the status quo pending final judgment on the merits, while making litigation more expensive, less reliable and less fair. If this case did not involve state regulation of abortion, it may be doubted that the Court would entertain, let alone adopt, such a departure from its precedents.

II

In this Court, appellants argue that the judgment of the Court of Appeals should be vacated and the District Court's denial of a preliminary injunction sustained. Appellants have stated that they "intend to present to the District Court a complete factual record which . . . could affect the disposition of this case," and have indicated some of the specific factual propositions they would seek to establish. Brief for Appellants 44–48. At oral argument, counsel for appellants reiterated that, with the exception of the second-physician requirement, "there are additional justifications by way of facts that we can offer" as to each of the challenged provisions. Tr. of Oral Argument 13. These assertions alone would justify vacating the judgment of the Court of Appeals insofar as that court did more than direct the entry of a preliminary injunction. In *Singleton v. Wulff*, 428 U.S., at 120, for example, this Court reversed the Court of Appeals' decision to reach the merits of that case, even though this Court had "no idea what evidence, if any, petitioner would, or could, offer in defense of this statute," because it was clear that "petitioner has had no opportunity to proffer such evidence." I would apply that reasoning here even if I were not persuaded that as to several of the challenged provisions additional factual development—for example, facts concerning the costs associated with the reporting and informed consent provisions, and the extent of the problems Pennsylvania was seeking to correct—

could affect the decision on the merits. Appellants should not have to prove that they are entitled to an opportunity to be heard.

Since it rendered "what amounts to a final declaratory judgment on the constitutionality of the statute," *ante*, at [300 n.1] (WHITE, J., dissenting), the Court of Appeals necessarily believed that in light of *Akron* and its companion cases appellees had established a sufficient likelihood of success on the merits to warrant issuance of a preliminary injunction. Pennsylvania contends that this ruling is erroneous even under the supervening decisions of this Court. In the alternative, Pennsylvania suggests that the facial constitutionality of the challenged provisions of its Abortion Act may be sustained on this record.

I agree with much of what JUSTICE WHITE has written in Part II of his dissenting opinion, and the arguments he has framed might well suffice to show that the provisions at issue are facially constitutional. Nonetheless, I believe the proper course is to decide this case as the Court of Appeals should have decided it, lest appellees suffer the very prejudice the Court sees fit to inflict on appellants. For me, then, the question is not one of "success" but of the "likelihood of success." In addition, because Pennsylvania has not asked the Court to reconsider or overrule *Roe v. Wade*, 410 U.S. 113 (1973), I do not address that question.

I do, however, remain of the views expressed in my dissent in *Akron*, 462 U.S., at 459–466. The State has compelling interests in ensuring maternal health and in protecting potential human life, and these interests exist "throughout pregnancy," *Id.*, at 461 (O'CONNOR, J., dissenting). Under this Court's fundamental-rights jurisprudence, judicial scrutiny of state regulation of abortion should be limited to whether the state law bears a rational relationship to legitimate purposes such as the advancement of these compelling interests, with heightened scrutiny reserved for instances in which the State has imposed an "undue burden" on the abortion decision. *Id.*, at 461–463 (O'CONNOR, J., dissenting). An undue burden will generally be found "in situations involving absolute obstacles or severe limitations on the abortion decision," not wherever a state regulation "may 'inhibit' abortions to some degree." *Id.*, at 464 (O'CONNOR, J., dissenting). And if a state law does interfere with the abortion decision to an extent that it becomes "necessary to apply an exacting standard of review," *id.*, at 467 (O'CONNOR, J., dissenting), the possibility remains that the statute will withstand the stricter scrutiny. See *id.*, at 473-474 (O'CONNOR, J., dissenting); *Ashcroft*, 462 U.S., at 505 (O'CONNOR, J., concurring in the judgment in part and dissenting in part).

These principles for evaluating state regulation of abortion were not newly minted in my dissenting opinion in *Akron*. Apart from *Roe's* outmoded trimester framework, the "unduly burdensome" standard had been articulated and applied with fair consistency by this Court in cases such as *Harris v. McRae*, 448 U.S. 297, 314 (1980), *Maher v. Roe*, 432 U.S. 464, 473 (1977), *Beal v. Doe*, 432 U.S. 438, 446 (1977), and *Bellotti v. Baird*, 428 U.S. 132, 147 (1976). In *Akron* and *Ashcroft* the Court, in my view, distorted and misapplied this standard, see *Akron*, 462 U.S., at 452–453 (O'CONNOR, J., dissenting), but made no clean break with precedent and indeed "follow[ed] this approach" in assessing some of the regulations before it in those cases. *Id.*, at 463 (O'CONNOR, J., dissenting).

The Court today goes well beyond mere distortion of the "unduly burdensome" standard. By holding that each of the challenged provisions is facially unconstitutional as a matter of law, and that no conceivable facts appellants might offer could alter this result, the Court appears to adopt as its new test a *per se* rule under which any regulation touching on abortion must be invalidated if it poses "an unacceptable danger of deterring the exercise of that right." *Ante*, at [280]. Under this prophylactic test, it seems that the mere possibility that some will be less likely to choose to have an abortion by virtue of the presence of a particular state regulation suffices to invalidate it. Simultaneously, the Court strains to discover "the anti-abortion character of the statute," *ante*, at [278], and, as JUSTICE WHITE points out, invents an unprecedented canon of construction under which "in cases involving abortion, a permissible reading of a statute is to be avoided at all costs." *Ante*, at [316] (WHITE, J., dissenting). I shall not belabor the dangerous extravagance of this dual approach, because I hope it represents merely a temporary aberration rather than a portent of lasting change in settled principles of constitutional law. Suffice it to say that I dispute not only the wisdom but the legitimacy of the Court's attempt to discredit and preempt state abortion regulation regardless of the interests it serves and the impact it has.

Under the "unduly burdensome" test, the District Judge's conclusion that appellees were not entitled to a preliminary injunction was clearly correct. Indeed, the District Judge applied essentially that test, after suggesting that no "meaningful distinction can be made between the plaintiffs' 'legally significant burden' and defendants' 'undue burden.'" 552 F. Supp. at 796. I begin, as does the Court, with the Act's informed consent provisions.

The Court condemns some specific features of the informed consent provisions in their entirety as irrelevant or distressing in some cases and as intruding on the relationship between the woman and her physician. JUSTICE WHITE convincingly argues that none of the Court's general criticisms is appropriate, since the information is clearly relevant in many cases and is calculated to inform rather than intimidate, and since all informed consent requirements must, from the very rationale for their existence, intrude to some extent on the physician's discretion to be the sole judge of what his or her patient needs to know. The "parade of horribles" the Court invalidated in *Akron*, 462 U.S., at 445, is missing here. For example, §3205(a)(iii) requires that the woman be informed, "when medically accurate," of the risks associated with a particular abortion procedure, and §3205(a)(v) requires the physician to inform the woman of "[t]he medical risks associated with carrying her child to term." This is the kind of balanced information I would have thought all could agree is relevant to a woman's informed consent.

I do not dismiss the possibility that requiring the physician or counselor to read aloud the State's printed materials if the woman wishes access to them but cannot read raises First Amendment concerns. Even the requirement that women who can read be informed of the availability of those materials, and furnished with them on request, may create some possibility that the physician or counselor is being required to "communicate [the State's] ideology." *Akron*, 462 U.S., at 472, n. 16 (O'CONNOR, J., dissenting); see *Wooley v. Maynard*, 430 U.S. 705 (1977). Since the Court of Appeals did not reach appellees' First Amendment claim, and since appellees do not raise it here, I need not decide whether this potential problem would be sufficiently serious to warrant issuance of a preliminary injunction as to those portions of §3205 that incorporate the printed information provisions of §3208. I note, however, that this is one of many points on which fuller factual development, including the actual contents of the printed materials, could affect resolution of the merits.

The Court singles out for specific criticism the required description, in the printed materials, of fetal characteristics at 2-week intervals. These materials, of course, will be shown to the woman only if she chooses to inspect them. If the materials were sufficiently inflammatory and inaccurate the fact that the woman must ask to see them would not necessarily preclude finding an undue burden, but there is no indication that this is true of the description of fetal characteristics the statute contemplates. Accordingly, I think it unlikely that appellees could succeed in making the threshold showing of an undue burden on this point, and the information is certainly rationally related to the State's interests in ensuring informed consent and in protecting potential human life. Similarly, I see little chance that appellees can establish that the abortion decision is unduly burdened by §3205's requirements that the woman be informed of the availability of medical assistance benefits and of the father's legal responsibility. Here again, the information is indisputably relevant in many cases and would not appear to place a severe limitation on the abortion decision.

The Court's rationale for striking down the reporting requirements of §3214, as JUSTICE WHITE shows, rests on an unsupported finding of fact by this Court to the effect that "[i]dentification is the obvious purpose of these extreme reporting requirements." *Ante*, at [280] (opinion of the Court). The Court's "finding," which is contrary to the preliminary finding of the District Judge that the statute's confidentiality requirements protected against any invasion of privacy that could burden the abortion decision, see 552 F. Supp., at 804, is simply another consequence of the Court's determination to prevent the parties from developing the facts. I do not know whether JUSTICE WHITE is correct in stating that "the provisions pose little or no threat to the woman's privacy," *ante*, at [312] (WHITE, J., dissenting), and I would leave that determination for the District Court, which can hear evidence on this point before making its findings. I do not, however, see a substantial threat of identification on the face of the statute, which does not require disclosure of the woman's identity to anyone, and which provides that reports shall be disclosed to the public only in "a form which will not lead to the disclosure of the identity of any person filing a report." §3214(e)(2). I therefore conclude that the District Judge correctly ruled that appellees are unlikely to succeed in establishing an undue burden on the abortion decision stemming from the possibility of identification.

I fully agree with JUSTICE WHITE that the Court has misconstrued the intended meaning of §3210(b)'s requirement that physicians employ the abortion method that is most likely to save the fetus unless, in the physician's good-faith judgment, that method "would present a significantly greater risk to the life or health of the pregnant woman." Since §3210(b) can fairly be read to require "only that the risk be a real and identifiable one," *ante*, at [313] (WHITE, J., dissenting), there is little possibility that a woman's abortion decision will be unduly burdened by risks falling below that threshold. Accordingly, §3210(b) should not be preliminarily enjoined, and I express no opinion as to the point at which a "trade-off" between the health of the woman and the survival of the fetus would rise to the level of an undue burden.

Since appellants and appellees agree that no further factfinding is needed concerning appellees' challenge to §3210(c)'s second-physician requirement, I am willing to assume that the merits of that challenge are properly before us. I have nothing to add to JUSTICE WHITE'S demonstration that this provision is constitutional under *Ashcroft* because the Act effectively provides for an exception making this requirement inapplicable in emergency situations. I likewise agree with JUSTICE WHITE that the preliminary injunction entered against enforcement of the Act's parental notice and consent provisions should be vacated, since, as in *Ashcroft*, there is no reason here to believe the State will not provide for the expedited procedures called for by its statute. See *Ashcroft*, 462 U.S., at 491, n. 16 (opinion of JUSTICE POWELL). I add only that the Court's explanation for its refusal to follow *Ashcroft*—that the new rules "should be considered by the District Court in the first instance," *ante*, at [274], n. 9—does not square with its insistence on resolving the rest of this case without giving the District Court an opportunity to do so.

In my view, today's decision makes bad constitutional law and bad procedural law. The "'undesired and uncomfortable straitjacket'" in this case, *ante*, at [277], is not the one the Court purports to discover in Pennsylvania's statute; it is the one the Court has tailored for the 50 States. I respectfully dissent.

Notes

1. The extraordinary importance of prompt resolution of the steel companies' claims' is shown by the fact that this Court granted certiorari before judgment in the Court of Appeals three days after the District Court ruled, and set the case for argument nine days later, "[d]eeming it best that the issues raised be promptly decided by this Court." 343 U.S., at 584.

APPENDIX THREE

In the Supreme Court of the United States October Term, 1985

No. 84–495

Richard Thornburgh, ET AL., Appellants

v.

American College of Obstetricians and Gynecologists, ET AL.

No. 84–1379

Eugene F. Diamond, ET AL., Appellants

v.

Allan G. Charles, ET AL.

ON APPEAL FROM THE UNITED STATES COURTS OF APPEALS FOR THE THIRD AND SEVENTH CIRCUITS

BRIEF FOR THE UNITED STATES AS AMICUS CURIAE IN SUPPORT OF APPELLANTS

INTEREST OF THE UNITED STATES

These cases involve the efforts of two state legislatures to balance the competing interests at stake in the abortion decision. Congress has in the past enacted legislation affecting that decision (see 42 U.S.C. 300a-6; Act of Nov. 20, 1979, Pub. L. No. 96–124, §109, 93 Stat. 926), and may do so again. This Court's continuing effort to define the perimeters of permissible abortion regulation has a direct impact upon the ability of the country's elected representatives—both state and federal—to deal with this important question of great public import and heated political debate.

SUMMARY OF ARGUMENT

The opinions of the courts below are multiply flawed. In their manifest eagerness to strike down the state statutes in question they transgress numerous canons of constitutional adjudication: provisions are construed so as to impugn rather than save their constitutionality; facts stipulated solely for purposes of a preliminary injunction are taken as dispositive for an ultimate judgment on the statute; and provisions repealed and substantially recast to meet constitutional objections are struck down in their earlier versions. More substantively, the courts below reach their conclusions as if this Court in *Roe v. Wade* has posited only one value, a woman's unfettered right to an abortion, rather than a balance of values which include the state's interest in maternal health and in unborn and future life. The harsh and one-sided nature of the decisions below may in part be a response to a change in emphasis in this Court's opinion in *Akron v. Akron Center for Reproductive Health*, which itself expressed considerable impatience with legislative attempts to balance the interests recognized in *Roe v. Wade*. To the extent this is so, these cases and *Akron* itself are not just wrong turns on a generally propitious journey but indications of an erroneous point of departure. Indeed, the textual, doctrinal and historical basis for *Roe v. Wade* is so far flawed and, as these cases illustrate, is a source of such instability in the law that this Court should reconsider that decision and on reconsideration abandon it.

DISCUSSION

A. In *Roe v. Wade*, 410 U.S. 113, 153 (1973), this Court held that the "right of privacy" emanating from the Due Process Clause "is broad enough to encompass a woman's decision whether or not to terminate her pregnancy." But the Court has consistently rejected the notion that "the Constitution requires abortions on demand" (*id.* at 208 (Burger, C.J., concurring)). Rather, the Court has held, in this and other contexts, that the right of privacy, "is not unqualified and must be considered against important state interests in regulation" (*id.* at 154).

Perhaps the dominant governmental interest recognized in the Court's opinions is the state's "unquestionably strong and legitimate interest in encouraging normal childbirth," an interest that "exist[s] throughout the course of the woman's pregnancy" (*Beal v. Doe*, 432 U.S. 438, 446 (1977)). And the Court has consistently recognized that the state has "an important and legitimate interest," which likewise exists throughout pregnancy, in safeguarding the health of the mother and in maintaining medical standards. *E.g., Roe v. Wade*, 410 U.S. at 154; *Doe v. Bolton*, 410 U.S. 179, 194–195 (1973); *Planned Parenthood of Central Missouri v. Danforth*, 428 U.S. 52, 80–81 (1976).

In evaluating state efforts to further these legitimate interests, this Court and its individual Justices have said that a regulation "is not unconstitutional unless it unduly burdens the right to seek an abortion." *E.g., Maher v. Roe*, 432 U.S. 464, 473 (1977) (original quotation marks omitted). Indeed, the Chief Justice has stated his understanding that "[t]he Court's holdings in *Roe v. Wade* * * * and *Doe v. Bolton* * * * simply require that a State not create an absolute barrier to a woman's decision to have an abortion" (*Maher v. Roe*, 432 U.S. at 481 (Burger, C.J., concurring)).

The decisions below are inconsistent with these principles and should be reversed. The courts of appeals betrayed unabashed hostility to state regulation of abortion and ill-disguised suspicion of state legislators' motives. The courts repeatedly failed "to give proper weight to the legislative decision, as expressed in the statute, to protect the life and health of the woman and the child subject to abortion" (84–495 J.S. App. 170a (Weis, J.)). A persistent theme of the decisions below is "the notion that normal rules of law, procedure and constitutional adjudication suddenly become irrelevant solely because a case touches on the subject of abortion" (*Danforth*, 428 U.S. at 98 (White, J., concurring and dissenting)). The decisions below thus not only "have far-reaching effects" on the abortion issue, but also "implicate the proper role of the states and the federal courts" under our Constitution (84–495 J.S. App. 172a–173a (Weis, J.)).

1. *No. 84–495.* The Third Circuit signaled its antipathy in the opening section of its opinion, in which it imputed to the Pennsylvania legislature "a pervasive invalid intent" to "restrict a pregnant woman's fundamental right to choose an abortion" (84–495 J.S. App. 31a, 32a). The court suggested that the legislature was somehow culpable for enacting "a complex and extensive regulatory scheme * * * containing numerous provisions which it had been advised skirted constitutional limits" (*id.* at 86a). The court faulted the legislature for passing the abortion bill "after scant debate" (*id.* at 13a) and for attaching it to another bill the court did not view as "germane" (*id.* at 12a & n.3). The court relied heavily (*id.* at 12a–13a) on newspaper accounts about a cosponsor's alleged opposition to *Roe v. Wade*. And even though the

case was on appeal from the district court's denial of a preliminary injunction,[1] the court of appeals reached out to render a final judgment holding most of the statute unconstitutional, asserting that "[t]he customary discretion accorded to a district court's ruling on a preliminary injunction yields to our plenary scope of review" (84-495 J.S. App. 21a).

The court's zeal to place the worst possible construction upon the Pennsylvania statute is evident from its treatment of the specific provisions challenged. That treatment is seriously at odds with this Court's abortion opinions and with basic principles of judicial review.

a. Section 3206(c) provides that a pregnant minor, without seeking parental consent, may petition the appropriate court to authorize an abortion upon a finding that she "is mature and capable of giving informed consent*** and has, in fact, given such consent" (18 Pa. Cons. Stat. Ann. (Purdon 1983)). This provision codifies the holding in *Bellotti v. Baird (Bellotti II)*, 443 U.S. 662, 648–651 (1979). The statute provides that such court proceedings "shall be confidential and shall be given such precedence*** as will ensure that the court may reach a decision promptly and without delay" (§3206 (f)). The judge must rule "within three business days of the date of application" (*ibid.*). The statute mandates an "expedited confidential appeal" if authorization is denied and directs the Pennsylvania Supreme Court to issue "such rules as may be necessary to***ensure confidentiality and*** promptness of disposition" (§3206 (h)).

The court of appeals "d[id] not invalidate section 3206" (84-495 J.S. App. 56a). The court nevertheless proceeded to enjoin the statute's enforcement "until the state promulgates [the] regulations" referred to above (*ibid.*). This Court has made it clear, however, that a state is not constitutionally required to have regulations on this subject, expressing confidence that state courts will expedite cases involving minors' consent consistently with this Court's decisions. *Bellotti II*, 443 U.S. at 645 & n.25. Accord, *Planned Parenthood Ass'n v. Ashcroft*, 462 U.S. 476, 491 n.16 (1983). The court of appeals' action in enjoining enforcement of a state law, without any finding that it contravenes federal law or the federal Constitution, is unprecedented and remarkable.

b. Section 3210(c) requires the attendance of a second physician at abortions performed after viability. This provision, like the provision at issue in *Ashcroft*, contains no explicit exception for medical emergencies (see 462 U.S. at 485 & n.8). The Court in *Ashcroft* inferred such an exception under the latter statute and held it valid (*ibid.*). The court of appeals refused to infer a comparable exception under Section 3210(c) here. It did so even though Section 3210(a) provides a "complete defense to any charge brought against a physician for violating the requirements of this section * * * that the abortion *was necessary to preserve maternal life or health*" (emphasis added). The court justified its holding by asserting that subsections (a) and (c) are "separated by [an] intervening provision [viz., subsection (b)] which on its face evinces the Pennsylvania legislature's unconstitutionally restrictive view of maternal health" (84–495 J.S. App. 73a). The court's insistence that the statute be construed so as to create rather than to remove constitutional problems inverts well-established canons of judicial review.

c. Section 3210(b) provides that the method of abortion used when the fetus is viable must be the one most likely to produce a live birth, unless that method would cause a "significantly greater" risk to the mother. The district court, in an effort to discharge its "oblig[ation] to give the statute [a] reasonable interpretation which avoids the danger of constitutional invalidity" (84–594 J.S. App. 247a–248a), interpreted "significantly greater" to mean "medically cognizable," and held the statute as thus interpreted valid under *Colautti v. Franklin*, 439 U.S. 379, 400 (1979). The court of appeals refused to adopt this construction, finding it "inconsistent with * * * the legislative intent," and accordingly declared the statute unconstitutional (84–495 J.S. App. 70a). It did so even though the district court has shown that its saving construction was supported by a dictionary definition of the relevant words (*id*. at 248a). And it did so without even considering the possibility of abstaining to ascertain whether the Pennsylvania courts might adopt the same construction that the district court did.

d. Section 3208, entitled "Printed Information," directs the Pennsylvania Department of Public Health to publish easily comprehensible pamphlets describing assistance available to pregnant women through public and private agencies. These pamphlets are to include the following statement: "The Commonwealth of Pennsylvania strongly urges you to contact [these agencies] before making a final decision about abortion" (§3208 (a) (1)). The statute also directs the Department to publish literature discussing the unborn child's probable anatomical characteristics and possibility of survival, provided that such material is "objective, nonjudgmental and designed to convey only accurate scientific information" (§3208 (a) (2)).

The court of appeals declared this statute unconstitutional (84–495 J.S. App. 58a–59a). It did not base this holding on a determination that the section, standing alone, was invalid. Indeed, such a determination would contravene this Court's ruling that a state may "make a value judgment favoring chilbirth over abortion, and * * * implement that judgment by the allocation of public funds" (*Maher v. Roe*, 432 U.S. at

474). The court of appeals based its holding, rather, on a determination that Section 3208 was "inextricably intertwined" (84–495 J.S. App. 58a) with another section which the court thought unconstitutional. The sole link between the two sections is a statutory cross-reference (see *id.* at 137a (Seitz, C.J., dissenting)). The court invalidated Section 3208 based on this suppposed "inextricable" connection even though the law contains an explicit severability clause (*ibid.*). The court's approach is unjustifiable and can only be explained as an attempt to censor printed matter the majority did not like.

e. Section 3205, entitled "Informed Consent," provides that a woman's consent to abortion will be deemed "voluntary and informed" only if the referring or the attending physician provides her with information about the relative medical risks, both physical and psychological, of abortion and childbirth. The doctor or his agent must also inform the woman of the availability of certain financial assistance and social services in the event of childbirth (§3205(a) (2) (i) and (ii)). Finally, the doctor or his agent must inform the woman that she has a right to review, but need not review, the printed materials described above (§3205 (a) (2) (iii), cross-referring to §3208).

The court of appeals held this statute unconstitutional, citing *Akron v. Akron Center for Reproductive Health, Inc.*, 462 U.S. 416 (1983). The court of appeals inferred that "'much of the information required * * * is designed not to inform the woman's consent but rather to persuade her to withhold it altogether'" (84–495 J.S. App. 48a (quoting 462 U.S. at 444)). And the court viewed the statute as mandating "a litany of information" that intrudes upon the attending physician's discretion (84–495 J.S. App. 48a-49a (quoting 462 at 444–445)).

The court of appeals plainly erred. Most of the information Pennsylvania requires is identical to that which the Court in *Akron* deemed "certainly * * * not objectionable," "probably * * * routinely made available to the patient," and "clearly * * * related to maternal health and to the State's legitimate purpose in requiring informed consent" (462 U.S. at 445–446 & n.37). It is true that Pennsylvania requires the doctor himself to provide the relevant medical information, permitting him to delegate to an assistant the provision of information about social services, financial assistance, and the like. Cf. *Akron*, 462 U.S. at 448–449 (holding that the physician generally must be allowed to "delegate [   ] the counselling task to another qualified individual"). But the division of labor Pennsylvania has adopted is surely a rational one, particularly in light of this Court's repeated stress on "the central role of the physician * * * in consulting with the woman about whether or not to have an abortion" (*Colautti*, 439 U.S. at 387).

The court of appeals likewise erred in holding that Pennsylvania cannot require that a woman be informed "[t]hat she has the right to review" certain printed materials (discussed above) published by the state health department. This information, unlike that deemed a "parade of horribles" in *Akron* (462 U.S. at 445), is required to be "objective, non judgmental and * * * accurate scientific information" (§3208 (a) (2)). Moreover, the woman is free to decide for herself whether or not she wants to read these pamphlets, and "nothing in the statute prevents the physician from advising that [she] not view [them] or disputing or supplementing them with his own information" (84–495 J.S. App. 140a (Seitz, C.J., dissenting)). This Court has repeatedly held that the state may promote maternal health by ensuring that a woman's abortion decision is truly knowing, voluntary, and informed. It cannot seriously be contended that a state, by offering a person the right to read objective, nonjudgmental materials before making a decision, would be held unconstitutionally to compel or coerce that person's decision in any other legal context.

f. Section 3214 (a) requires that "[a] report of each abortion performed * * * be made to the department on forms prescribed by it." The physician must report routine statistical information about each abortion, such as the patient's age and marital status (but not her identity), the type of abortion procedure used, and any medical complications resulting therefrom. He must also report the basis for his determination "that a child is not viable," and, if he determines that the fetus is viable, to report "the basis for his determination that the abortion is necessary to preserve maternal life or health." (§3214 (a) (8), cross-referring to §3211).

The court of appeals held this statute unconstitutional. While acknowledging that this Court has approved recordkeeping and reporting requirements for abortions, it asserted that "[t]he nature and complexity of [Pennsylvania's] requirements * * * have crossed the permissible threshold" (84–495 J.S. App. 80a). It reasoned that Pennsylvania's law would "have a significant impact on the woman's abortion decision" by "increas[ing] the costs of * * * abortions" by an unspecified amount (*id.* at 80a–81a).

The court of appeals' reasoning is seriously flawed. The statistical information Pennsylvania requires to be reported is information that "most physicians would obtain as a matter of course, or which is easily obtained through simpl[e] questions or observation" (84–495 J.S. App. 148a (Seitz, C.J., dissenting)). The court of appeals had no basis for distinguishing Pennsylvania's recordkeeping requirements from those approved in *Danforth*. Compare 428 U.S. at 79-81. The parties' stipulation that Pennsylvania's requirements would increase abortion costs by an unspecified amount—recordkeeping requirements always increase costs, a fact that obviously was equally true in *Danforth*—is irrelevant absent evidence about the magnitude of those expenses. Indeed, a host of state laws (be they laws or regulatory requirements) impose increased costs on providers of medical services, and it could scarcely be contended that such laws are therefore unconstitutional. In any event, the record in this case contains no evidence about the actual costs imposed by Pennsylvania's reporting requirements, and the court of appeals thus had "no way of knowing what cost increase is attributable to [them]" (84-495 J.S. App. 149a (Seitz, C.J., dissenting)). Cf. *Ashcroft*, 462 U.S. at 489-490 (noting district court's findings as to cost of pathology reports and holding that those costs imposed "a relatively insignificant burden").

The court of appeals likewise erred in holding that Pennsylvania cannot require doctors to report the basis for their determinations about fetal viability and danger to maternal health. It is far-fetched to suggest, as did the court of appeals (84-495 J.S. App. 81a), that such reporting violates this Court's "directive that a physician be accorded broad discretion" in making these determinations. Obviously, a doctor does not have "discretion" to make unjustifiable and unsupportable judgments about life and death, and it is neither an affront nor an unreasonable burden to require that he rationally explain the basis for such decisions. Nor can it seriously be contended that the need to furnish such explanations unconstitutionally "chills" physicians' willingness to perform abortions. It is hard to see how Pennsylvania can enforce its legitimate interest in protecting life if it is foreclosed from seeking such information.

2. *No. 84-1379.* The Seventh Circuit, ruling unanimously, struck down four sections of the Illinois Abortion Law. The Court's decision ignores elementary principles of jurisdiction, comity and federalism in its relentless determination to invalidate the challenged provisions at all costs.

a. Section 6 (4) of the Illinois Abortion Law, as enacted in 1979, prescribed a standard of care for a doctor performing an abortion when there existed "a possibility known to him" of fetal viability (84-1379 J.S. App. 8). On November 16, 1979, four days before Section 6 (4)'s effective date, the district court issued a preliminary injunction against its enforcement, finding that it incorporated an unconstitutional definition of "viability" (*id.* at 3). In October 1983, the district court converted the preliminary injunction into a permanent injunction (579 F. Supp. 464, 470-471 (N.D. Ill. 1983). On June 30, 1984, while the instant appeal was pending in the Seventh Circuit, the Illinois legislature amended Section 6 (4) (see 84-1379 J.S. App. 9, 58-59). The court of appeals recognized that this amendment "substantially altered" Section 6 (4) and the court specifically "decline[d] to evaluate [the] constitutionality" of the current version of the statute (84–1379 J.S. App. 9).

The court of appeals, however, proceeded to declare the repealed version of Section 6 (4) unconstitutional. Rejecting the State's suggestion of mootness, the court likened the legislature's 1984 revision of the statute to "a defendant's voluntary abandonment" of prior unconstitutional conduct (84–1379 J.S. App. 18). The court theorized that the Illinois legislature "could reenact" the repealed version of Section 6 (4), and was persuaded that "such a result would not be unlikely" inasmuch as the legislature had amended Section 6 (4) twice during the previous five years (84–1379 J.S. App. 19–20). The court concluded that the State had failed to prove that it would not "return to its old ways" if plaintiffs' challenge were dismissed (*id.* at 20). The court also suggested that the 1983 version of the statute might have residual "chilling effects" despite its repeal (*ibid.*).

The court's reasoning is remarkable. The old version of Section 6 (4) had been under continuous injunction from the day it was enacted until the day it was repealed. The statute thus could never have been applied to anyone, and the controversy concerning its validity was accordingly moot. Although this Court has recognized a narrow exception to the mootness doctrine where defendants "voluntarily abandon" challenged conduct for the purpose of evading judicial review (*City of Mesquite v. Aladdins's Castle, Inc.*, 455 U.S. 283 (1982)), we know of no instance, and the court of appeals cited none, where this exception has been held to cover a statutory amendment by a state legislature, which, of course, is not even a "defendant" here.

The court of appeals, moreover, had absolutely no basis for concluding that reenactment of the defunct, allegedly unconstitutional statute was likely. The legislature's previous amendments to the law surely provided no basis for that conclusion, since those amendments, as the court itself recognized, represented faithful and repeated attempts "to alter the contours of [the] statute to reflect the latest judicial pronouncements in the area of abortion and privacy" (84–1379 J.S. App. 20). More generally, principles of federalism and comity make it wholly inappropriate for a federal court to presume that a state legislature and governor will act in bad faith by repealing and then reenacting a statute for the purpose of evading judicial review.[2]

b. Section 6 (1) of the Illinois Abortion Law, as amended in 1979, prescribed a standard of care for a doctor performing an abortion "after the fetus is known to be viable" (84–1379 J.S. App. 6). On November 16, 1979, four days before the statute became effective, the district court preliminarily enjoined its enforcement, finding that it incorporated an unconstitutional definition of viability (*id.* at 3). In September 1983, the Illinois legislature amended the definition of viability, providing that a fetus is viable "when, in the medical judgment of the attending physician based on the particular facts of the case before him, there is a reasonable likelihood of sustained survival of the fetus outside the womb, with or without artificial support" (*id.* at 7, 58). On October 14, 1983, the district court sustained the amended definition of viability, held that Section 6 (1) was thus constitutional, and lifted the preliminary injunction (579 F. Supp. at 466, 469). On June 30, 1984, while the instant appeal was pending in the Seventh Circuit, the Illinois legislature amended Section 6 (1) (see 84–1379 J.S. App. 7, 57–58). The court of appeals recognized that this amendment "substantially transformed section 6 (1)" and the court "accordingly decline[d] to discuss the constitutionality" of the current version (*id.* at 7).

Once again, however, the court of appeals proceeded to declare the repealed version of the statute unconstitutional. Rejecting the State's suggestion of mootness, the court noted that old Section 6 (1) had operative effect for the eight-month period between October 14, 1983, and June 30, 1984. The court observed that the statute of limitations had not expired with respect to events occurring during that period, and hence suggested that the State "could prosecute plaintiffs * * * if [they] violated [the repealed] section while it remained in effect" (84–1379 J.S. App. 15). The court found "this possibility insufficiently speculative to render [their] challenge * * * moot" (*id.* at 16).

The court's reasoning is flawed. The State explicitly advised the court of appeals that it would not initiate prosecutions of the type appellees assertedly feared (see 84–1379 J.S. 42, 48). Moreover, appellees brought a facial challenge to Section 6 (1) and did not allege that they performed any late-term abortions during the eight-month period in question (see *id.* at 43). The possibility that appellees might be prosecuted under the old statute is thus too conjectural to satisfy Article III requirements. See, *e.g.*, *Los Angeles v. Lyons*, 461 U.S. 95, 101–110 (1983); *Poe v. Ullman*, 367 U.S. 497, 507 (1961).

On the merits, the court of appeals held the old version of Section 6 (1) unconstitutionally vague. That statute made it illegal, in the case of a pregnancy termination "after the fetus is known to be viable," for [a]ny physician or person assisting in such a pregnancy termination" intentionally to fail to manifest a specified standard of care. The court found the statute vague because it "does not specify * * * which party, physician or assistant, must make this viability determination" (84–1379 J.S. App. 26).

As noted above, the Illinois legislature in September 1983 had amended the statute's definition of "viability" so as to make the determination of viability depend on "the medical judgment *of the attending physician."* It would have required no great leap of logic for the court of appeals thence to infer that the legislature meant the determination of the attending physician, not of his assistant, to govern under old Section 6 (1). Indeed, the 1984 amendment to Section 6 (1) makes this explicit. See 84–1379 J.S. App. 57–58. We think that a fair reading of the statute compelled this construction of the 1983 version. In any event, this construction was plainly permitted, and the court of appeals was obliged to adopt that permissible construction under the well-settled principle that federal courts should construe state statutes in a manner favoring their constitutionality.

c. Section 2 (10) of the Illinois Abortion Law defines an "abortifacient" as any substance or device "known to cause fetal death." Section 11 (d) requires any person who prescribes or administers a substance or device "which he knows to be an abortifacient" to tell the recipient "that it is an abortifacient." Intentional or reckless failure to provide this information is a misdemeanor.

The court of appeals held these two provisions unconstitutional (84–1379 J.S. App. 43). The court did not suggest that Section 2 (10)'s definition of "abortifacient" is inaccurate. Nor did it suggest that it is unconstitutional for a state to require a doctor who performs an abortion, or who prescribes an abortifacient, to tell his patient what he is doing. Indeed, a state in regulating abortions indisputably may require "the giving of information to the patient as to just what [will] be done and as to its consequences" (*Danforth*, 428 U.S. at 67 n.8). Rather, the court invalidated these two provisions because Section 2 (10), in defining "abortifacient," refers to "fetal death," and because *another* section of the statute—Section 2 (9), which was repealed in September 1983—formerly defined "fetus" as "a human being from fertilization until birth" (see 84–1379 J.S. App. 39–40, 60). Reading these three sections together, the court concluded that Section 11 (d) unconstitutionally "foist[s] upon the pregnant woman [the State's] view that life begins at conception" (84–1379 J.S. App. 39 (citing *Akron*, 462 U.S. at 444)).

This line of reasoning is strained indeed. Section 11 (d) simply requires that a doctor, when administering something that is likely to destroy the fetus, tell his patient that he is administering something that is likely to destroy the fetus. Destruction of the fetus in such circumstances is obviously a "consequence" of which the pregnant woman may be informed (*Danforth*, 428 U.S. at 67 n.8). Section 11 (d) does not say that the doctor must use the words "abortifacient" or "fetal death"; he is free to get the message across in any way he chooses. Moreover, the doctor is not required to refer to, or to say anything about, the definition of "fetus" formerly contained in Section 2 (9). The pregnant woman presumably knows what a "fetus" is; if not, the doctor is free to explain it in his own words. All Section 11 (d) requires is that the doctor tell her that she is about to have an abortion if that is what she is about to have.[3]

Section 11 (d) is an entirely reasonable provision designed to ensure that women seeking birth control assistance understand the difference between "abortifacients" and "contraceptives." The difference is significant for many women, whether for physical, moral, or religious reasons, and the state plainly has a legitimate interest in ensuring that this difference is explained to them so that they may make an informed choice. In adopting a strained and illogical construction of Section 11 (d), the court of appeals ignored both the State's legitimate interests and proper principles of judicial review.

B. The approach of the courts below betrays in our view an extreme and unseemly hostility to legitimate state regulation of abortion. By subjecting innocuous, even repealed, statutes to strained interpretations, apparently for no other reason than to invalidate them, the courts seemed determined to make regulations so difficult to sustain that abortions before the third trimester will become available virtually "on demand" (*Roe v. Wade*, 410 U.S. at 208 (Burger, C.J., concurring)). In so doing, the courts relied heavily on this Court's decision in *Akron*. See, *e.g.*, 84–495 J.S. App. 20a-21a, 24a-25a, 46a-47a, 48a-49a, 79a; 84–1379 J.S. App. 30, 35-36, 38-39. It is perhaps not fanciful to suggest that the courts below may have thought they detected in *Akron* an undercurrent of impatience with state efforts to regulate abortion, and to have taken their cue from that insight.

We believe that *Akron* does represent something of a departure from the Court's previous abortion decisions, both in the standard of review it applies and in the diminished weight it seems to attach to a state's legitimate interests in this area. In reviewing the instant cases, therefore, the Court may find it appropriate to consider whether *Akron* sent an erroneous message to the lower federal courts. There are several respects in which we think that might have happened.

1. This Court in *Roe v. Wade* held that the states have legitimate interests in protecting fetal life and preserving maternal health, and that these interests become sufficiently "compelling" at some point during pregnancy to justify restrictions on, or outright proscription of, abortion. Until *Akron*, however, the Court had not suggested that a state's choice among various alternative means of achieving a given "compelling" objective had *itself* to be supported by a compelling state

interest. Rather, provided that the state was pursuing a "compelling" objective (*e.g.*, health), a particular regulation was deemed valid if it was "reasonably related" to that objective (*e.g.*, was a rational health regulation) and did not "unduly burden" the woman's freedom of choice respecting abortion. See, *e.g.*, *Danforth*, 428 U.S. at 80; *Beal v. Doe*, 432 U.S. at 445; *Maher v. Roe*, 432 U.S. at 473.

The *Akron* decision seems to signal a departure from this analytical framework. Certain passages in that opinion suggest, for example, that a state, in crafting a regulation designed to protect maternal health, must demonstrate a "compelling interest" in selecting one of several options, each of which represents a rational means of achieving the state's goal. This is most evident in the Court's treatment of Akron's "informed consent" provisions. The ordinance required "the attending physician" to inform his patient of the relative risks and consequences of pregnancy and abortion (462 U.S. at 446). The Court acknowledged that this information was "clearly related to maternal health and to the State's legitimate purpose in requiring informed consent" (*ibid.*). The Court acknowledged the importance of having this information conveyed by a "well-trained and competent counselor []" (*id.* at 449 n. 41). The Court acknowledged that its earlier decisions had "stressed repeatedly the central role of the physician * * * in consulting with the woman about whether or not to have an abortion" (*id.* at 447 (original quotation marks omitted)). And the Court found nothing in the record to "suggest that ethical physicians will charge more for adhering to this typical element of the physician-patient relationship" (*ibid.*). Yet the Court nevertheless held the ordinance unconstitutional because it required the attending physician to make the communication, rather than permitting his assistant to do so. The Court was "not convinced * * * that there is as vital a state need for insisting" that the information be conveyed by the one rather than by the other. (462 U.S. at 448).

This holding, in our view, cannot be squared with the Court's previous opinions. A requirement that *the physician* convey the medical information was surely "reasonably related" to Akron's compelling health objective, and that requirement was not shown to have increased the cost of abortions by a magnitude sufficient to impose an "undue burden" on pregnant women's freedom of choice. The regulation should accordingly have been sustained.

2. Prior to *Akron*, this Court had consistently recognized that a State may legitimately "make a value judgment favoring childbirth over abortion" (*Maher v. Roe*, 432 U.S. at 474). "The Constitution," the Court had said, "does not compel a state to fine-tune its statutes so as to encourage or facilitate abortions," and hence the fact that a

regulation "may inhibit some [women] from seeking abortions is not a valid basis to void the statute" (*H.L. v. Matheson*, 450 U.S. 398, 413 (1981)). To the contrary, the Court had held that "state action 'encouraging childbirth except in the most urgent circumstances' is 'rationally related to the legitimate governmental objective of protecting potential life'" (*ibid.*, quoting *Harris v. McRae*, 448 U.S. 297, 325 (1980)).

Certain passages in *Akron* again seem to signal a departure from these principles. The Court in *Akron* suggested, for example, that a state regulation is invalid if it is "designed to influence the woman's informed choice between abortion or childbirth" (462 U.S. at 444 (footnote omitted)). On that premise, the Court struck down provisions requiring that certain information be furnished to a woman contemplating an abortion, reasoning that the information was "designed * * * to persuade her to withhold" her consent to that procedure (*ibid.*).

Once a woman steps into an abortion clinic, however, there is no way a state can promote its legitimate policy of "encouraging childbirth" without at the same time "discouraging abortion." A woman who enters "an abortion clinic, where abortions for pregnant minors frequently take place," is presumably inclined to terminate her pregnancy, and it is "unlikely that she will obtain adequate counsel from the attending physician at an abortion clinic," much less be dissuaded from her proposed course. *Bellotti II*, 443 U.S. at 641 (original quotation marks omitted). Indeed, as a doctor at one of the clinics involved in *Akron* testified, when a teenager showed up at the clinic he assumed the decision was made: "When you go to a bar, you go there to drink" (81–746 Resp. Br. 20). Obviously, no state can promote a policy of "encouraging normal childbirth" in such circumstances unless it is allowed to place a counterweight in the other side of the scales.

The *Akron* majority thus had little basis in precedent for suggesting that state action is unconstitutional per se if it is "designed to influence the woman's informed choice between abortion or childbirth." If the state's interest in encouraging chilbirth is to mean anything, and if the woman's consent to abortion is to be truly informed, the state must be allowed, in a reasoned and objective way, to tell its side of the story, and a story favoring childbirth is a permissible story for it to tell. Of course, should the state convey that message in an inaccurate or overbearing fashion, or otherwise attempt to compel or coerce the woman's decision, her decision would not be "knowing, intelligent, and voluntary" (*Danforth*, 428 U.S. at 90 (Stewart, J., concurring)), and the state's action would constitute "an unduly burdensome interference with her freedom to decide whether to terminate her pregnancy" (*Maher v. Roe*, 432 U.S. at 474). But an effort by the state to influence a pregnant woman to choose cildbirth instead of abortion, in a manner that does not impair her freedom of choice, can hardly be thought to erect an unconstitutional obstacle.

3. Prior to *Akron*, this Court's abortion opinions generally reflected the well-settled rule that federal courts should accord state statutes a sympathetic construction that favors their constitutionality. See, *e.g.*, *Danforth*, 428 U.S. at 64; *Bellotti II*, 443 U.S. at 645 & n.25; *H.L. v. Matheson*, 450 U.S. at 406, 407 & n.14, 412. Once again, however, the *Akron* opinion seems to suggest a more hostile approach. This is perhaps most evident in the majority's treatment of Akron's regulation requiring that physicians performing abortions "insure that the remains of the unborn child are disposed of in a humane and sanitary manner" (462 U.S. at 451). The city averred that this regulation was designed simply "to preclude the mindless dumping of aborted fetuses onto garbage piles" (*ibid.* (original quotation marks omitted)). The Court nevertheless held the regulation unconstitutionally vague, speculating that "[t]he phrase 'humane and sanitary' does, as the Court of Appeals noted, suggest a possible intent to mandate some sort of decent burial of [the] embryo" (*ibid.* (original quotation marks omitted)).

This approach is difficult to reconcile with the Court's previous opinions. Akron's ordinance was surely susceptible of a constitutional construction. The phrase "humane and sanitary" appears in countless laws regulating health and safety. Congree has even mandated the "humane * * * disposal of excess wild free-roaming horses and burros" (43 U.S.C. 1901 (a) (6)). As a familiar regulatory formula, the phrase "humane and sanitary" resembles the phrase "informed consent," which the Court in *Danforth* held not to be vague (see 428 U.S. at 67 n.8). In striking down the Akron formula based on speculation that the draftsmen of the ordinance might have intended to mandate "some sort of decent burial" (462 U.S. at 451), the Court in *Akron* may have invited the kind of unsympathetic statutory construction, the temptation to impugn legislative motives, that the courts of appeals engaged in here.

C. Having said this, candor compels us to state our conviction that *Akron* is a symptom, not the source, of the problem. As the decisions below demonstrate, the constitutional inquiry mandated by *Roe v. Wade* is not easy for courts to conduct in a principled fashion. The key factors in the equation—viability, trimesters, the right to terminate one's pregnancy—have no moorings in the text of our Constitution or in familiar constitutional doctrine. Because the parameters of the inquiry are indeterminate, courts are disposed to indulge in a free-ranging, essentially legislative, process of devising regulatory schemes that reflect their notions of morality and social justice. The result has been a set of judicially-crafted rules that has become increasingly more intricate and complex, taking courts further away from what they do best and into the realm of what legislatures do best.

We recognize that the principle of *stare decisis*, furthering as it does the policies of continuity and consistency of adjudication, weighs against reconsidering recent precedents. See *Atascadero State Hospital v. Scanlon*, [105 S.Ct. 3142, 3148-49 n.3 (1985)]; *Akron*, 462 U.S. at 420 & n.1. This principle, however, does not count so strongly in constitutional litigation, where short of a constitutional amendment, this Court is the only body capable of effecting a needed change. See *Akron*, 462 U.S. at 420; *Glidden Co. v. Zdanok*, 370 U.S. 530, 543 (1962). Moreover, this Court must respond to obligations that transcend the institutional concerns underlying the doctrine of *stare decisis. See Erie R. Co. v. Tompkins*, 304 U.S. 64, 77-78 (1938) ("If only a question of statutory construction were involved, we should not be prepared to abandon a doctrine so widely applied throughout nearly a century. But the unconstitutionality of the course pursued has now been made clear and compels us to do so.") (Brandeis, J.)). Where a judicial formulation affecting the allocation of constitutional powers has proven "unsound in principle and unworkable in practice," where it "leads to inconsistent results at the same time that it disserves principles of democratic self-governance," this Court has not hesitated to reconsider a prior decision. *Garcia v. San Antonio Metropolitan Transit Authority*, [105 S.Ct. 1005, 1016 (1985)].

1. To provide a regime for delimiting the permissible scope of abortion regulation, *Roe v. Wade* divided pregnancy into three trimesters, with radically different consequences for state regulatory power in each. This analytical framework has proved inherently unworkable. Subsequent developments, both technological and medical, have demonstrated the arbitrariness of these lines: the Court "simply concluded that a line must be drawn, *** and proceeded to draw that line" (*Garcia*, [105 S.Ct. at 1014] (original quotation marks omitted)). Arbitrary line drawing may occasionally be necessary to make explicit constitutional rights efficacious, but such arbitrariness gains the appearance of legislation pure and simple where the subject is one upon which the Constitution is silent.

The Court in *Roe v. Wade* properly recognized that the states have a strong interest in safeguarding maternal health, but it is difficult to grasp why the compelling quality of this interest should undergo a radical change at the end of the first trimester. The Court made a determination—basically one of legislative fact—that "until the end of the first trimester mortality in abortion may be less than mortality in normal childbirth" (410 U.S. at 149, 163). The legislative nature of this finding is shown by "evidence that developments in the past decade, particularly the development of a much safer method for performing second-trimester abortion, * * * have extended the period in which abortions are safer than childbirth" (*Akron*, 462 U.S. at 429 n.11). The fact that *Akron*, despite this evidence, retained the end of the first trimester as the sharply determinative point demonstrates that point's essential arbitrariness. As Justice O'Connor wrote in dissent, "The fallacy inherent in the *Roe* framework is apparent: just because the State has a compelling interest in ensuring maternal safety once an abortion may be more dangerous than childbirth, it simply does not follow that the State has *no* interest before that point that justifies state regulation to ensure that first-trimester abortions are performed as safely as possible" (*id*. at 460 (emphasis in original)).

It was similarly arbitrary for the Court in *Roe v. Wade* to determine that the state's legitimate interest "in protecting prenatal life" (410 U.S. at 150, 153–154) undergoes a constitutionally significant change at the point of fetal viability. There is no obvious constitutional connection between the ability of a fetus to survive outside the womb, and the magnitude of a state's lawful concern to protect future life. As Justice O'Connor said in her *Akron* dissent, "[P]otential life is no less potential in the first weeks of pregnancy than it is at viability or afterward. * * * The choice of viability as the point at which the state interest in *potential* life becomes compelling is no less arbitrary than choosing any point before viability or any point afterward" (462 U.S. at 461 (emphasis in original)).

The "viability" standard is particularly unworkable as a constitutional reference point because it changes with advances in technology. The "increasingly earlier fetal viability" demonstrated in recent scientific studies (462 U.S. at 457 (O'Connor, J., dissenting)) obviously owes to improvements in medical techniques, and not to any change in our perceptions about how fully developed or worthy of life a fetus is at any point in time. It is disturbing to attribute constitutional significance to a point which, besides being in motion rather than being fixed, has its movement dictated by advances in engineering rather than by forces more familiar to traditional judicial analysis.

The arbitrary nature of *Roe v. Wade's* analytical framework is reflected in the increasingly complex linedrawing of its progeny. A state may require that certain information be furnished to a woman by a doctor or his assistant (*Akron*, 462 U.S. at 448), but may not require that such information be furnished to her by the doctor himself (*id*. at 449). A state may require that second-trimester abortions be performed in clinics (*Simopoulos v. Virginia*, 462 U.S. 506 (1983)), but may not require that they be performed in hospitals (*Akron*, 462 U.S. at 437–439). As each set of these subtle distinctions was crafted, still more unanswered questions were posed. During the decade since *Roe v. Wade* the adversaries in the abortion debate have come back again and again, asking this Court to spin an ever-finer web of regulations. The adversaries are back again today. They are sure to return. Each time, the set of rules will get longer and more intricate. This is an inappropriate burden to impose on any court, or on any Constitution.

2. The second, compelling ground for our urging reconsideration of *Roe v. Wade* is our belief that the textual, historical and doctrinal basis of that decision is so far flawed[4] that this Court should overrule it and return the law to the condition in which it was before that case was decided.

There is no explicit textual warrant in the Constitution for a right to an abortion. It is true, of course, that words, and certainly the words of general constitutional provisions, do not interpret themselves. That being said, the further afield interpretation travels from its point of departure in the text, the greater the danger that constitutional adjudication will be like a picnic to which the framers bring the words and the judges the meaning. Constitutional interpretation retains the fullest measure of legitimacy when it is disciplined by fidelity to the framers' intention as revealed by history, or, failing sufficient help from history, by the interpretative tradition of the legal community. That tradition is illuminated not only by court decisions, but by the practice of lawyers and legislatures "in the compelling traditions of the legal profession." *Rochin v. California*, 342 U.S. 165, 171 (1952) (Frankfurter, J.).

We respectfully submit that by these criteria *Roe v. Wade* is extraordinarily vulnerable. It stands as a source of trouble in the law not only on its own terms, but also because it invites confusion about the sources of judicial authority and the direction of this Court's own future course. *Stare decisis* is a principle of stability. A decision as flawed as we believe *Roe v. Wade* to be becomes a focus of instability, and thus is less aptly sheltered by that doctrine from criticism and abandonment.

a. The ultimate textual source for *Roe v. Wade* (410 U.S. at 129) is the Fourteenth Amendment's guarantee: "nor shall any State deprive any person of * * * liberty * * * without due process of law." It is late in the day to argue that this provision should be limited to its apparent textual meaning: government's actually taking hold of a person, as to confine him, without fair procedures. The expansive possibilities of "due process," however, early offered temptations which by all accounts led to one of the most troubled and demoralizing episodes in our constitutional history, during which the Court repeatedly frustrated the workings of the ordinary democratic process by imposing its own debatable and parochial view of appropriate social policy. *E.g.*, *Adkins v. Children's Hospital*, 261 U.S. 525 (1923); *Lochner v. New York*, 198 U.S. 45 (1905). The now prevailing doctrine that the Due Process Clause incorporates particular protections of the Bill of Rights, however controversial on historical grounds,[5] was plainly intended to have the function of reining in such judicial extravagance and reanchoring the interpretation of that Clause in the constitutional text—though somewhat downstream of it historical starting point. See *Adamson v. California*, 332 U.S. 46, 69-72 (1947) (Black, J., dissenting).

Viewed in this context, *Roe v. Wade* seems particularly ill-founded. Due process analysis, while it must recognize the need to go beyond scrutiny of the few relevant words of the Clause, must nevertheless seek a connection with the intentions of those who framed and ratified the constitutional text. As this Court acknowledged in *Roe v. Wade* (410 U.S. at 138-139), however, and as Justice Rehnquist emphasized in dissent (*id*. at 174-176 & n.1), state laws condemning or limiting abortion were very general at the time the Fourteenth Amendment was adopted. Indeed, the period between 1860 and 1880 witnessed "the most important burst of anti-abortion legislation in the nation's history" (J. Mohr, *Abortion in America* 200 (1978)). Nor does the tenor and contemporaneous understanding of those laws leave much doubt that they were directed, not only at protecting maternal health, but also at what was widely viewed as a moral evil comprehending the destruction of actual or potential human life (see Mohr at 35-36) and the undermining of family values in whose definition and reenforcement the state has always had a significant stake. It is fair to conclude that those who drafted and voted for the Fourteenth Amendment would have been surprised indeed to learn that they had put any part of such subjects beyond the pale of state legislative regulation.

Surely this historical context of the Due Process Clause is relevant to its interpretation. The most usual and straightforward use of history is to illuminate the intention of controversial constitutional texts. The debate about the practices contemporaneous with the adoption of the Establishment Clause was waged precisely because it has been thought to bear on that Clause's meaning: either to show acceptance of considerable state involvement in religion (see *Lynch v. Donnelly*, [465 U.S. 668, 673-78 (1984)]; *Marsh v. Chambers*, 463 U.S. 783, 787-791 (1983)), or to demonstrate that such involvement had fostered a controversy the Clause was meant to resolve. History similarly has been invoked as dispositive in regard to the acceptability of the death penalty under the Eighth Amendment: How could framers who before, during and after that Amendment's adoption regularly acquiesced in the application of capital punishment be taken to have condemned this practice as cruel and unusual? See *Gregg v. Georgia*, 428 U.S. 153, 176-177 (1976) (plurality opinion); *Furman v. Georgia*, 408 U.S. 238, 380 (1972) (Burger, C.J., dissenting); *id.* at 408 n.6 (Blackmun, J., dissenting). History has regularly been invoked to elucidate the meaning of the Fifth Amendment's guarantee against self-incrimination (see *Kastiger v. United States*, 406 U.S. 441, 443-447 (1972); *Miranda v. Arizona*, 384 U.S. 436, 458-460 (1966)), and the Sixth Amendment's guarantee of trial by jury. See *Williams v. Florida*, 399 U.S. 78, 86-103 (1970); *Duncan v. Louisana*, 391 U.S. 145, 151-154 (1968). In all these instances the use of history was straightforward. The purpose for which history is invoked in *Roe v. Wade*, by contrast, is far from evident. The Court's opinion appears to acknowledge the relevance of history, yet it reaches a conclusion in direct variance with the historical facts recited.

b. History is invoked in another way to take account of developments in society and the law. Such an approach has seemed particularly plausible in determining the application of the Fourth Amendment's protections to such undreamt-of developments as wire-tapping, electronic surveillance, the searches of automobiles and airplanes. History in this sense appears as a vector, in which the original understanding is seen as the point of departure for developing values implied and inchoate at the point of origin. But whether the vector is held to lead to a right to attend criminal trials (*Richmond Newspapers, Inc. v. Virginia*, 448 U.S. 555, 557-580 (1980)) or a right to travel (*Shapiro v. Thompson*, 394 U.S. 618, 630 (1969)), the Court has always taken pains to trace its point of origin back to specific constitutional provisions by a route either inferential or historical.

In *Roe v. Wade*, by contrast, the connections by either route were wholly missing and the Court was forced to leap to its conclusion. Certainly the course of legal attitudes and practice, "the compelling traditions of the legal profession" (*Rochin v. California*, 342 U.S. at 171), permit no extrapolation from the past to the Court's conclusion in *Roe v. Wade*. The story traced by the Court does not show a steady and growing acceptance of a point of view until the practice in a few jurisdictions can be characterized as anomalous. At most, the historical account in *Roe v. Wade* shows an ebb and flow of condemnation and concern about the practice of abortion. More accurately, it would seem that the passage of the Fourteenth Amendment roughly coincided with the rise of particular *stringency* in abortion laws, and that, between

1868 and 1973, such stringent laws appeared as a general feature of the legal landscape, representing by the Court's own count the policy "in a majority of the States." 410 U.S. at 118. This historical trajectory does not support the conclusion for which it was adduced.

c. There remains the inferential route, by which a specific constitutional text is seen to harbor the germ of a theory that establishes a general and fundamental right. The classic statement of this line of reasoning is found in Justice Harlan's dissent in *Poe v. Ulman*, 367 U.S. at 541–543. He wrote that "the liberty guaranteed by the Due Process Clause * * * is not a series of isolated points pricked out in terms of" the particular rights enumerated in the first eight Amendments. Rather, he said, liberty "is a rational continuum which, broadly speaking, includes a freedom from all substantial arbitrary impositions and purposeless restraints" (*ibid.*).

As Justice Harlan was at pains to insist, however, even this process of inferential extrapolation is directly rooted in textually specified constitutional values. The same connection "to what went before" is insisted upon in *Griswold v. Connecticut*, 381 U.S. 479, 484–485 (1965). The invocation in *Roe v. Wade* of both the particular concept of privacy and of this general mode of constitutional analysis, far from being anchored in text, history, or precedent, is an abrupt departure from the Court's prior decisions.[6] Indeed, all of the "privacy" cases that the court cited in *Roe v. Wade* were applications of accepted principles, whether of equal protection[7] or of freedom of expression at the core of the First Amendment.[8] Neither equal protection, nor intrusion upon the home, nor freedom to think or promulgate ideas is involved in laws regulating abortion.

d. There can be no doubt of the strength of the conviction held by some that free access to abortion is a fundamental expression of individual freedom, and that such freedom is the first principle of a just society. A conviction of self-evidence may well accompany a view so strongly held. Yet this conviction does not constitute constitutional argument. It is at best an intuition based in controversial moral and social theories of the good life and of an individual's situation in society, theories "which a large part of the country does not entertain." *Lochner v. New York*, 198 U.S. at 75 (Holmes, J., dissenting). And when controversial but seemingly self-evident convictions are translated directly into constitutional doctrine, we risk repeating the whole lamentable story surrounding *Lochner* for which Justice Holmes (*id.* at 76) composed the epitaph at its birth: "[The Constitution] is made for people of fundamentally differing views, and the accident of our finding certain opinions natural and familiar or novel and even shocking ought not to conclude our judgment upon the question whether statutes embodying them conflict with the Constitution of the United States."

As in logic contradictory premises can be used to prove anything, so in constitutional law principles that are ill-founded can be used to justify any conclusion, and thus rob the law of its intrinsically compelling force. And when constitutional law, which is above ordinary politics, seeks to settle disputes of value and vision which are the stuff of politics, both law and politics are more not less subject to the kind of intense pressures which have characterized the abortion debate since *Roe v. Wade.*

CONCLUSION

The portions of the court of appeals' judgments that invalidate appellants' abortion regulations should be reversed.

Respectfully submitted.

Charles Fried
Acting Solicitor General

Richard K. Willard
Acting Assistant Attorney General

Carolyn B. Kuhl
Deputy Assistant Attorney General

John F. Cordes
John M. Rogers
Attorneys

JULY 1985

Notes

1. The district court had granted a preliminary injunction as to one section of the statute, but the State conceded the invalidity of that section on appeal (84-495 J.S. App. 18a, 33a-34a).

2. Appellants suggest (84-1379 J.S. 43) that, while the controversy as to the old version of Section 6 (4) is moot, the controversy as to its current version remains alive, since the court of appeals' rationale for invalidating the former would also apply to the latter. Although we sympathize with appellants' desire to obtain guidance from this Court, we cannot agree with this submission.

The court of appeals expressly "decline[d] to evaluate [the] constitutionality" of the current provision (84-1379 J.S. App. 9), and this Court "reviews judgments, not statements in opinions" (*Black v. Cutter Laboratories*, 351 U.S. 292, 297 (1956)).

3. In any event, the court of appeals wholly ignored the fact that the statute's allegedly improper definition of "fetus" was repealed in September 1983. Since then, the statute has defined "fetus" as "an individual organism of the species homo sapiens from fertilization until live birth" (84-1379 J.S. App. 60). It cannot seriously be contended that this definition impermissibly adopts any particular "theory of life" (*Roe v. Wade*, 410 U.S. at 162).

4. This judgment is shared by a broad spectrum of constitutional scholars. See, *e.g.*, J.H. Ely, *Democracy and Distrust* 2-3, 248 n.52 (1980); Gunther, *Some Reflections on the Judicial Role: Distinctions, Roots, and Prospects*, 1979 Wash. U.L.Q. 817, 819; Burt, *The Constitution of the Family*, 1979 Sup. Ct. Rev. 329, 371-373; A. Bickel, *The Morality of Consent* 27-29 (1975); Epstein, *Substantive Due Process by Any Other Name: The Abortion Cases*, 1973 Sup. Ct. Rev. 159; Wellington, *Common Law Rules and Constitutional Double Standards: Some Notes on Adjudication*, 83 Yale L.J. 21, 297-311 (1973); Ely, *The Wages of Crying Wolf: A Comment on Roe v. Wade*, 82 Yale L.J. 920 (1973).

5. See, *e.g.*, Fairman, *Does the Fourteenth Amendment Incorporate the Bill of Rights? The Original Understanding*, 2 Stan. L. Rev. 5 (1949).

6. As Dean Ely explained, this Court's invalidation in *Griswold* of a statute regulating the *use* of contraceptives, as opposed to their manufacture or sale, indicated an underlying concern that enforcement of the statute "*would have been virtually impossible* without the most outrageous sort of governmental prying into the privacy of the home." 82 Yale L.J. at 929-930 (emphasis in original). A statute limiting a medical procedure performed by a doctor in a clinic or hospital is simply not analogous; abortion statutes could obviously be enforced without the necessity of repulsive searches. Fourth Amendment policies accordingly provide no support for the holding in *Roe v. Wade*.

7. *Skinner v. Oklahoma*, 316 U.S. 535, 538 (1942) (criminal sterilization act violated equal protection by distinguishing without an adequate basis between persons convicted of larceny and embezzlement); *Loving v. Virginia*, 388 U.S. 1, 12 (1967) (statute prohibiting interracial marriages involved "invidious racial discriminations"); *Eisenstadt v. Baird*, 405 U.S. 438, 446-455 (1972) (statute prohibiting distribution of contraceptives violated equal protection by treating married and unmarried women differently without a rational basis).

8. *Meyer v. Nebraska*, 262 U.S. 390, 400 (1923) (invalidating law prohibiting the teaching of foreign languages in private elementary schools because "[m]ere knowledge of the German language cannot reasonably be regarded as harmful"); *Pierce v. Society of Sisters*, 268 U.S. 510 (1925) (invalidating statute requiring all children to attend public schools); *Prince v. Massachusetts*, 321 U.S. 158, 164 (1944) (prosecution of Jehovah's Witness under statute prohibiting sale by minors of periodicals implicates but does not violate freedom of religion); *Stanley v. Georgia*, 394 U.S. 557 (1969) (reversing criminal conviction for mere possession of films in defendant's home).

Table of Cases

Index